WE ARE HERE FOREVER

This is a work of fiction. All names, places, and characters are products of the author's imagination or are used fictitiously. Any resemblance to real people, places, or events is entirely coincidental.

Library of Congress Cataloging in Publication Number: 2018961371

ISBN: 978-1-68369-120-4

Printed in China

Typeset in Canoodle and Sketchnote

Designed by Aurora Parlagreco
Production management by John J. McGurk

Quirk Books
215 Church Street
Philadelphia, PA 19106
quirkbooks.com

10 9 8 7 6 5 4 3 2 1

For readers of the webcomic; Roomba; my parents; Nick, Sam, Kelly, Perry, and Eden

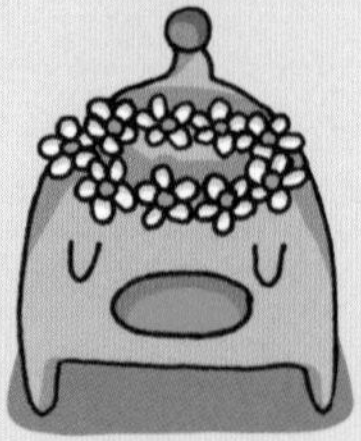

WELCOME, HUMAN PERSONS, TO THE WORLD OF *WE ARE HERE FOREVER*!

HELLO!

The book you're about to read is a history book . . . but not *human* history. *We Are Here Forever* is a collection of stories about purple creatures called the Puramus and their time on Earth after humanity has disappeared. No one seems to know how the Puramus ended up in this empty post-apocalyptic world. To provide an overview of their history, the book's twelve chapters include chronological jumps, and they're not always forward in time. As a reader, you can simply enjoy the adventures of these well-intentioned goofballs as they explore and learn. Or, for those who prefer to read more closely, clues to their mysterious origins are there to discover.

We human beings like to consider ourselves indispensable, but the Pura live on without us for hundreds, maybe thousands, of years. Do they learn from our mistakes? Or does developing a civilization automatically bring with it the hang-ups and conflicts that we, too, have struggled with?

We Are Here Forever began as a webcomic in 2016, but this collection of stories stands on its own. You don't have to do any homework before jumping in. As for fans of the webcomic, enjoy the never-before-seen tales. Newcomers, if you like what you see, explore the webcomic for more. Everyone wins!

Whether you're coming to the Puramus for the first time or already follow their escapades online, their interlocking antics form a saga filled with humor and mystery. Not all pieces of the puzzle are on the table. Maybe they never will be . . .

Thanks for picking up this book. As Boop would say: "This is nice."

—Michelle

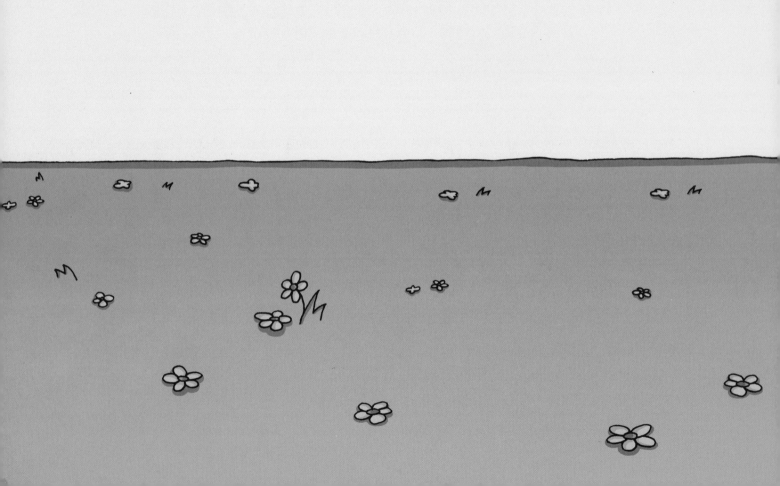

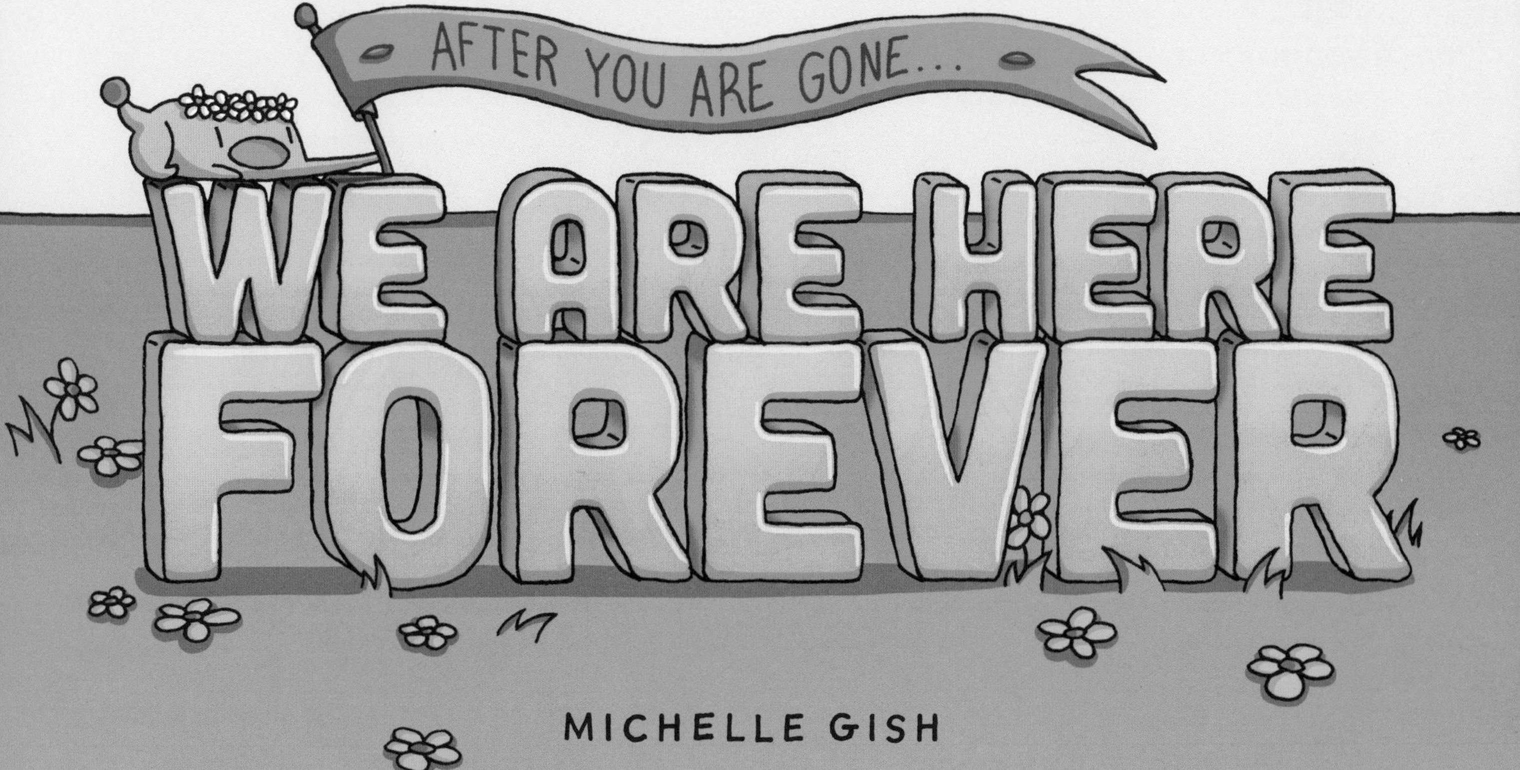
AFTER YOU ARE GONE...
WE ARE HERE
FOREVER

MICHELLE GISH

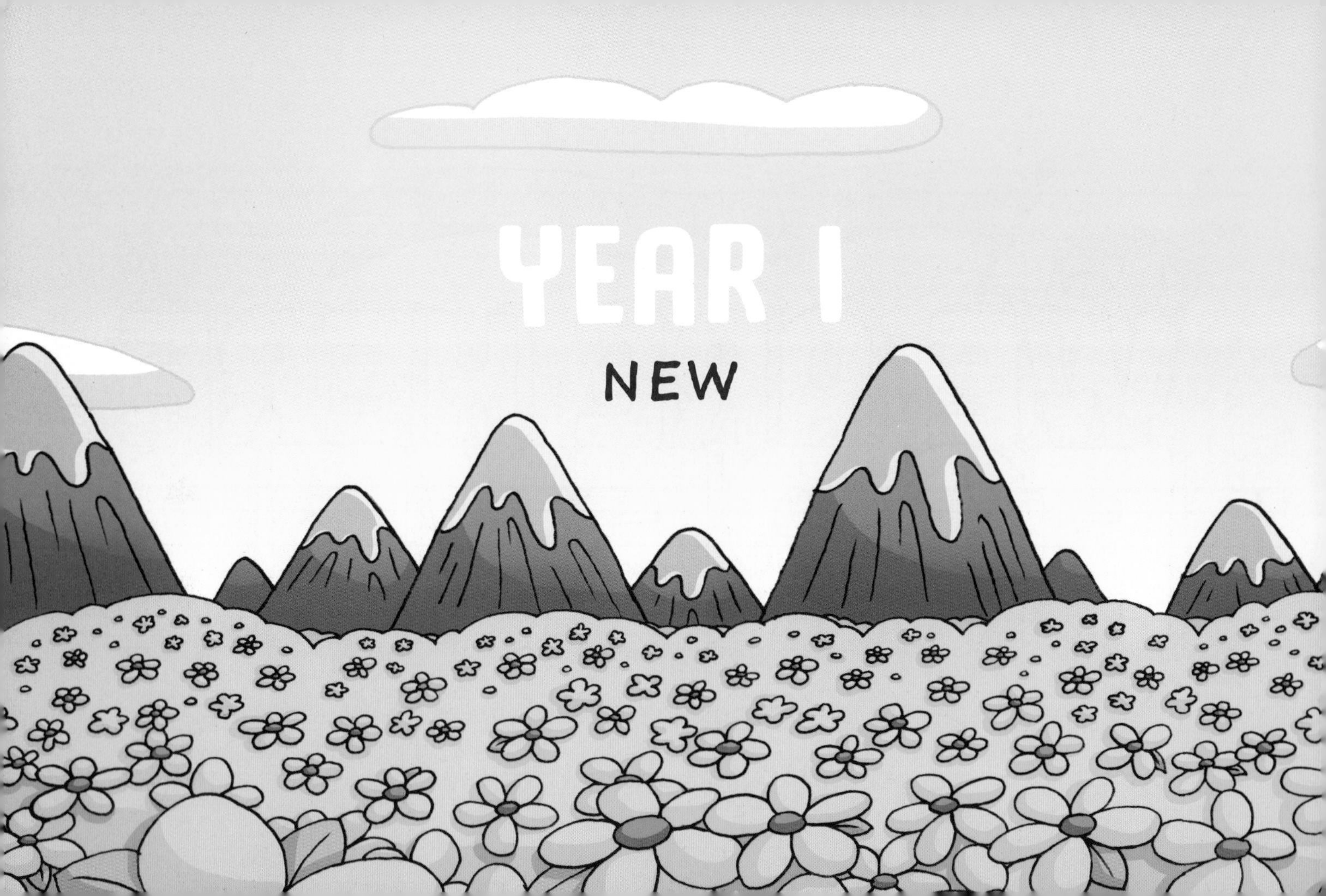
YEAR 1
NEW

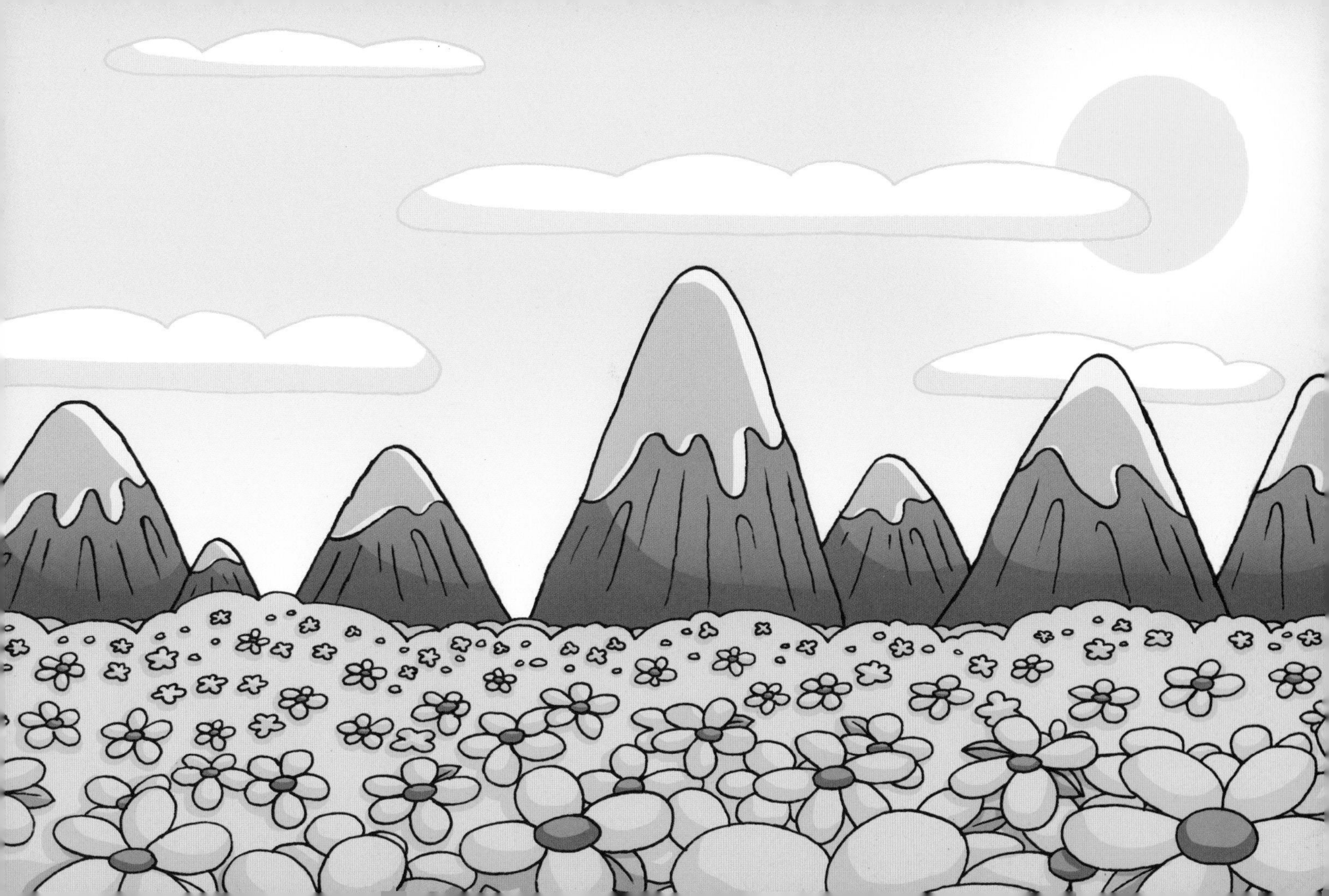

CHAPTER ONE

—

FRIENDS
AND FLOWERS

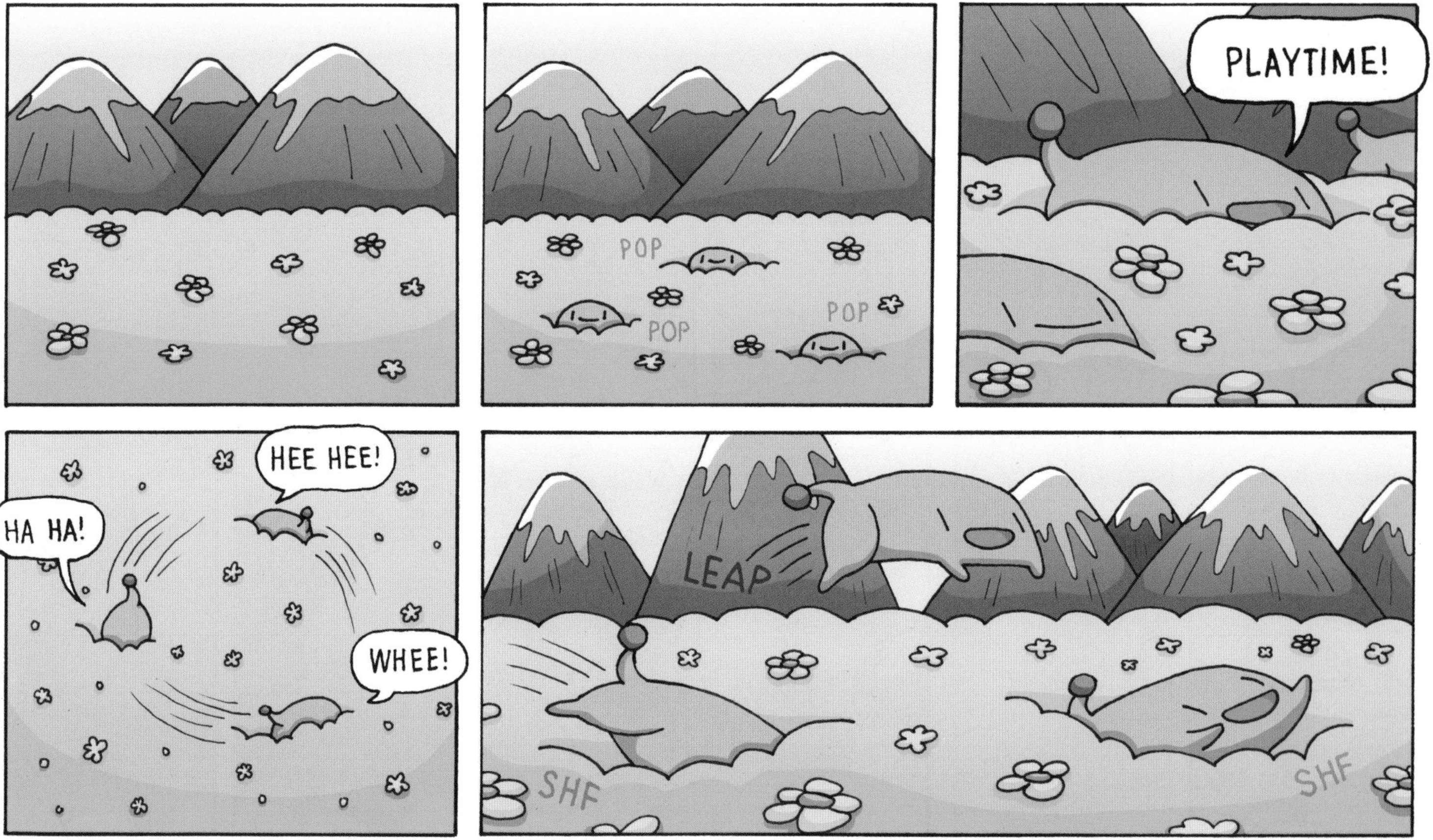

POP
POP
POP
PLAYTIME!
HA HA!
HEE HEE!
WHEE!
LEAP
SHF
SHF

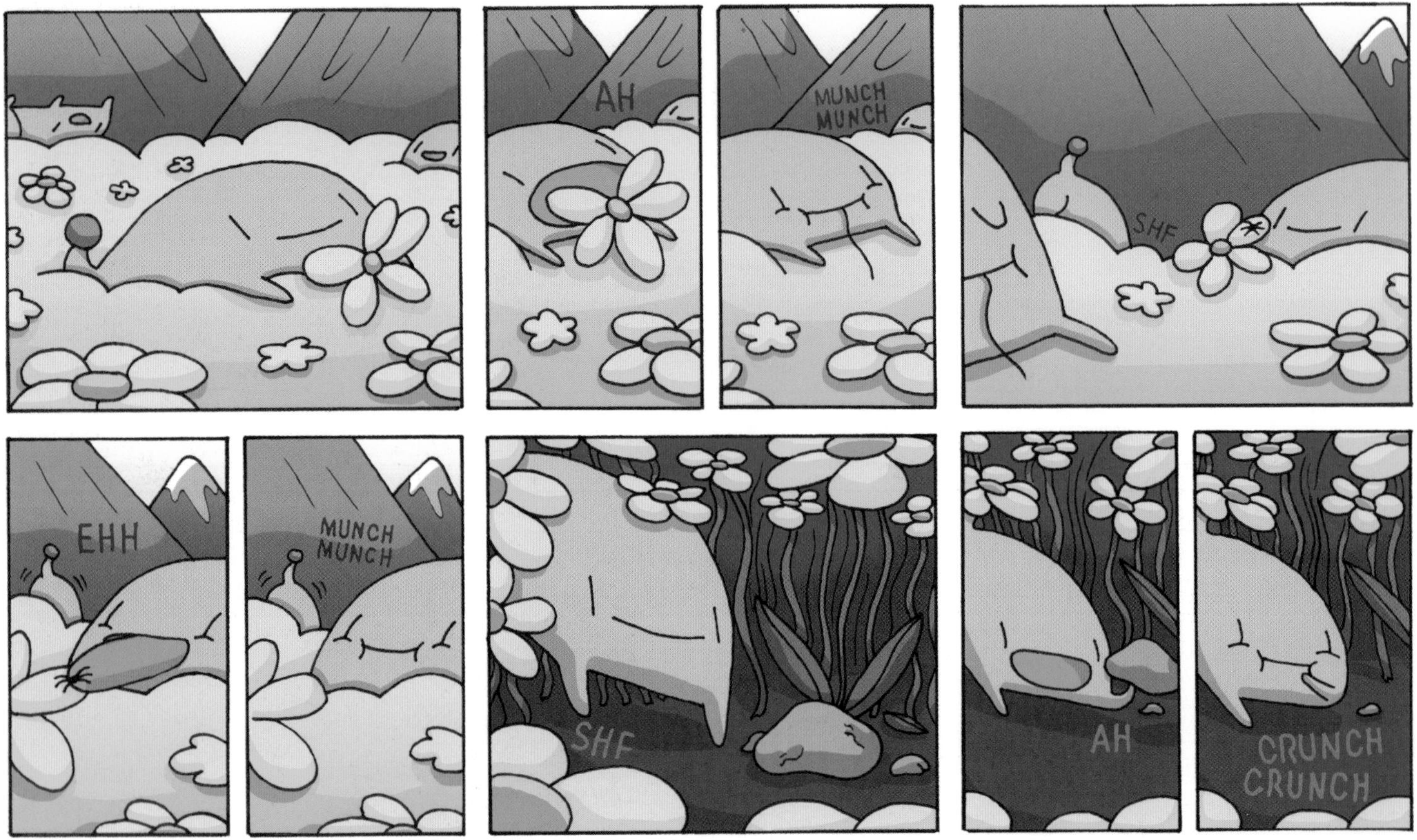
AH
MUNCH MUNCH
SHF
EHH
MUNCH MUNCH
SHF
AH
CRUNCH CRUNCH

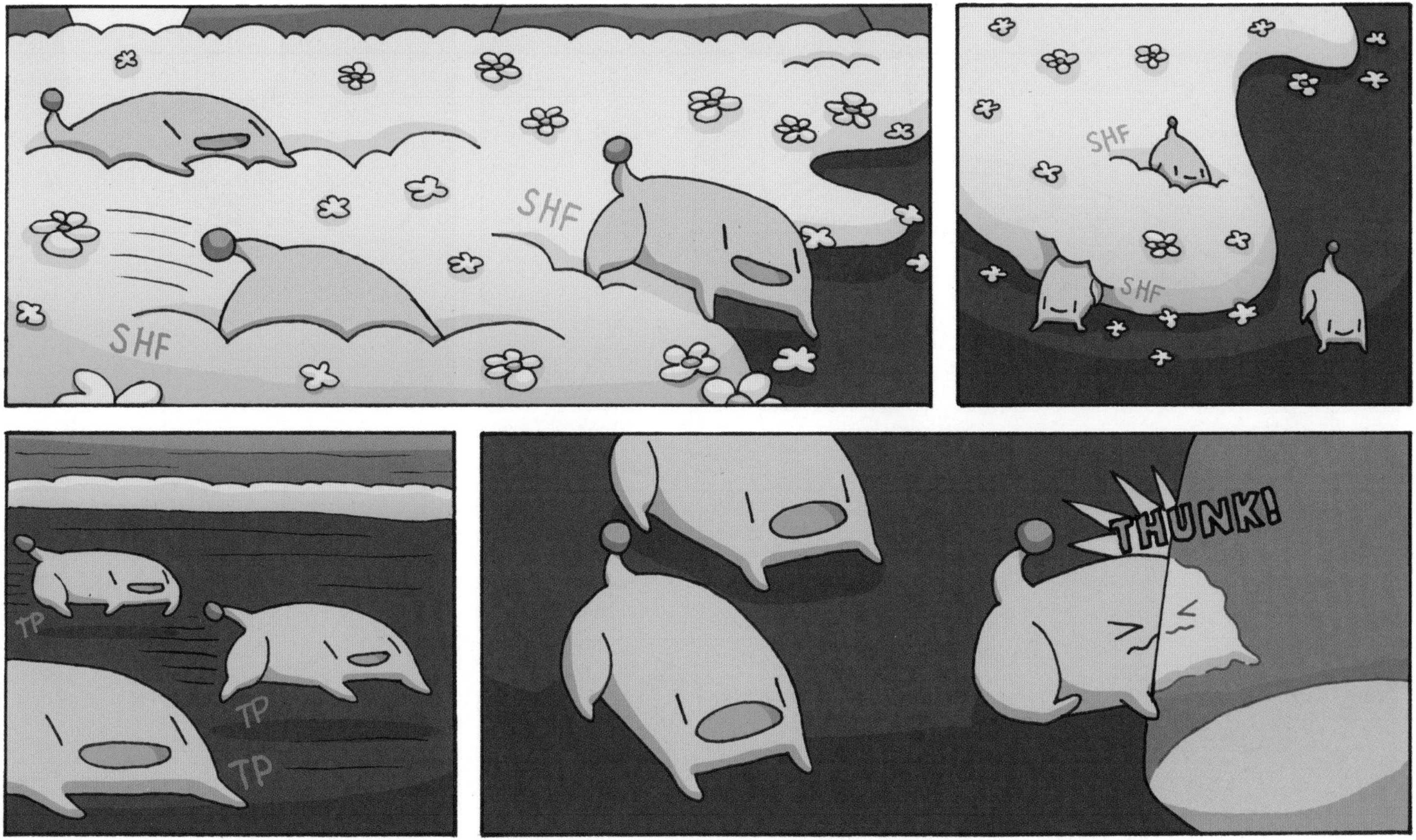

SHF
SHF
SHF
SHF
TP
TP
TP
THUNK!

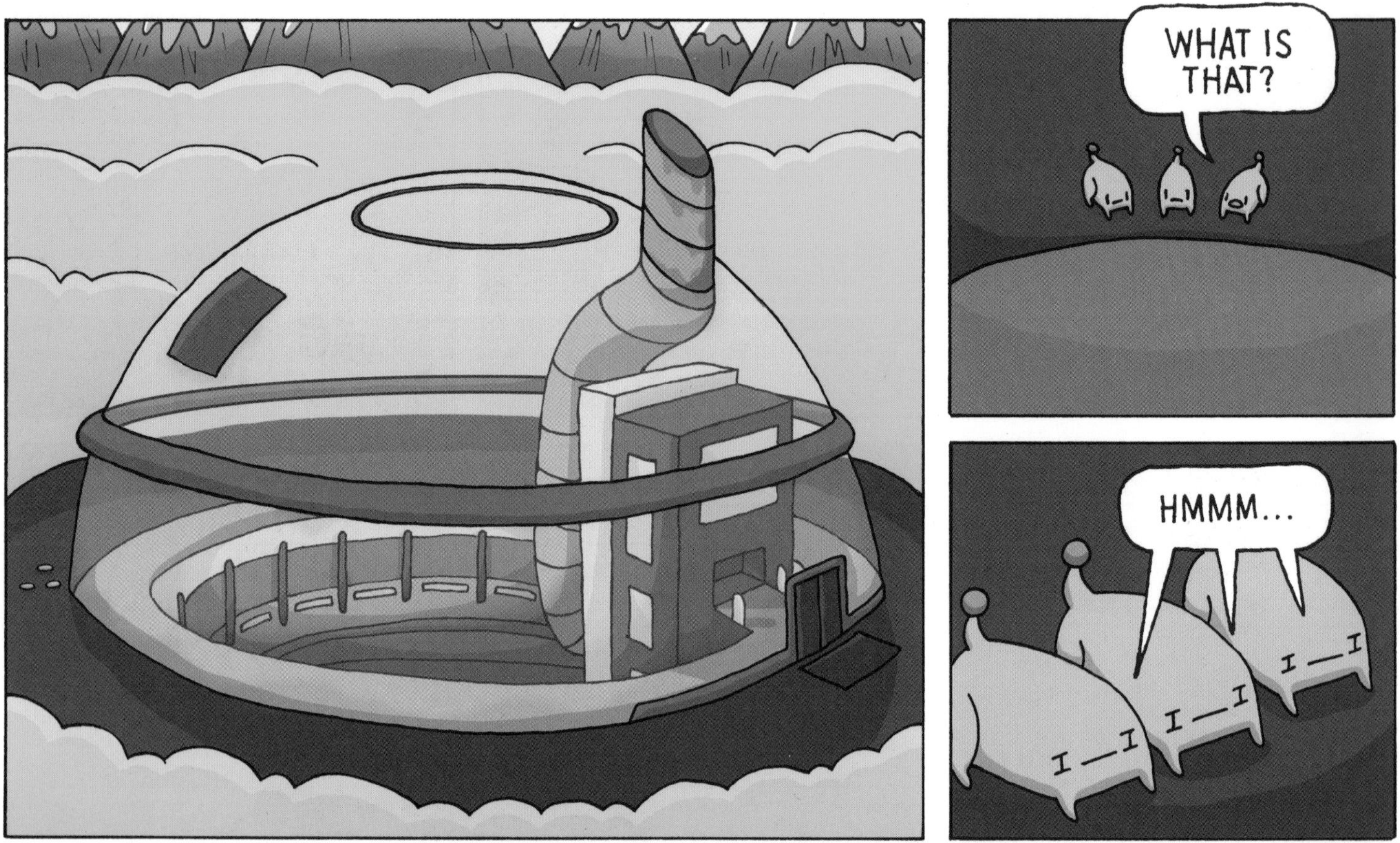
WHAT IS THAT?
HMMM...

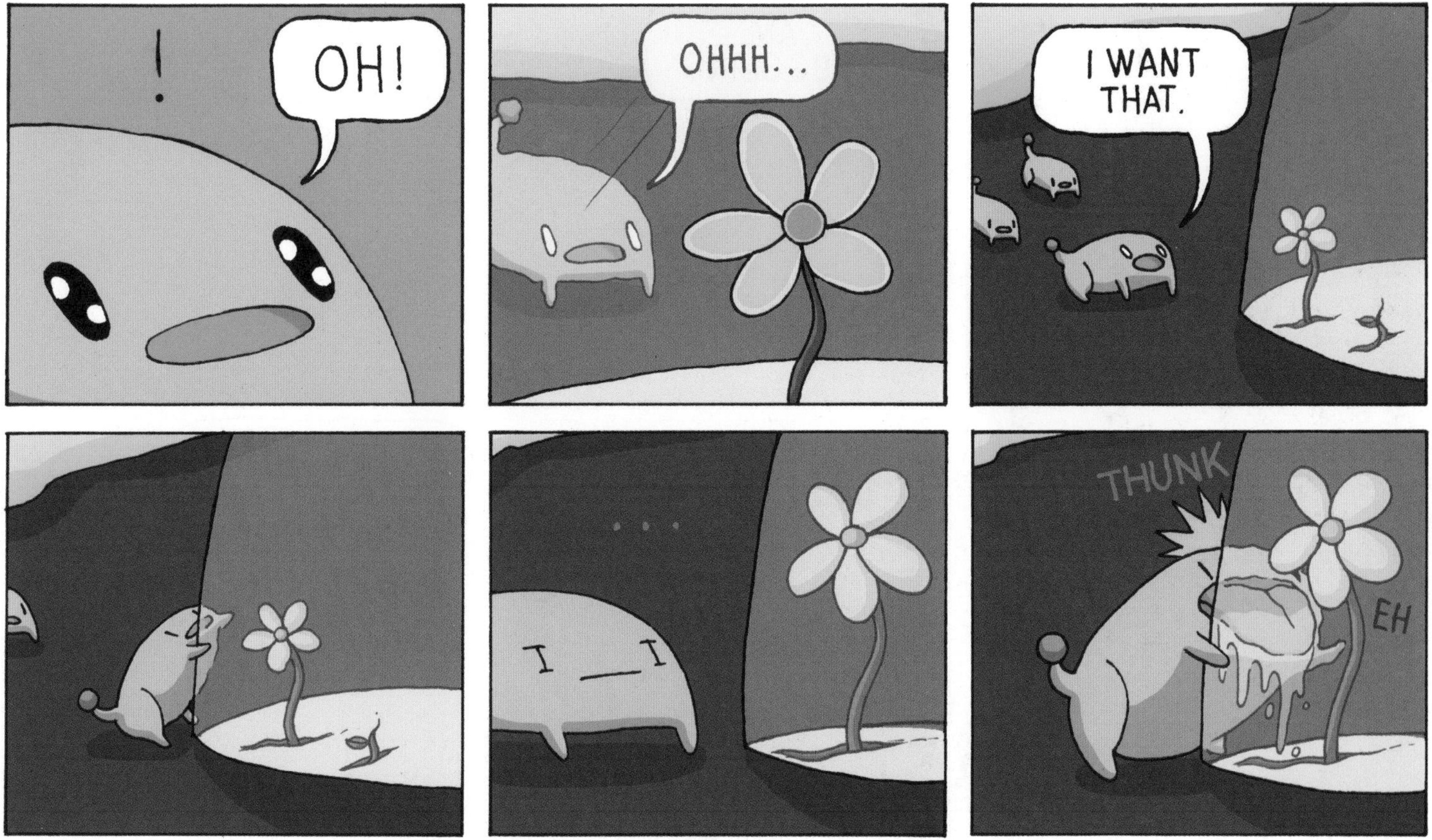
!
OH!
OHHH...
I WANT THAT.
...
THUNK
EH

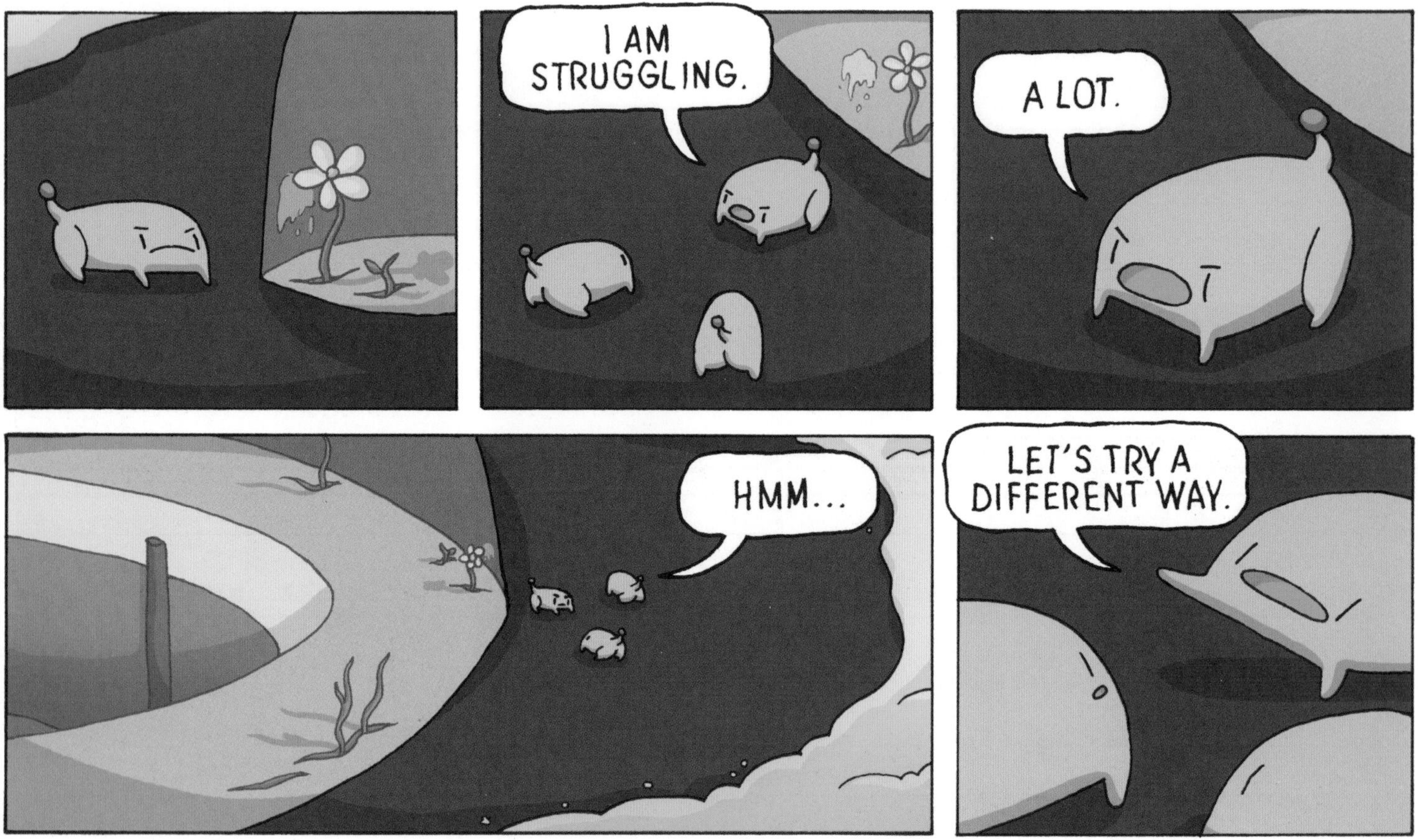
I AM STRUGGLING.
A LOT.
HMM...
LET'S TRY A DIFFERENT WAY.

LOOK!
EASY.
TOUCH
BZZZZZZT!

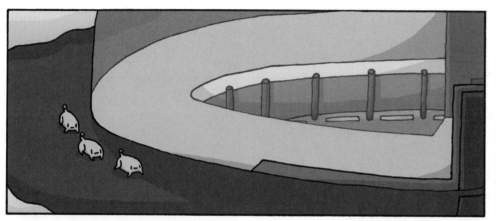

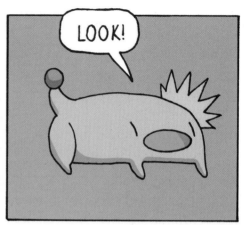

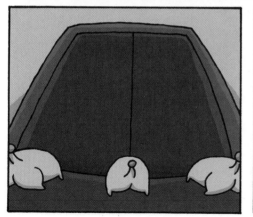

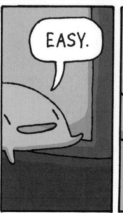

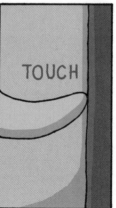

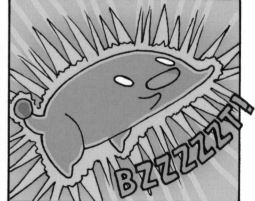

HAH?!
TOUCH
BZZZZZZT!
TOUCH
BZZZZZZT!
I AM FEELING ANGER.
TSS
...
I NEED IDEAS.
HMM...

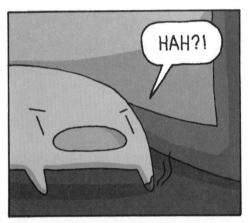

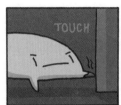

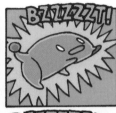

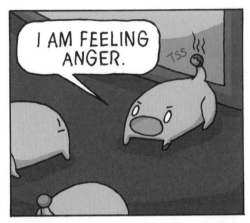

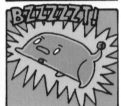

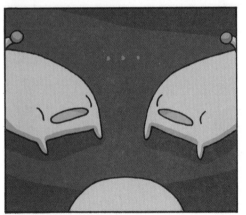

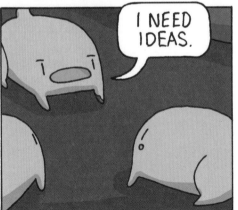

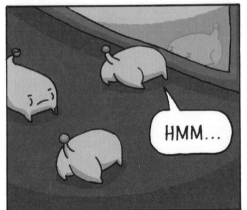

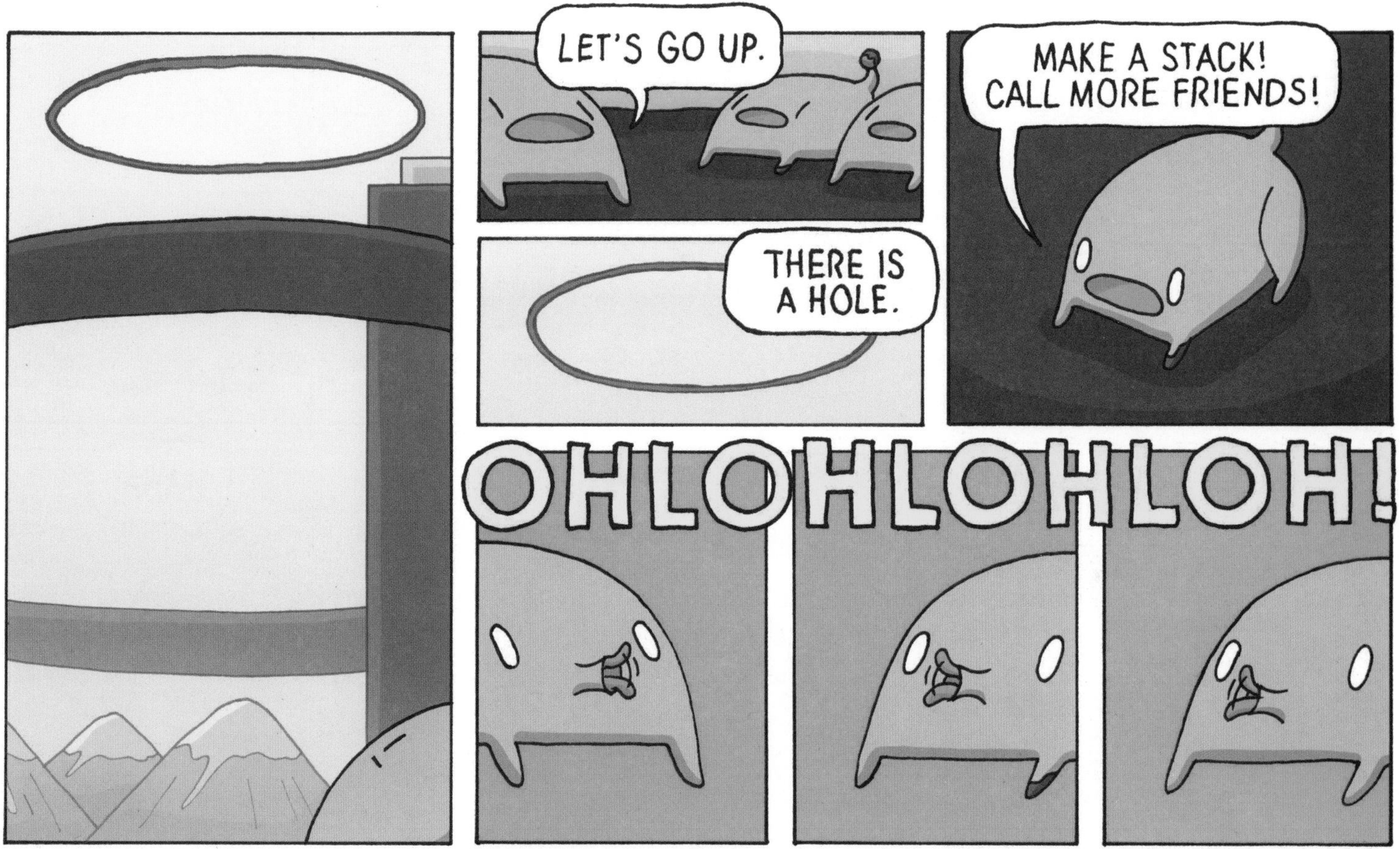
LET'S GO UP.
THERE IS A HOLE.
MAKE A STACK! CALL MORE FRIENDS!
OHLOHLOHLOH!

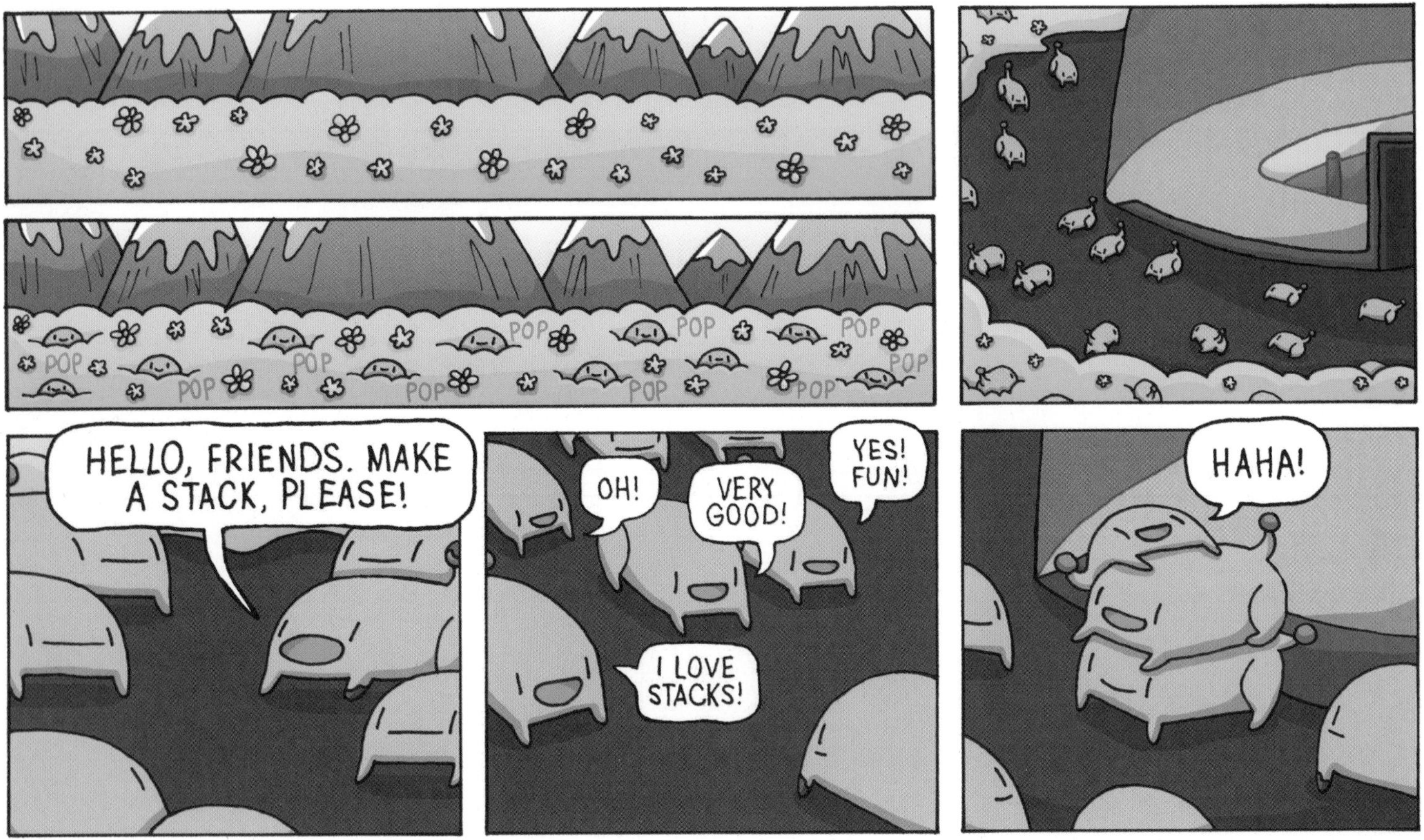
POP
POP
POP
POP
POP
POP
POP
POP
POP
POP
HELLO, FRIENDS. MAKE A STACK, PLEASE!
OH!
VERY GOOD!
YES! FUN!
I LOVE STACKS!
HAHA!

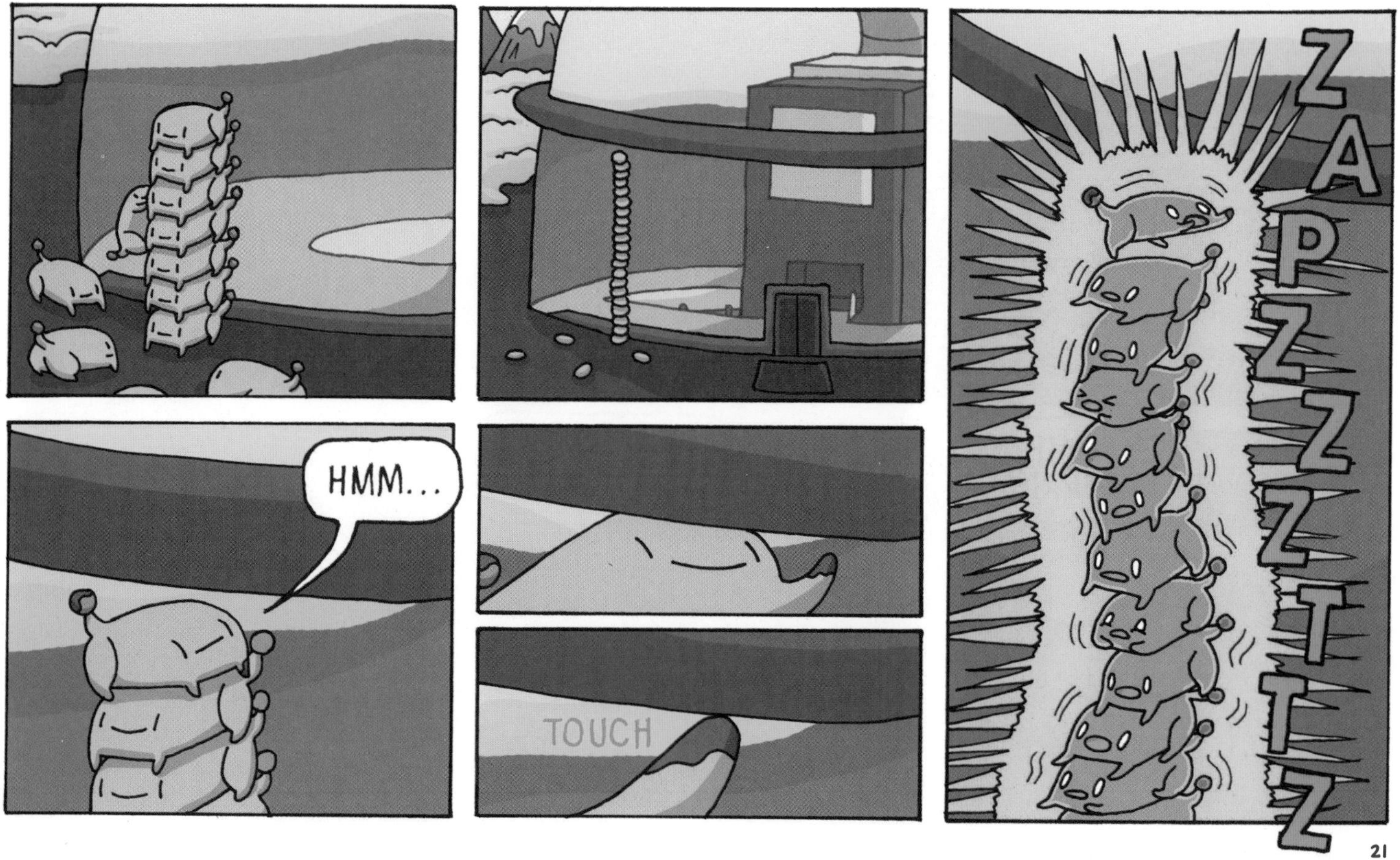
HMM...
TOUCH
ZAPZZZZTTTZ

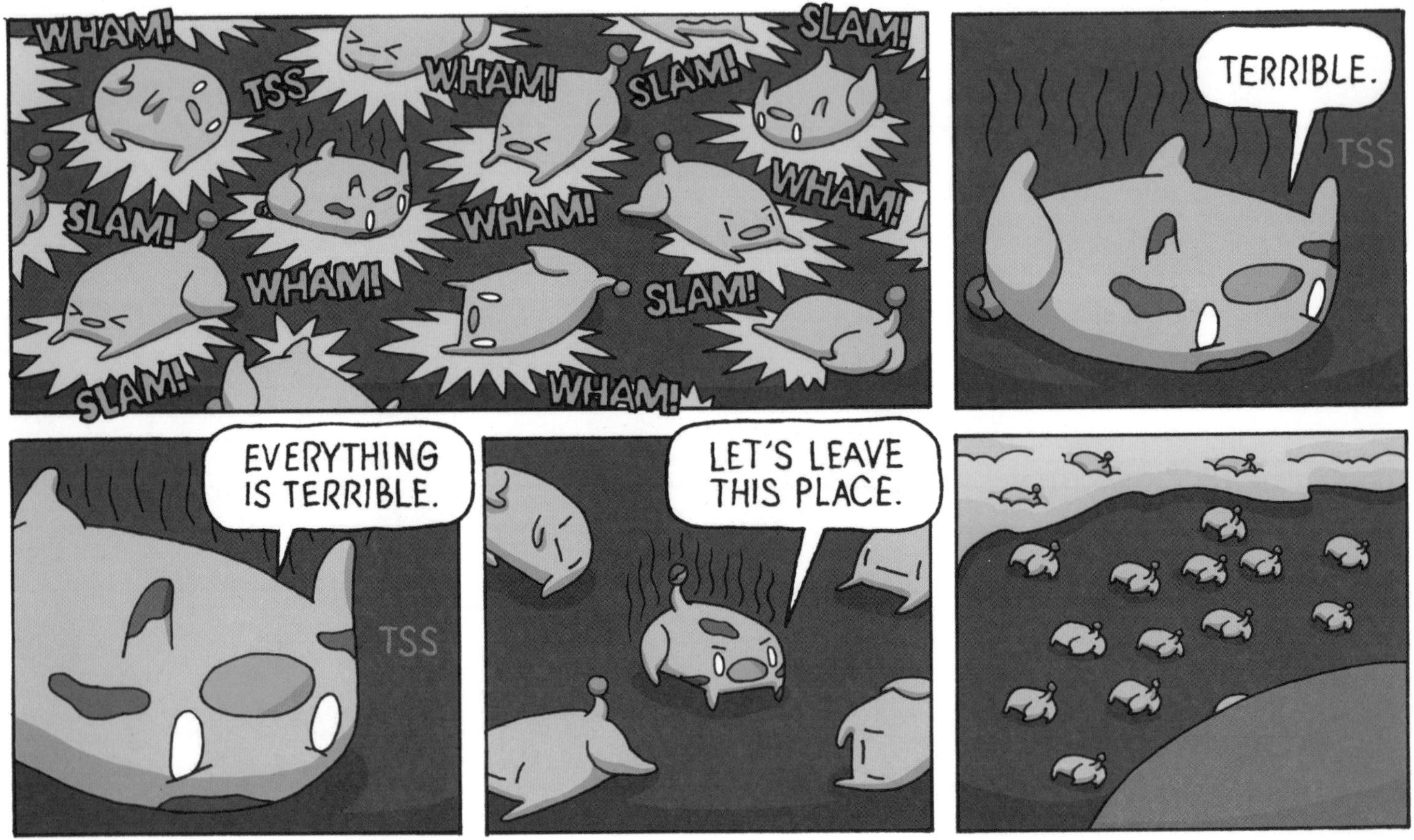
WHAM!
TSS
WHAM!
SLAM!
SLAM!
SLAM!
WHAM!
WHAM!
WHAM!
SLAM!
SLAM!
WHAM!
TERRIBLE.
TSS
EVERYTHING IS TERRIBLE.
TSS
LET'S LEAVE THIS PLACE.

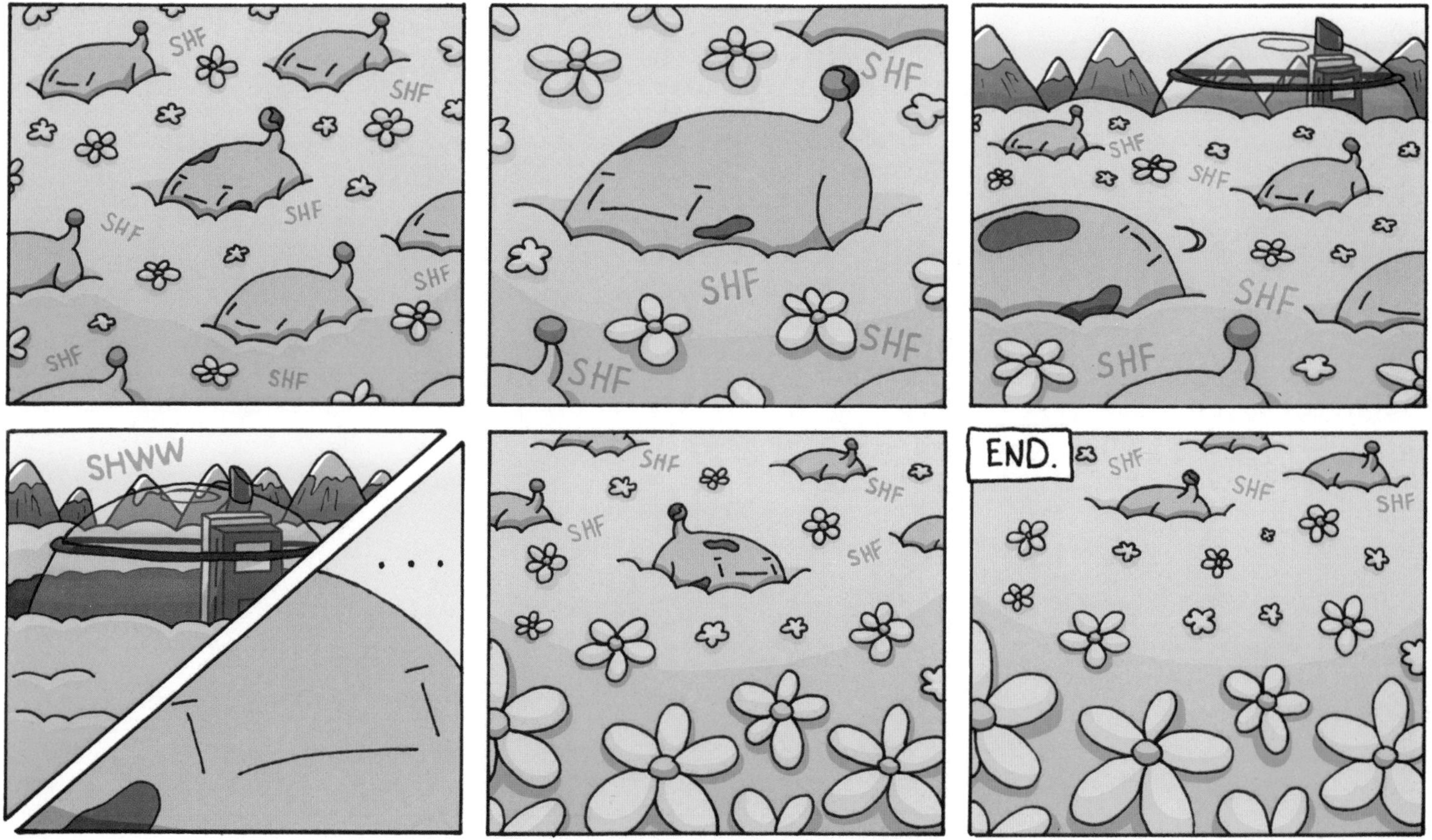
SHF
SHF
SHF
SHF
SHF
SHF
SHF
SHF
SHF
SHF
SHF
SHF
SHF
SHF
SHF
SHF
SHWW
. . .
SHF
SHF
SHF
SHF
END.
SHF
SHF
SHF

CHAPTER TWO

—

YUMMY SCARY

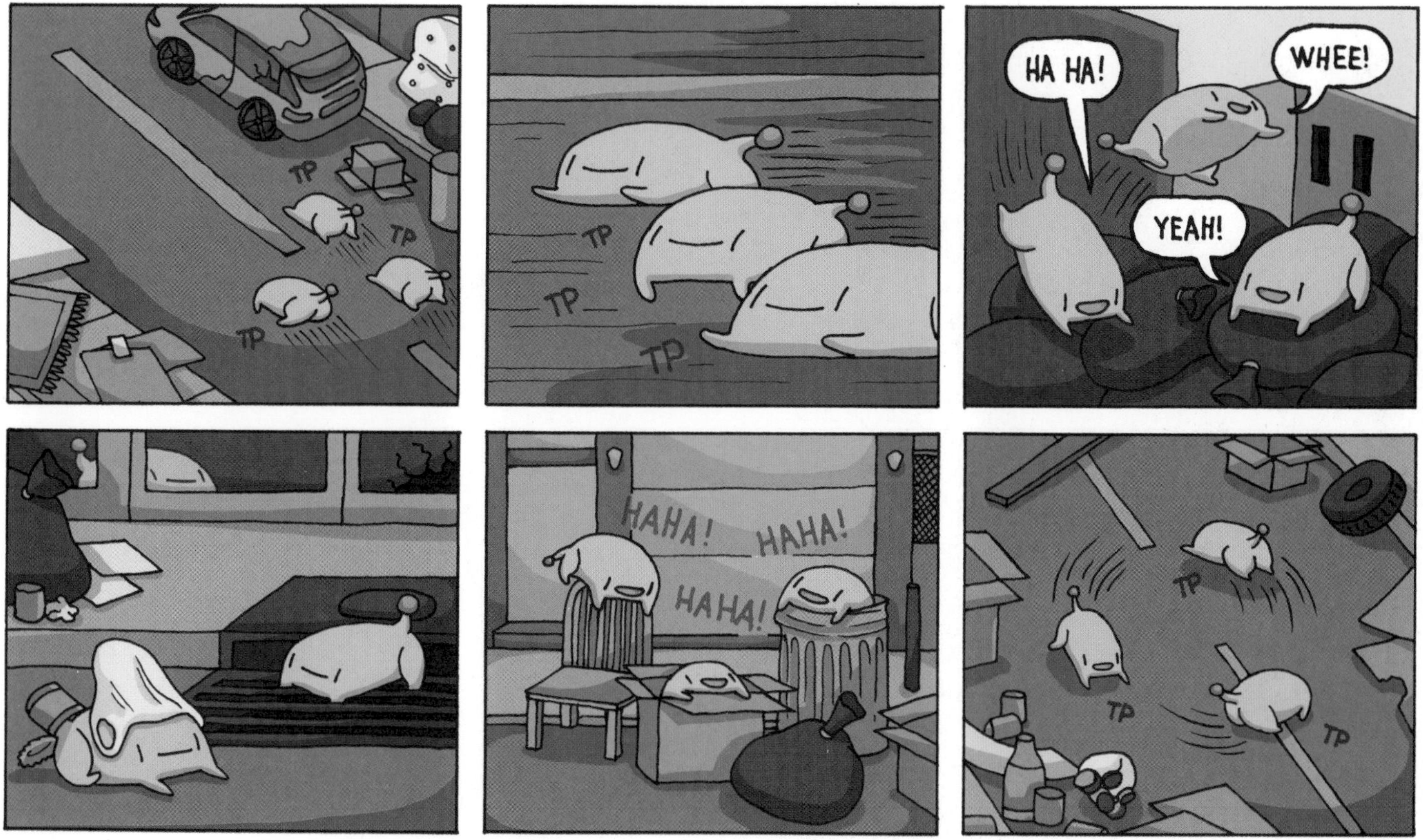
TP
TP
TP
TP
TP
TP
TP
HA HA!
WHEE!
YEAH!
HAHA!
HAHA!
HAHA!
TP
TP
TP

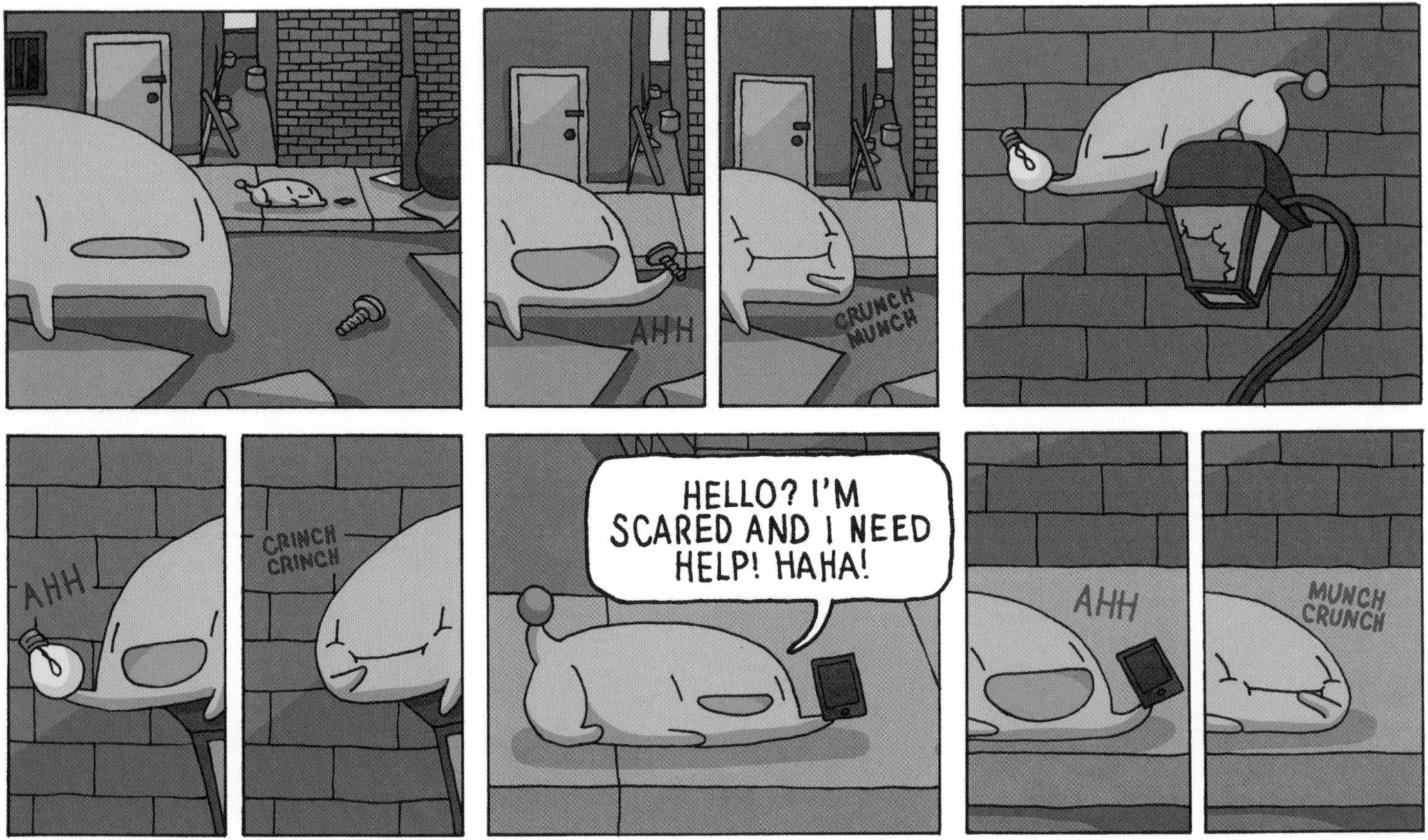
AHH
CRUNCH MUNCH
AHH
CRINCH CRINCH
HELLO? I'M SCARED AND I NEED HELP! HAHA!
AHH
MUNCH CRUNCH

OH!
!
SQUARES.

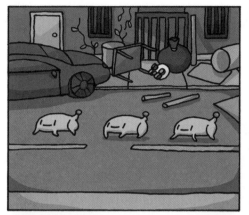

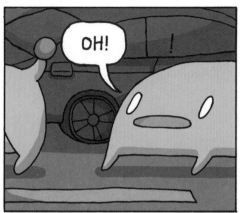

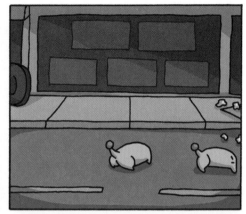

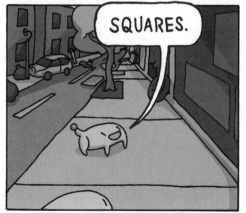

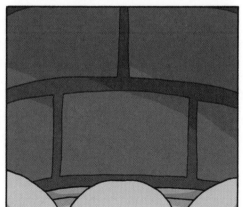

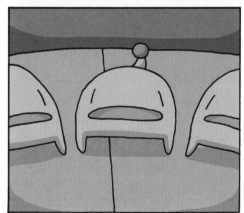

FFFSSSSSSSS!!!!
AGGHH!! AGHH!! AGHHH!!
TP
TP
TP
FFSSS!!
THAT RUINED OUR GOOD TIME.

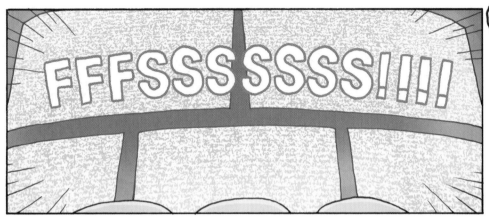

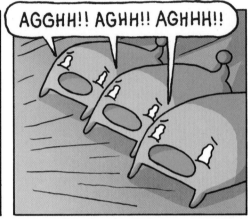

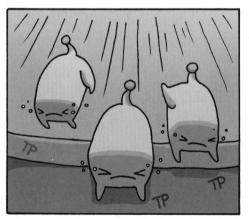

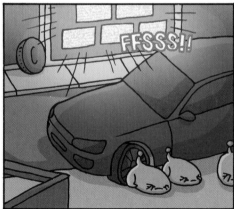

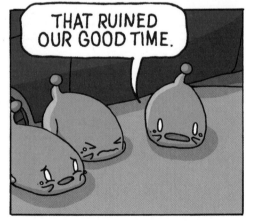

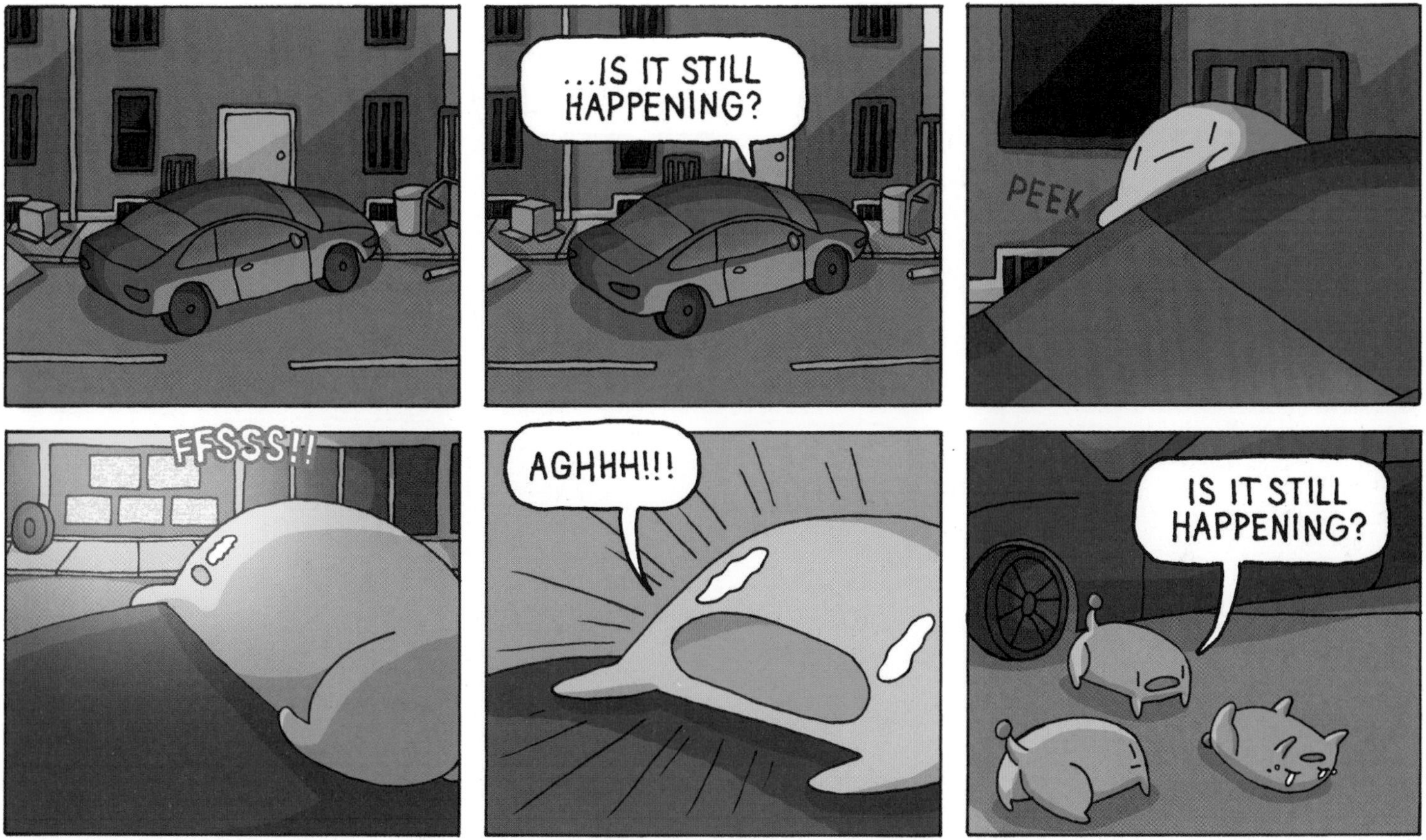
...IS IT STILL HAPPENING?
PEEK
FFSSS!!
AGHHH!!!
IS IT STILL HAPPENING?

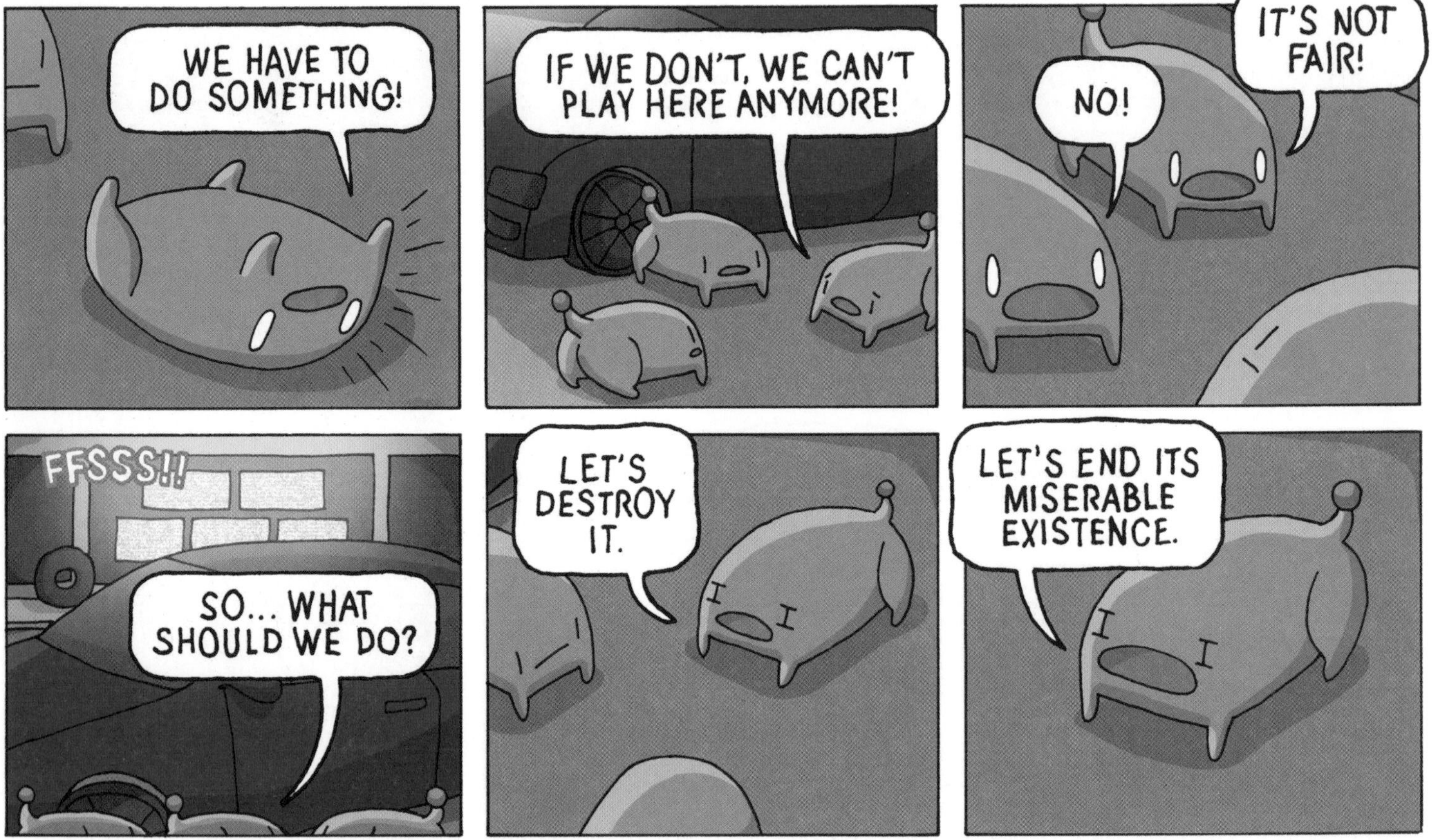
WE HAVE TO DO SOMETHING!
IF WE DON'T, WE CAN'T PLAY HERE ANYMORE!
NO!
IT'S NOT FAIR!
FFSSS!!
SO... WHAT SHOULD WE DO?
LET'S DESTROY IT.
LET'S END ITS MISERABLE EXISTENCE.

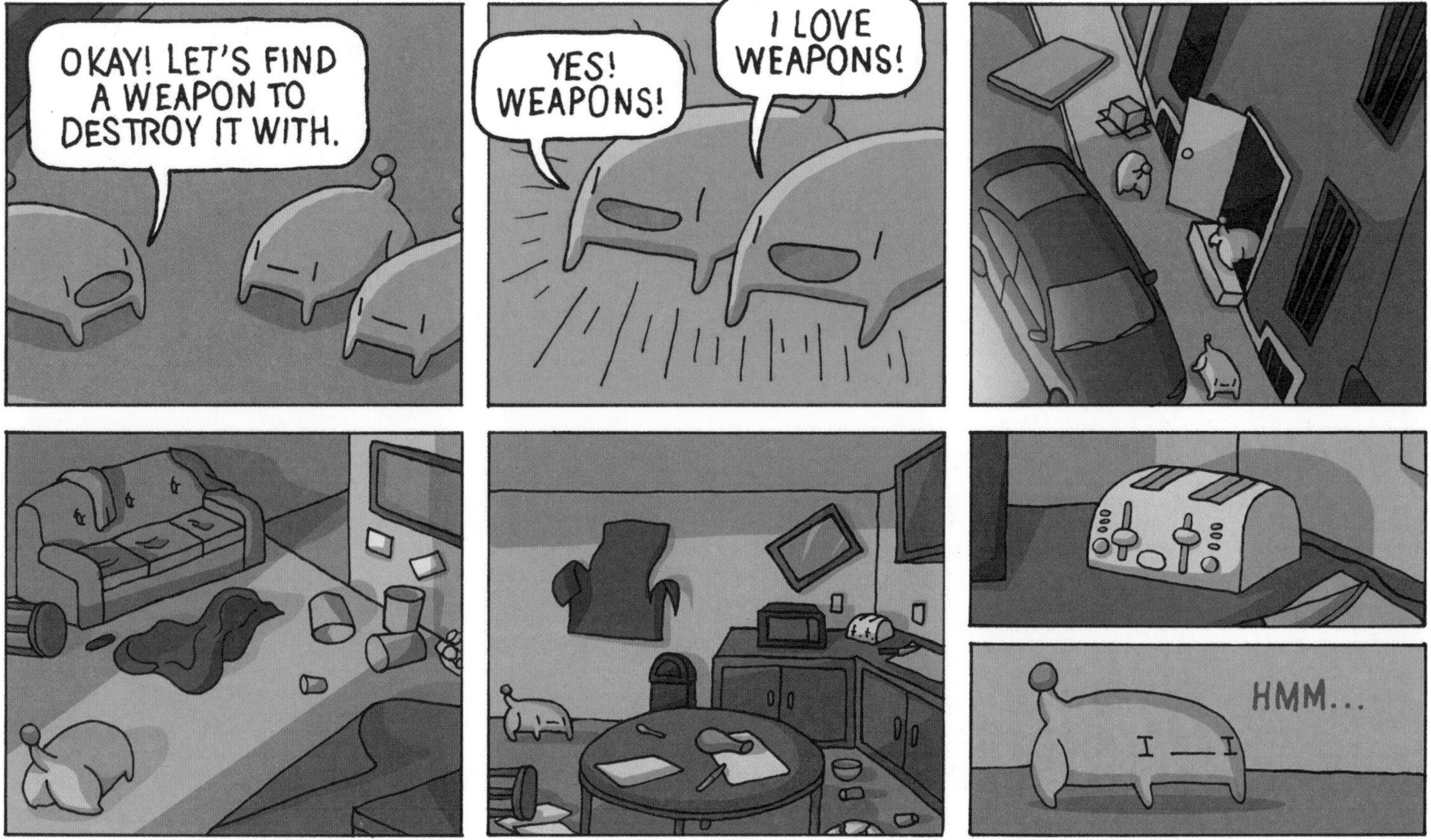
OKAY! LET'S FIND A WEAPON TO DESTROY IT WITH.
YES! WEAPONS!
I LOVE WEAPONS!
HMM...

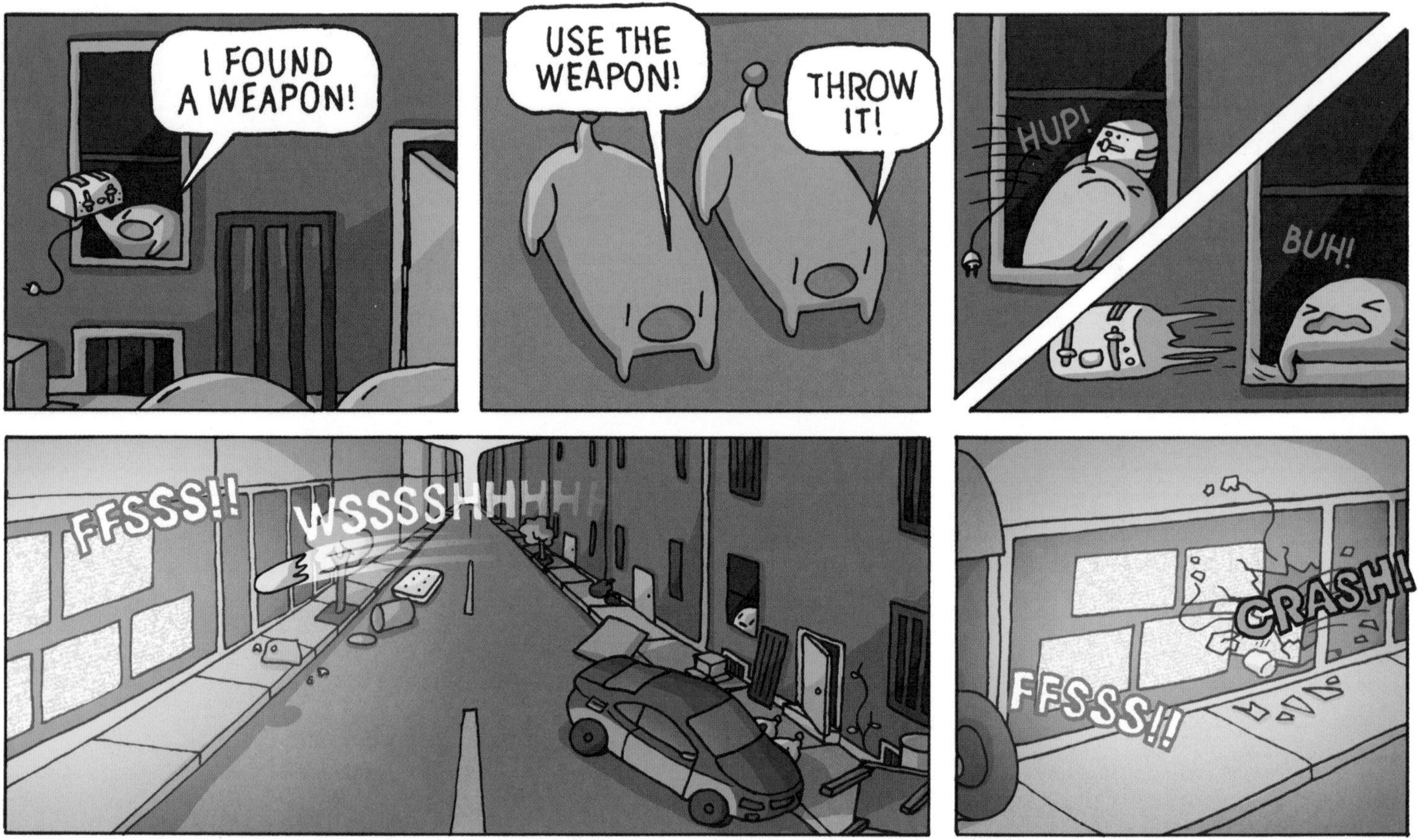
I FOUND A WEAPON!
USE THE WEAPON!
THROW IT!
HUP!
BUH!
FFSSS!!
WSSSSHHHHH
CRASH!
FFSSS!!

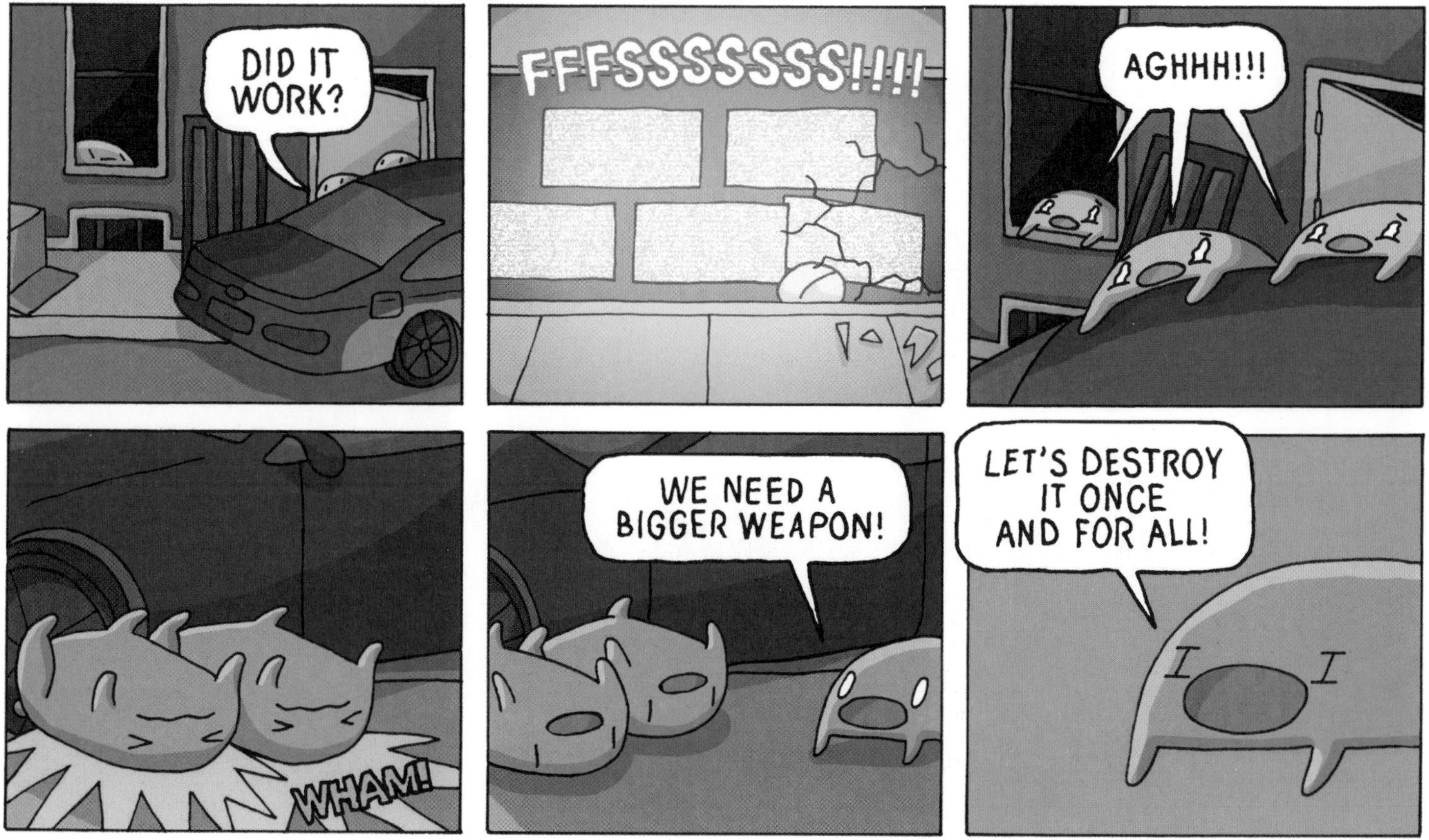
DID IT WORK?
FFFSSSSSSS!!!!
AGHHH!!!
WHAM!
WE NEED A BIGGER WEAPON!
LET'S DESTROY IT ONCE AND FOR ALL!

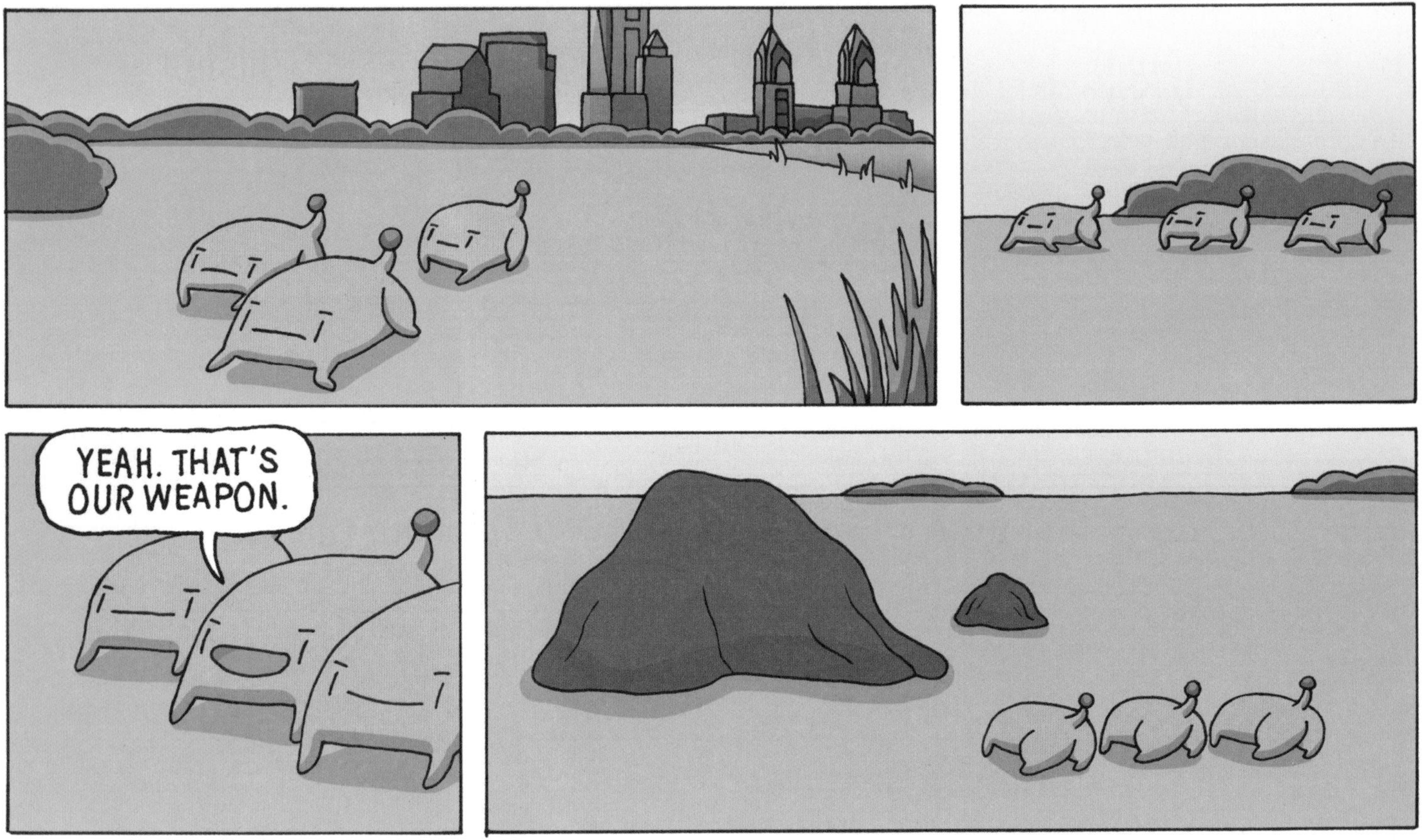
YEAH. THAT'S OUR WEAPON.

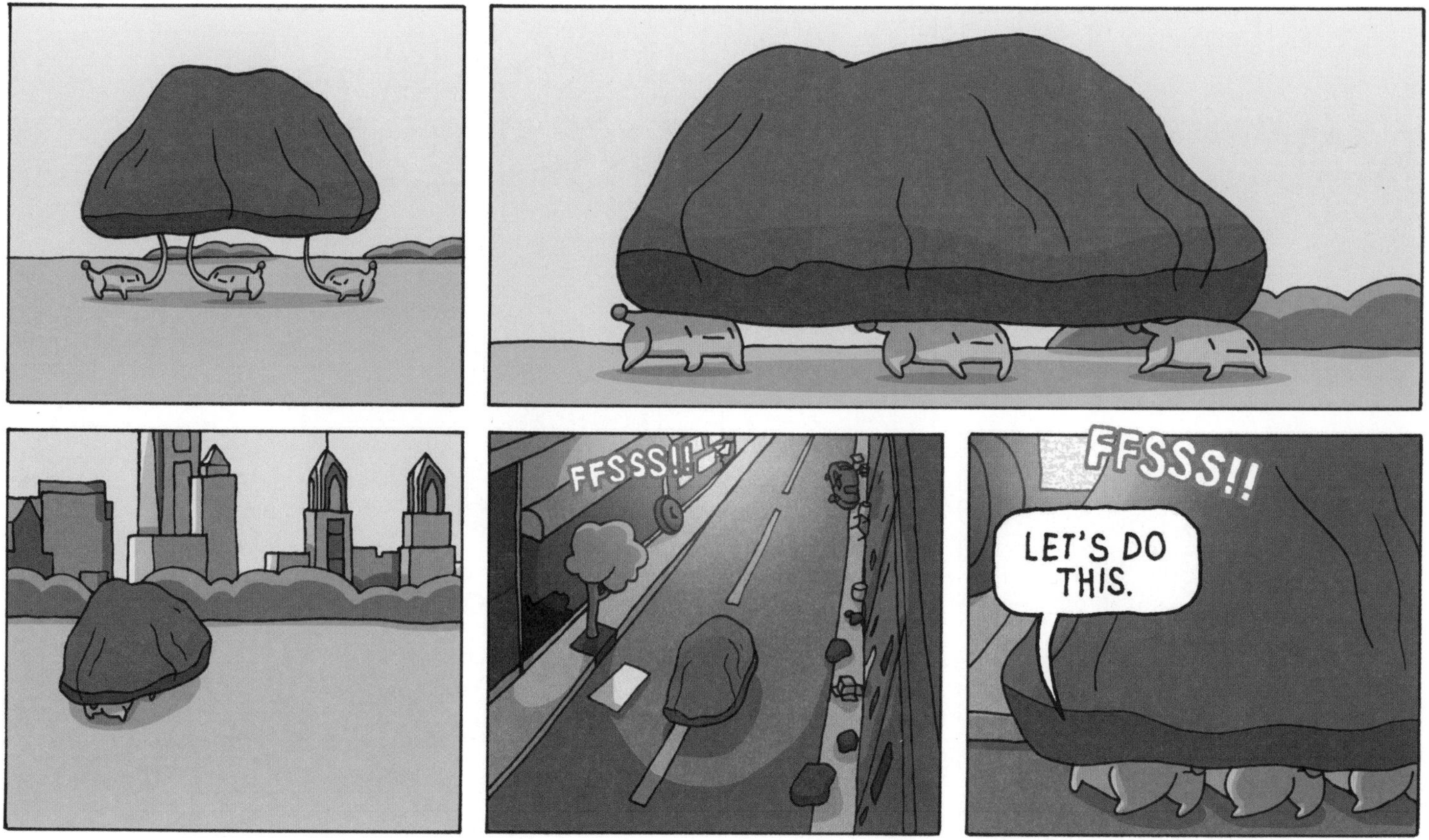
FFSSS!!
FFSSS!!
LET'S DO THIS.

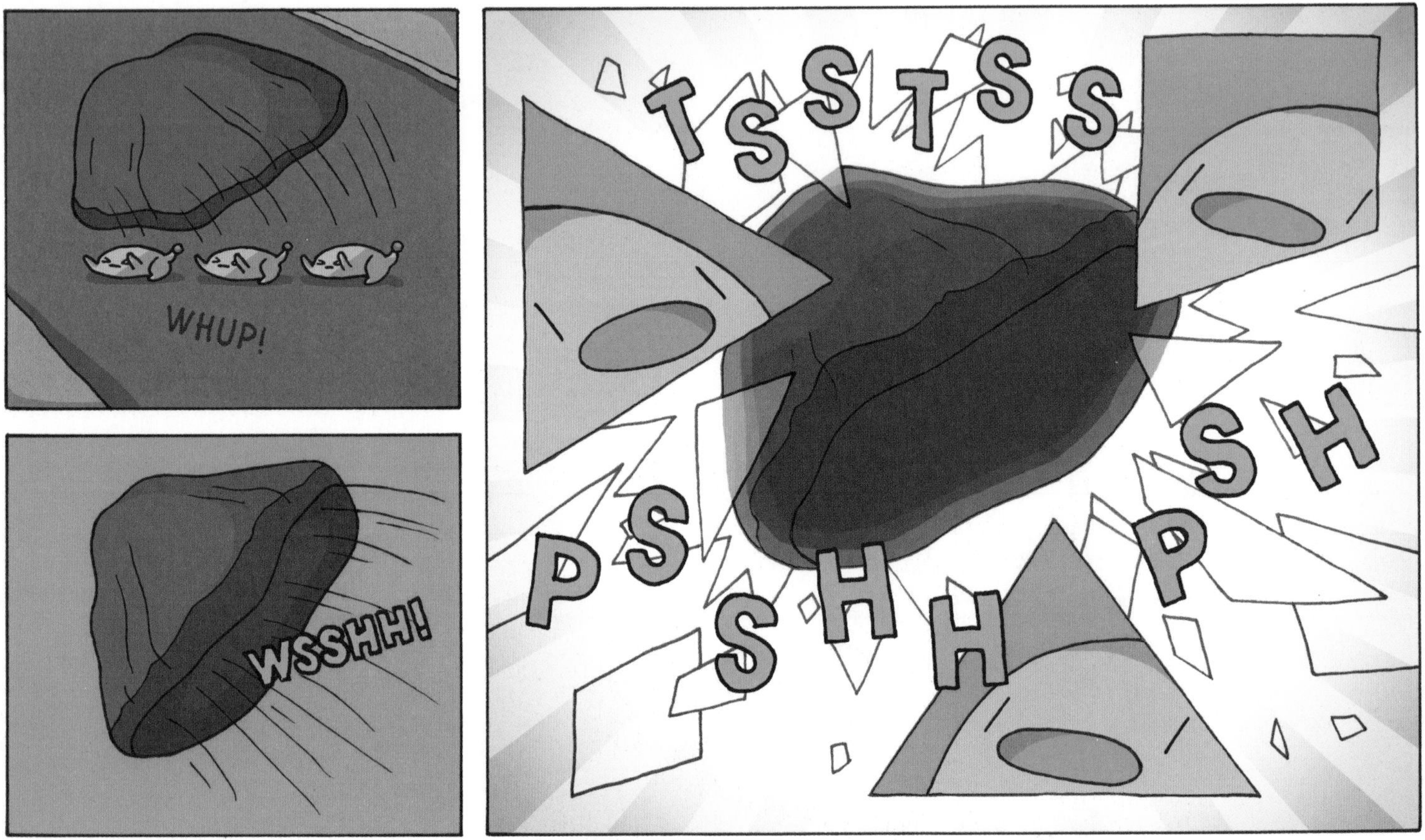
WHUP!
WSSHH!
TSSTSS
PSSHH
PSH

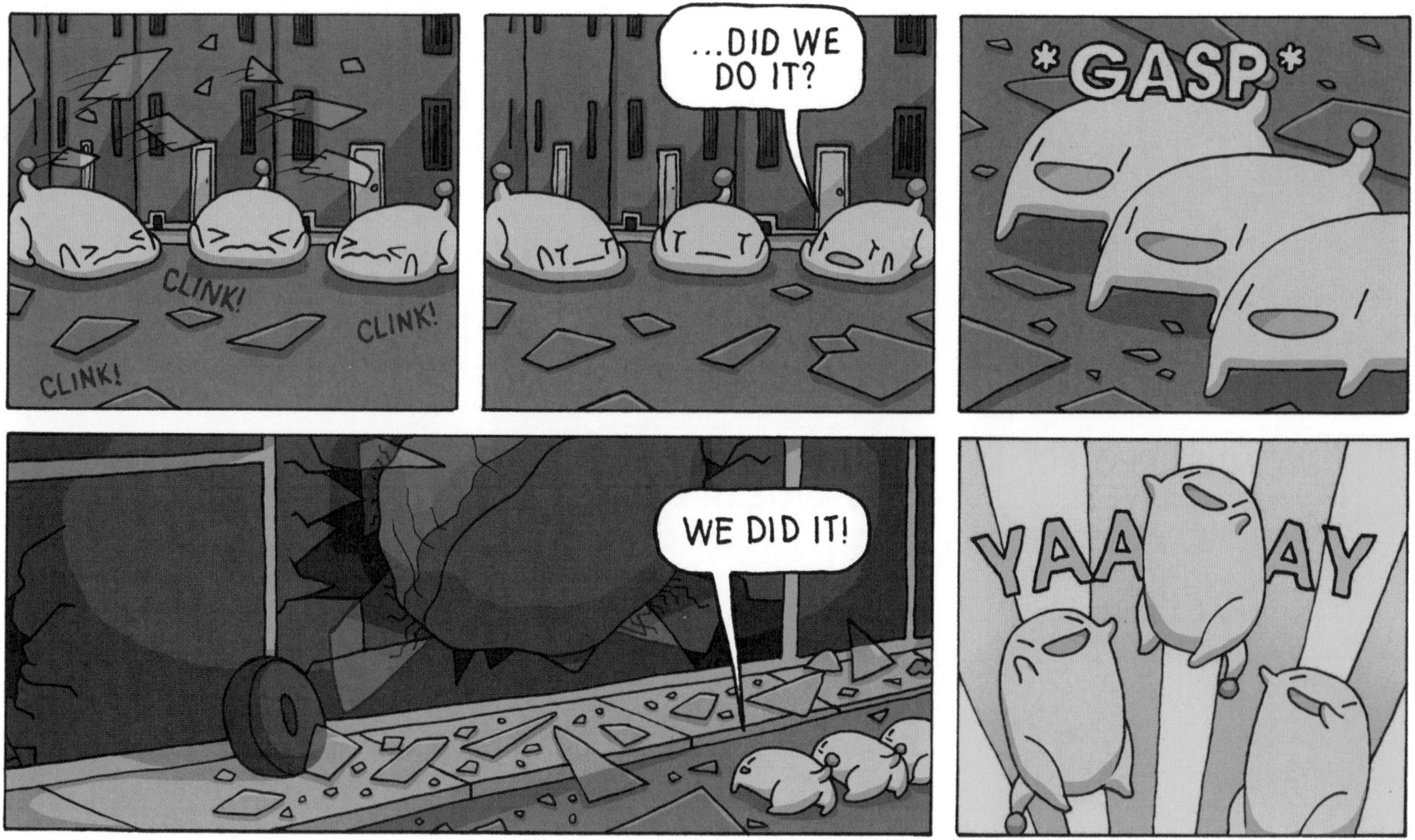
CLINK!
CLINK!
CLINK!
...DID WE DO IT?
GASP
WE DID IT!
YAA AY

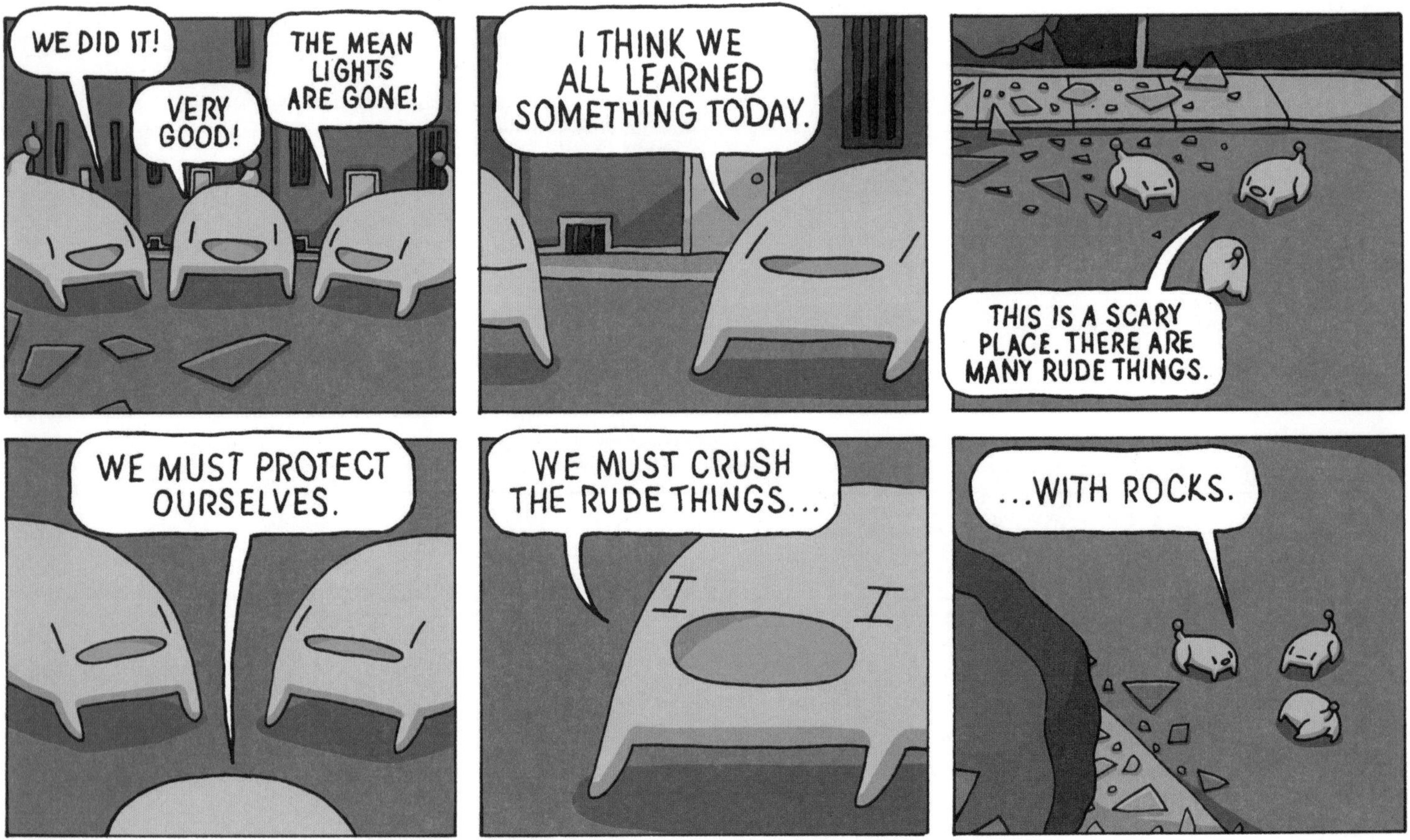
WE DID IT!
VERY GOOD!
THE MEAN LIGHTS ARE GONE!
I THINK WE ALL LEARNED SOMETHING TODAY.
THIS IS A SCARY PLACE. THERE ARE MANY RUDE THINGS.
WE MUST PROTECT OURSELVES.
WE MUST CRUSH THE RUDE THINGS...
...WITH ROCKS.

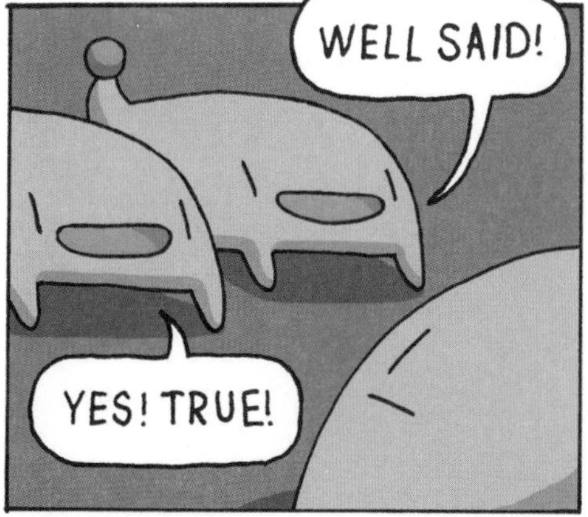
WELL SAID!
YES! TRUE!

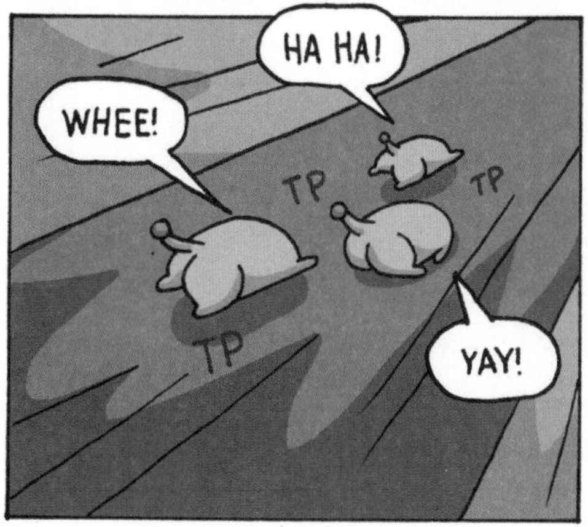
WHEE!
HA HA!
TP
TP
TP
YAY!

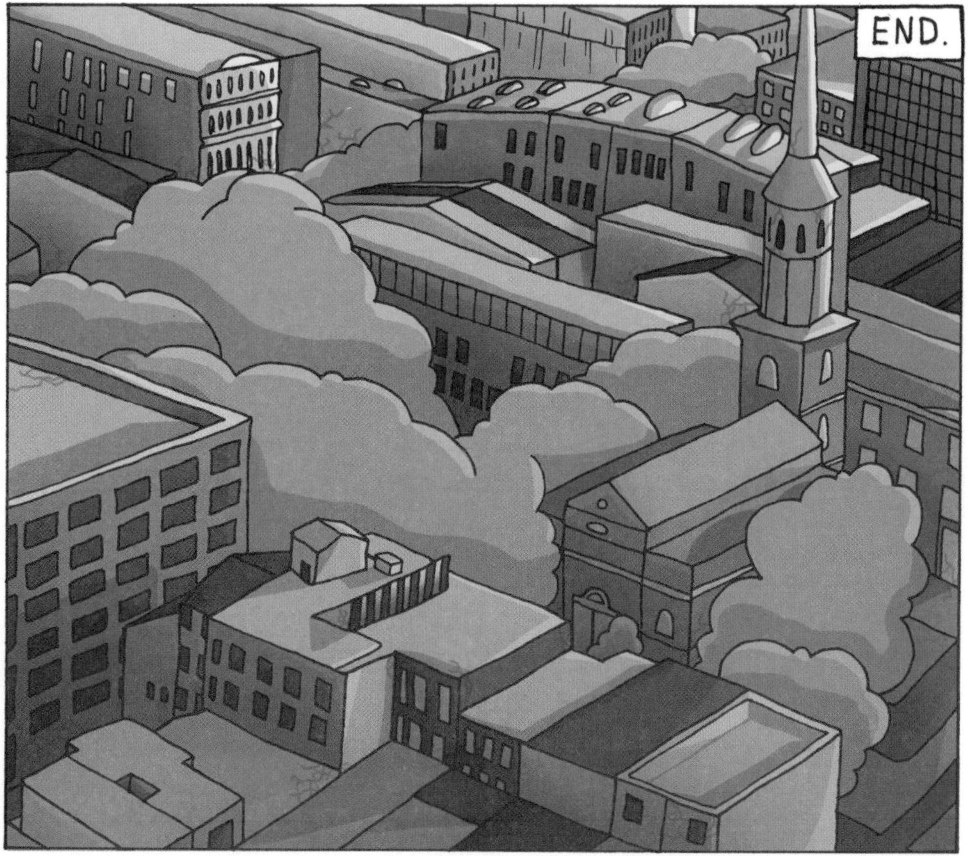
END.

CHAPTER THREE

—

MAMA BIRD, TEACH ME HOW TO FLY

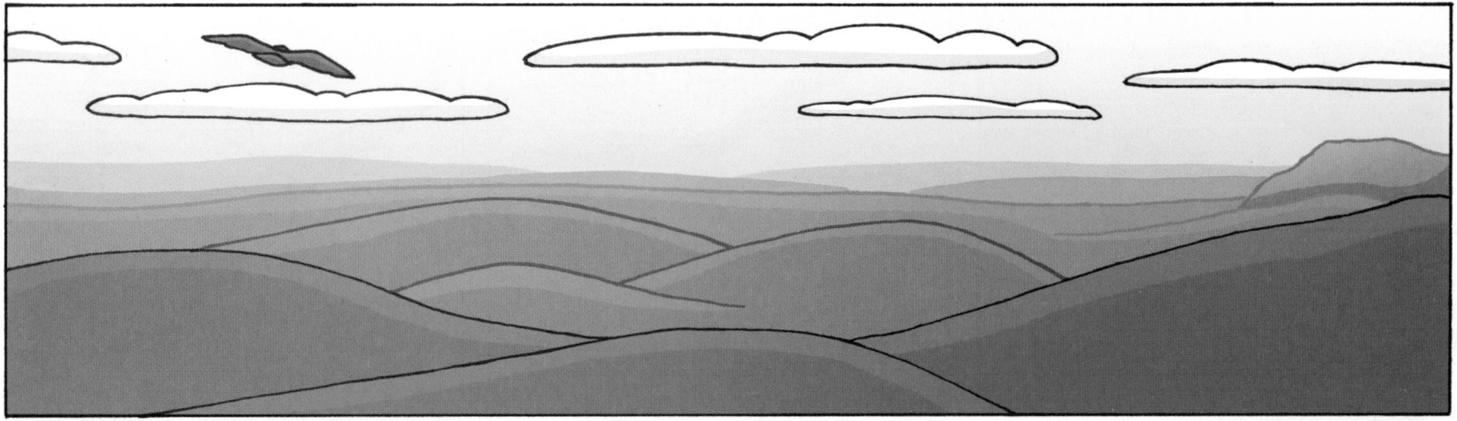

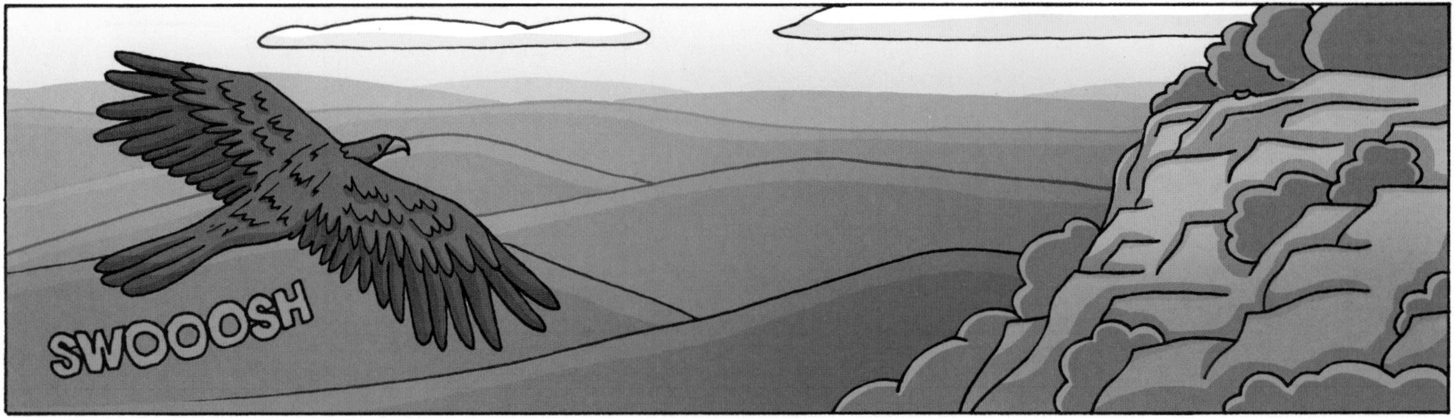
SWOOOSH

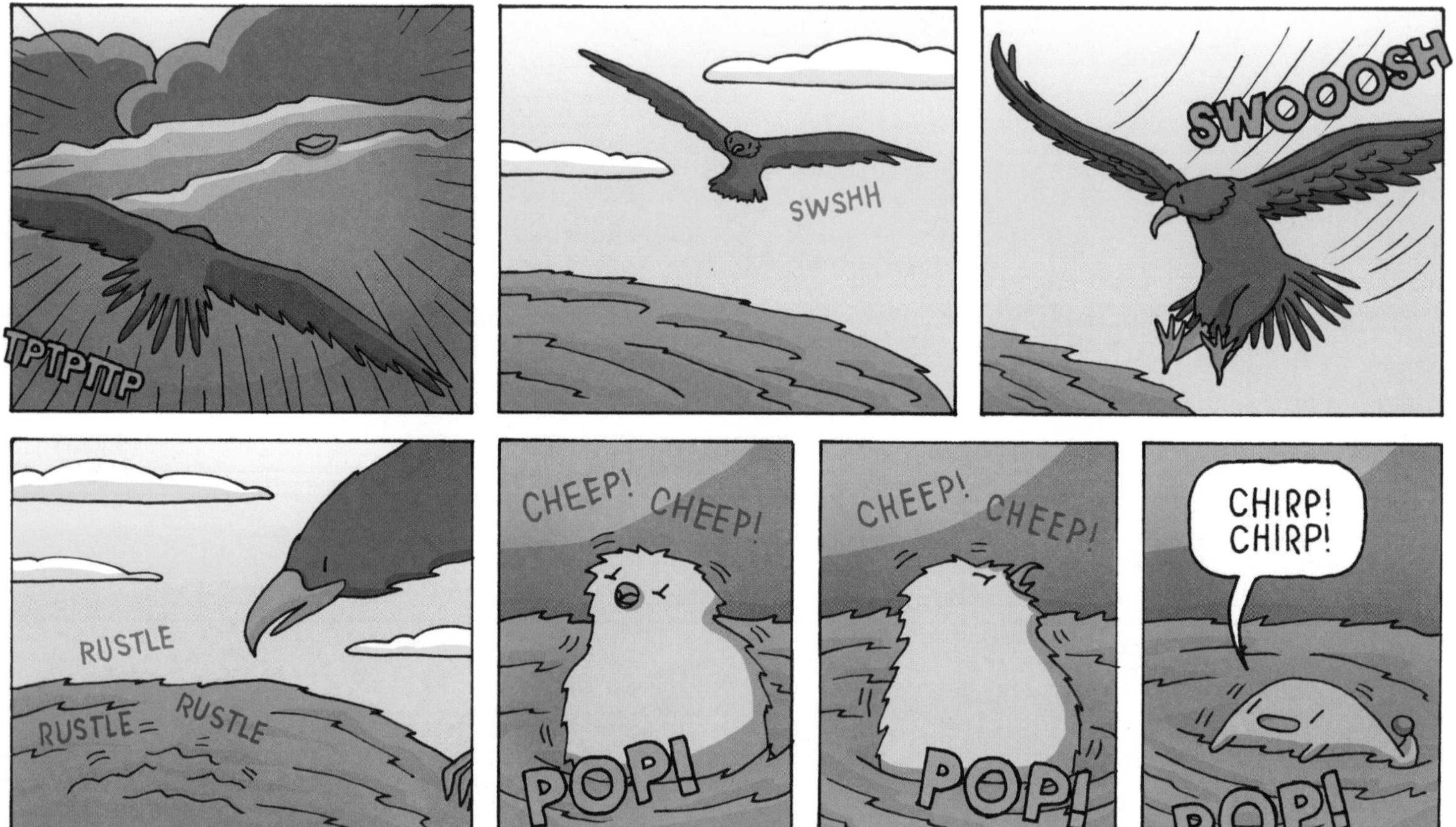
TPTPTTP
SWSHH
SWOOOSH
RUSTLE
RUSTLE
RUSTLE
CHEEP!
CHEEP!
POP!
CHEEP!
CHEEP!
POP!
CHIRP! CHIRP!
POP!

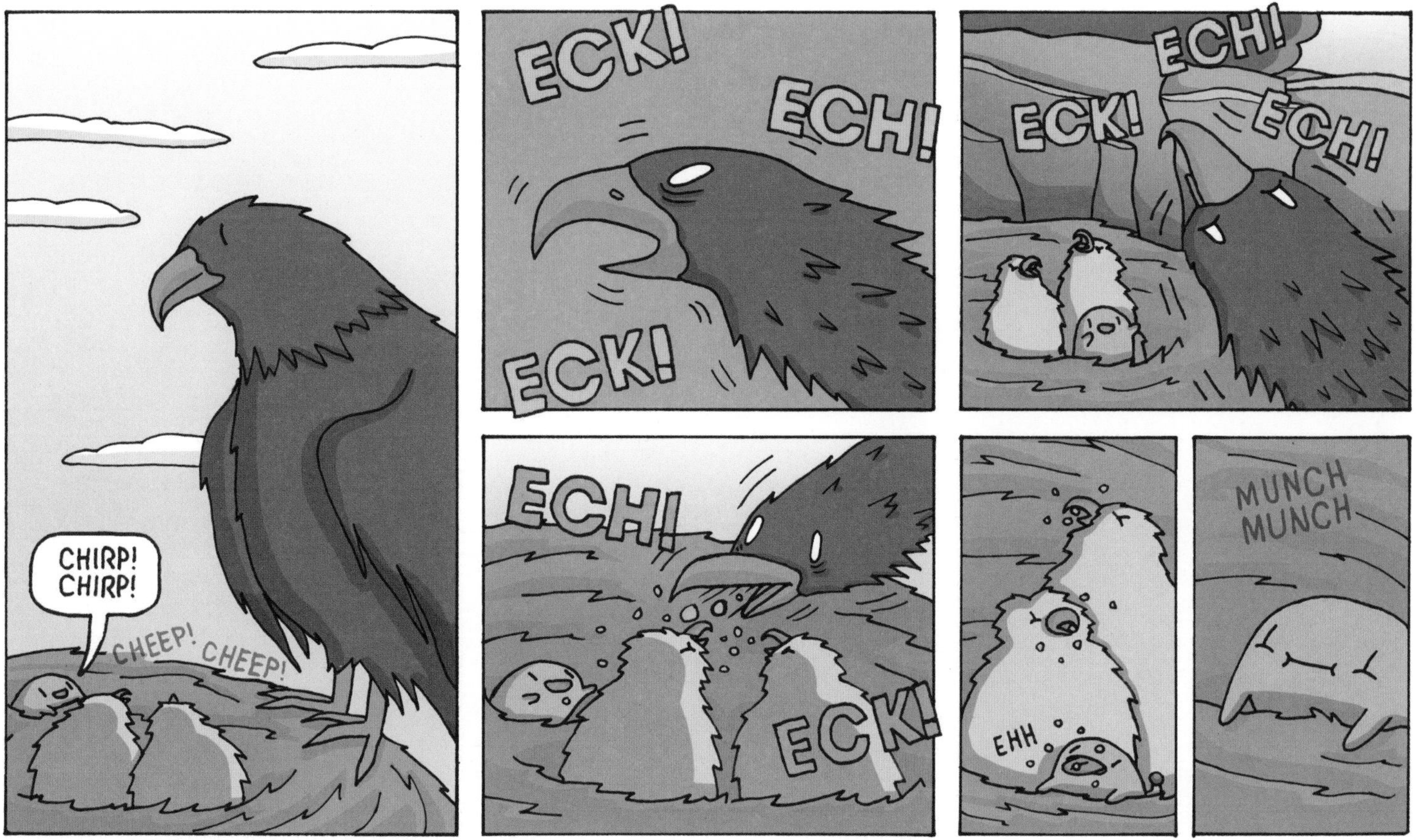
CHIRP! CHIRP!
CHEEP! CHEEP!
ECK!
ECH!
ECK!
ECH!
ECK!
ECH!
ECH!
ECK!
EHH
MUNCH MUNCH

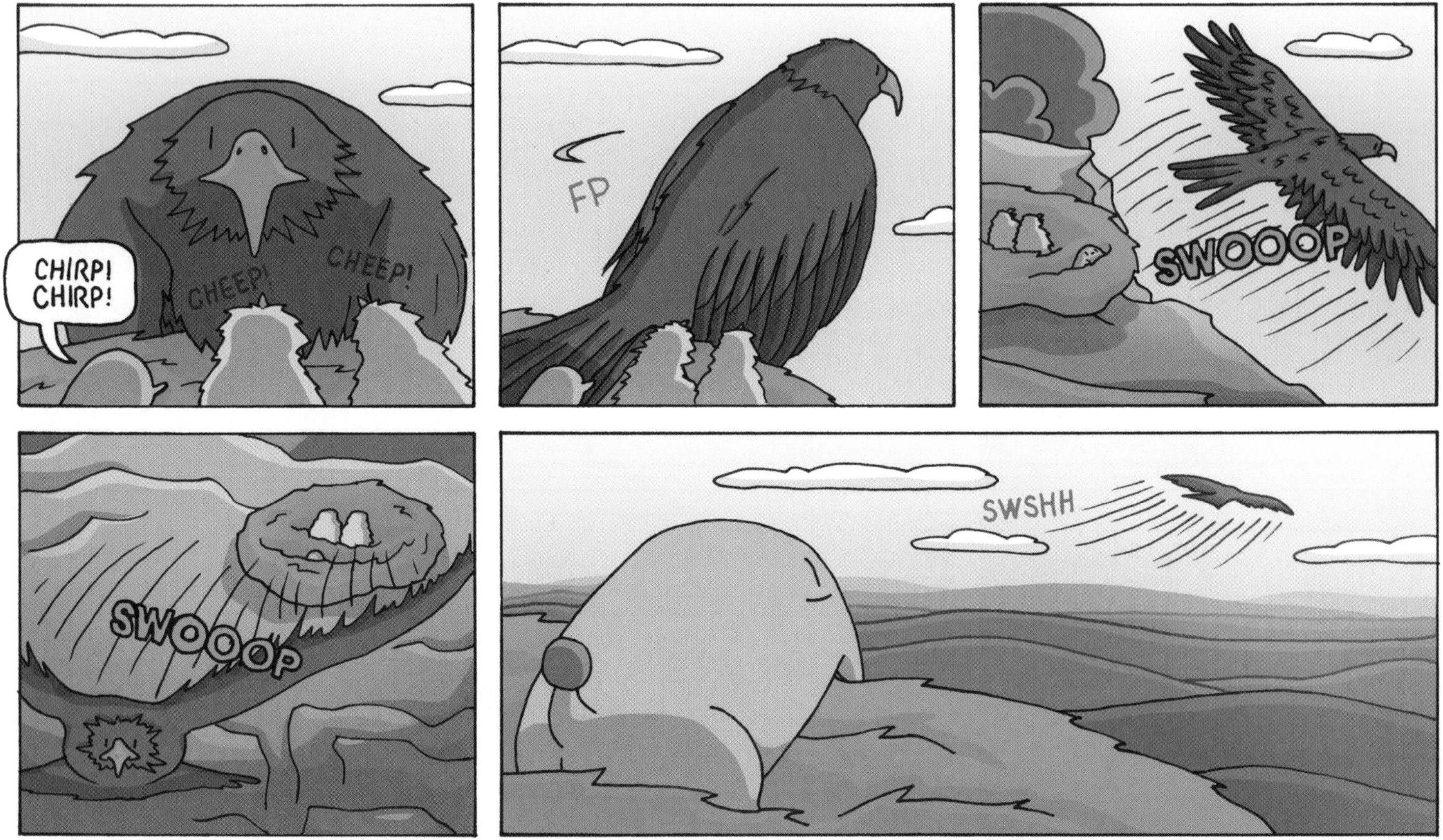
CHIRP! CHIRP!
CHEEP!
CHEEP!
FP
SWOOOP
SWOOOP
SWSHH

Z Z Z
Z Z Z
Z Z Z
Z Z Z

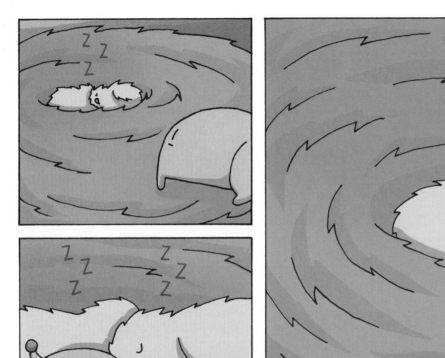

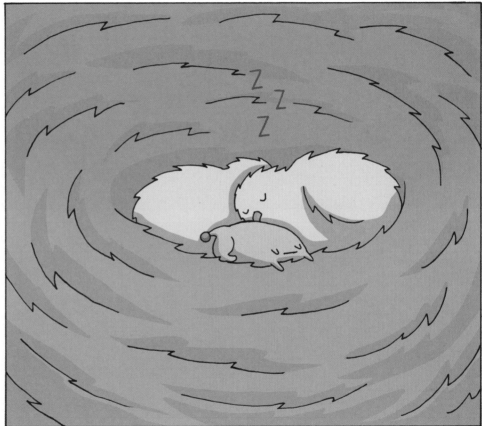

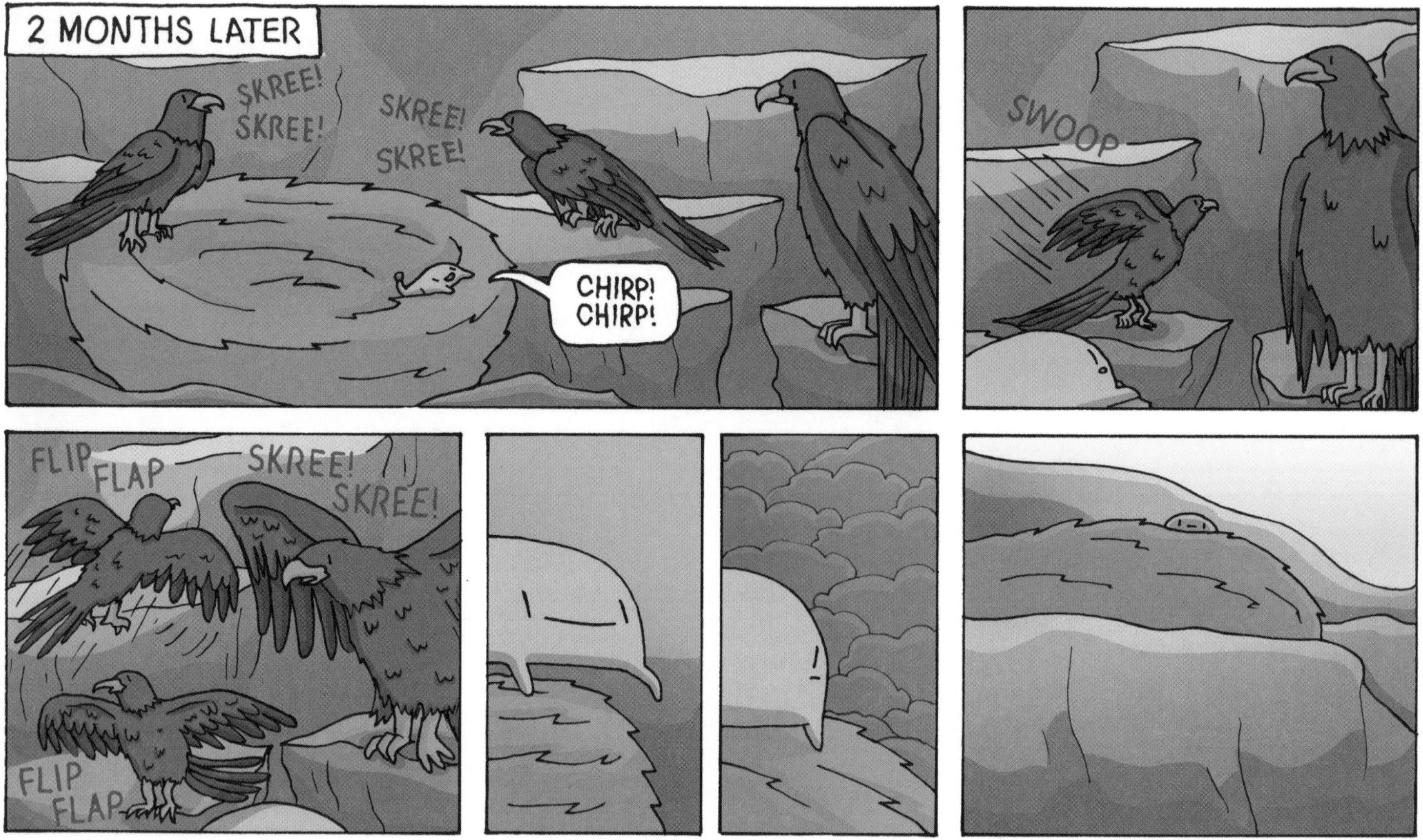
2 MONTHS LATER
SKREE! SKREE!
SKREE! SKREE!
CHIRP! CHIRP!
SWOOP
FLIP FLAP
SKREE! SKREE!
FLIP FLAP

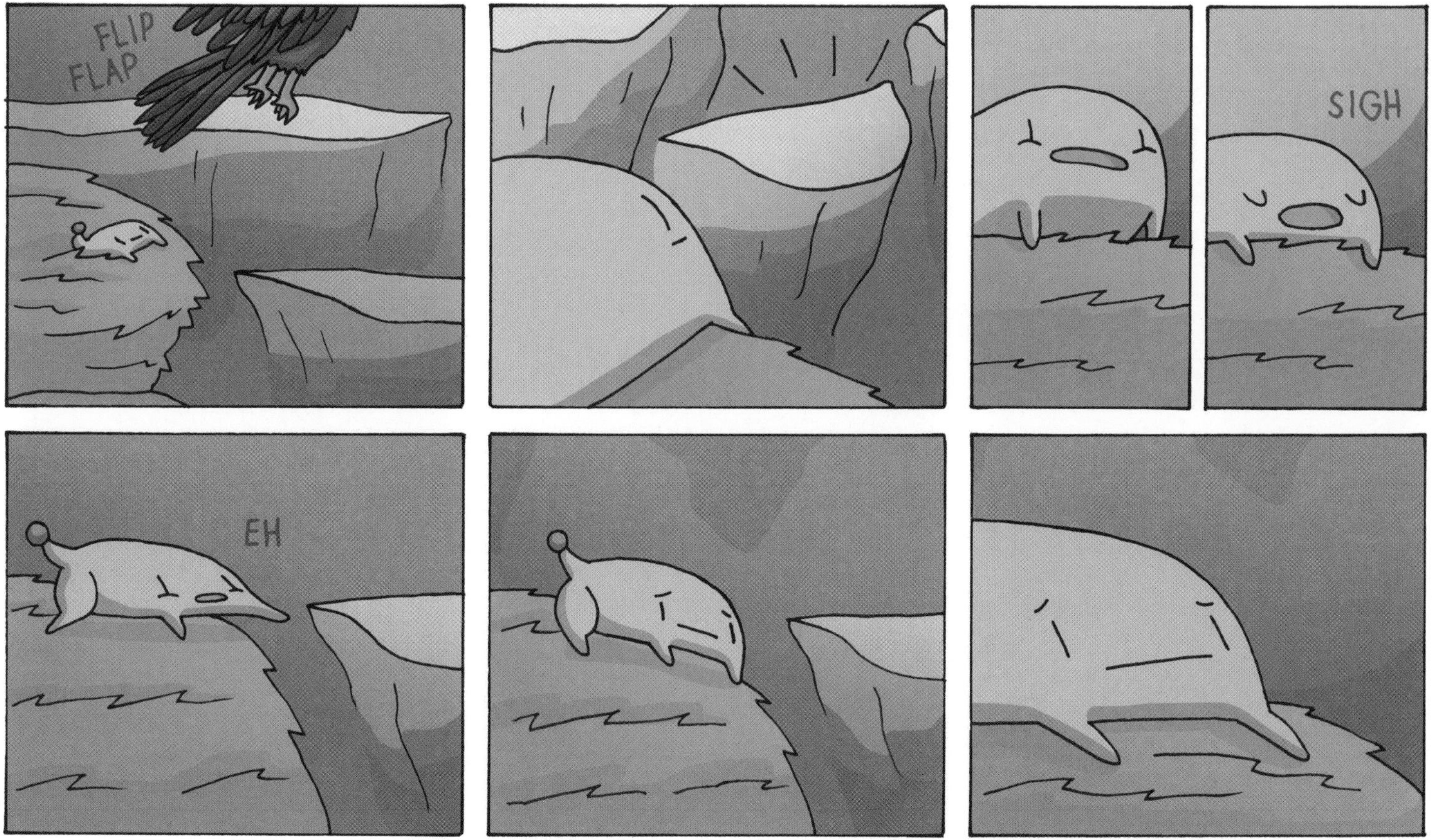
FLIP
FLAP
SIGH
EH

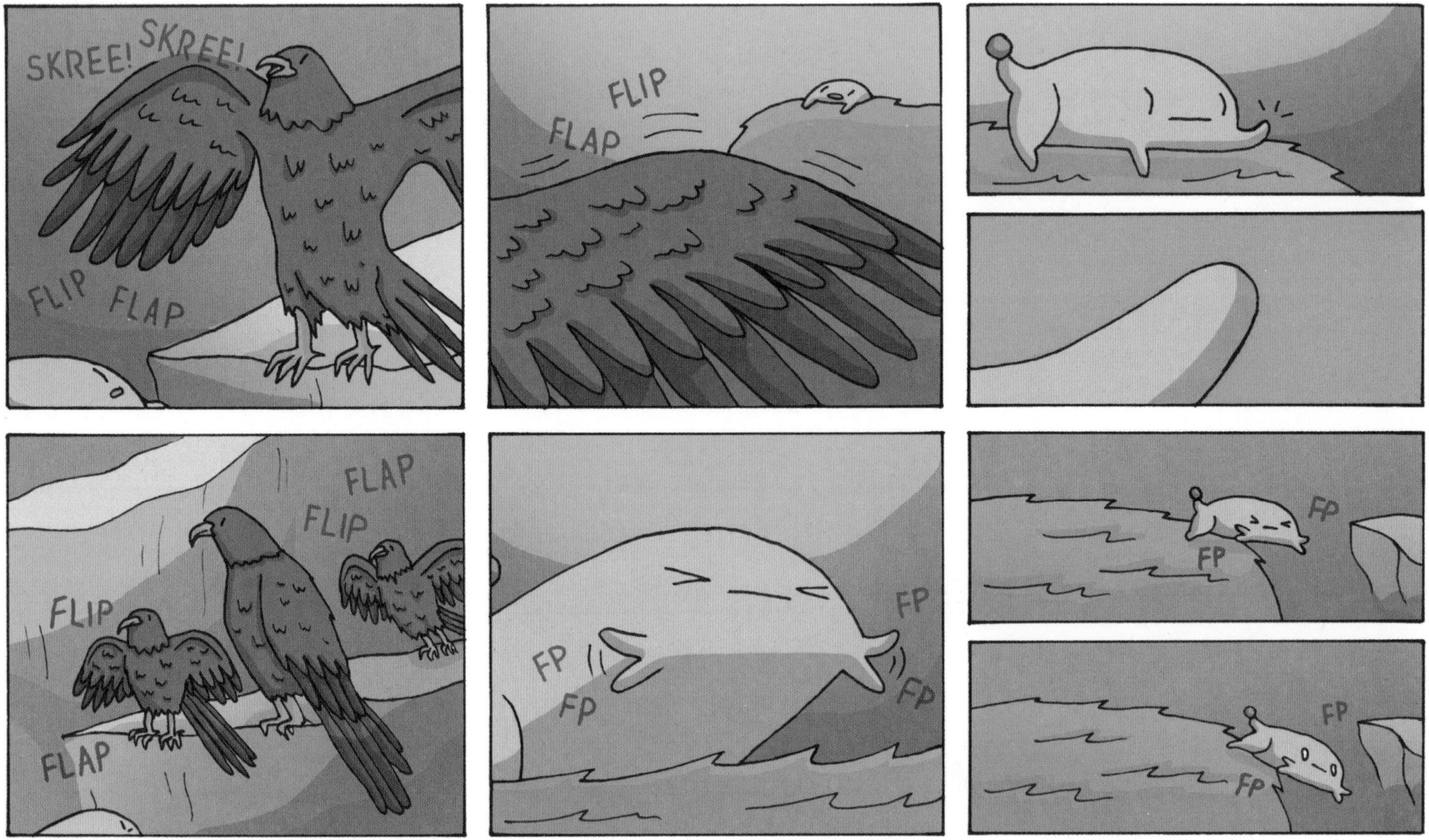

SKREE! SKREE!
FLIP FLAP
FLIP
FLAP
FLIP
FLAP
FLIP
FLAP
FP
FP
FP
FP
FP
FP
FP
FP

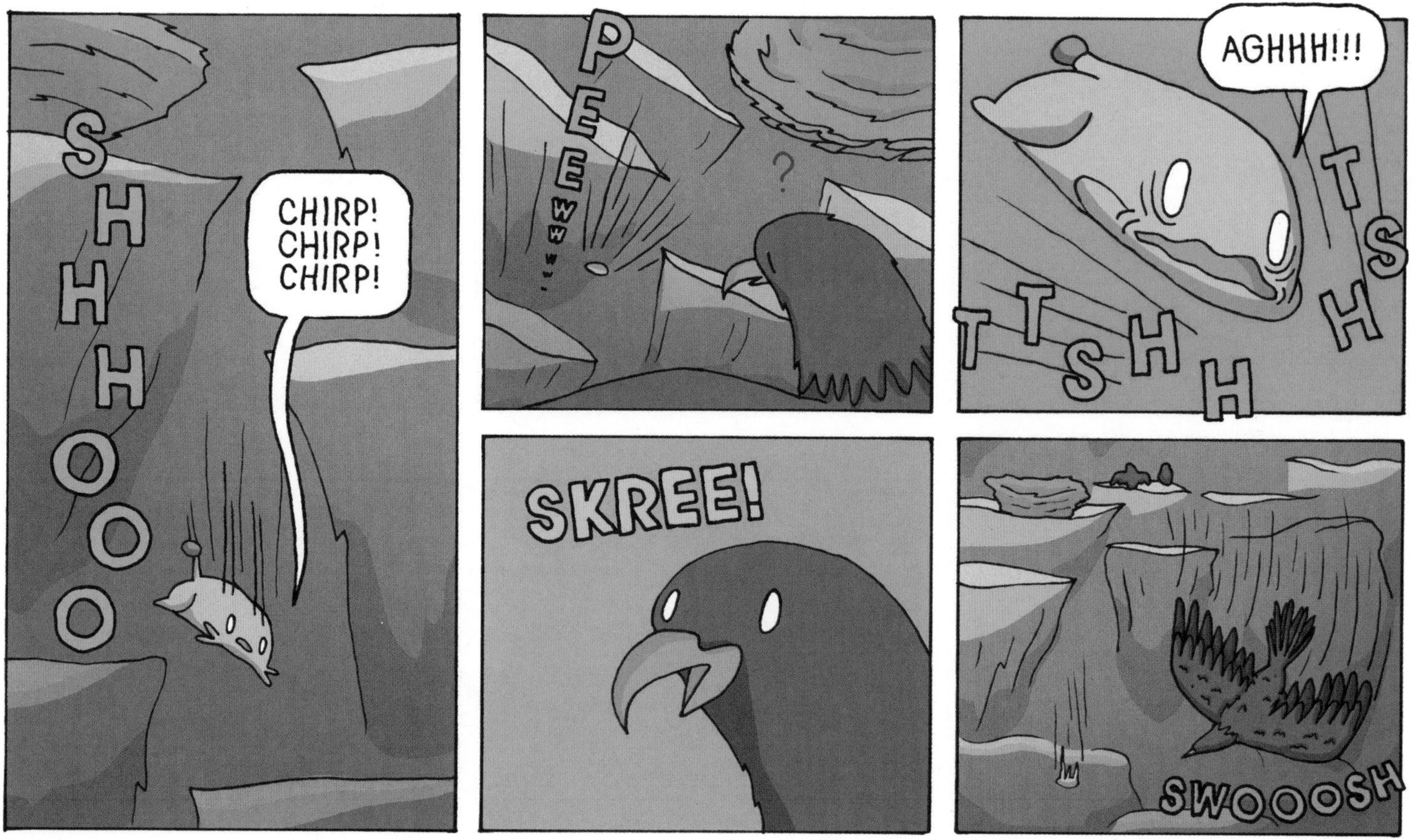
SHHHOOO
CHIRP! CHIRP! CHIRP!
PEEWWW
?
AGHHH!!!
TTSHHHST
SKREE!
SWOOOSH

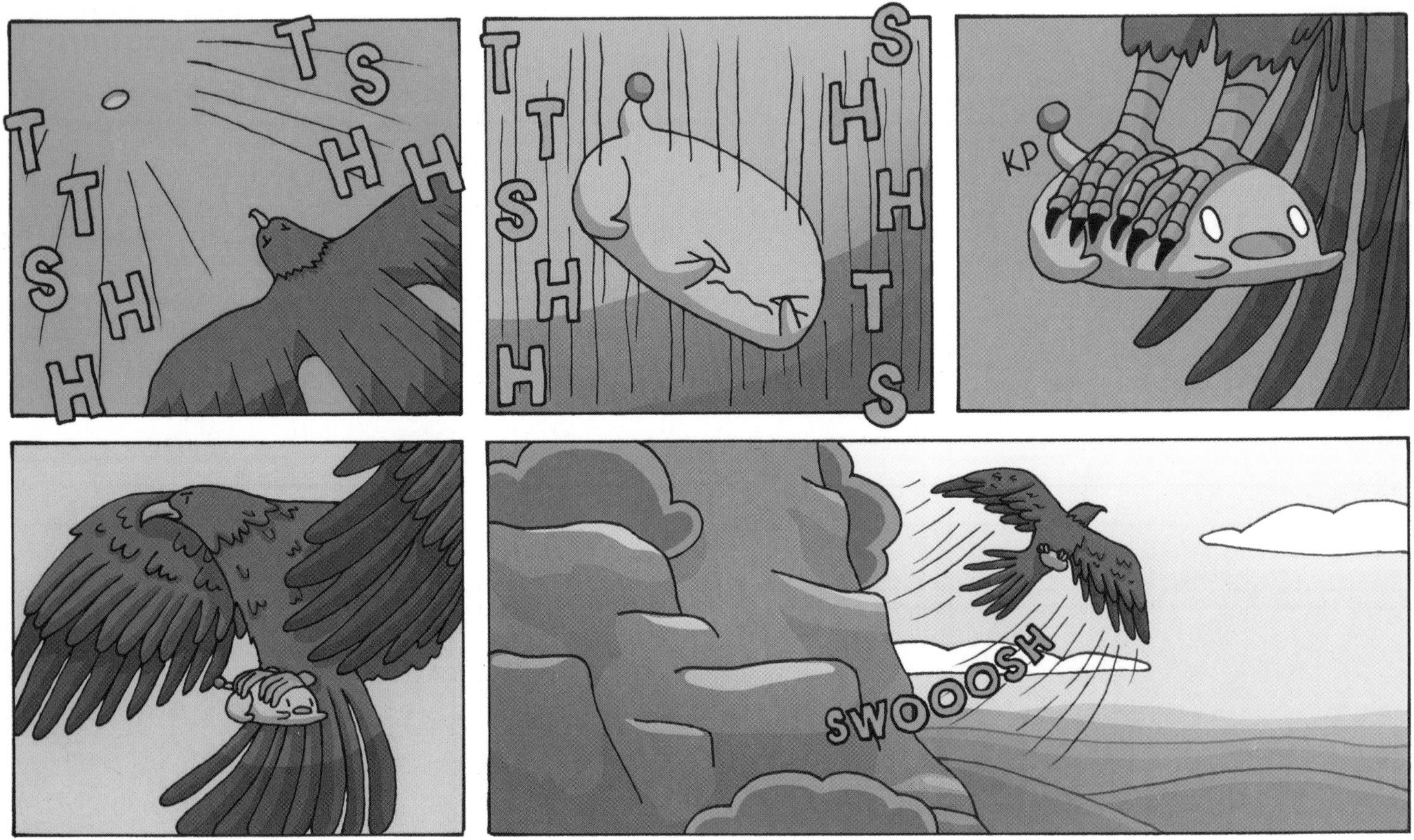
TSHH
TSHH
TSHH
TSHH
KP
SWOOOSH

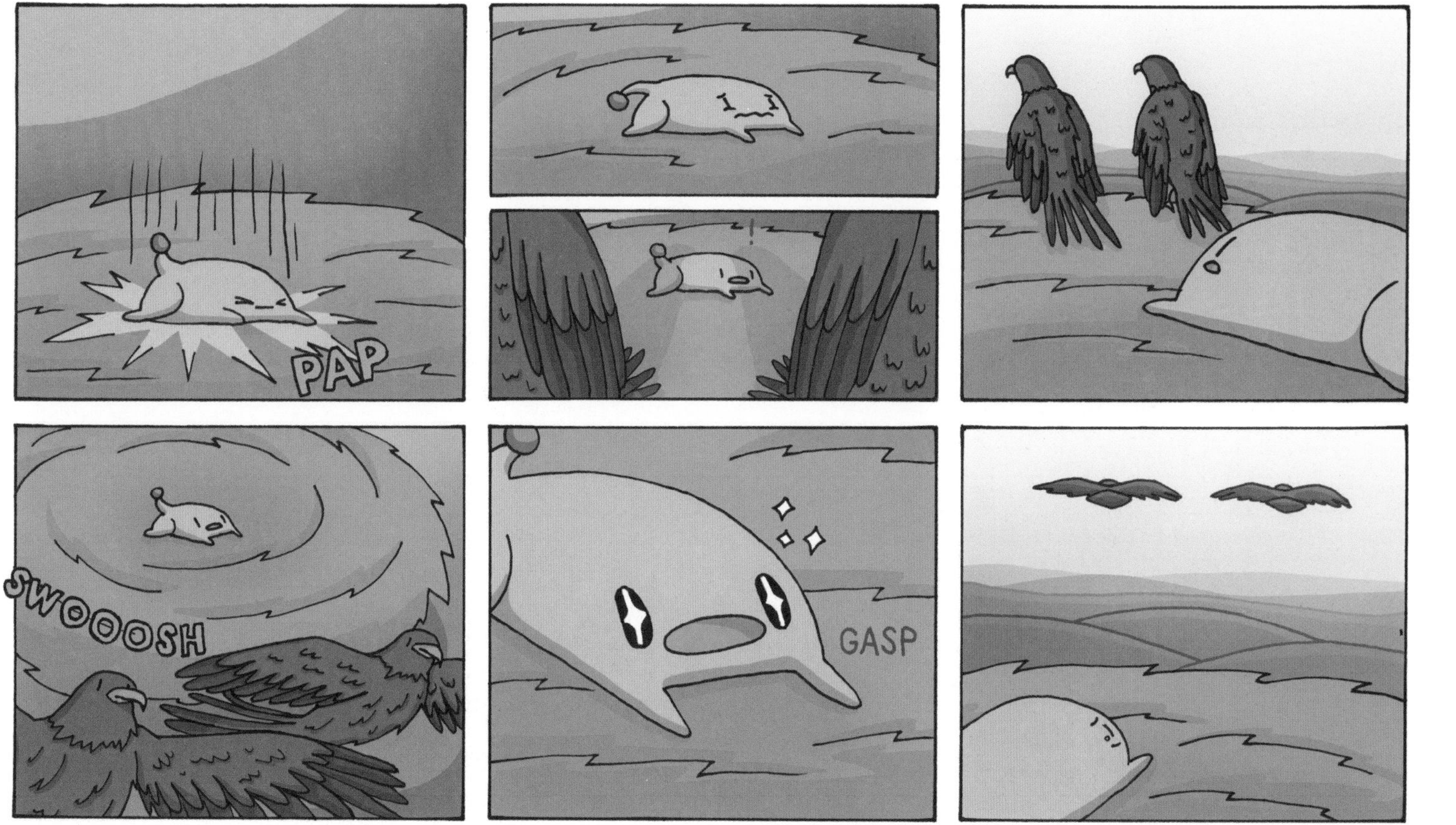
PAP
!
SWOOOSH
GASP

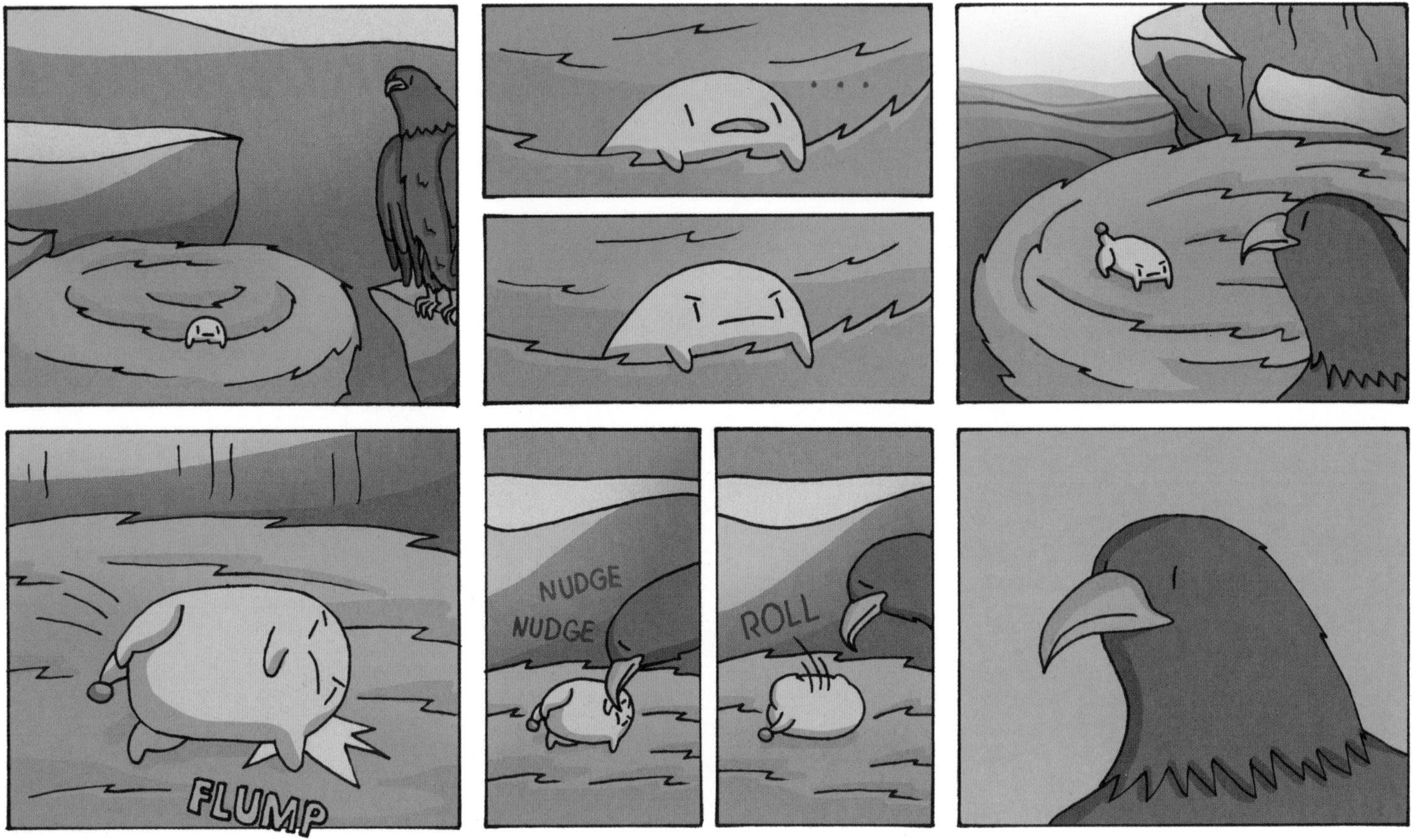
...
FLUMP
NUDGE
NUDGE
ROLL

KP
SWOOOSH
SSSHHHOOOO
SSHOOOO
FP
FP
FP
FP
SSHOO

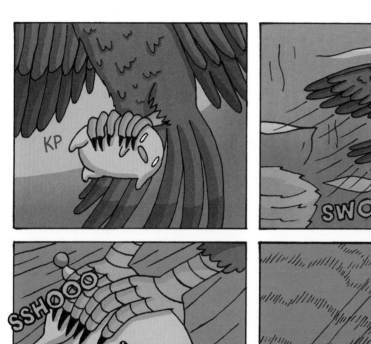

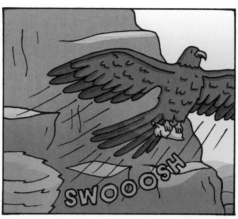

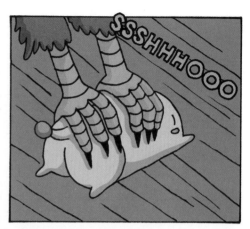

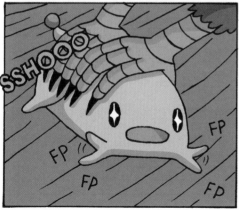

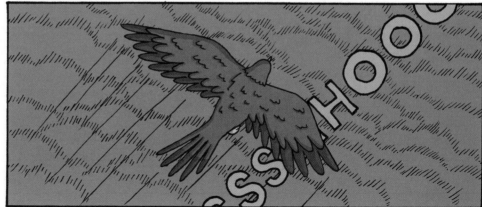

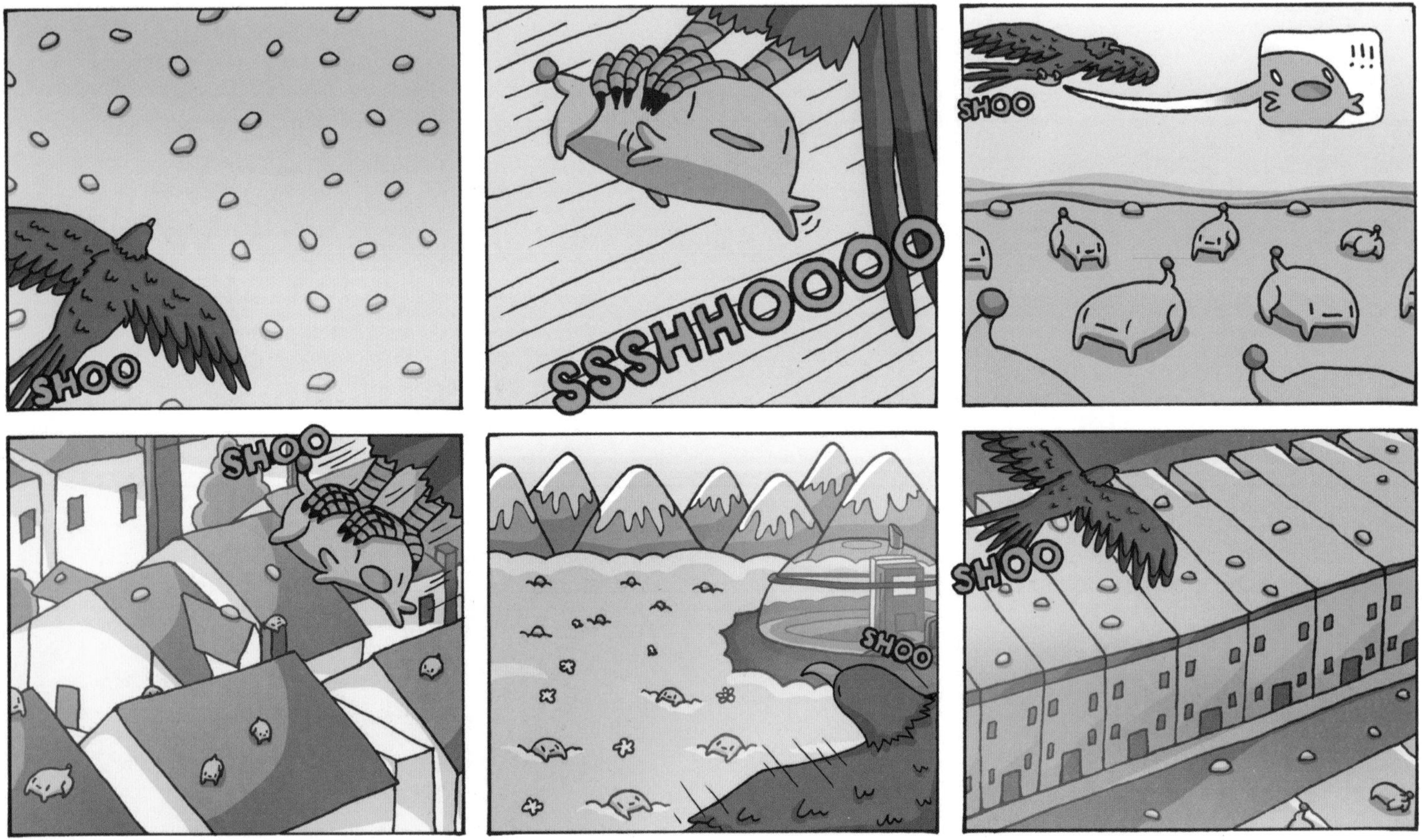
SHOO
SSSHHOOOOO
SHOO
!!!
SHOO
SHOO
SHOO

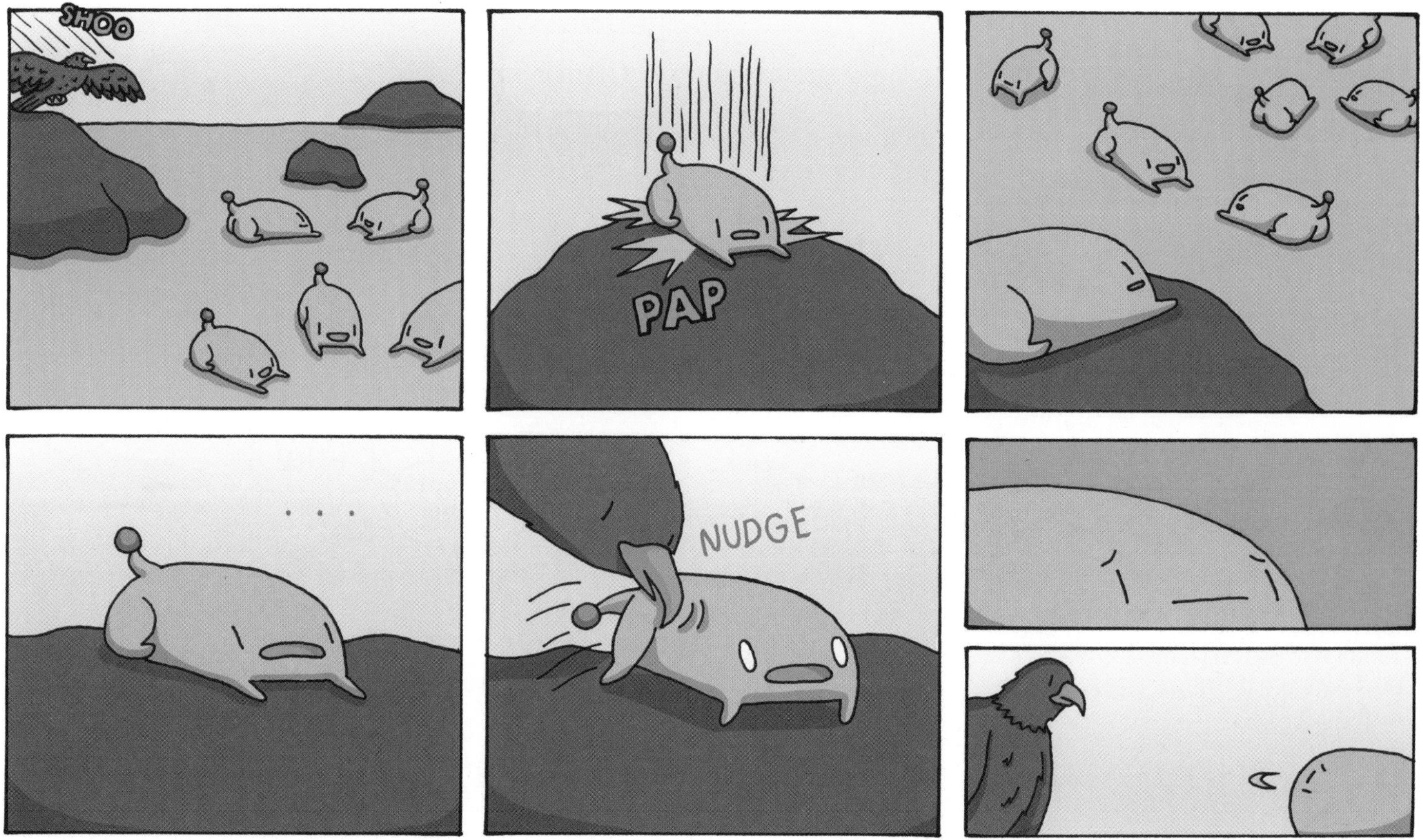
SHOO
PAP
. . .
NUDGE

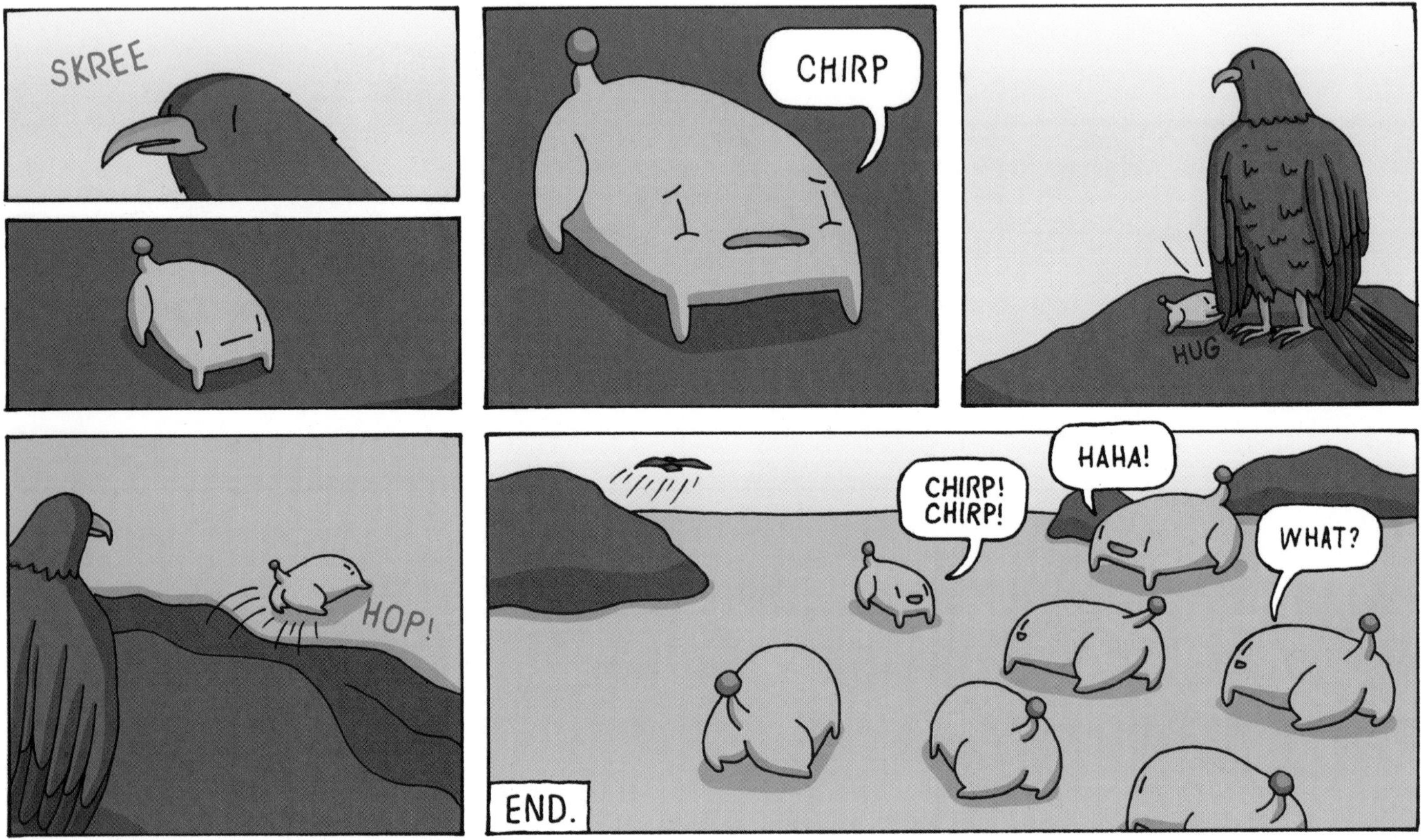
SKREE
CHIRP
HUG
HOP!
CHIRP! CHIRP!
HAHA!
WHAT?
END.

YEAR 147

KING

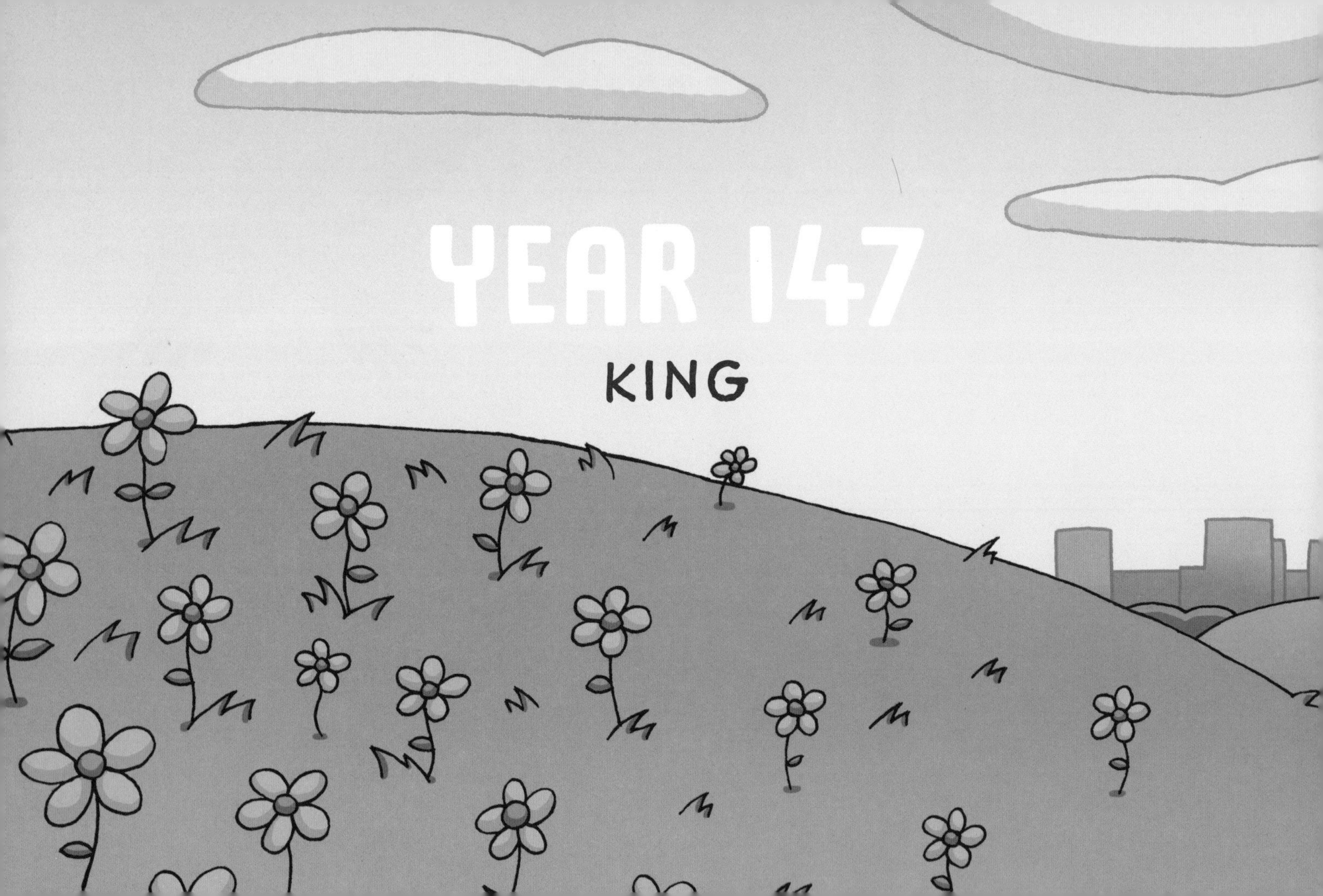

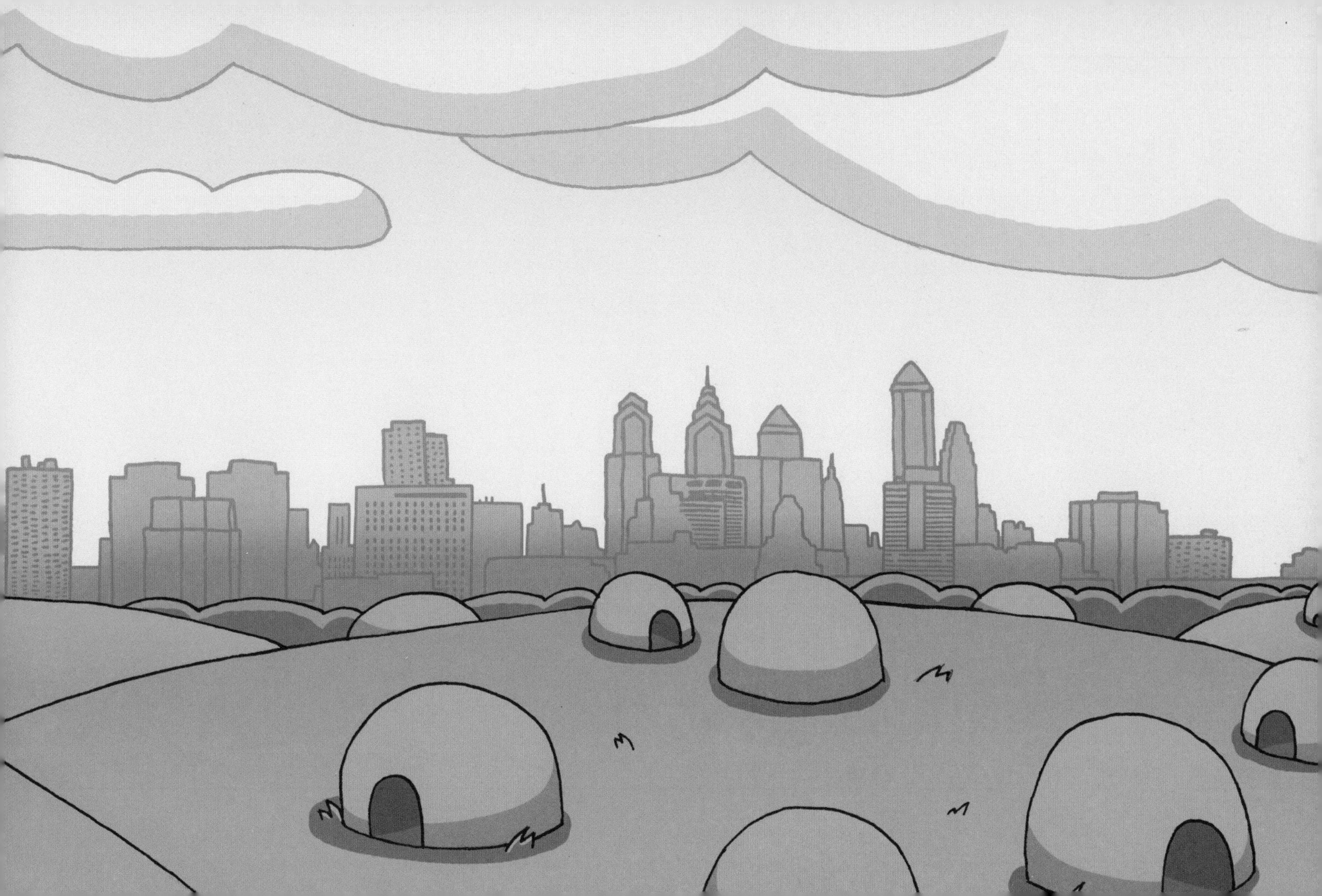

CHAPTER FOUR

—

KING WANTS A NEW FLARG

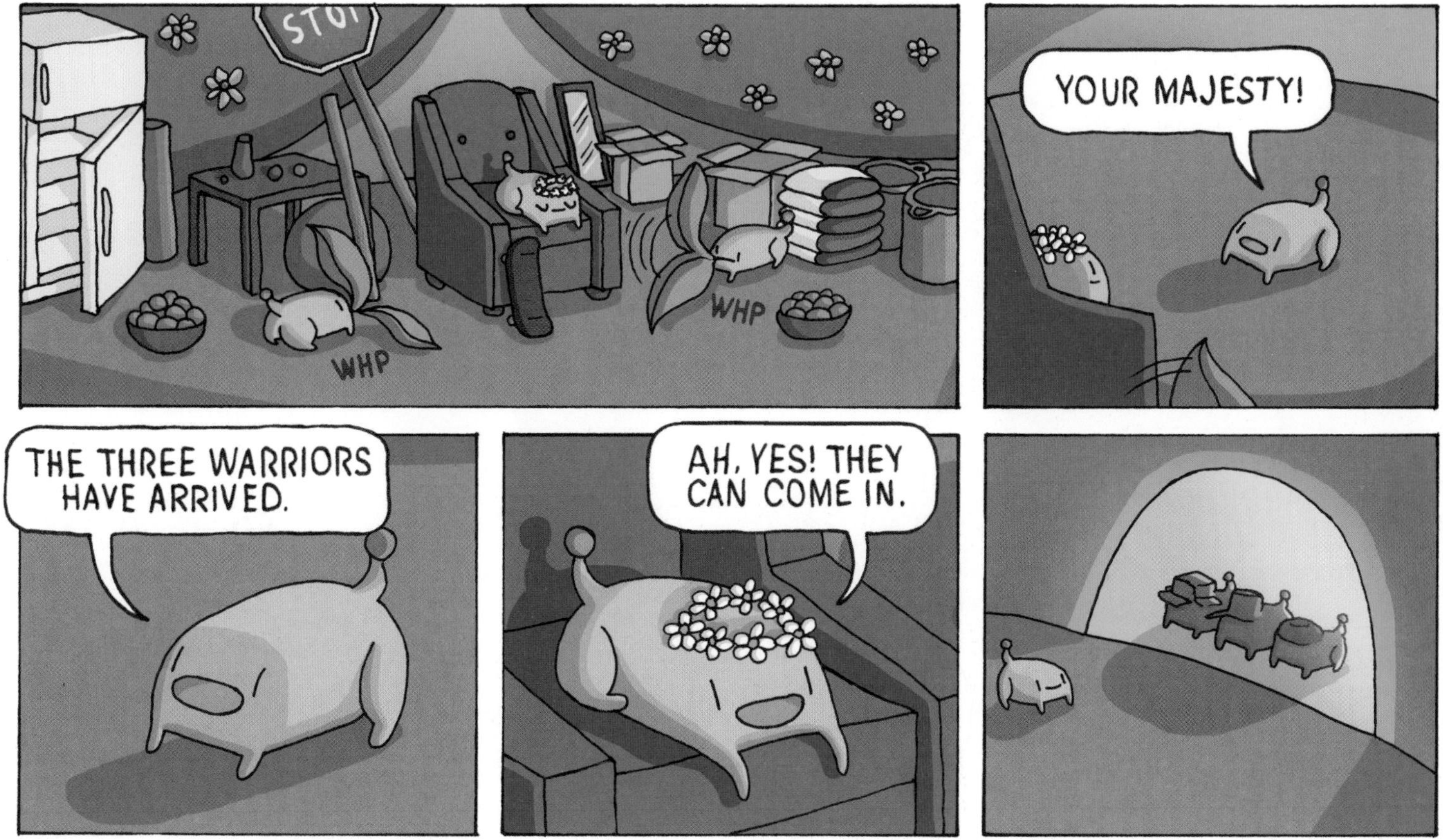

WHP
WHP
YOUR MAJESTY!
THE THREE WARRIORS HAVE ARRIVED.
AH, YES! THEY CAN COME IN.

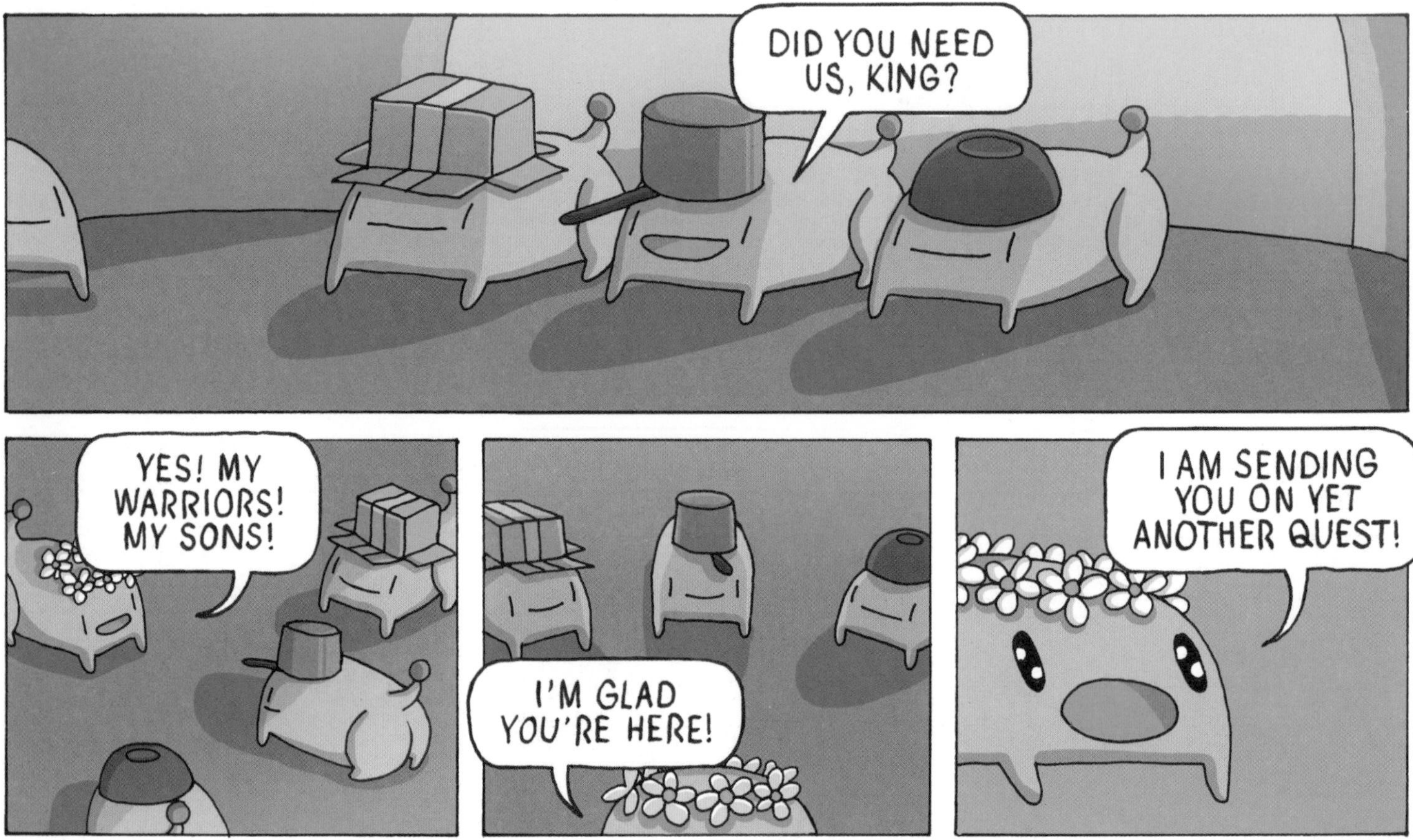
DID YOU NEED US, KING?
YES! MY WARRIORS! MY SONS!
I'M GLAD YOU'RE HERE!
I AM SENDING YOU ON YET ANOTHER QUEST!

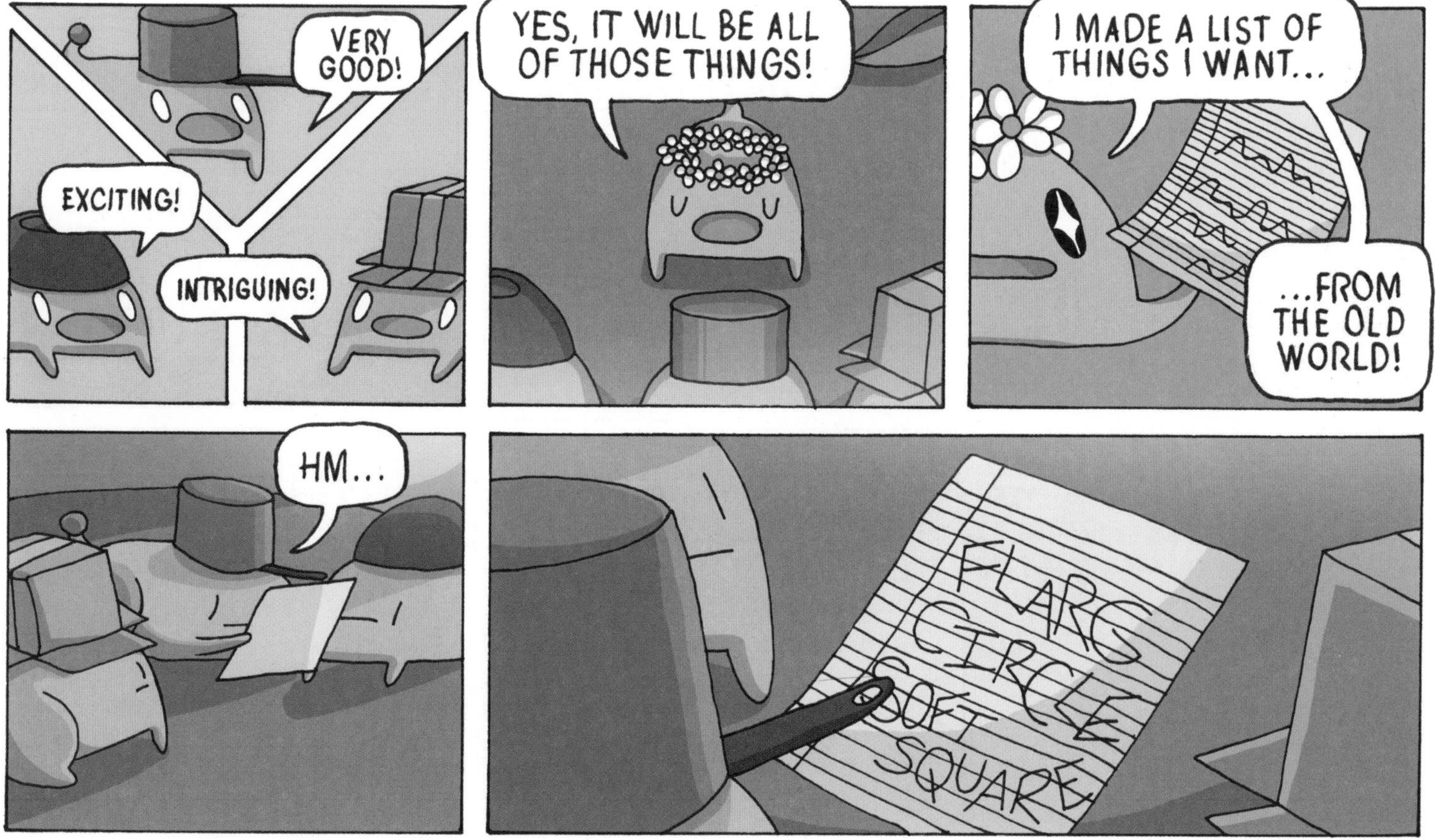
VERY GOOD!
EXCITING!
INTRIGUING!
YES, IT WILL BE ALL OF THOSE THINGS!
I MADE A LIST OF THINGS I WANT...
...FROM THE OLD WORLD!
HM...
FLARG
CIRCLE
SOFT
SQUARE

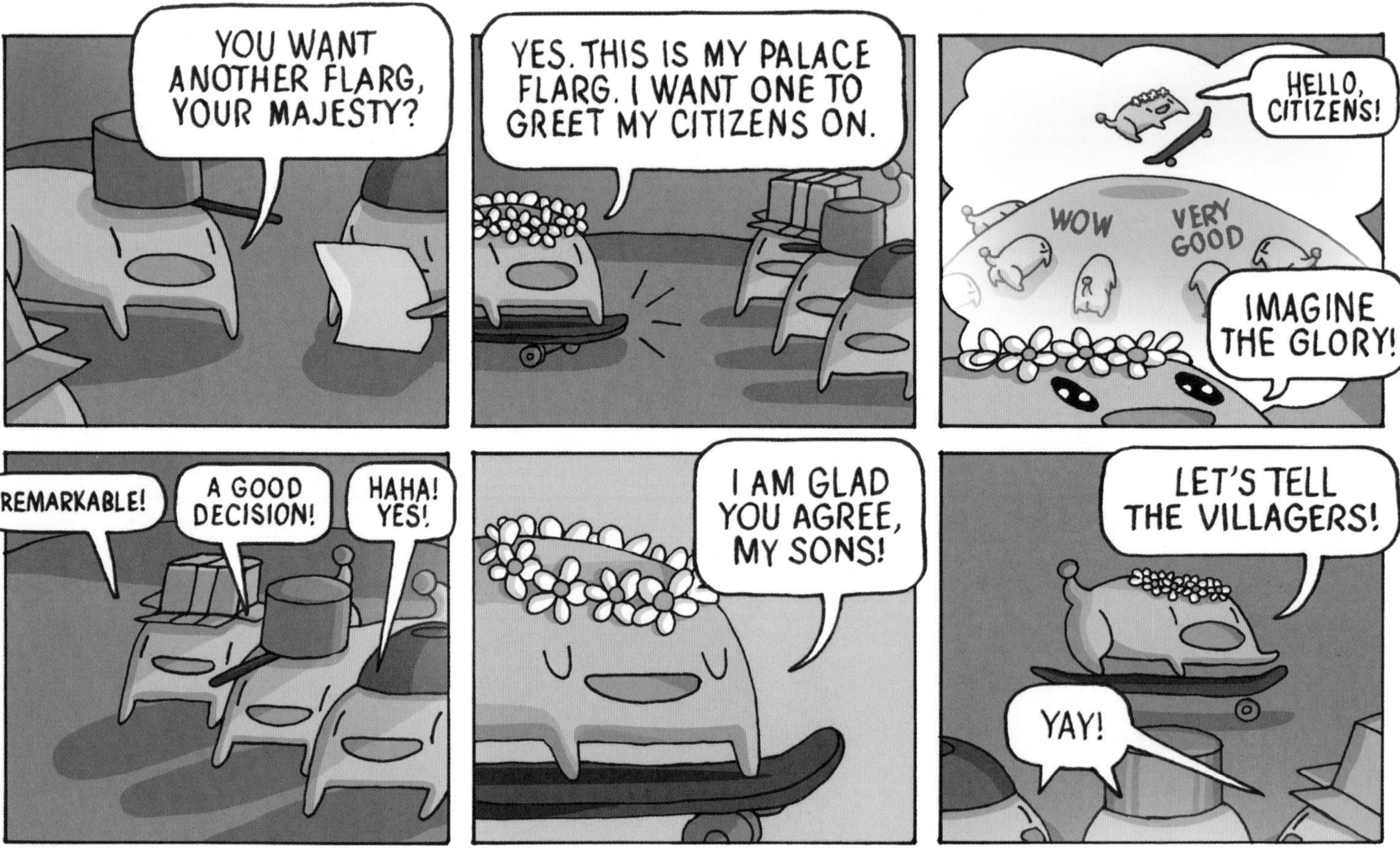
YOU WANT ANOTHER FLARG, YOUR MAJESTY?
YES. THIS IS MY PALACE FLARG. I WANT ONE TO GREET MY CITIZENS ON.
HELLO, CITIZENS!
WOW
VERY GOOD
IMAGINE THE GLORY!
REMARKABLE!
A GOOD DECISION!
HAHA! YES!
I AM GLAD YOU AGREE, MY SONS!
LET'S TELL THE VILLAGERS!
YAY!

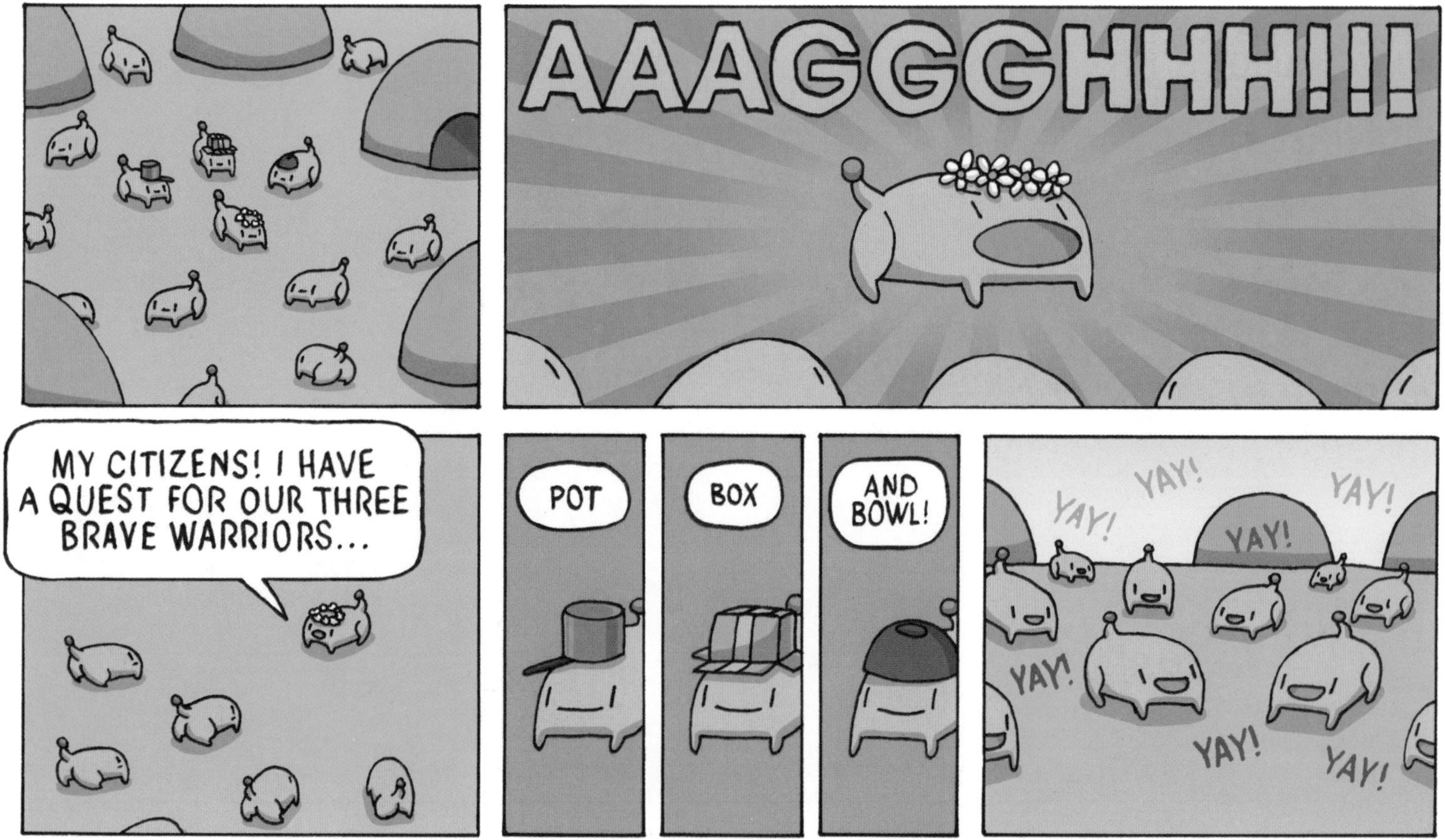
AAAGGGHHH!!!
MY CITIZENS! I HAVE A QUEST FOR OUR THREE BRAVE WARRIORS...
POT
BOX
AND BOWL!
YAY!
YAY!
YAY!
YAY!
YAY!
YAY!
YAY!

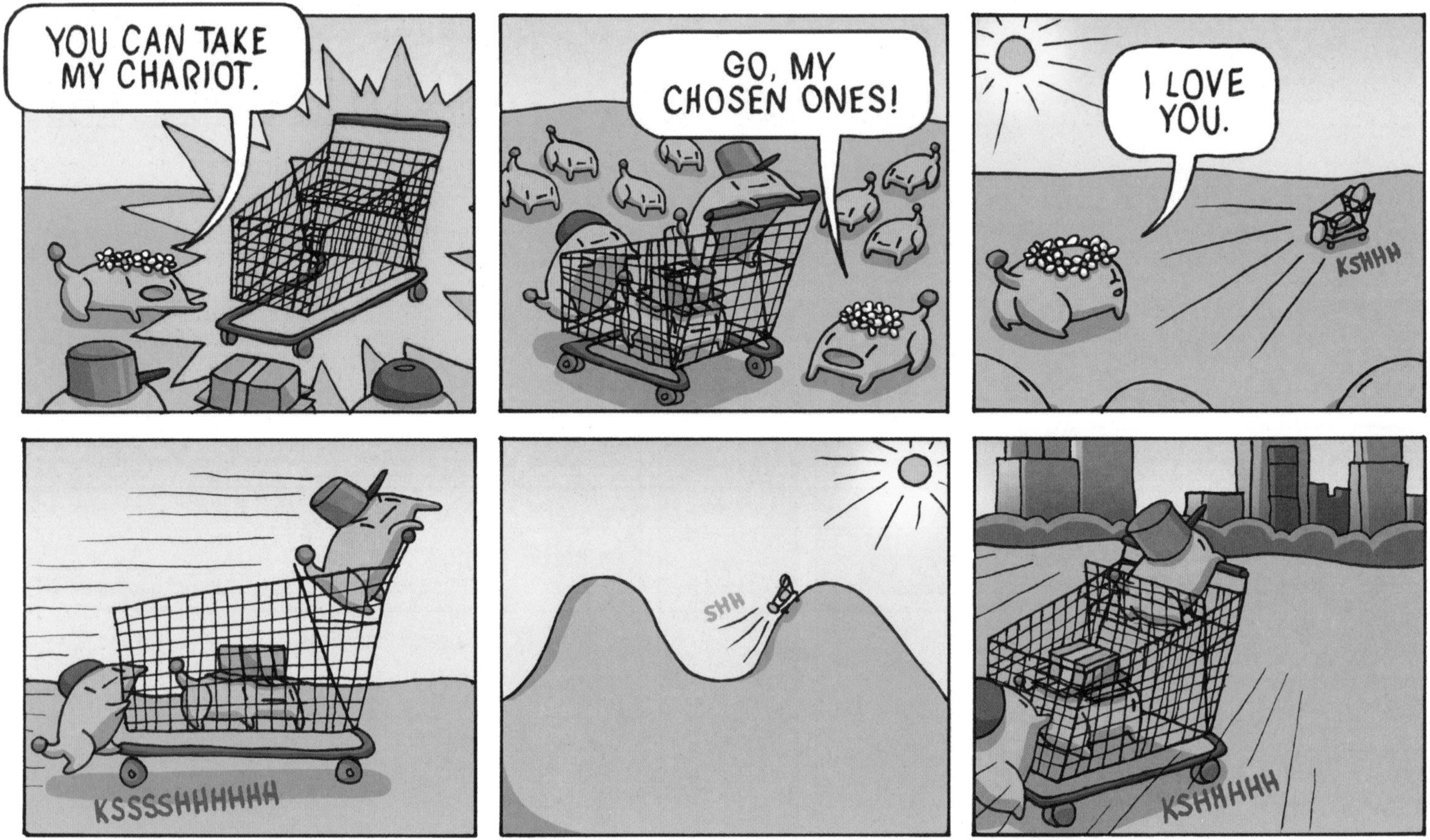
YOU CAN TAKE MY CHARIOT.
GO, MY CHOSEN ONES!
I LOVE YOU.
KSHHH
KSSSSHHHHHH
SHH
KSHHHHH

KSHHHHH

LET'S STOP HERE.

BOX, YOU WILL GET THE CIRCLE.

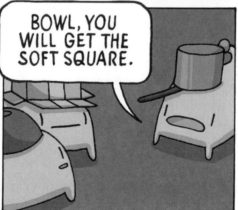

BOWL, YOU WILL GET THE SOFT SQUARE.

I WILL GET THE FLARG.

IT IS MY DESTINY.

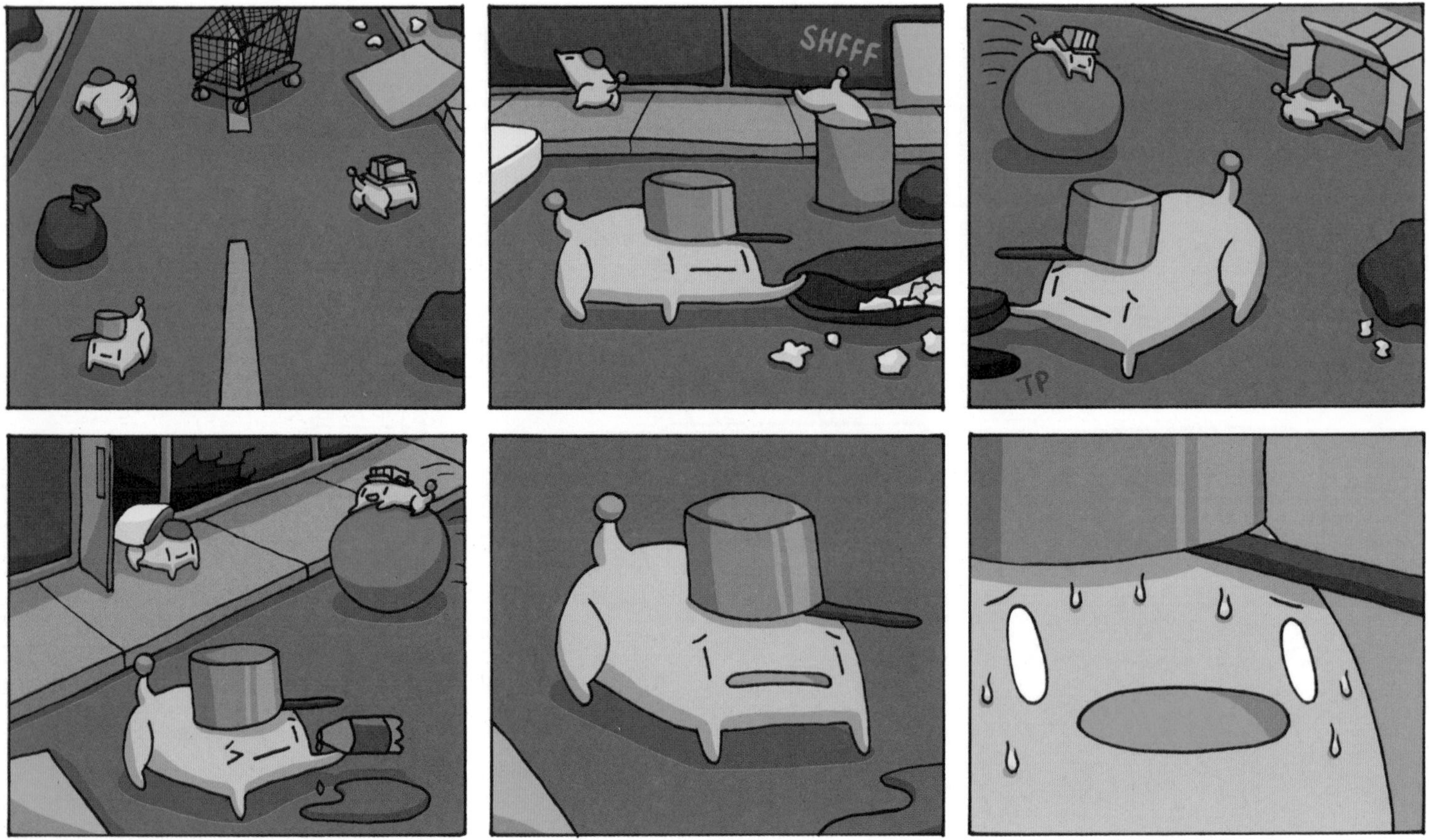
SHFFF
TP

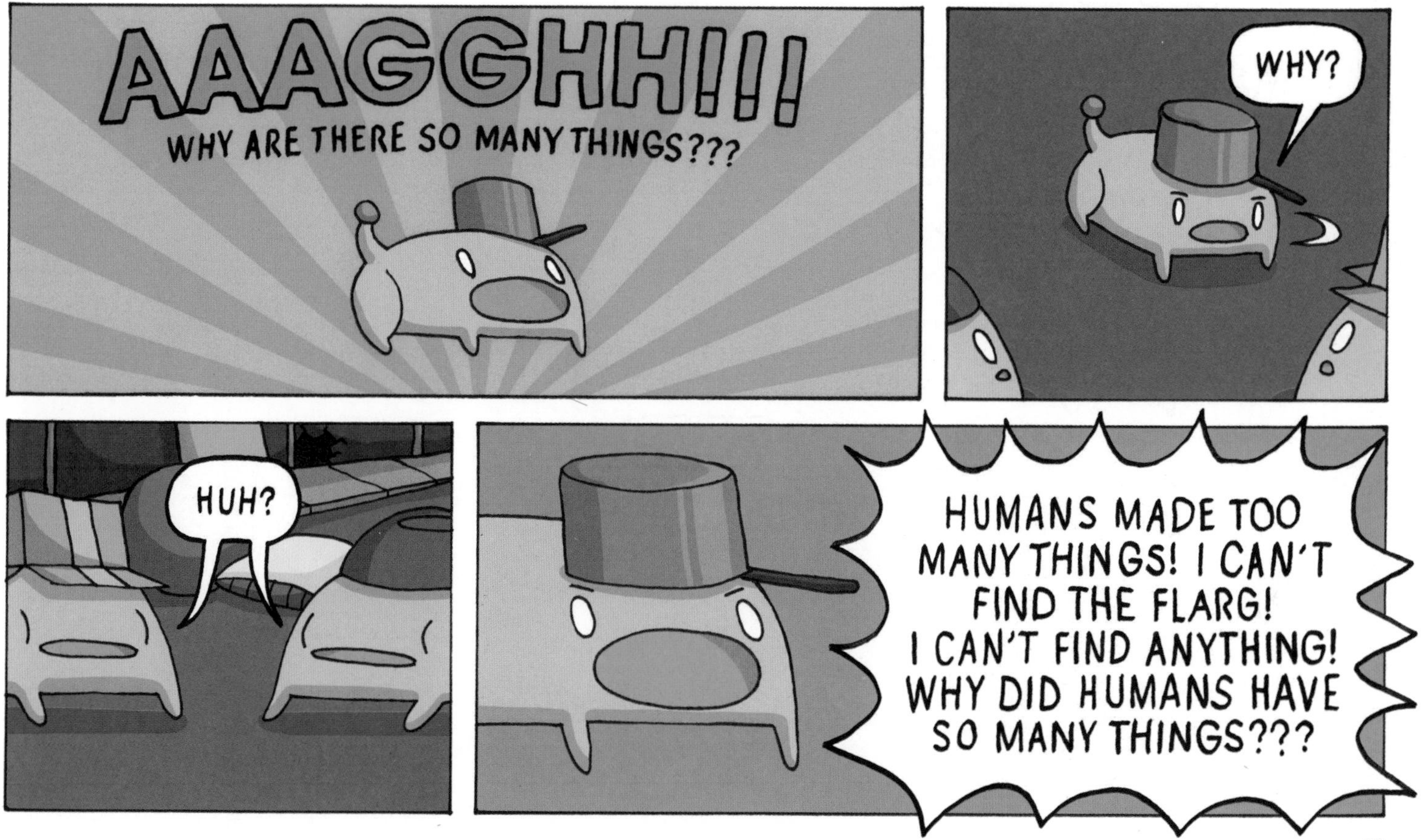
AAAGGHH!!!
WHY ARE THERE SO MANY THINGS???
WHY?
HUH?
HUMANS MADE TOO MANY THINGS! I CAN'T FIND THE FLARG! I CAN'T FIND ANYTHING! WHY DID HUMANS HAVE SO MANY THINGS???

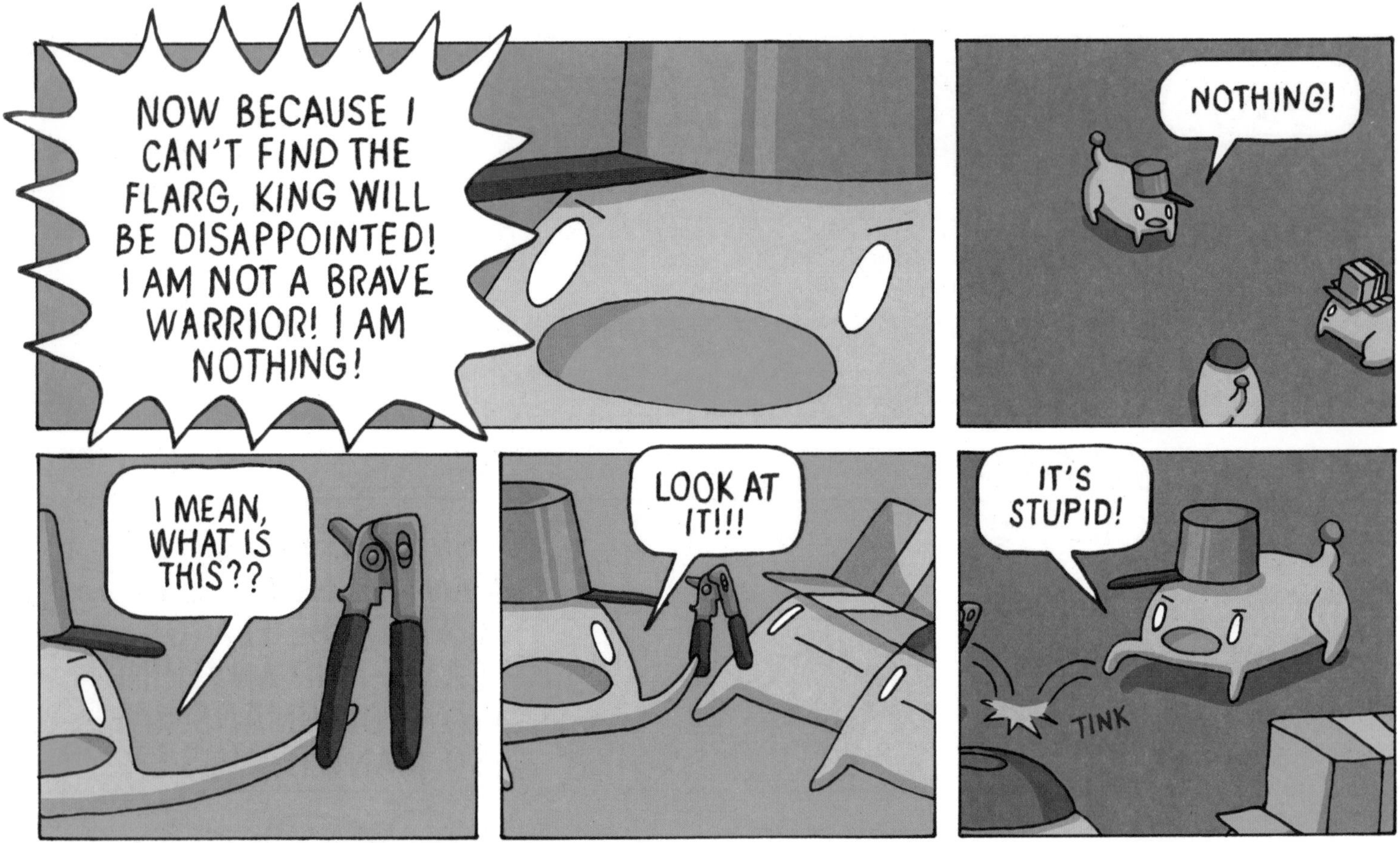
NOW BECAUSE I CAN'T FIND THE FLARG, KING WILL BE DISAPPOINTED! I AM NOT A BRAVE WARRIOR! I AM NOTHING!
NOTHING!
I MEAN, WHAT IS THIS??
LOOK AT IT!!!
IT'S STUPID!
TINK

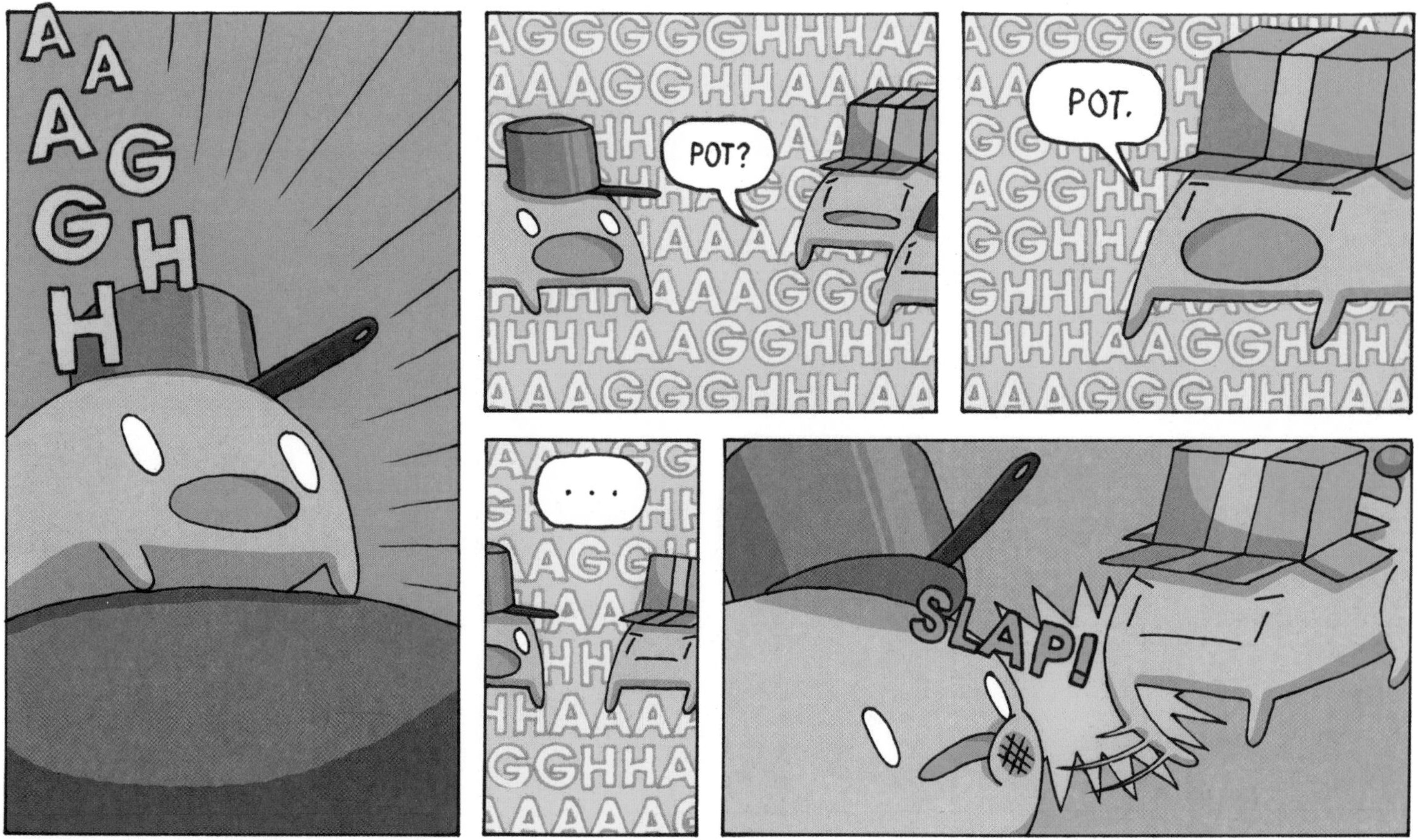
AAAGGHH
POT?
POT.
. . .
SLAP!

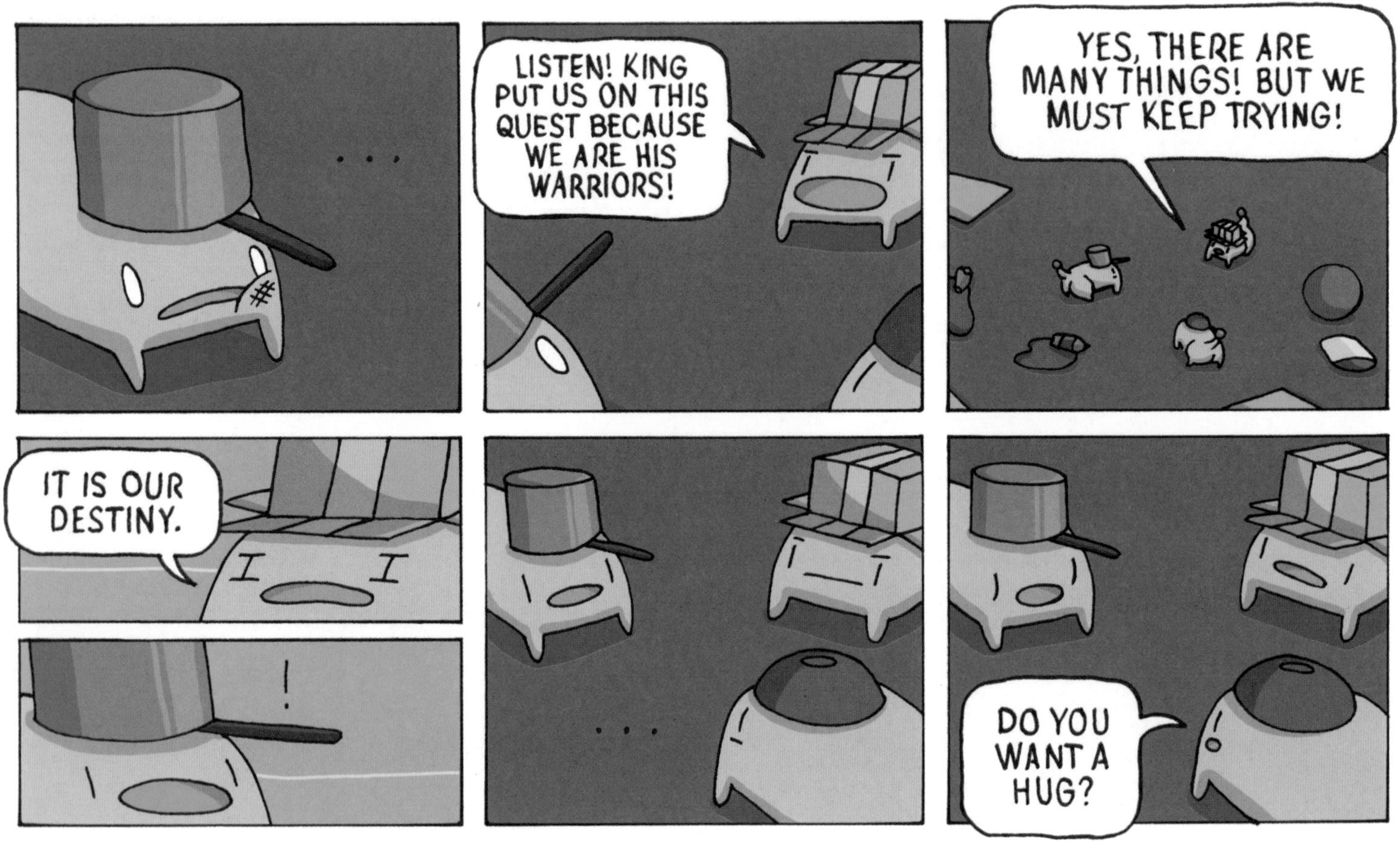
. . .
LISTEN! KING PUT US ON THIS QUEST BECAUSE WE ARE HIS WARRIORS!
YES, THERE ARE MANY THINGS! BUT WE MUST KEEP TRYING!
IT IS OUR DESTINY.
!
. . .
DO YOU WANT A HUG?

POWER HUG!
LET'S DO THIS!
KSHHHHH
KSHHHHH
STOP THE CARRIAGE!

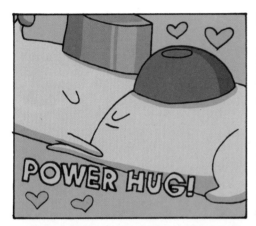

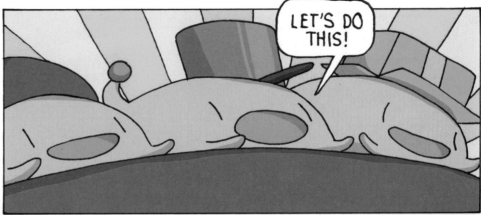

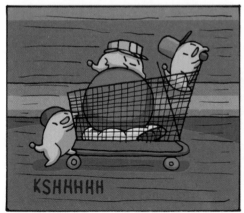

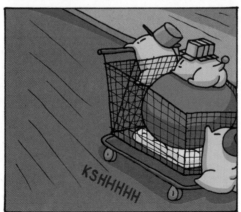

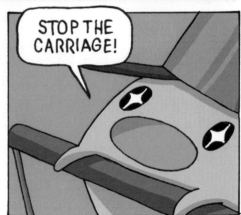

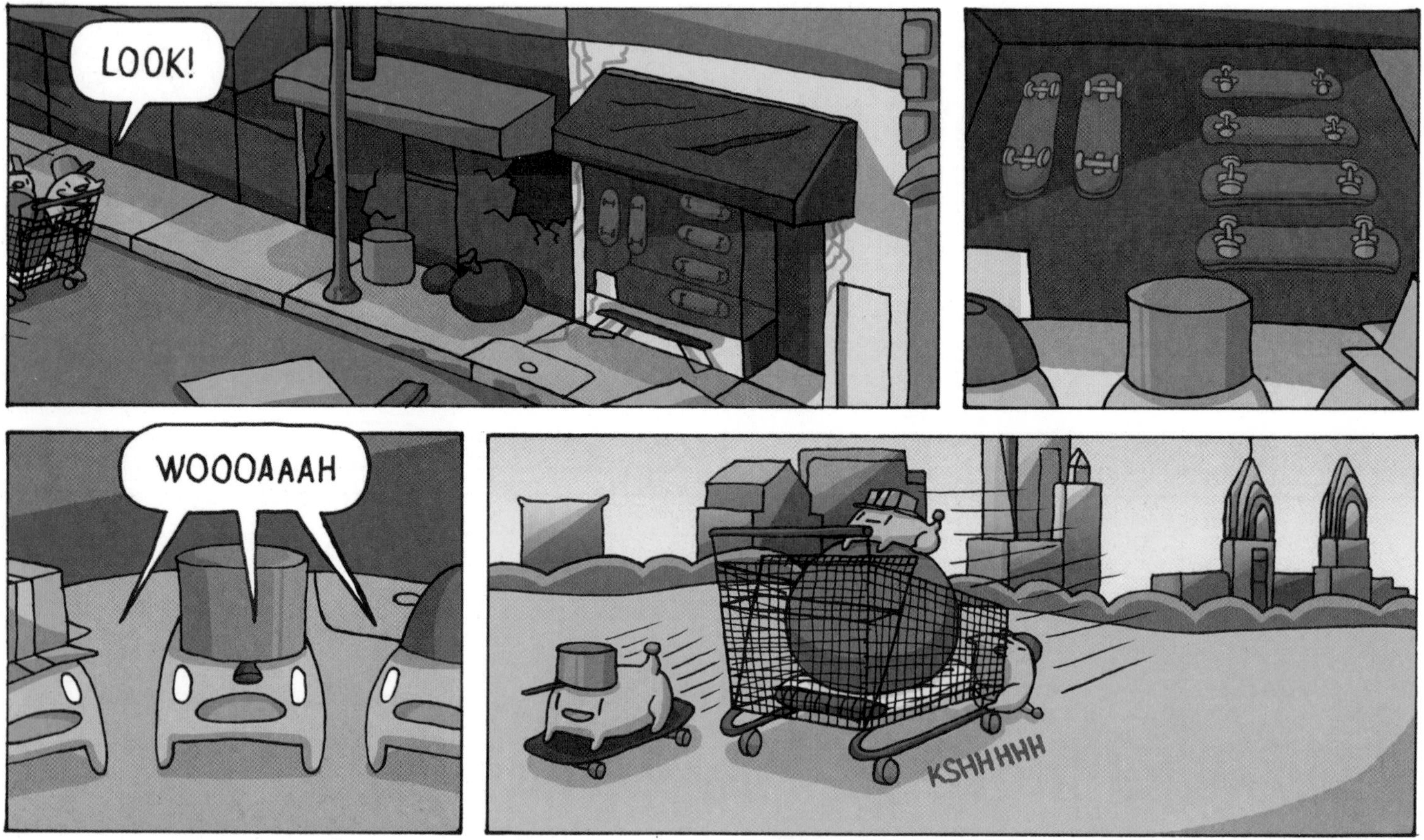
LOOK!
WOOOAAAH
KSHHHHH

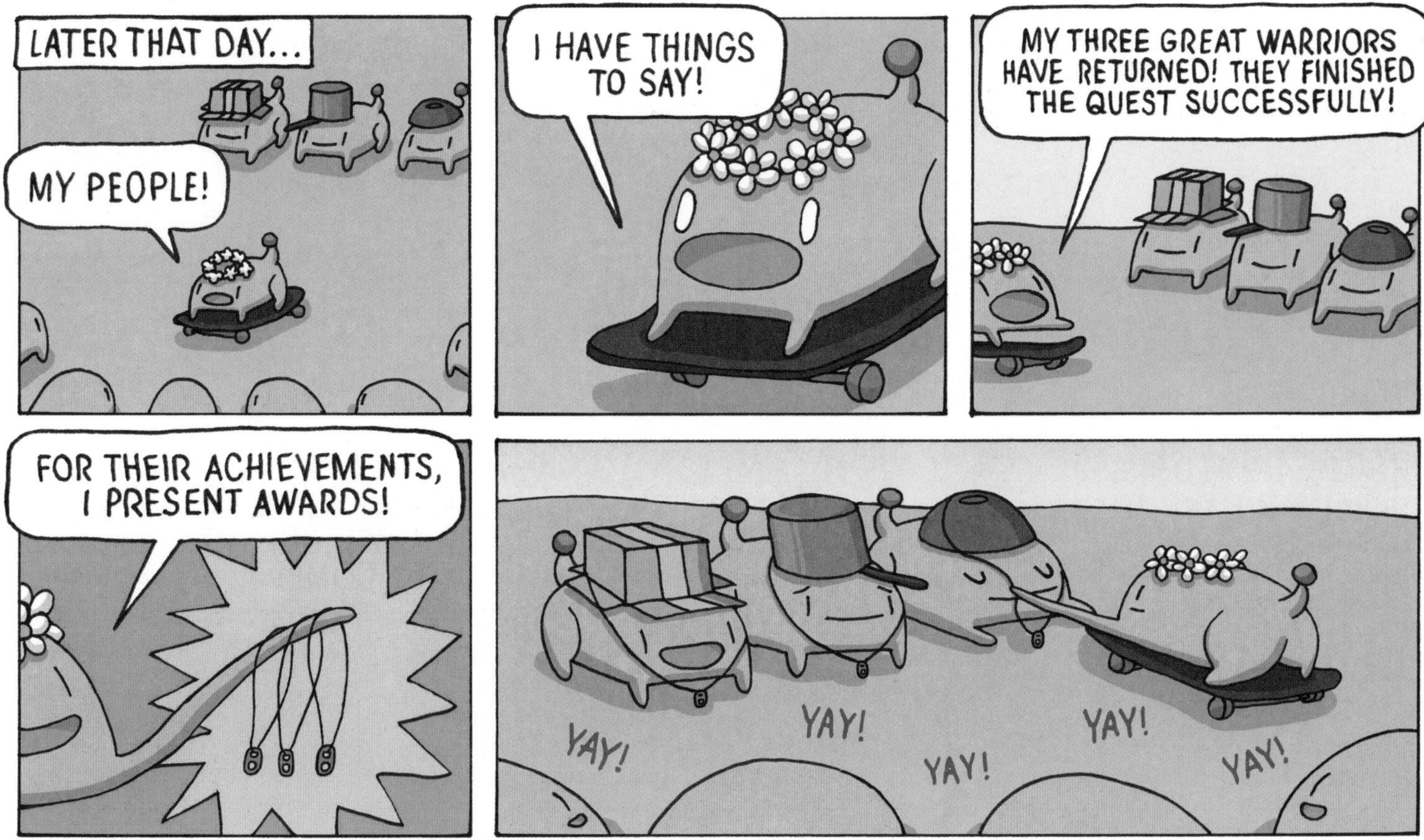
LATER THAT DAY...
MY PEOPLE!
I HAVE THINGS TO SAY!
MY THREE GREAT WARRIORS HAVE RETURNED! THEY FINISHED THE QUEST SUCCESSFULLY!
FOR THEIR ACHIEVEMENTS, I PRESENT AWARDS!
YAY!
YAY!
YAY!
YAY!
YAY!

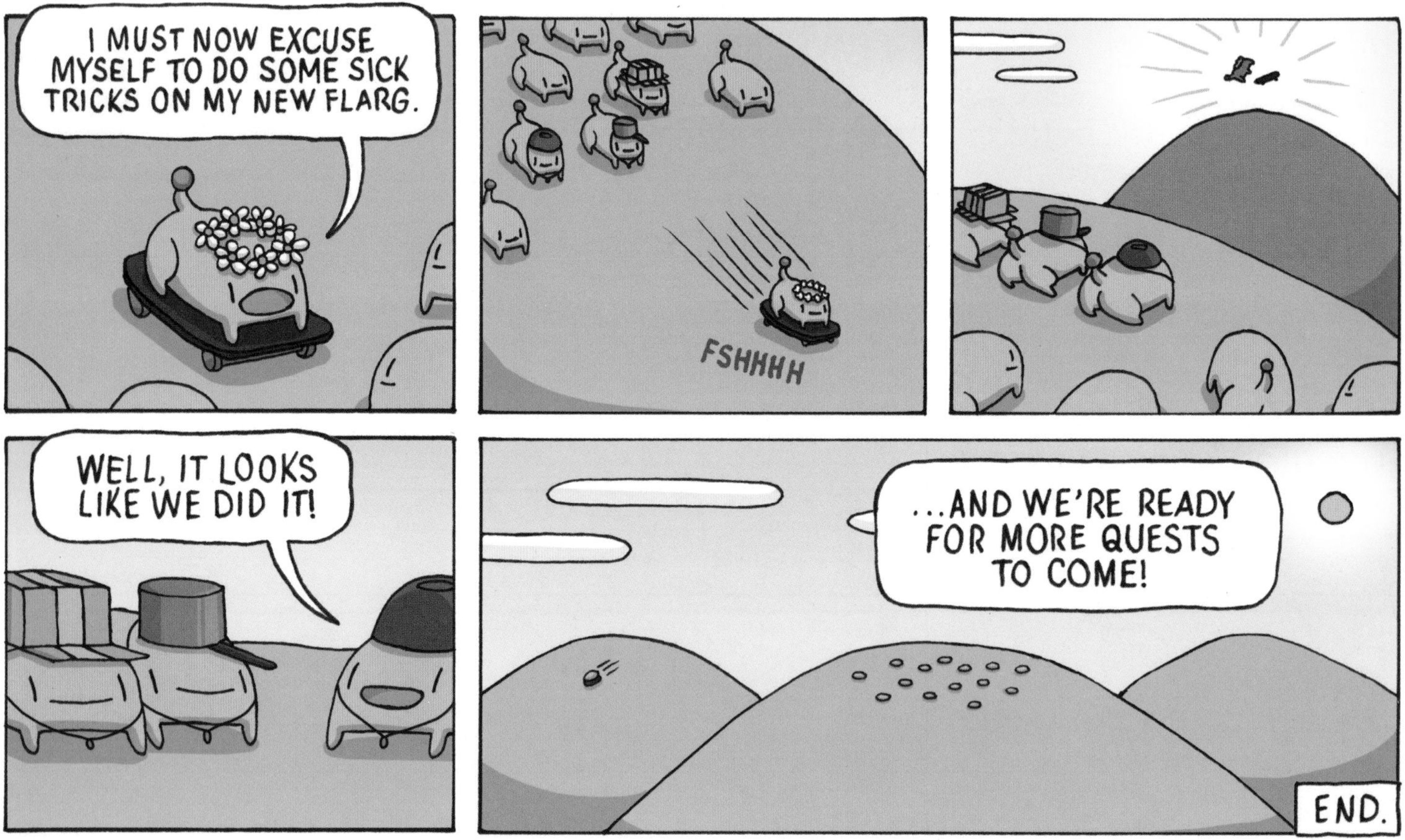
I MUST NOW EXCUSE MYSELF TO DO SOME SICK TRICKS ON MY NEW FLARG.
FSHHHH
WELL, IT LOOKS LIKE WE DID IT!
...AND WE'RE READY FOR MORE QUESTS TO COME!
END.

CHAPTER FIVE

—

LET'S BUILD A THING

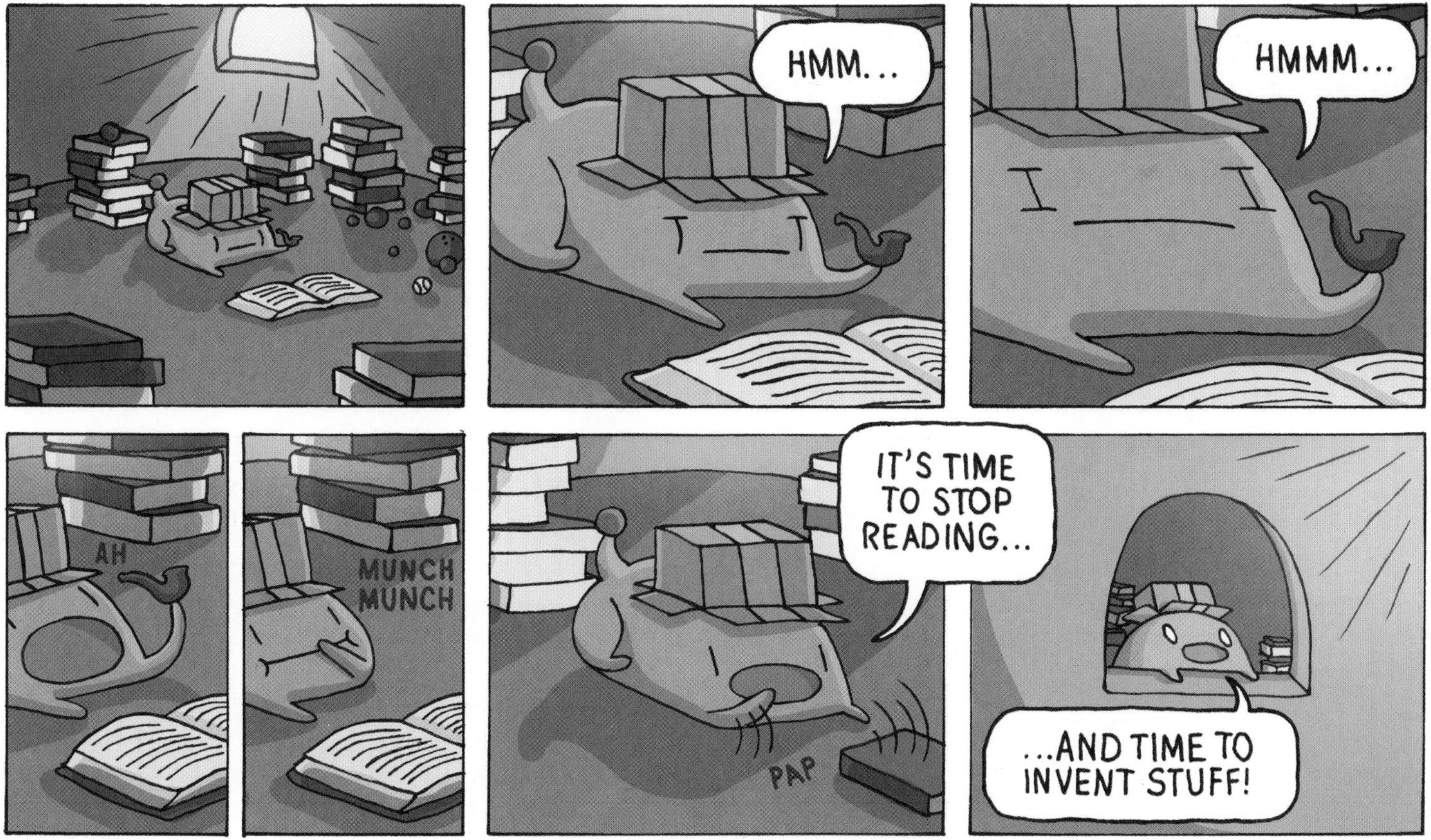
HMM...
HMMM...
AH
MUNCH MUNCH
IT'S TIME TO STOP READING...
PAP
...AND TIME TO INVENT STUFF!

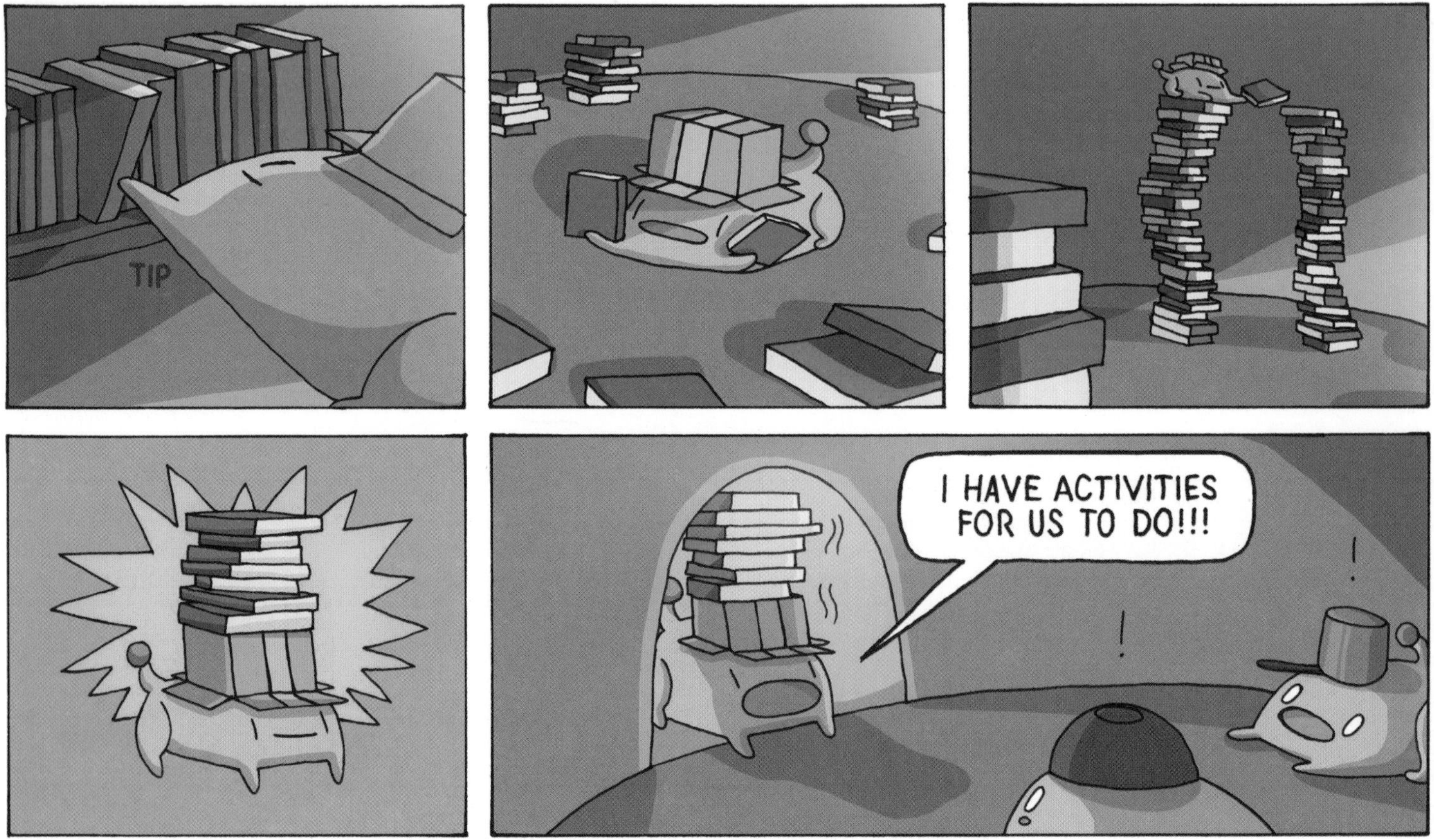
TIP
I HAVE ACTIVITIES FOR US TO DO!!!
!
!

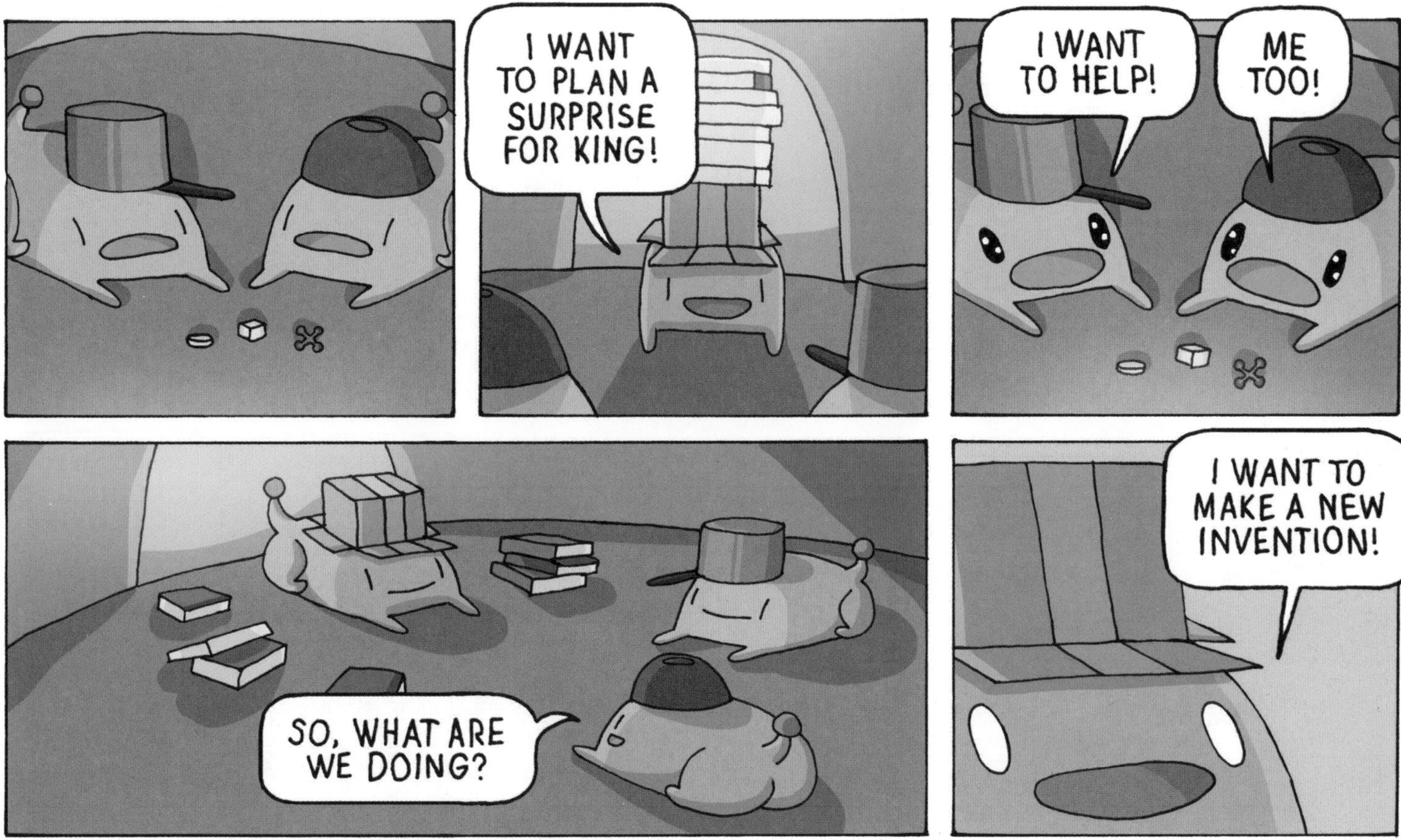
I WANT TO PLAN A SURPRISE FOR KING!
I WANT TO HELP!
ME TOO!
SO, WHAT ARE WE DOING?
I WANT TO MAKE A NEW INVENTION!

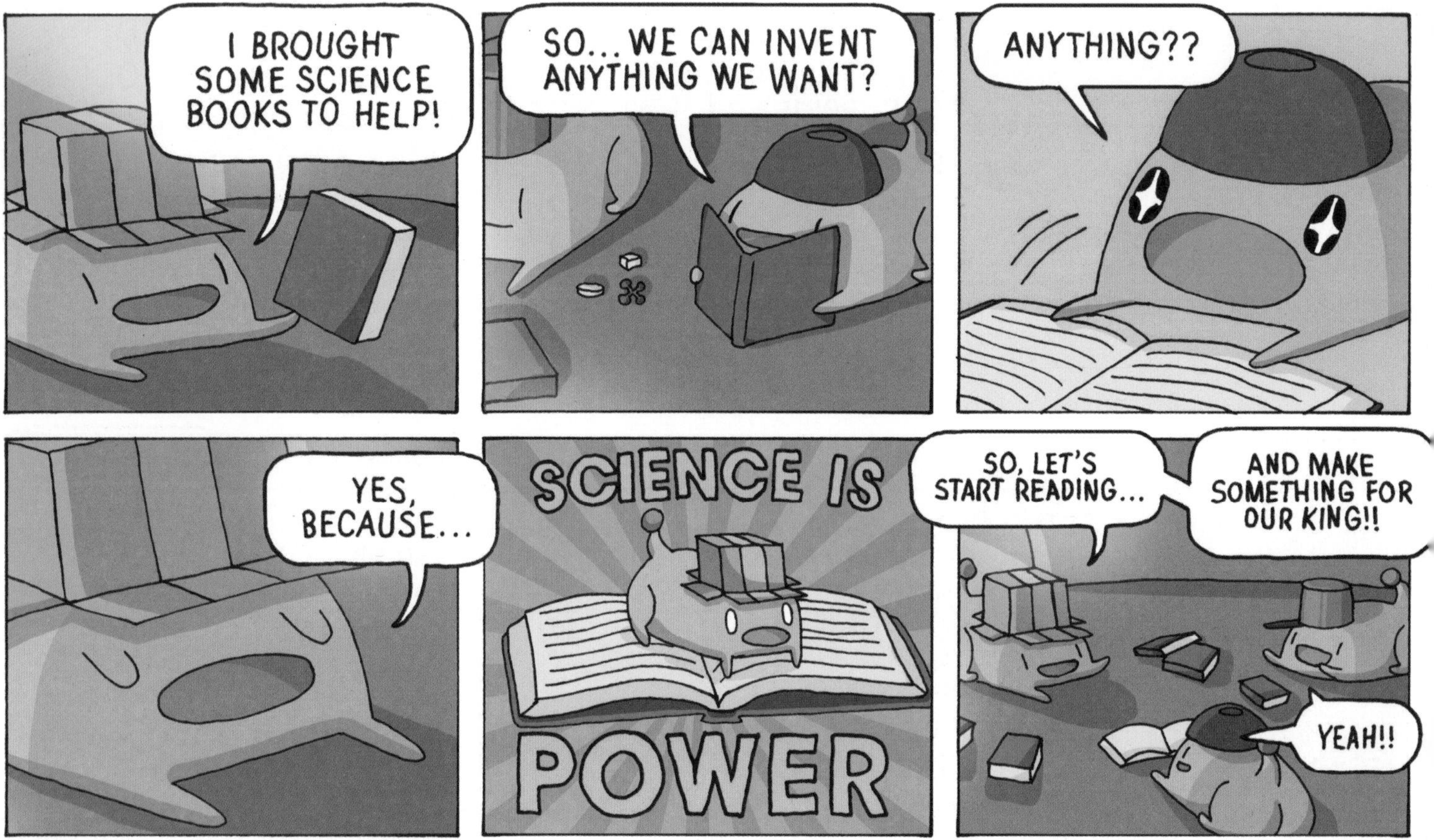

I BROUGHT SOME SCIENCE BOOKS TO HELP!
SO... WE CAN INVENT ANYTHING WE WANT?
ANYTHING??
YES, BECAUSE...
SCIENCE IS POWER
SO, LET'S START READING...
AND MAKE SOMETHING FOR OUR KING!!
YEAH!!

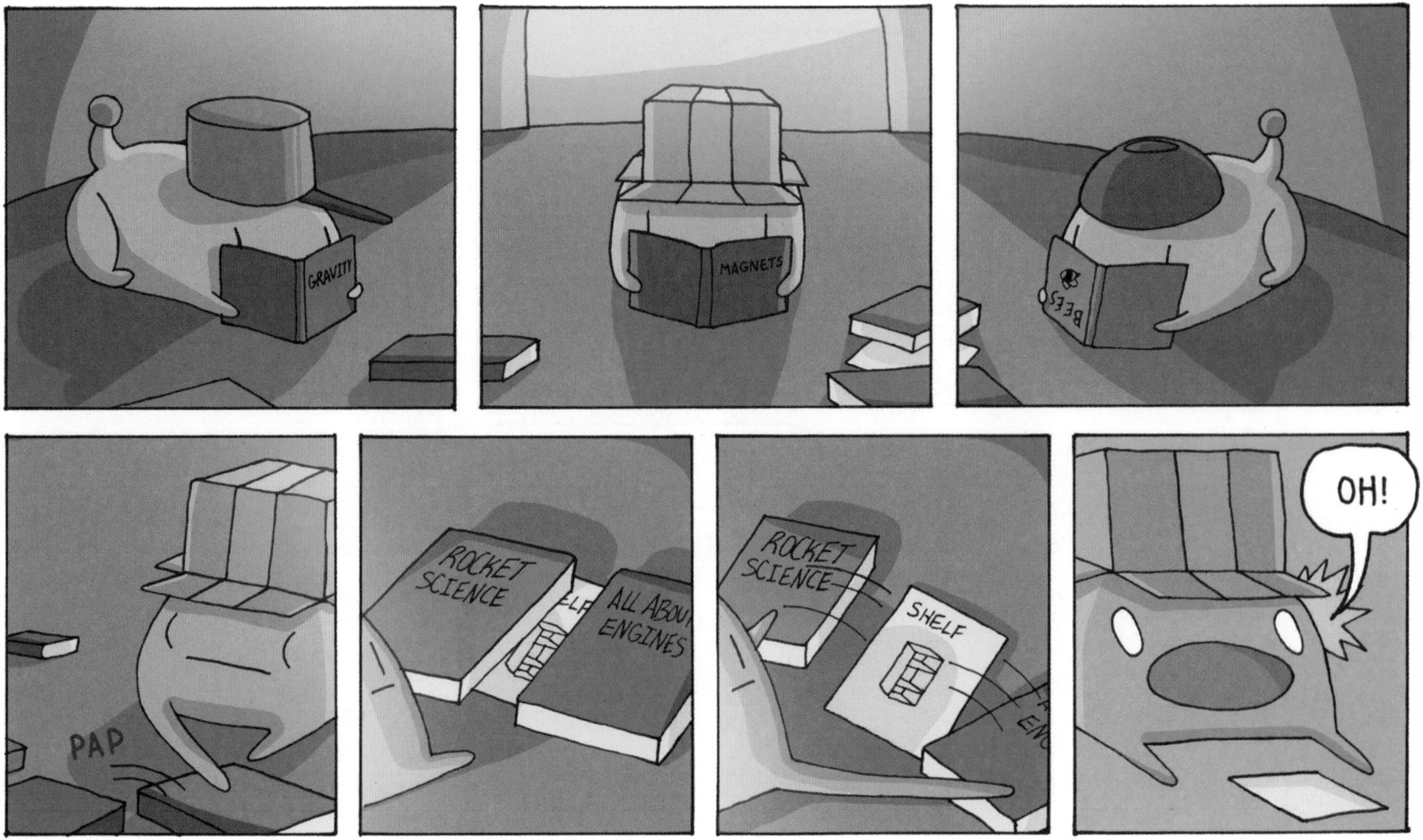
GRAVITY
MAGNETS
BEES
PAP
ROCKET SCIENCE
ALL ABOUT ENGINES
ROCKET SCIENCE
SHELF
OH!

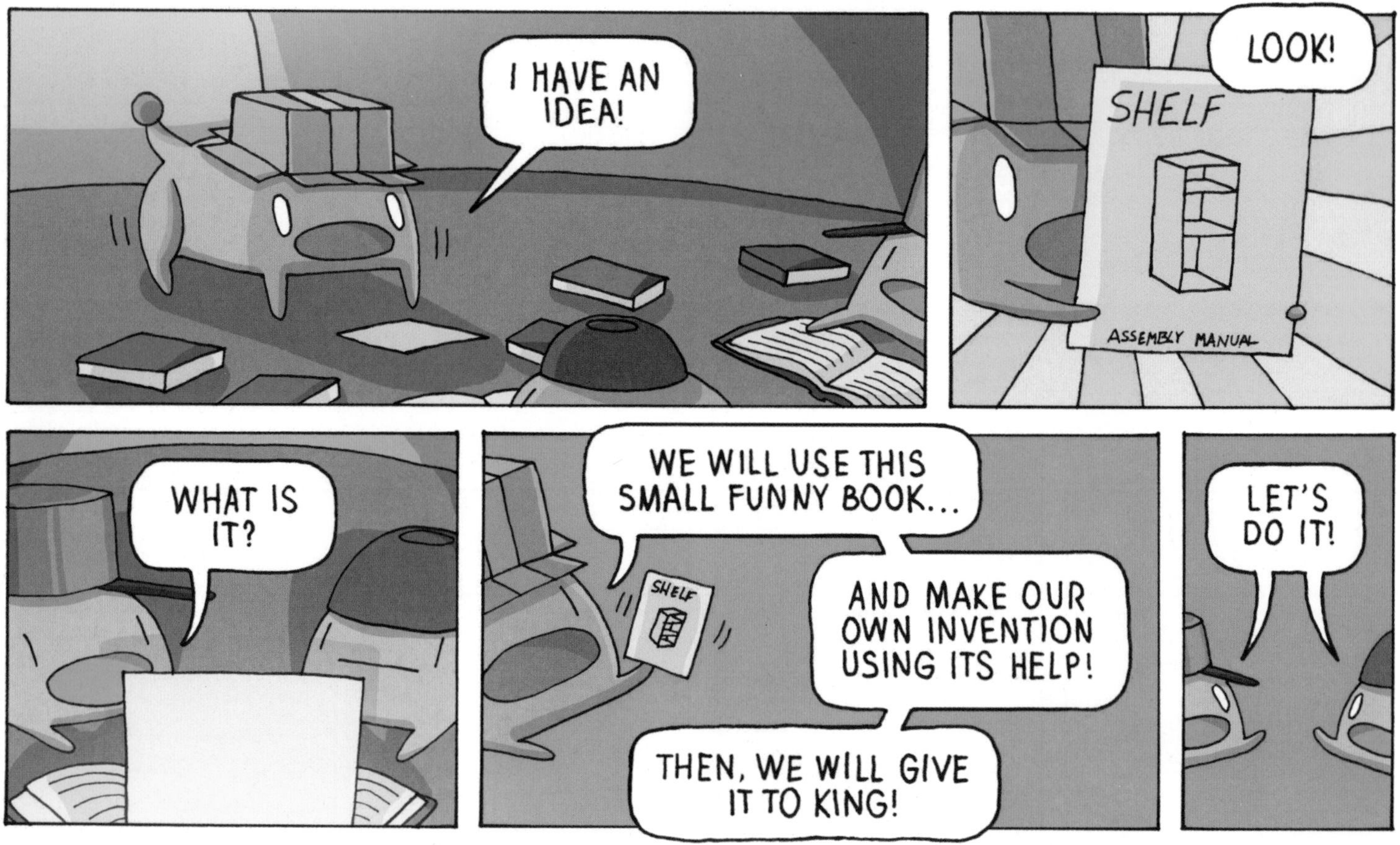
I HAVE AN IDEA!
LOOK!
SHELF
ASSEMBLY MANUAL
WHAT IS IT?
WE WILL USE THIS SMALL FUNNY BOOK...
SHELF
AND MAKE OUR OWN INVENTION USING ITS HELP!
THEN, WE WILL GIVE IT TO KING!
LET'S DO IT!

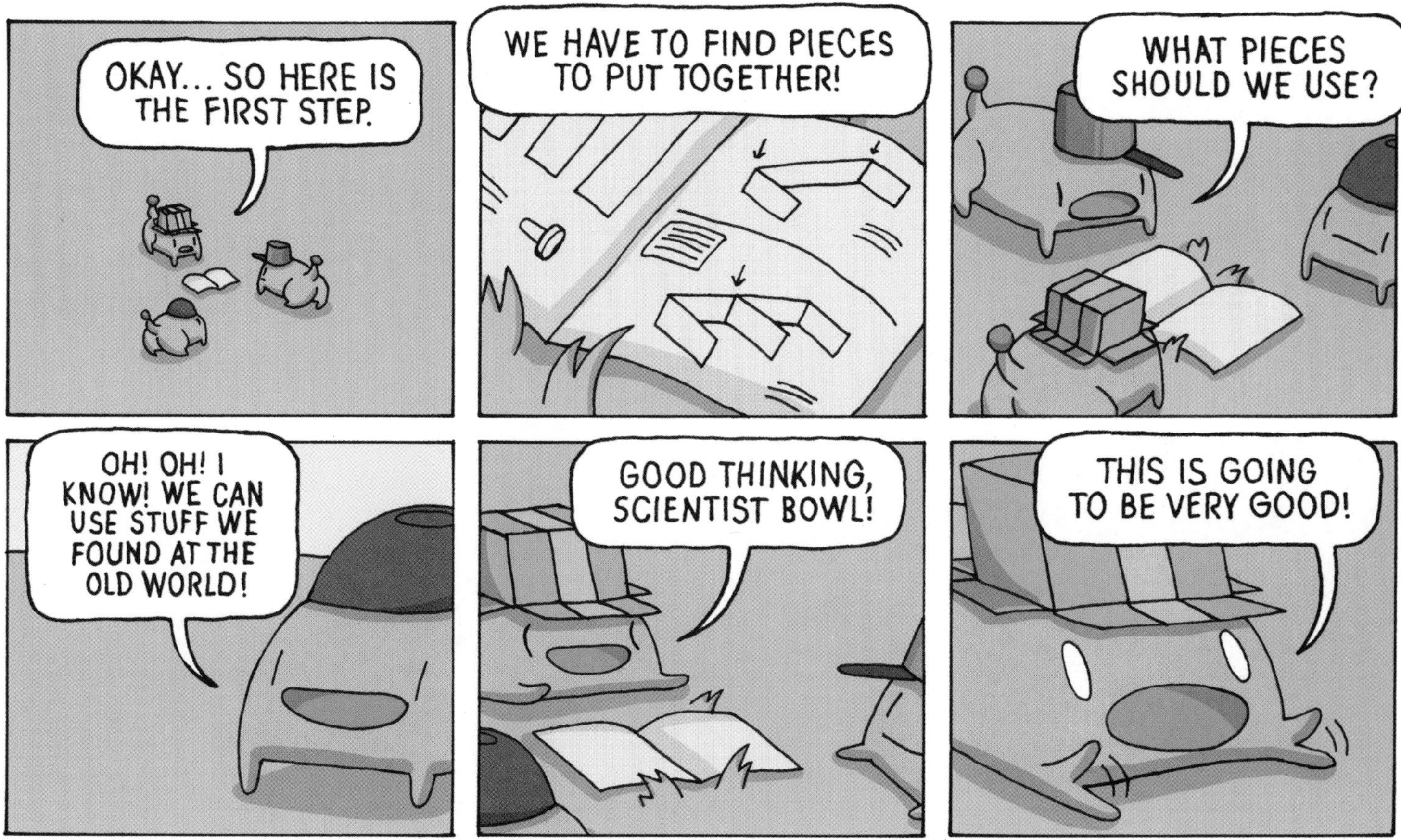
OKAY... SO HERE IS THE FIRST STEP.
WE HAVE TO FIND PIECES TO PUT TOGETHER!
WHAT PIECES SHOULD WE USE?
OH! OH! I KNOW! WE CAN USE STUFF WE FOUND AT THE OLD WORLD!
GOOD THINKING, SCIENTIST BOWL!
THIS IS GOING TO BE VERY GOOD!

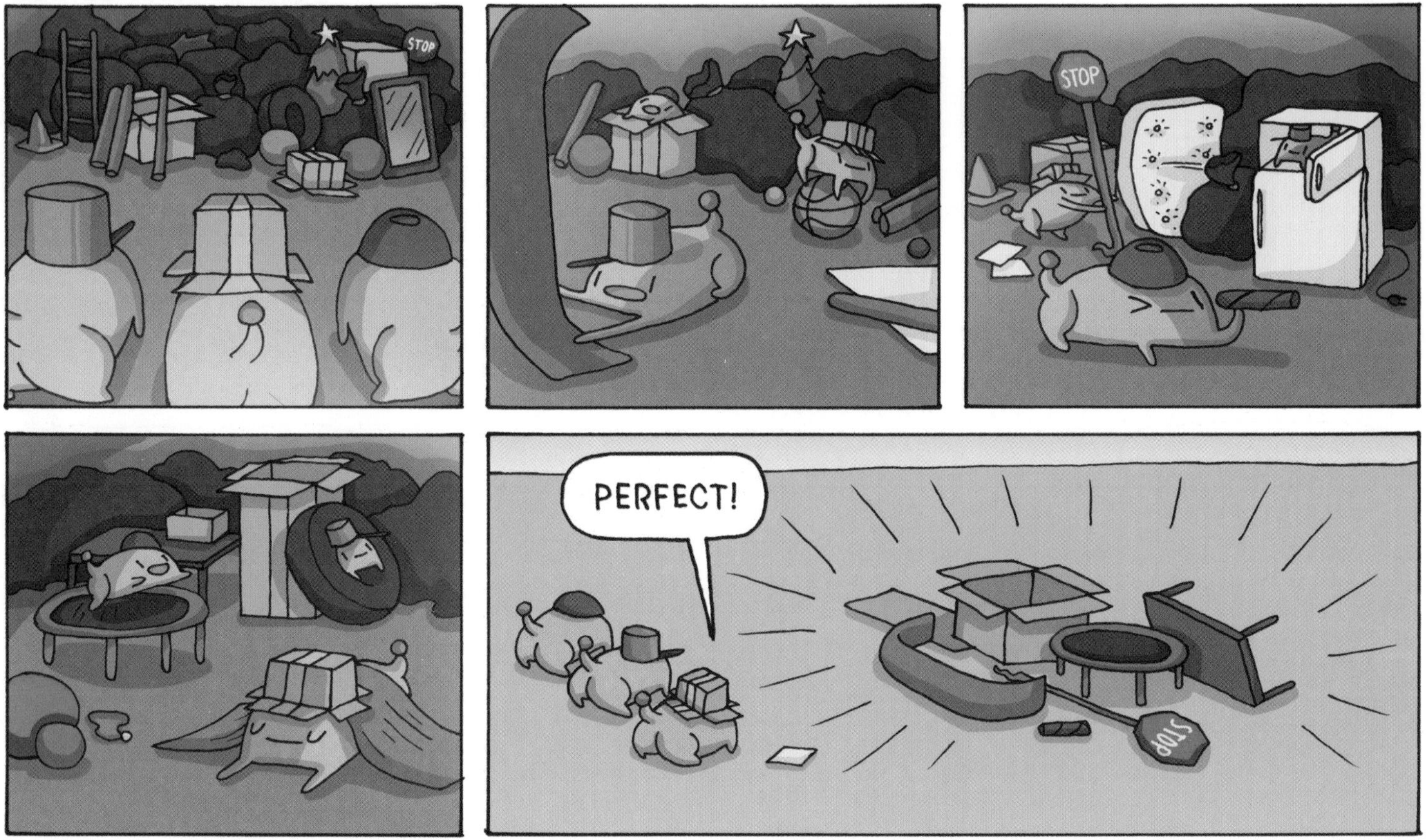
STOP
STOP
PERFECT!
STOP

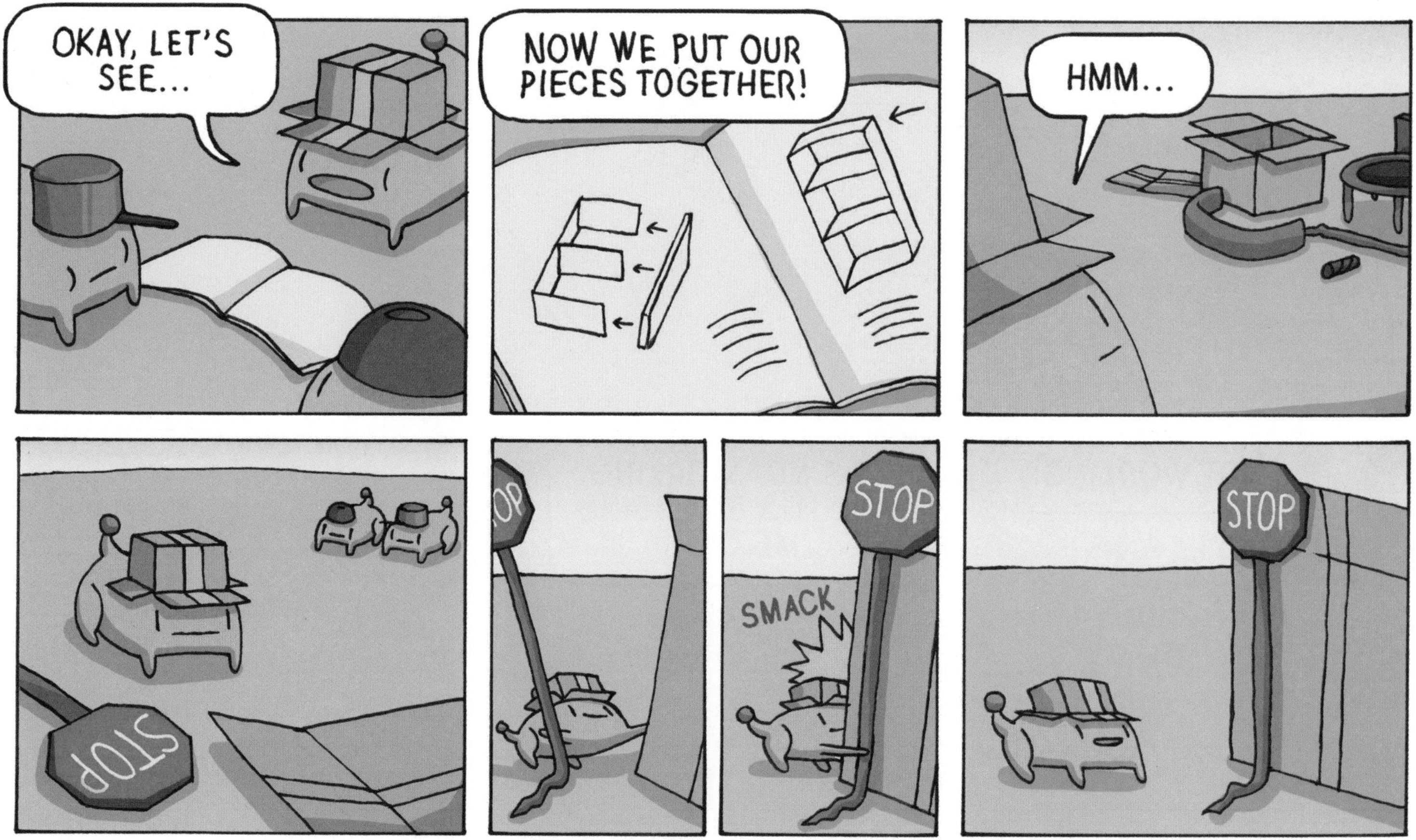
OKAY, LET'S SEE...
NOW WE PUT OUR PIECES TOGETHER!
HMM...
STOP
OP
SMACK
STOP
STOP

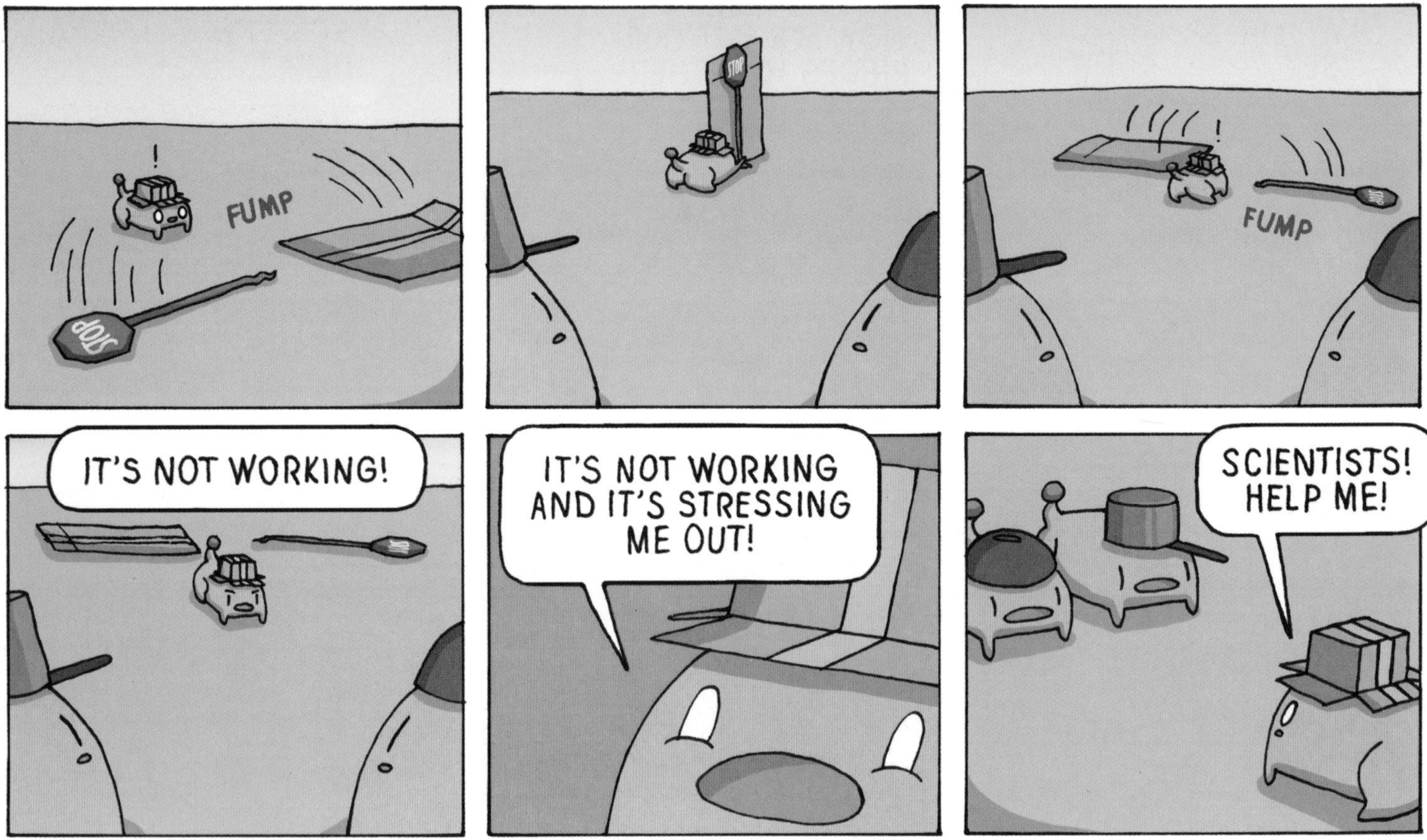
!
FUMP
STOP
STOP
!
STOP
FUMP
IT'S NOT WORKING!
IT'S NOT WORKING AND IT'S STRESSING ME OUT!
SCIENTISTS! HELP ME!

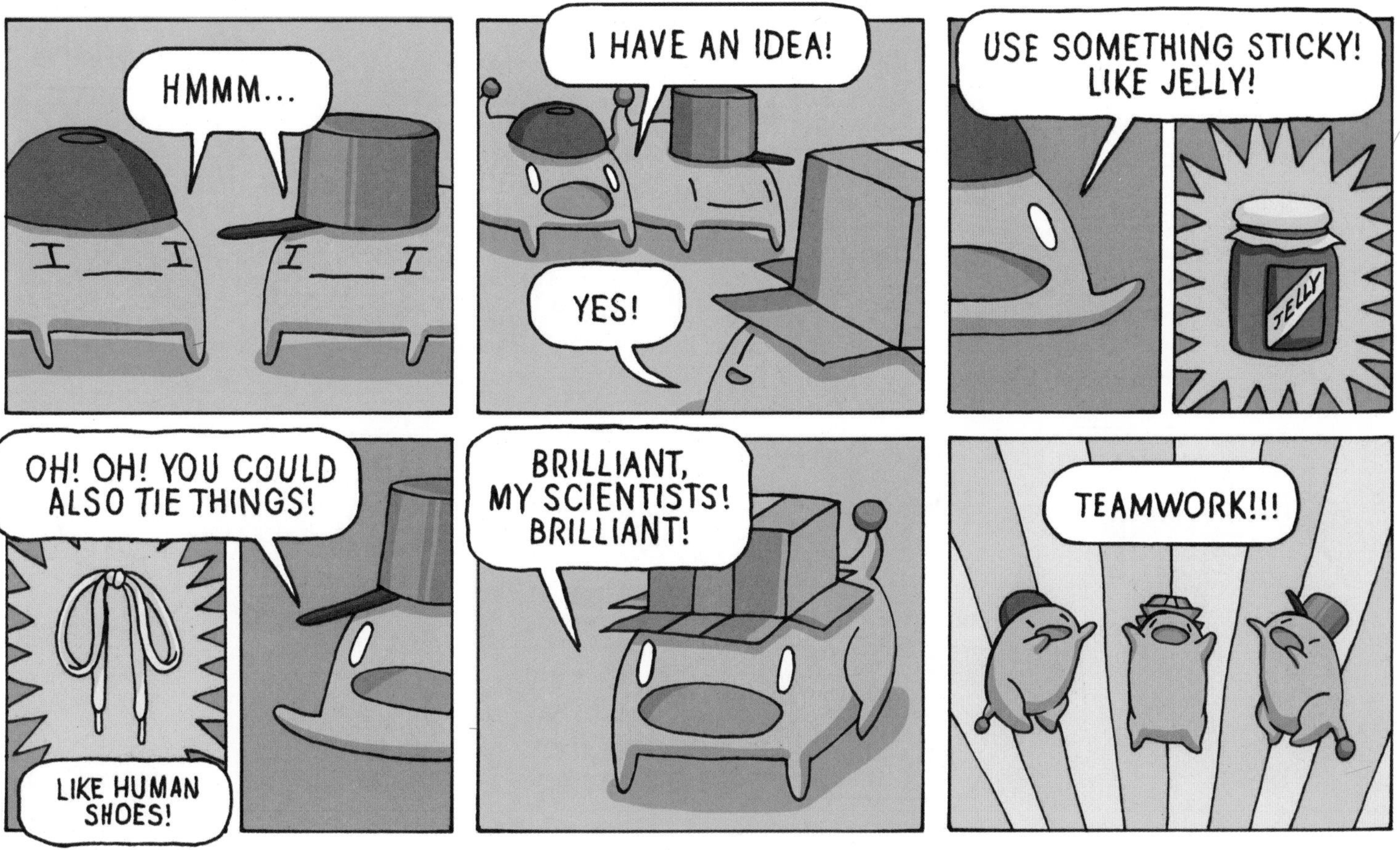

HMMM...
I HAVE AN IDEA!
YES!
USE SOMETHING STICKY! LIKE JELLY!
JELLY
OH! OH! YOU COULD ALSO TIE THINGS!
LIKE HUMAN SHOES!
BRILLIANT, MY SCIENTISTS! BRILLIANT!
TEAMWORK!!!

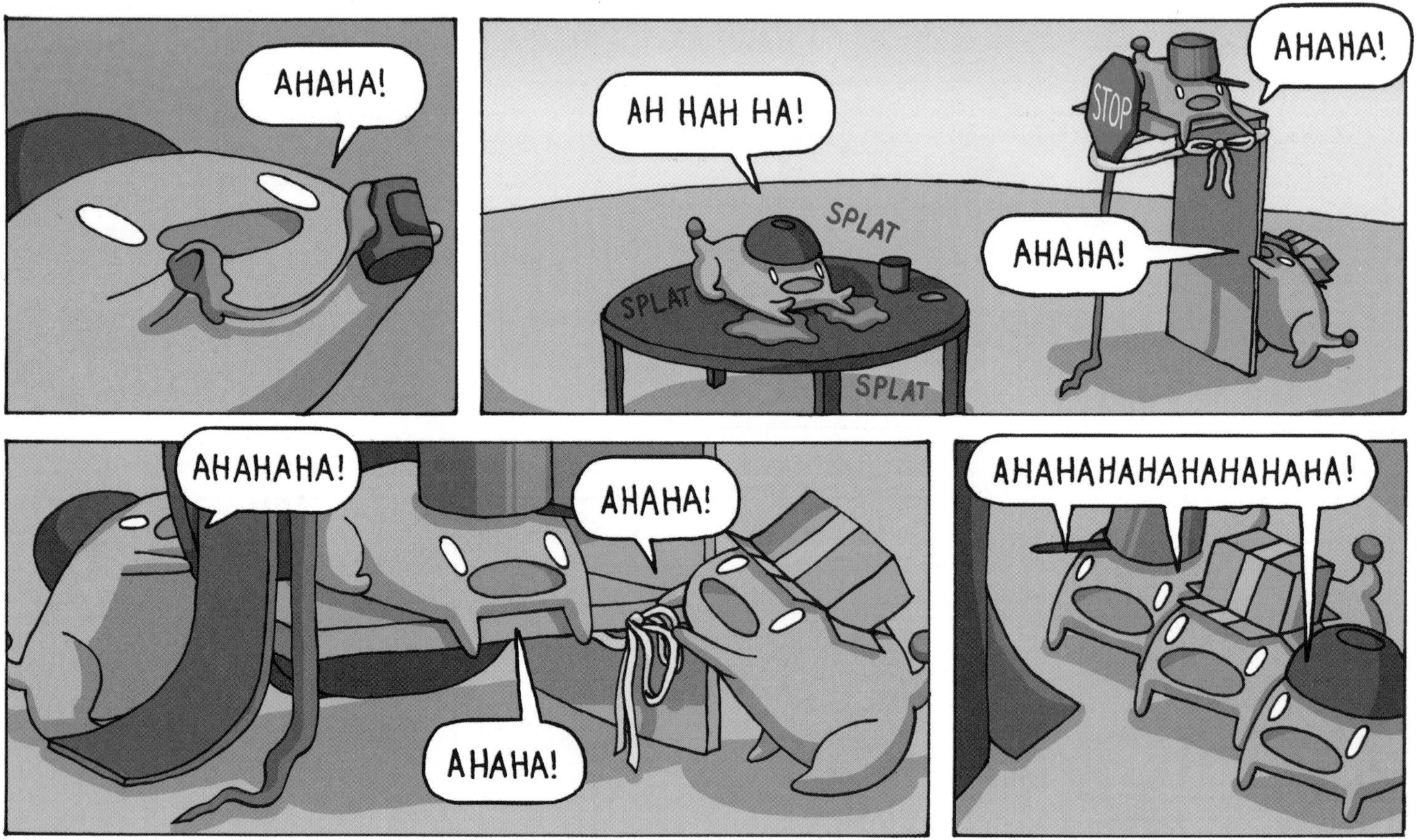
AHAHA!
AH HAH HA!
SPLAT
SPLAT
SPLAT
AHAHA!
AHAHA!
AHAHAHA!
AHAHA!
AHAHA!
AHAHAHAHAHAHAHAHA!

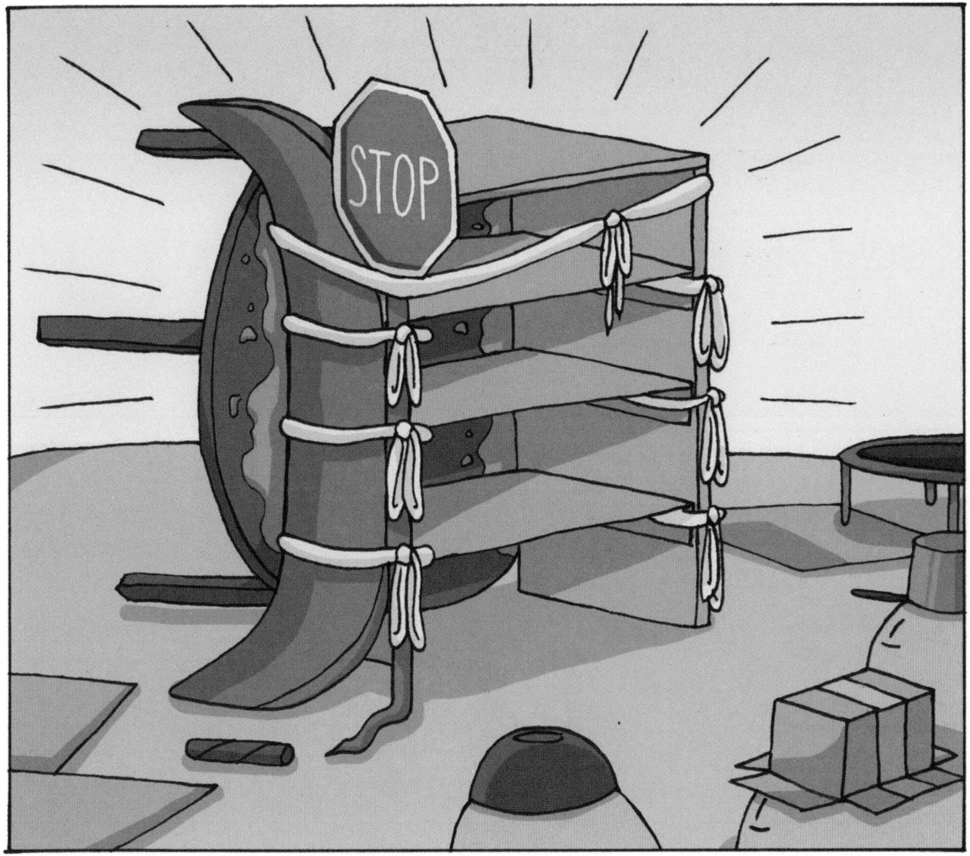
STOP

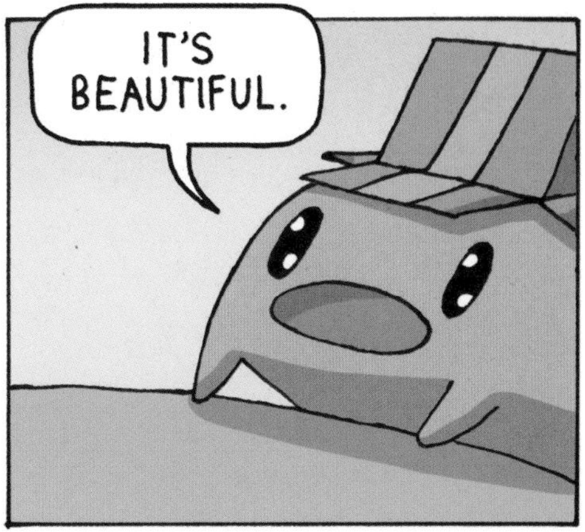
IT'S BEAUTIFUL.

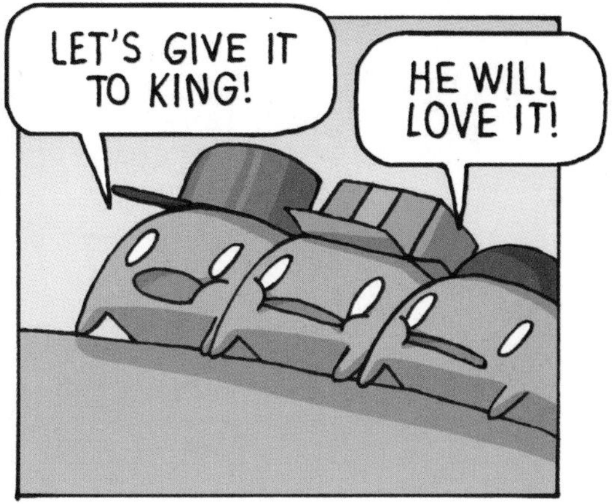
LET'S GIVE IT TO KING!
HE WILL LOVE IT!

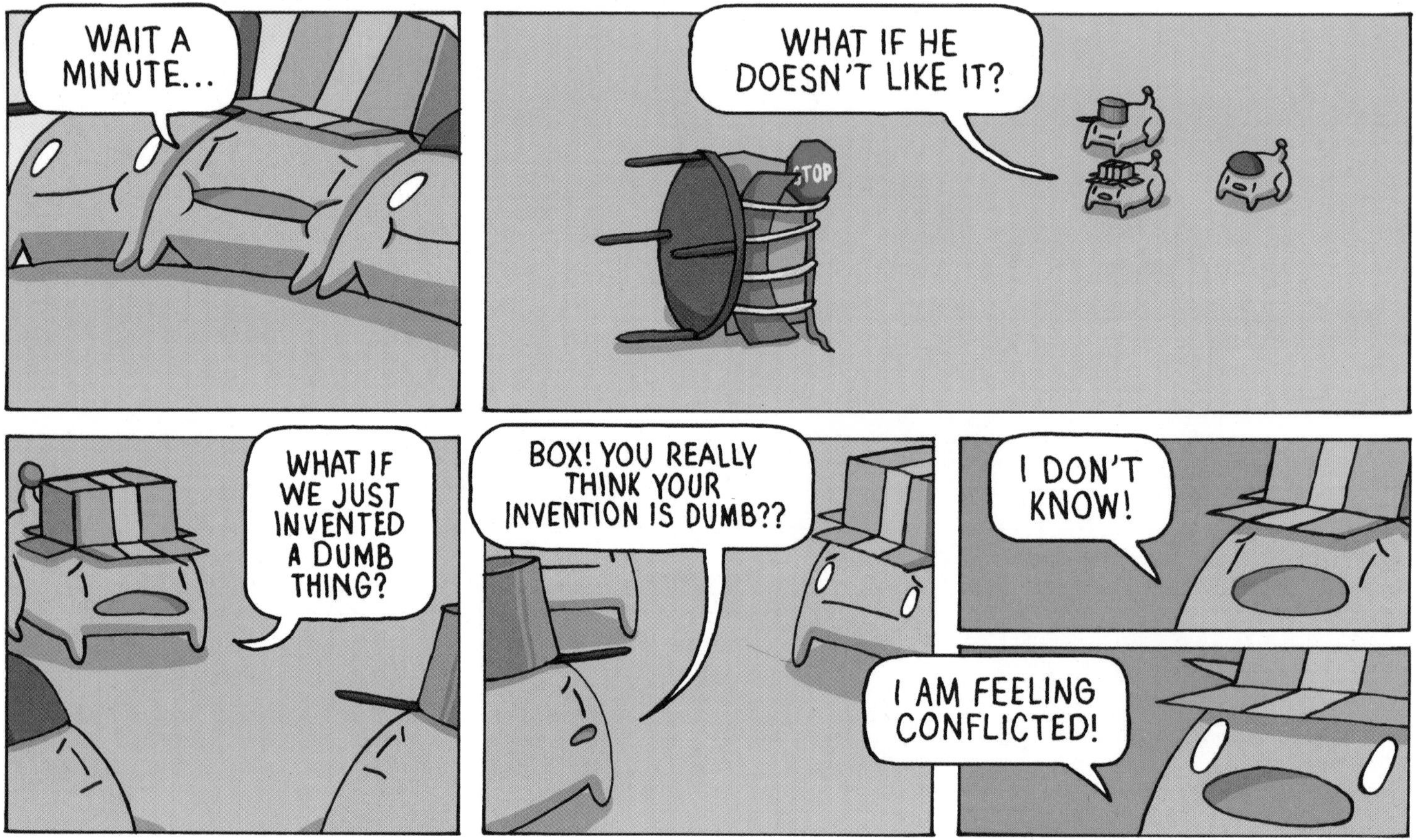

WAIT A MINUTE...
WHAT IF HE DOESN'T LIKE IT?
STOP
WHAT IF WE JUST INVENTED A DUMB THING?
BOX! YOU REALLY THINK YOUR INVENTION IS DUMB??
I DON'T KNOW!
I AM FEELING CONFLICTED!

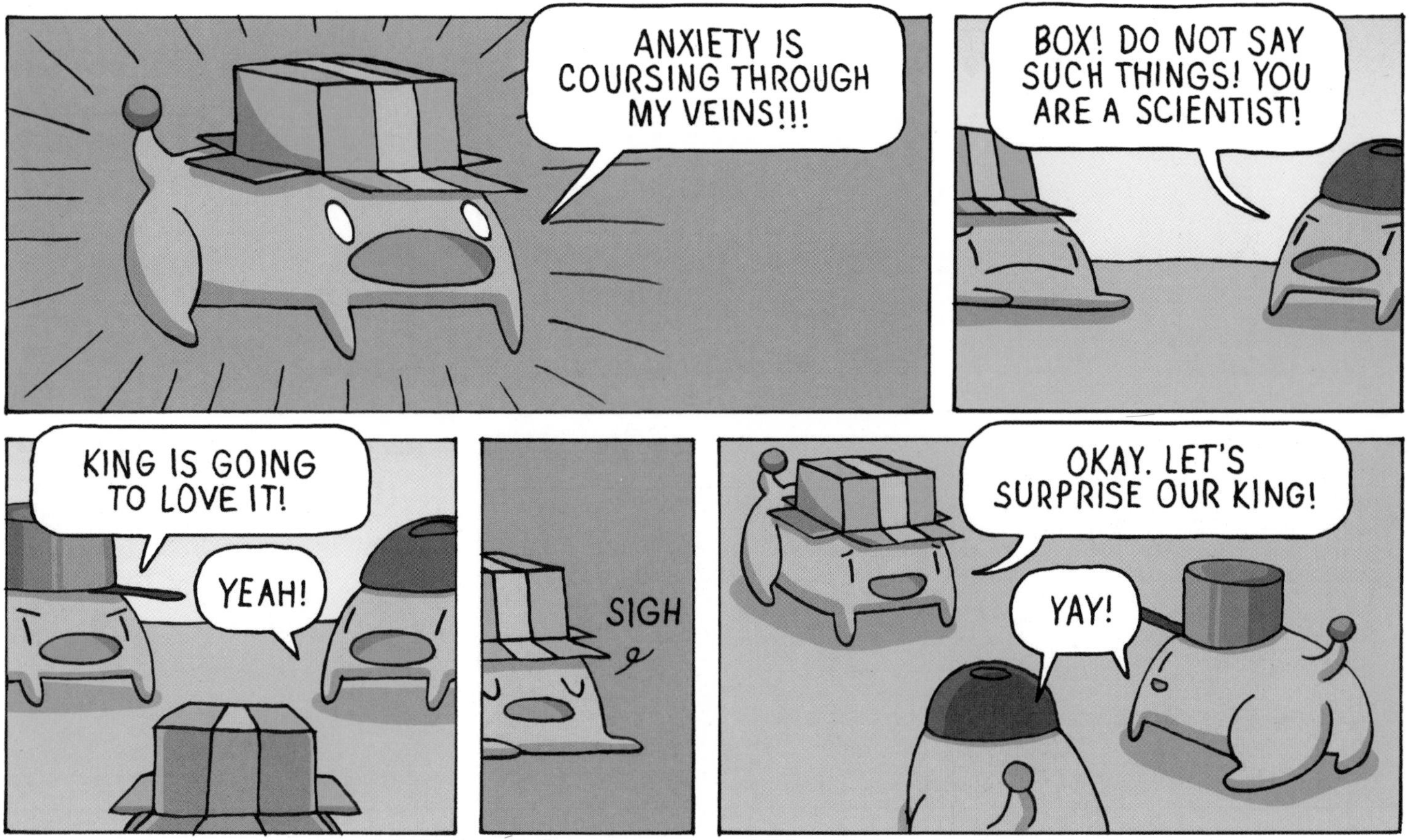
ANXIETY IS COURSING THROUGH MY VEINS!!!
BOX! DO NOT SAY SUCH THINGS! YOU ARE A SCIENTIST!
KING IS GOING TO LOVE IT!
YEAH!
SIGH
OKAY. LET'S SURPRISE OUR KING!
YAY!

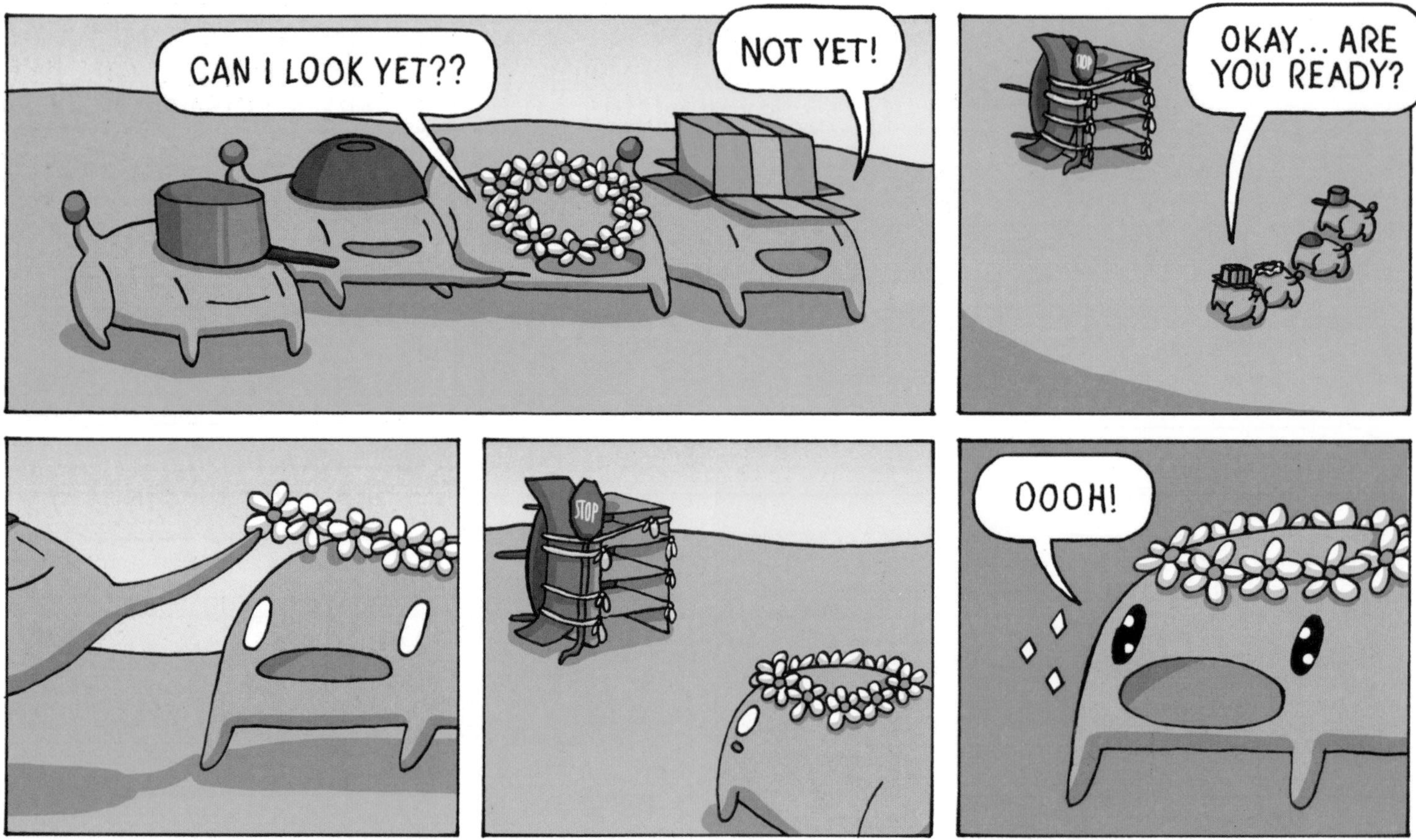
CAN I LOOK YET??
NOT YET!
OKAY... ARE YOU READY?
STOP
OOOH!

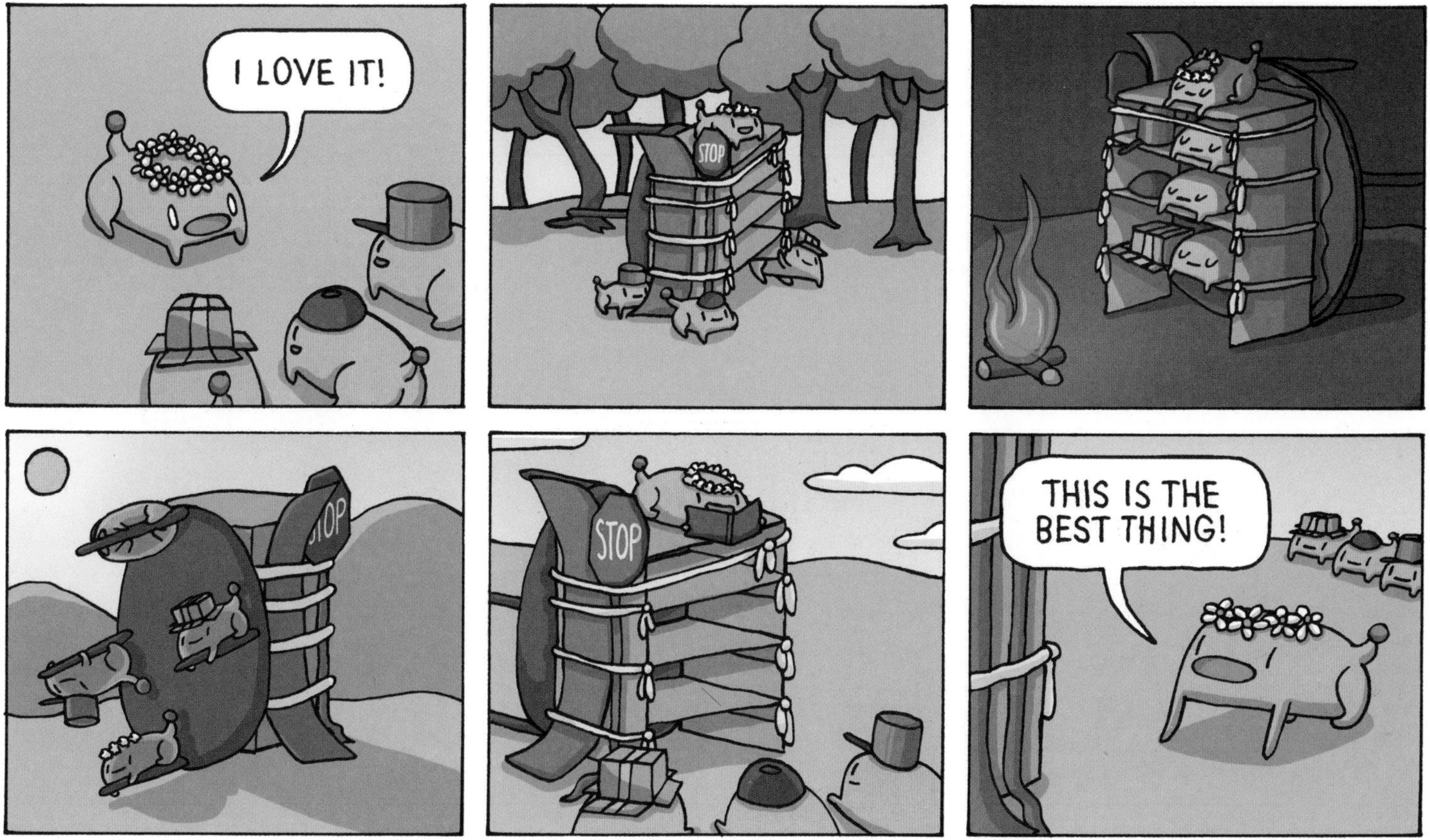
I LOVE IT!
STOP
STOP
STOP
THIS IS THE BEST THING!

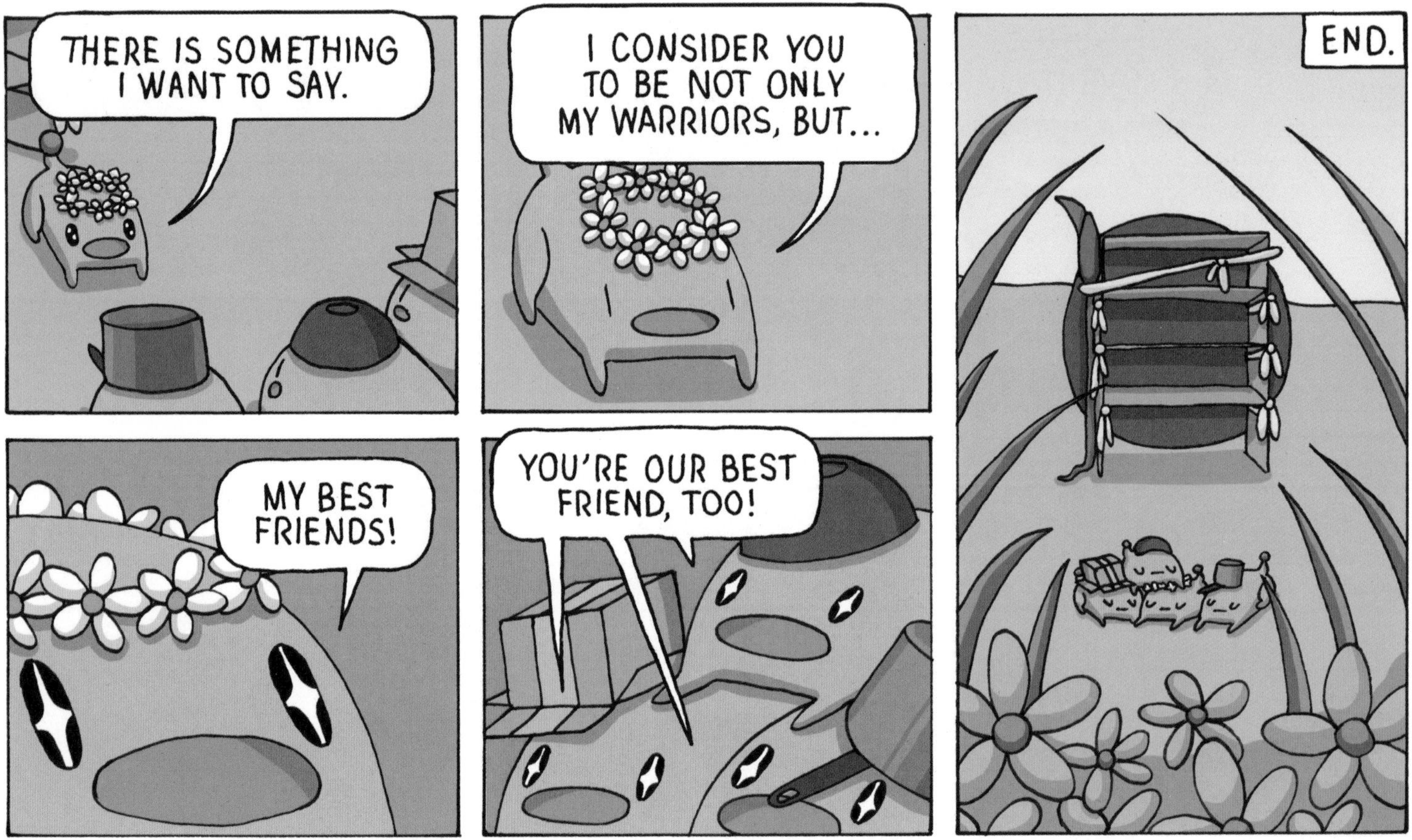
THERE IS SOMETHING I WANT TO SAY.
I CONSIDER YOU TO BE NOT ONLY MY WARRIORS, BUT...
END.
MY BEST FRIENDS!
YOU'RE OUR BEST FRIEND, TOO!

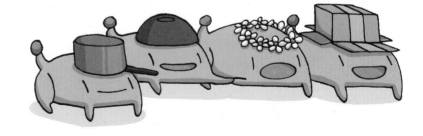

CHAPTER SIX

—

WAR

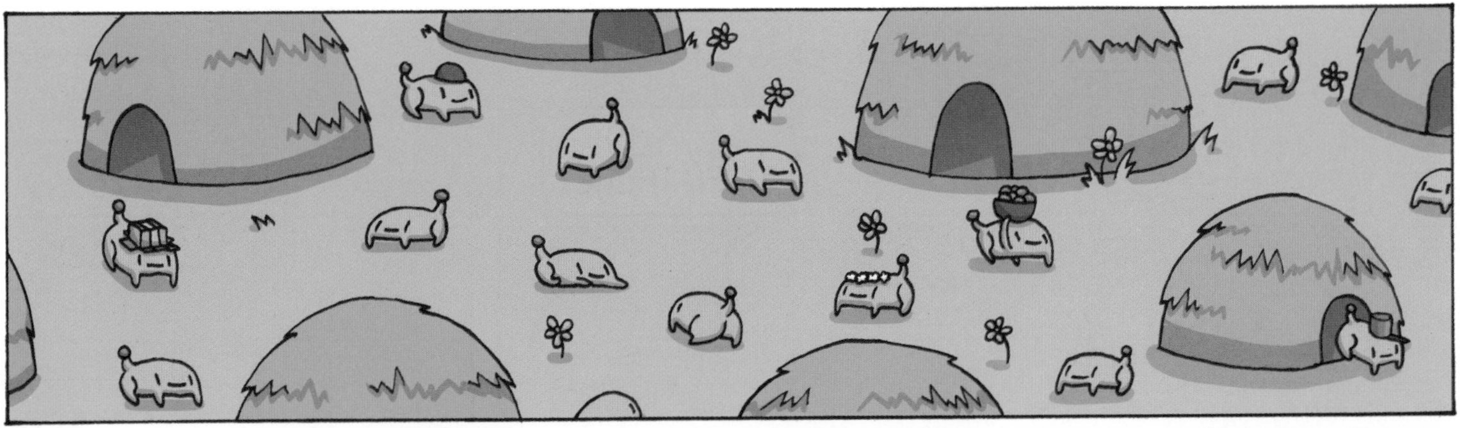

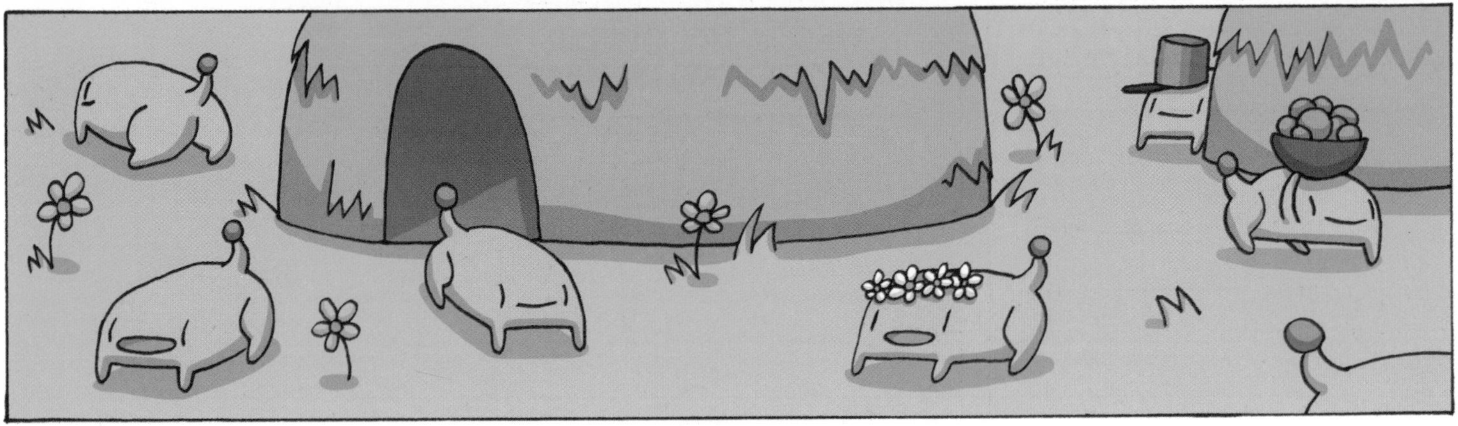

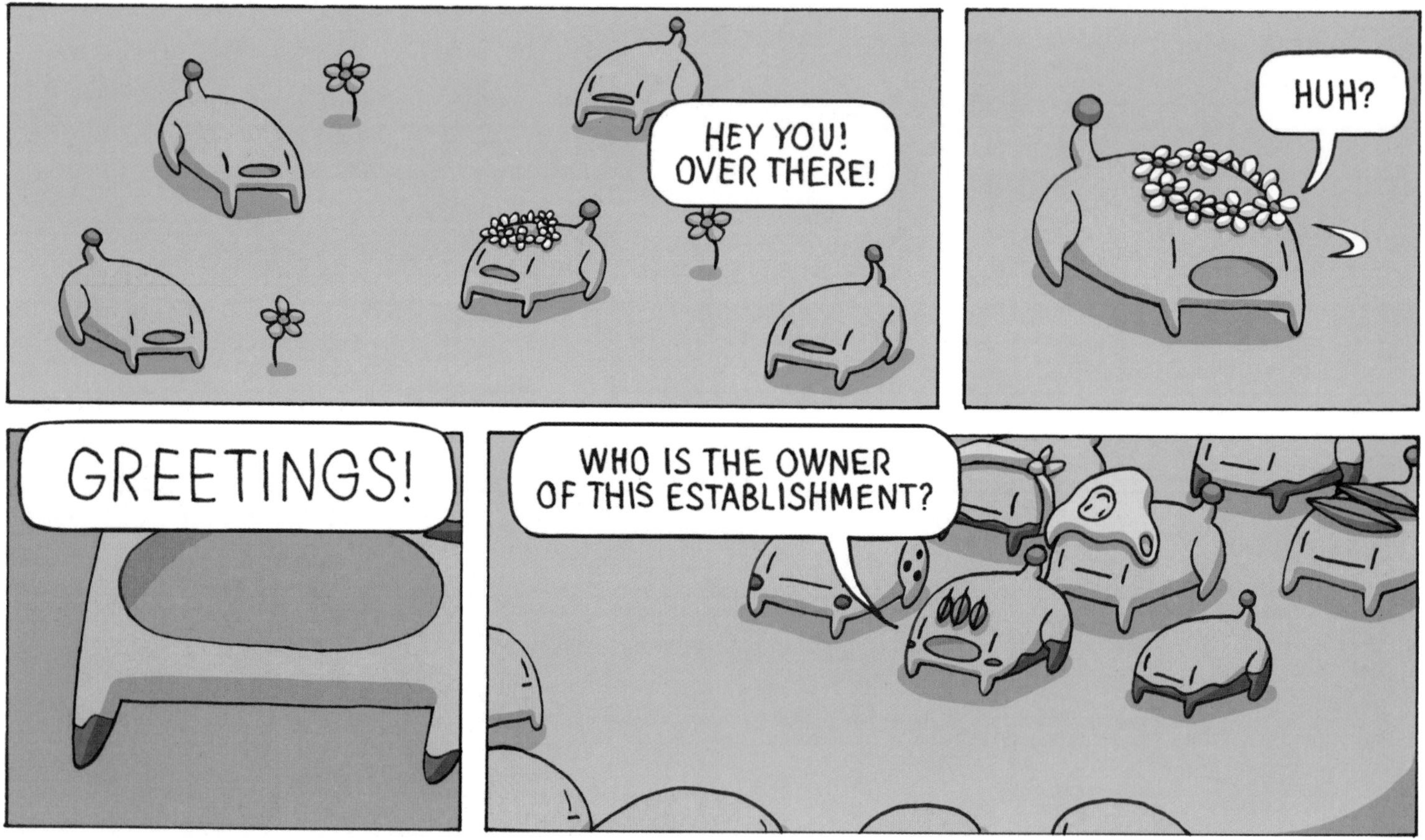
HEY YOU! OVER THERE!
HUH?
GREETINGS!
WHO IS THE OWNER OF THIS ESTABLISHMENT?

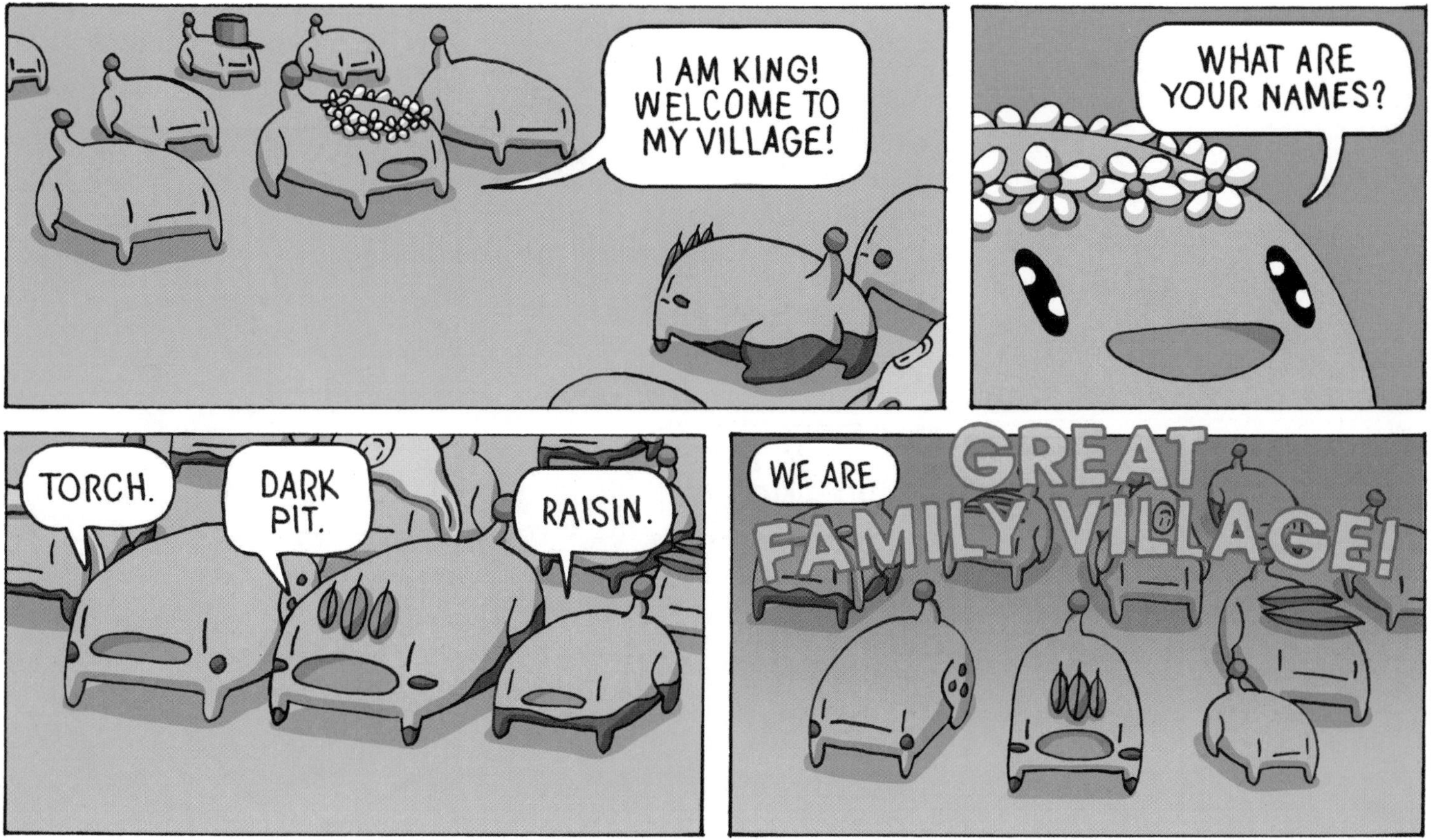
I AM KING! WELCOME TO MY VILLAGE!
WHAT ARE YOUR NAMES?
TORCH.
DARK PIT.
RAISIN.
WE ARE
GREAT FAMILY VILLAGE!

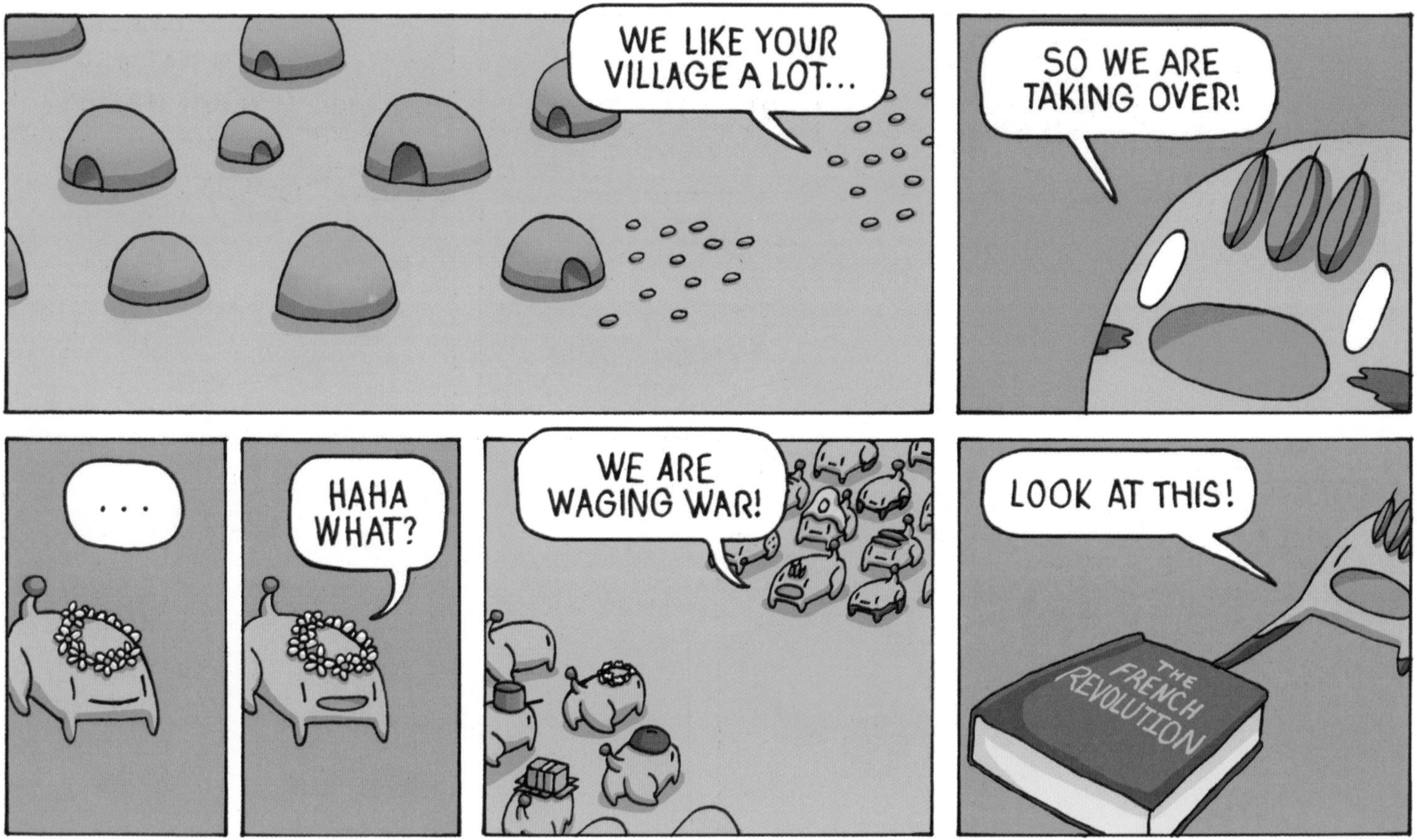
WE LIKE YOUR VILLAGE A LOT...
SO WE ARE TAKING OVER!
...
HAHA WHAT?
WE ARE WAGING WAR!
LOOK AT THIS!
THE FRENCH REVOLUTION

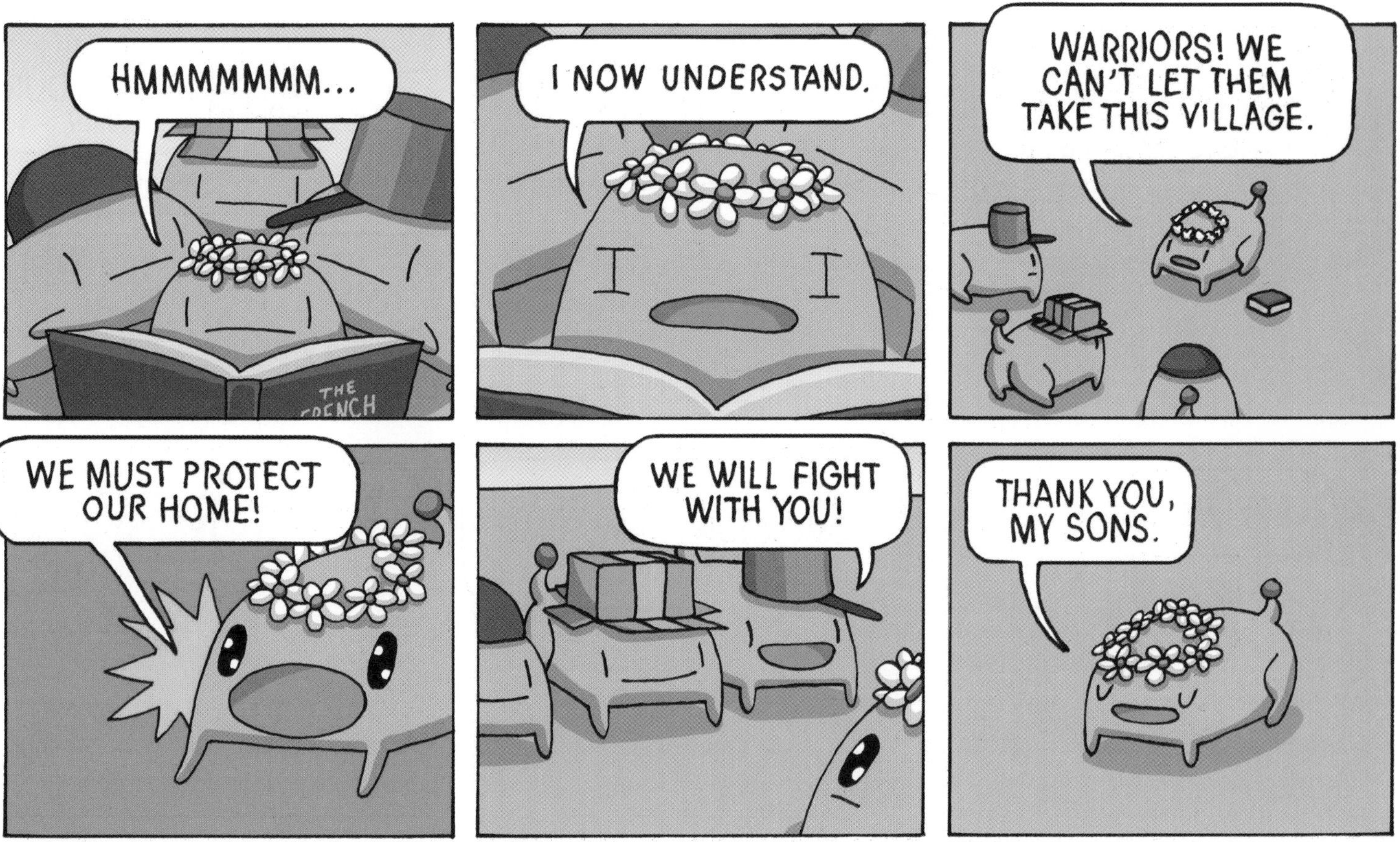
HMMMMMMM...
THE FRENCH
I NOW UNDERSTAND.
WARRIORS! WE CAN'T LET THEM TAKE THIS VILLAGE.
WE MUST PROTECT OUR HOME!
WE WILL FIGHT WITH YOU!
THANK YOU, MY SONS.

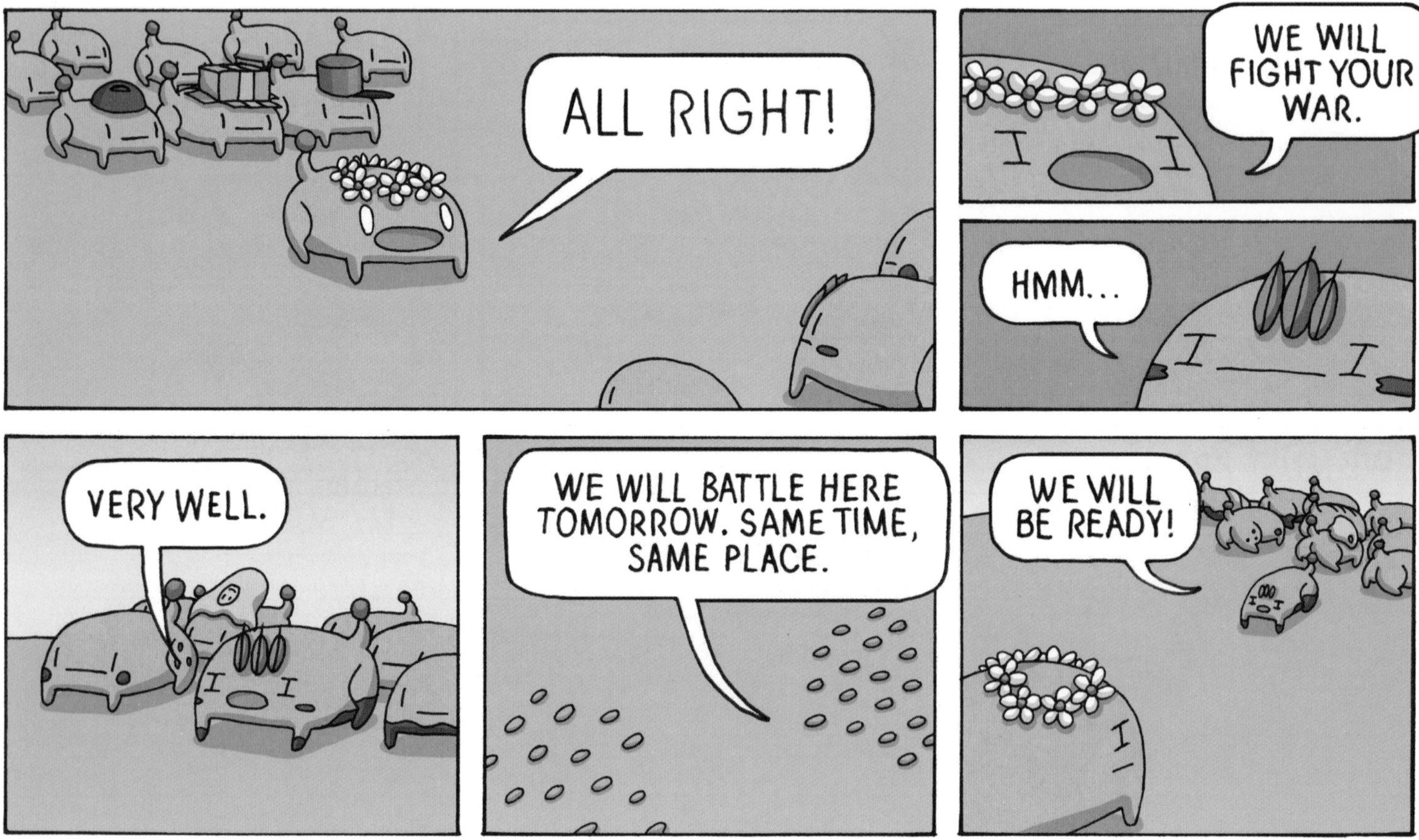
ALL RIGHT!
WE WILL FIGHT YOUR WAR.
HMM...
VERY WELL.
WE WILL BATTLE HERE TOMORROW. SAME TIME, SAME PLACE.
WE WILL BE READY!

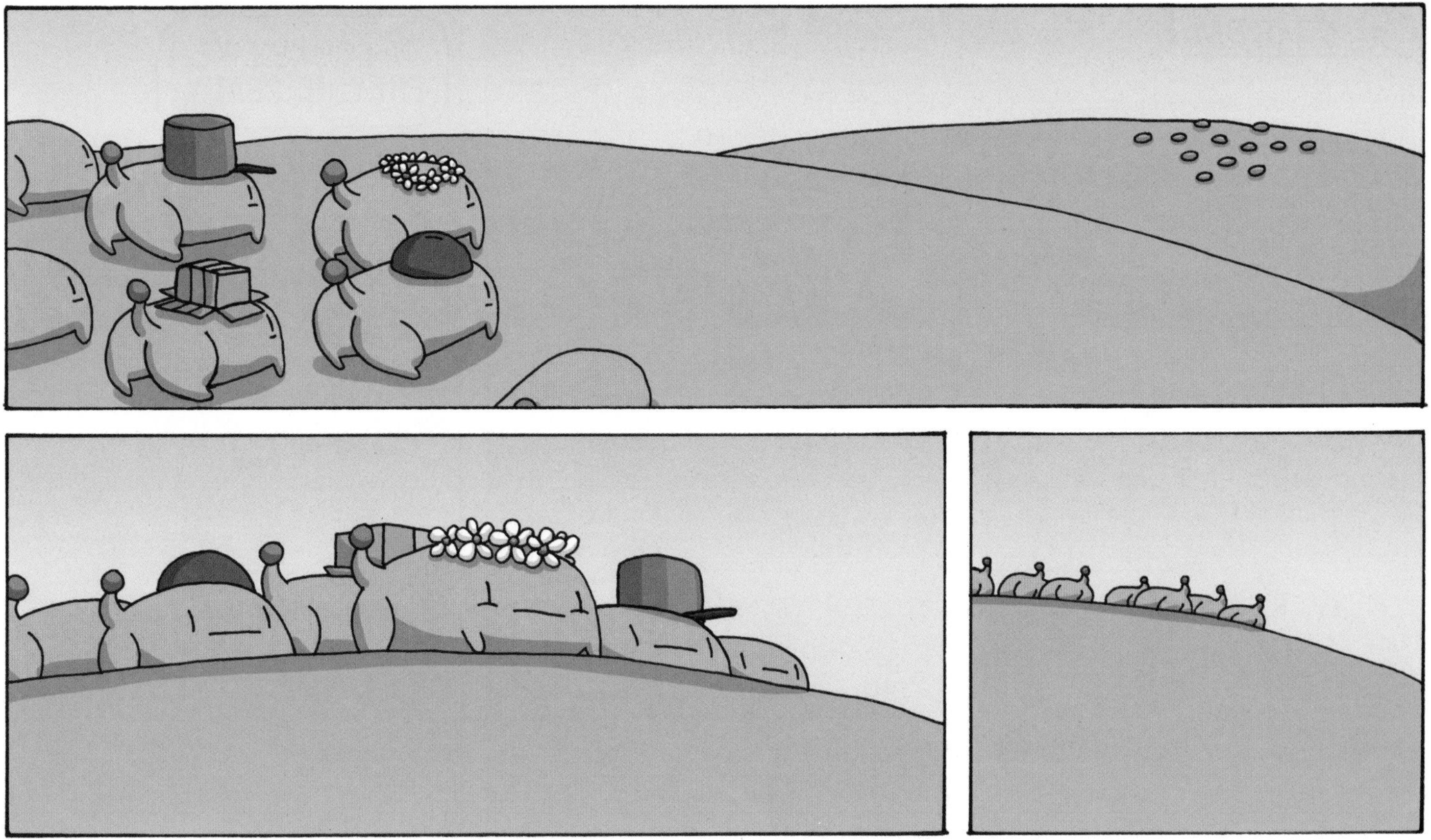

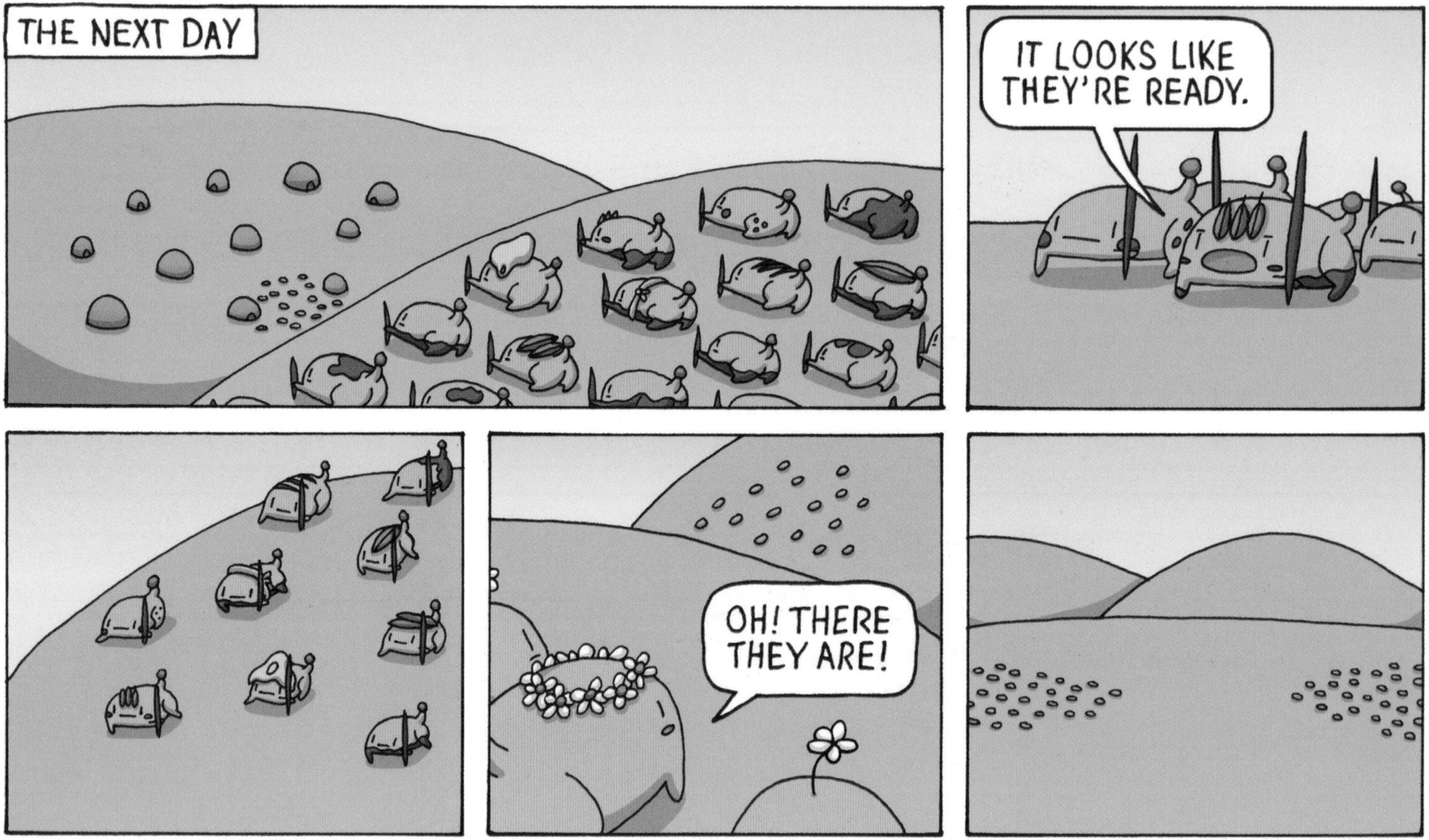
THE NEXT DAY
IT LOOKS LIKE THEY'RE READY.
OH! THERE THEY ARE!

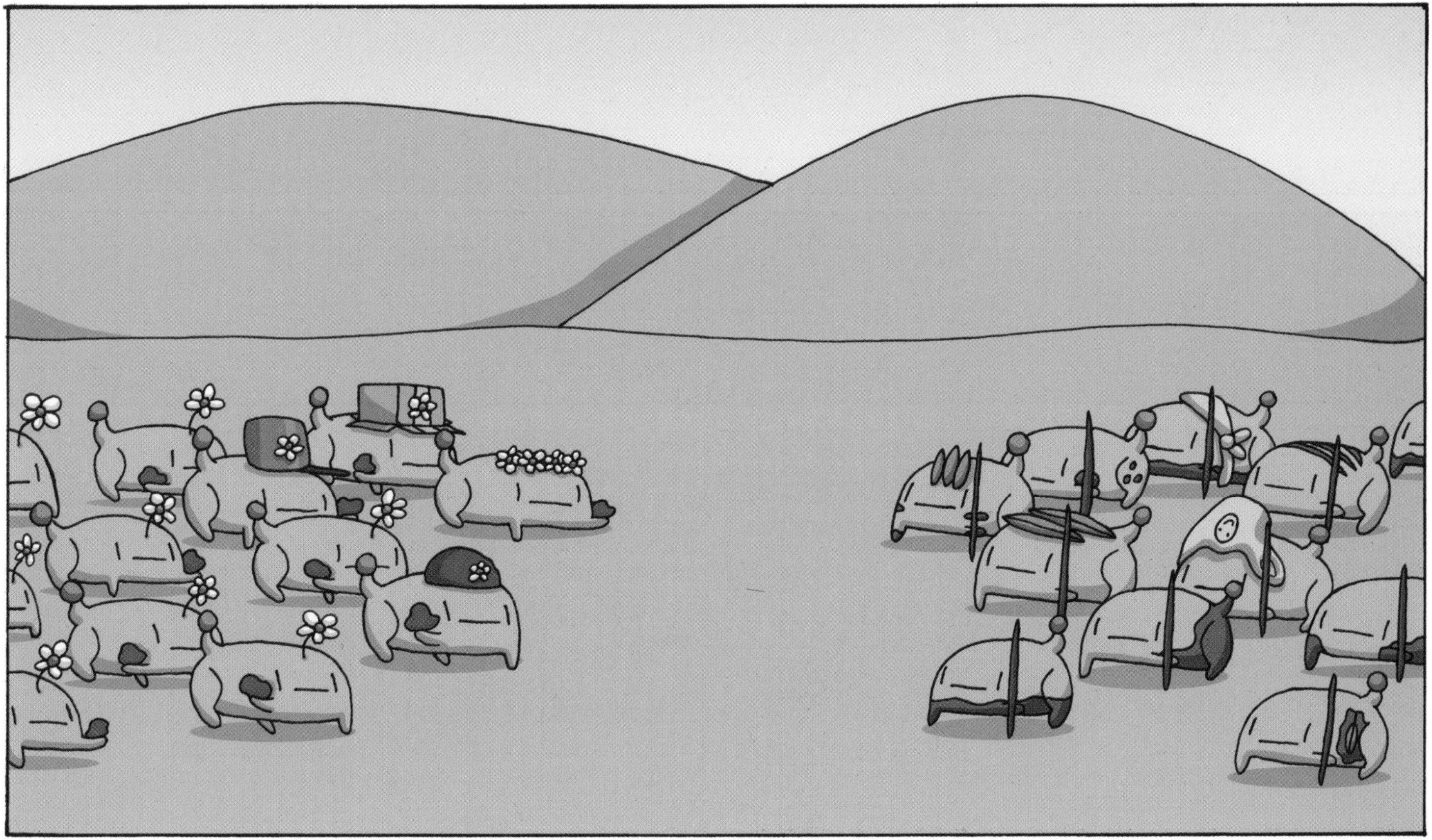

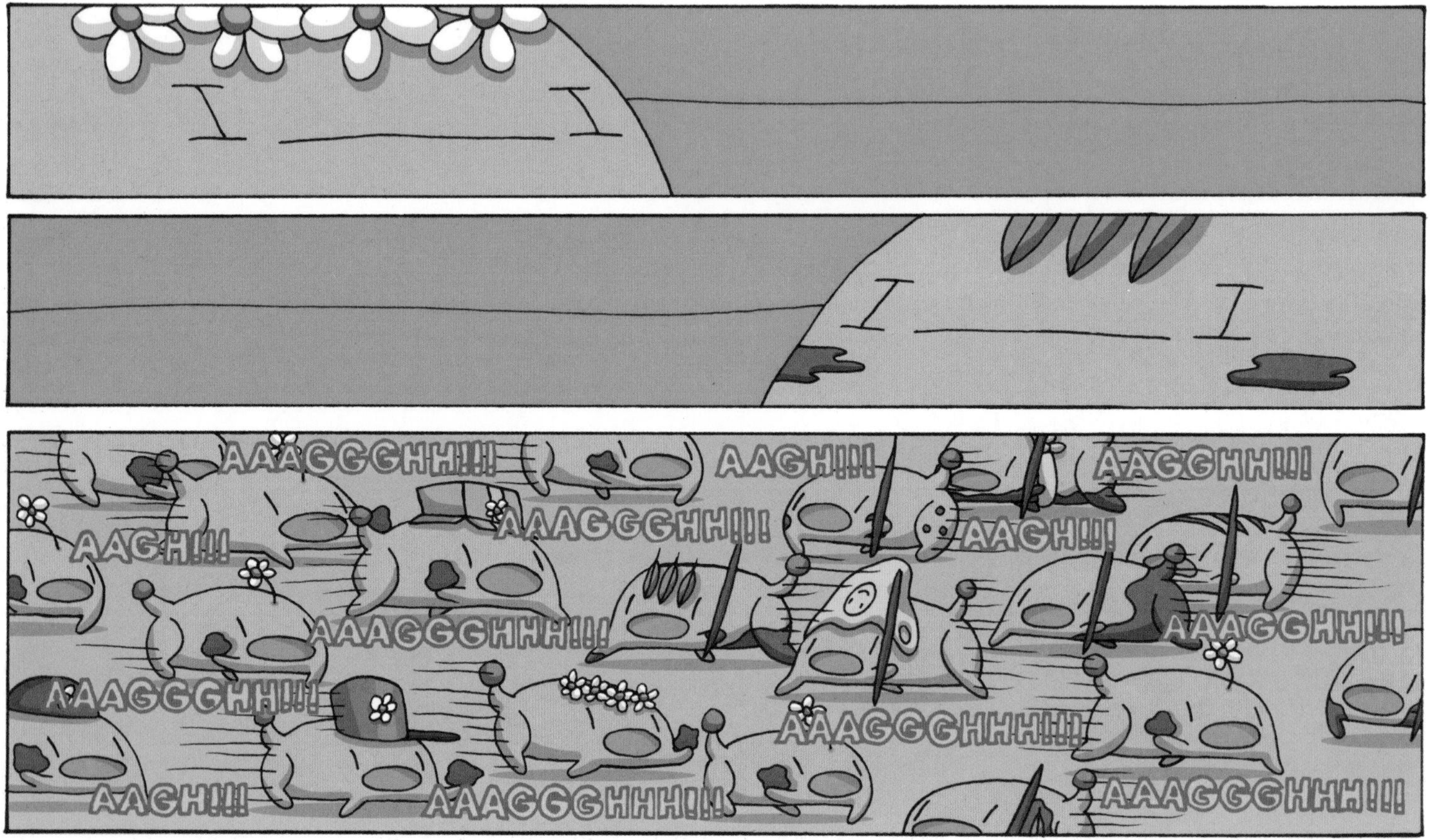
AAAGGGHH!!!
AAGH!!!
AAGGHH!!!
AAGH!!!
AAAGGGHH!!!
AAGH!!!
AAAGGGHHH!!!
AAAGGHH!!!
AAAGGGHH!!!
AAAGGGHHH!!!
AAGH!!!
AAAGGGHHH!!!
AAAGGGHHH!!!

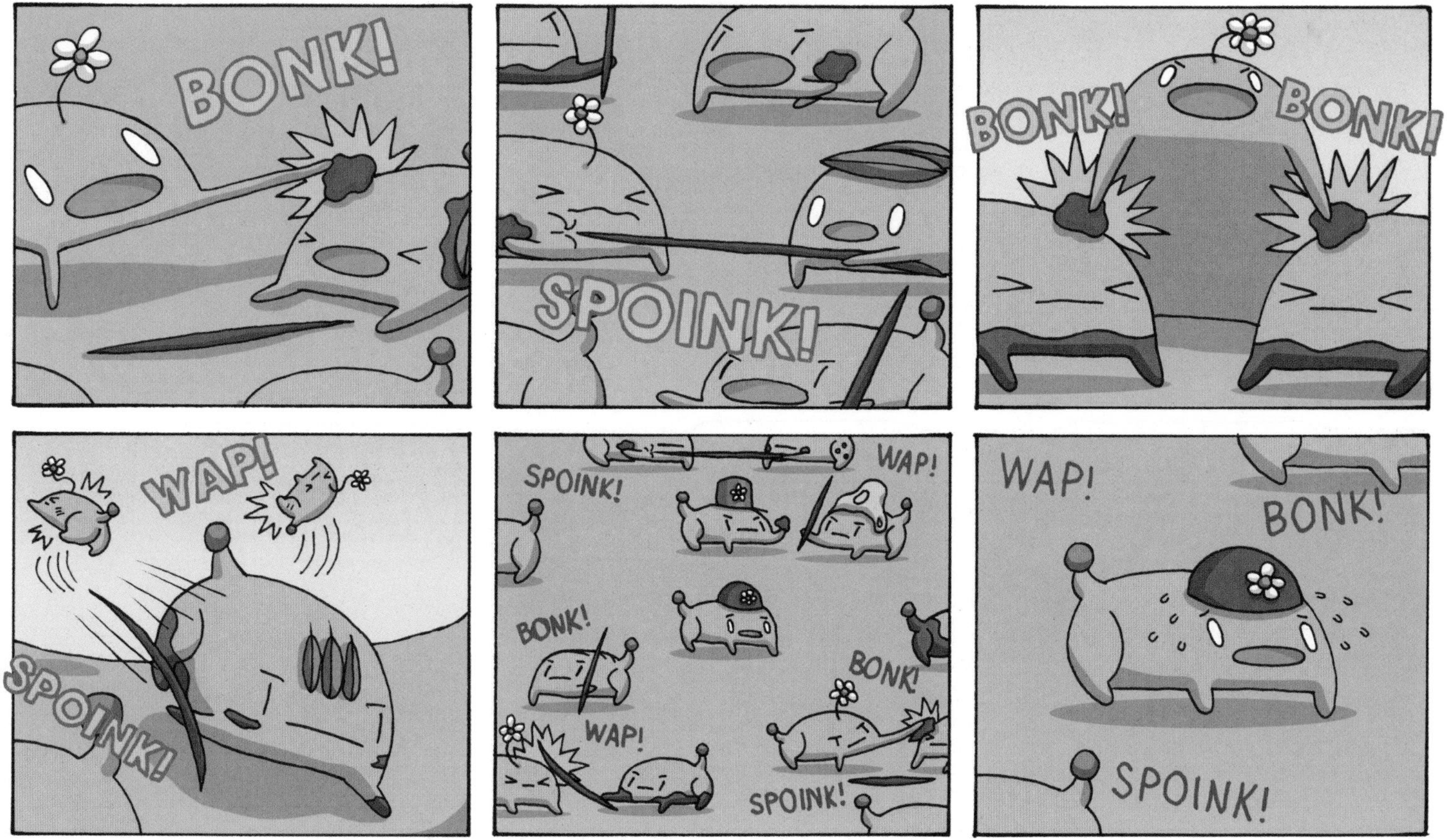
BONK!
SPOINK!
BONK!
BONK!
WAP!
SPOINK!
SPOINK!
WAP!
BONK!
BONK!
WAP!
SPOINK!
WAP!
BONK!
SPOINK!

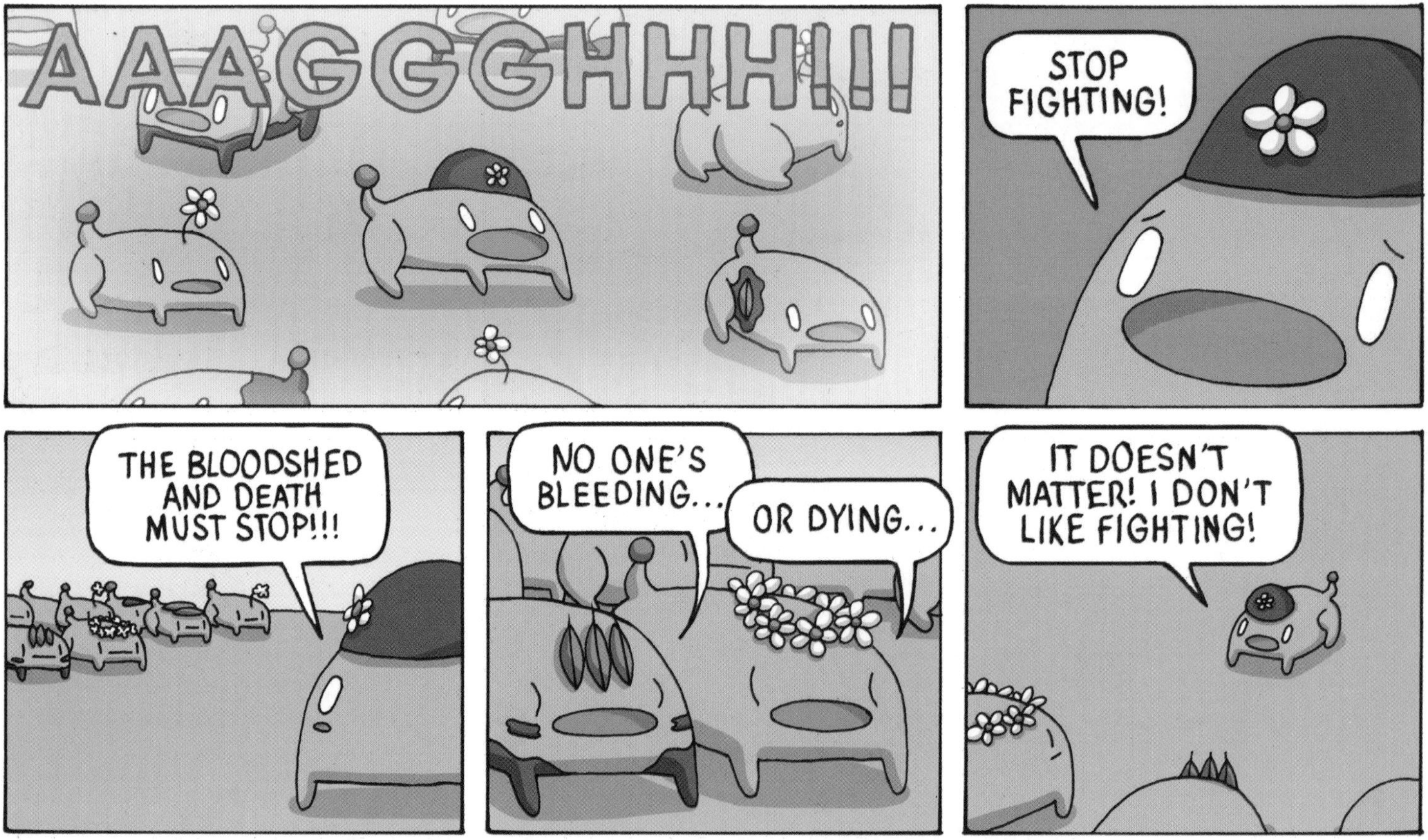
AAAGGGHHHH!!!
STOP FIGHTING!
THE BLOODSHED AND DEATH MUST STOP!!!
NO ONE'S BLEEDING...
OR DYING...
IT DOESN'T MATTER! I DON'T LIKE FIGHTING!

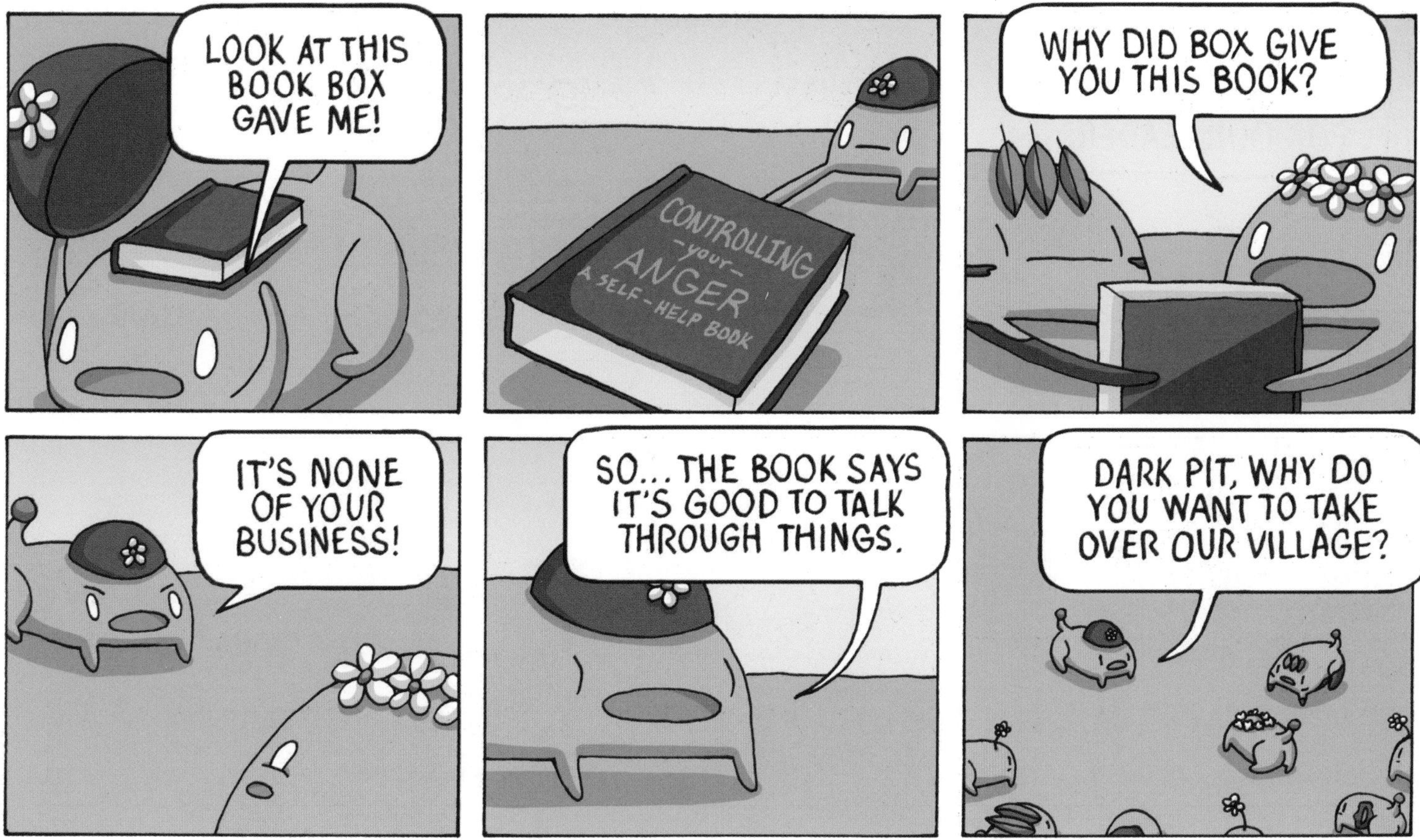
LOOK AT THIS BOOK BOX GAVE ME!
CONTROLLING -your- ANGER A SELF-HELP BOOK
WHY DID BOX GIVE YOU THIS BOOK?
IT'S NONE OF YOUR BUSINESS!
SO... THE BOOK SAYS IT'S GOOD TO TALK THROUGH THINGS.
DARK PIT, WHY DO YOU WANT TO TAKE OVER OUR VILLAGE?

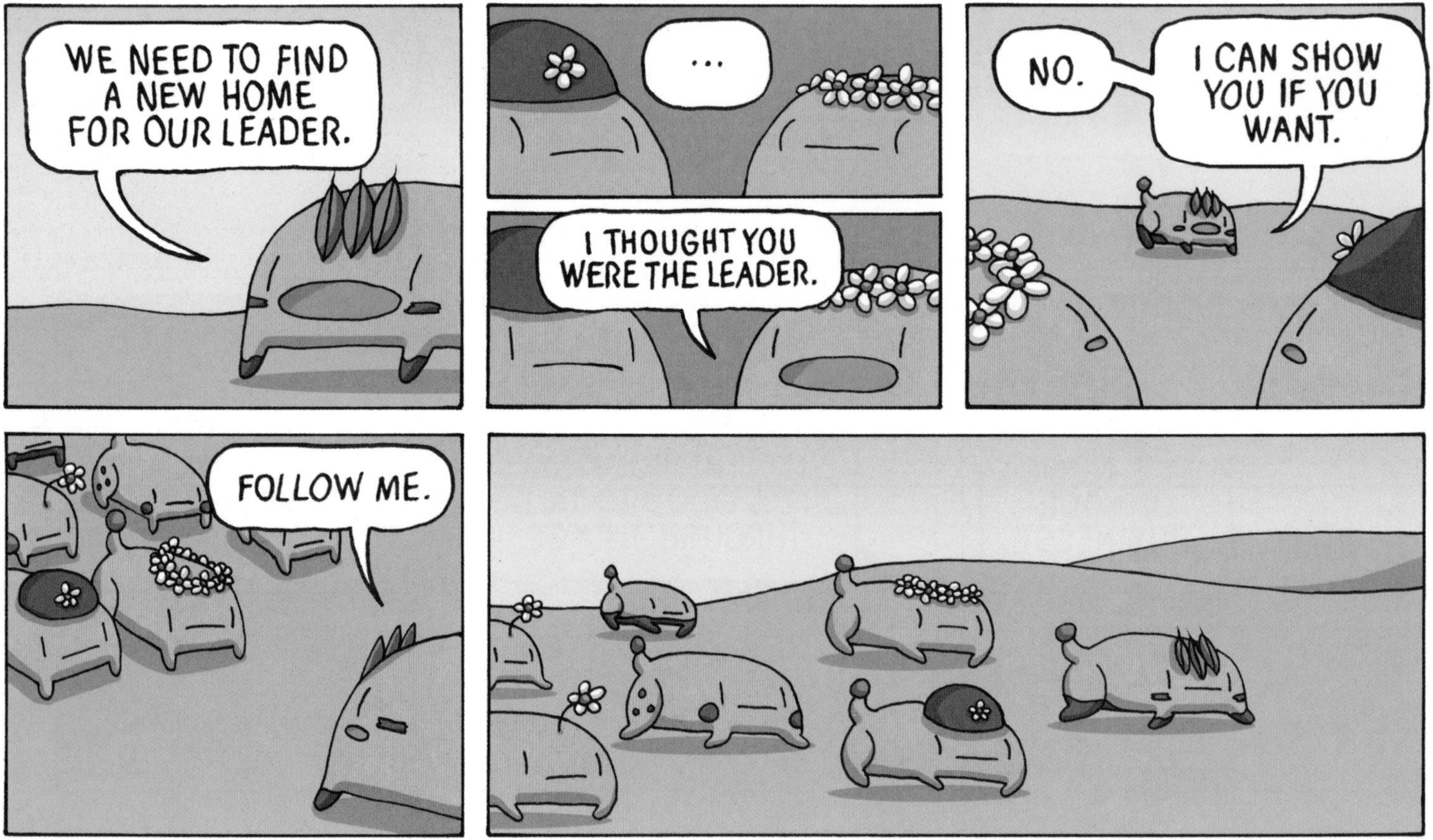
WE NEED TO FIND A NEW HOME FOR OUR LEADER.
...
I THOUGHT YOU WERE THE LEADER.
NO.
I CAN SHOW YOU IF YOU WANT.
FOLLOW ME.

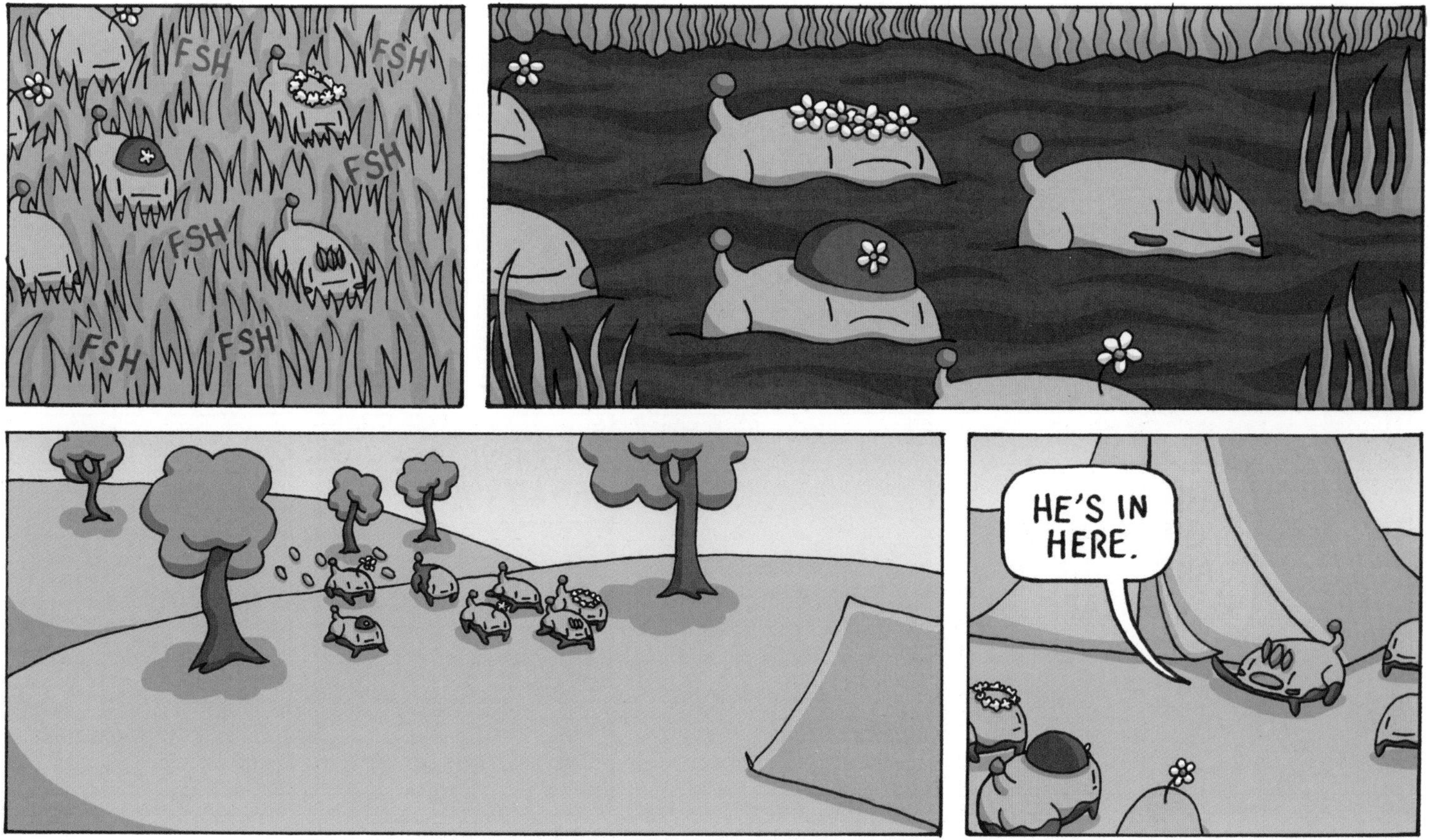
FSH
FSH
FSH
FSH
FSH
FSH
HE'S IN HERE.

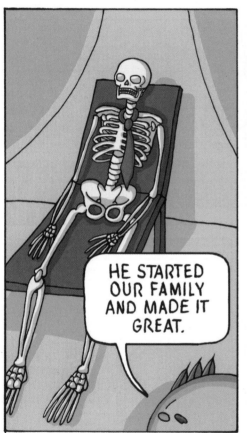

HE STARTED OUR FAMILY AND MADE IT GREAT.

OH! YOU HAVE A HUMAN PERSON.

YES. WE PROMISED TO PROTECT EACH OTHER.

YOUR VILLAGE CAN LIVE WITH US.

REALLY?!

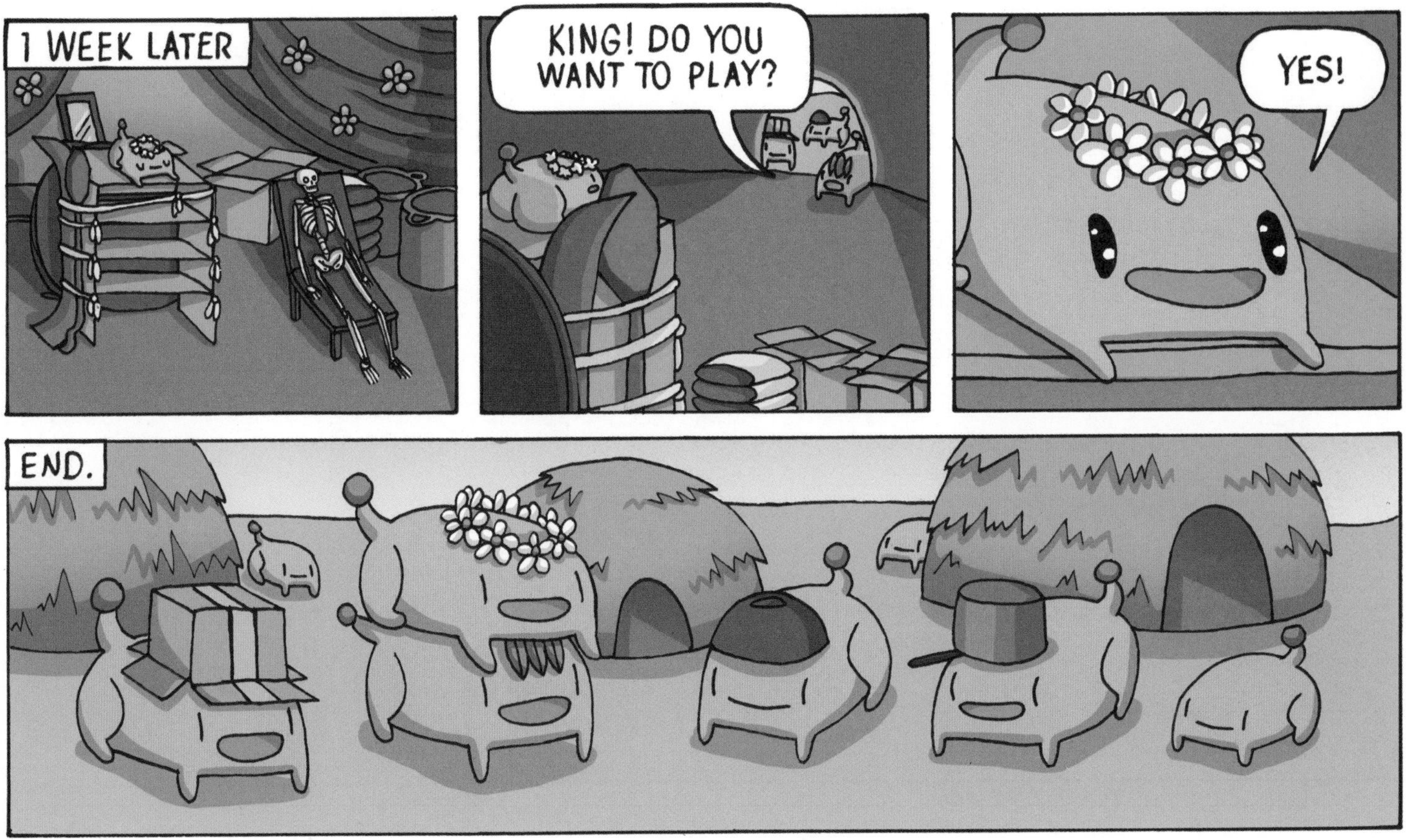
1 WEEK LATER
KING! DO YOU WANT TO PLAY?
YES!
END.

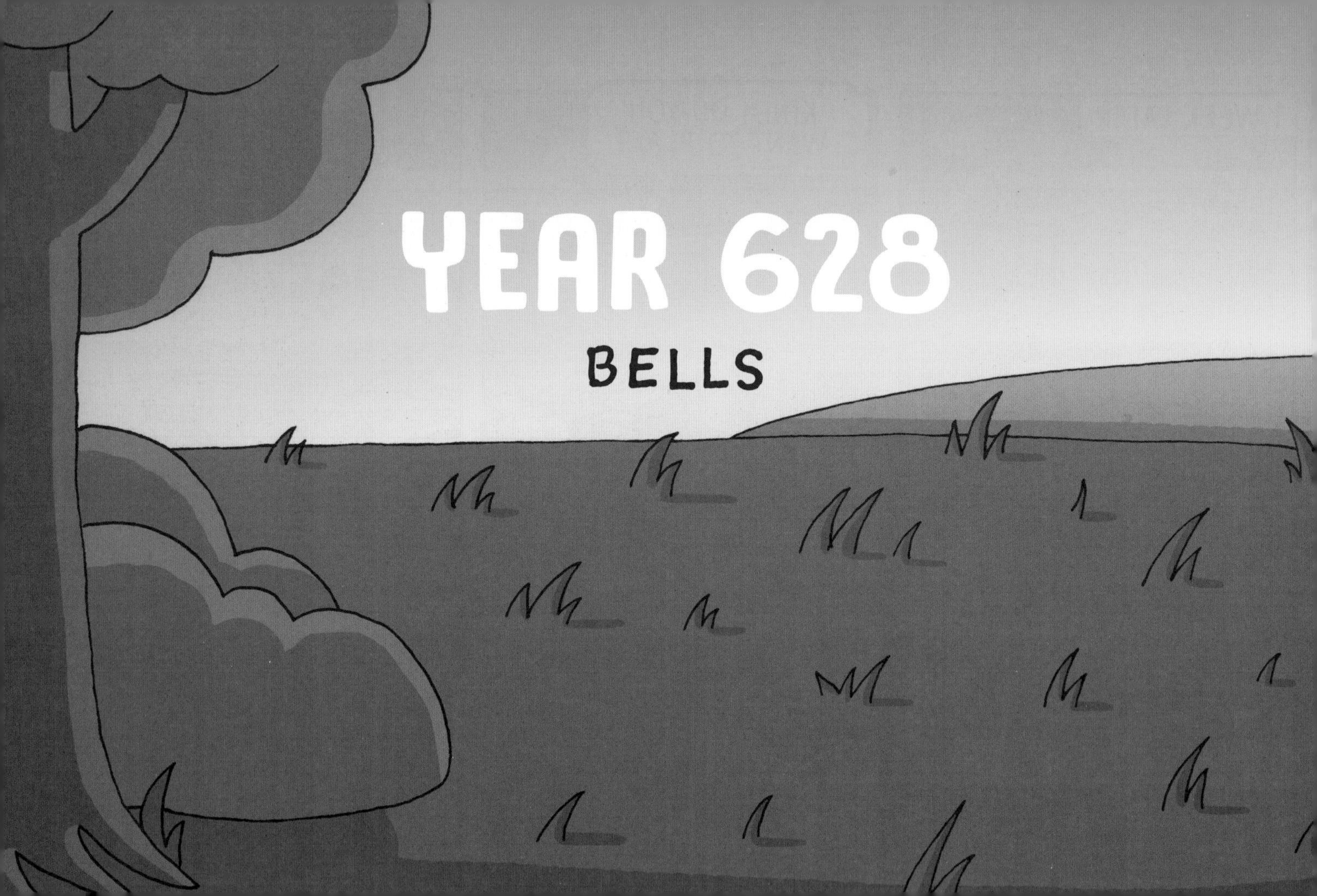
YEAR 628
BELLS

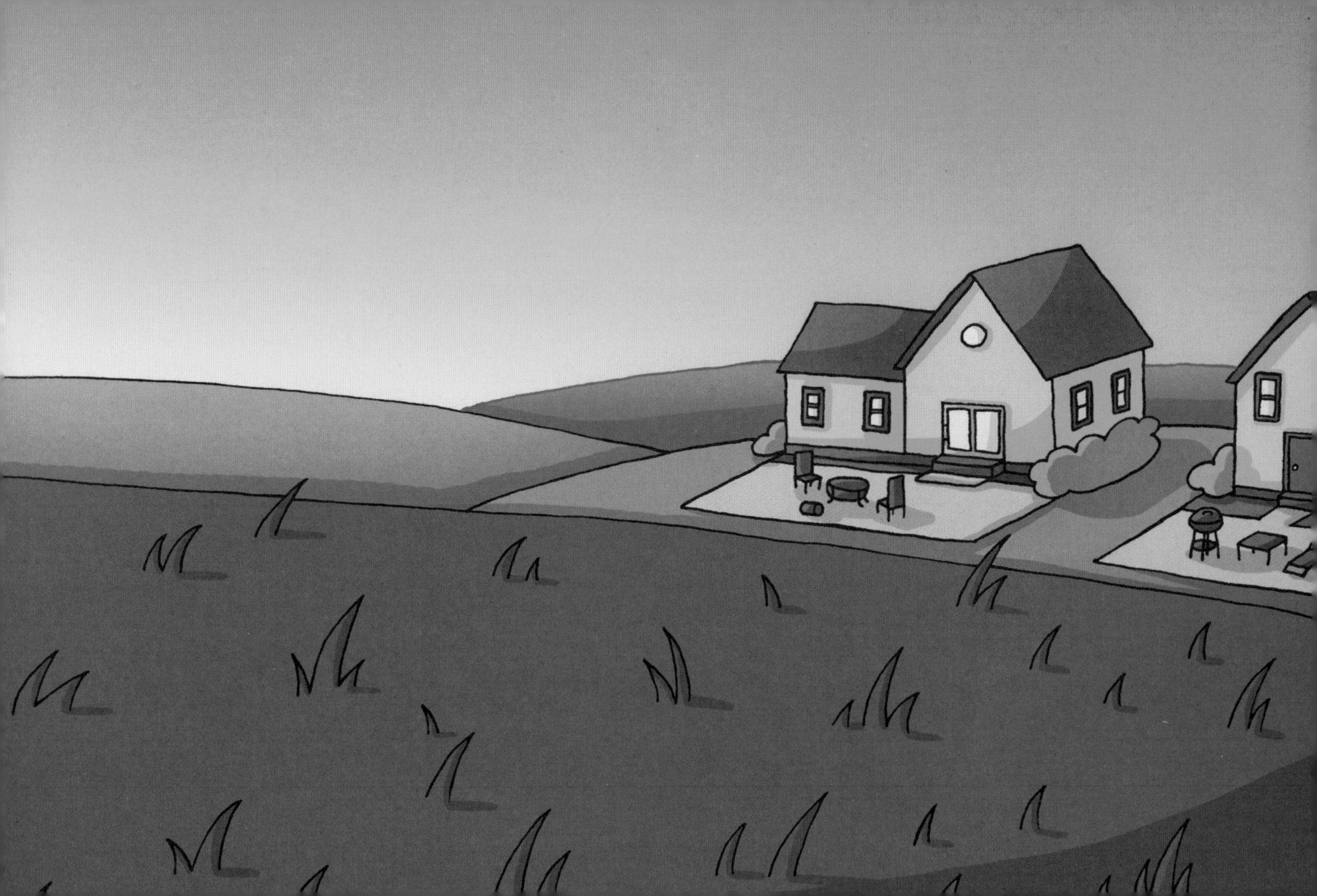

CHAPTER SEVEN

—

WHAT IS ART?

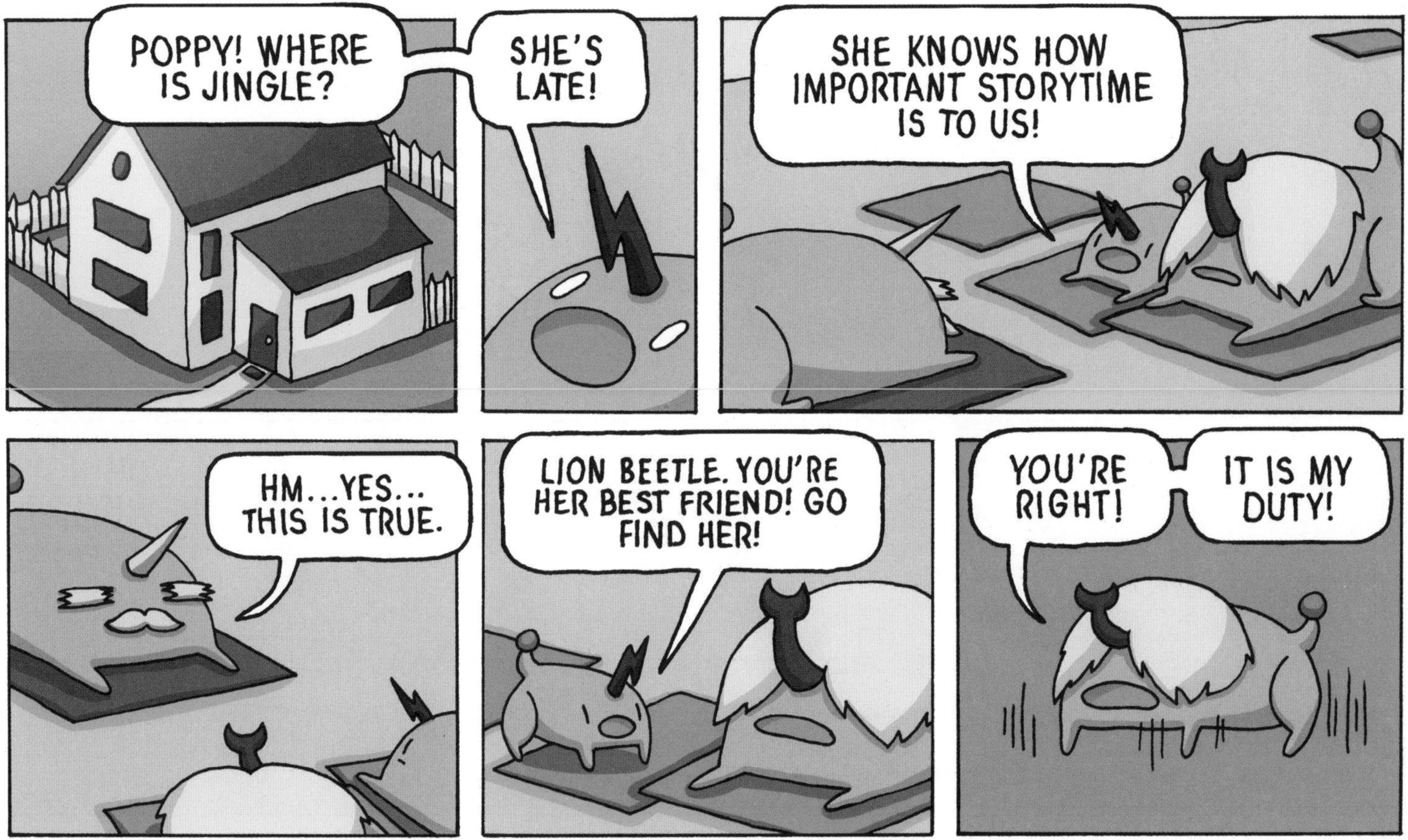
POPPY! WHERE IS JINGLE?
SHE'S LATE!
SHE KNOWS HOW IMPORTANT STORYTIME IS TO US!
HM...YES... THIS IS TRUE.
LION BEETLE. YOU'RE HER BEST FRIEND! GO FIND HER!
YOU'RE RIGHT!
IT IS MY DUTY!

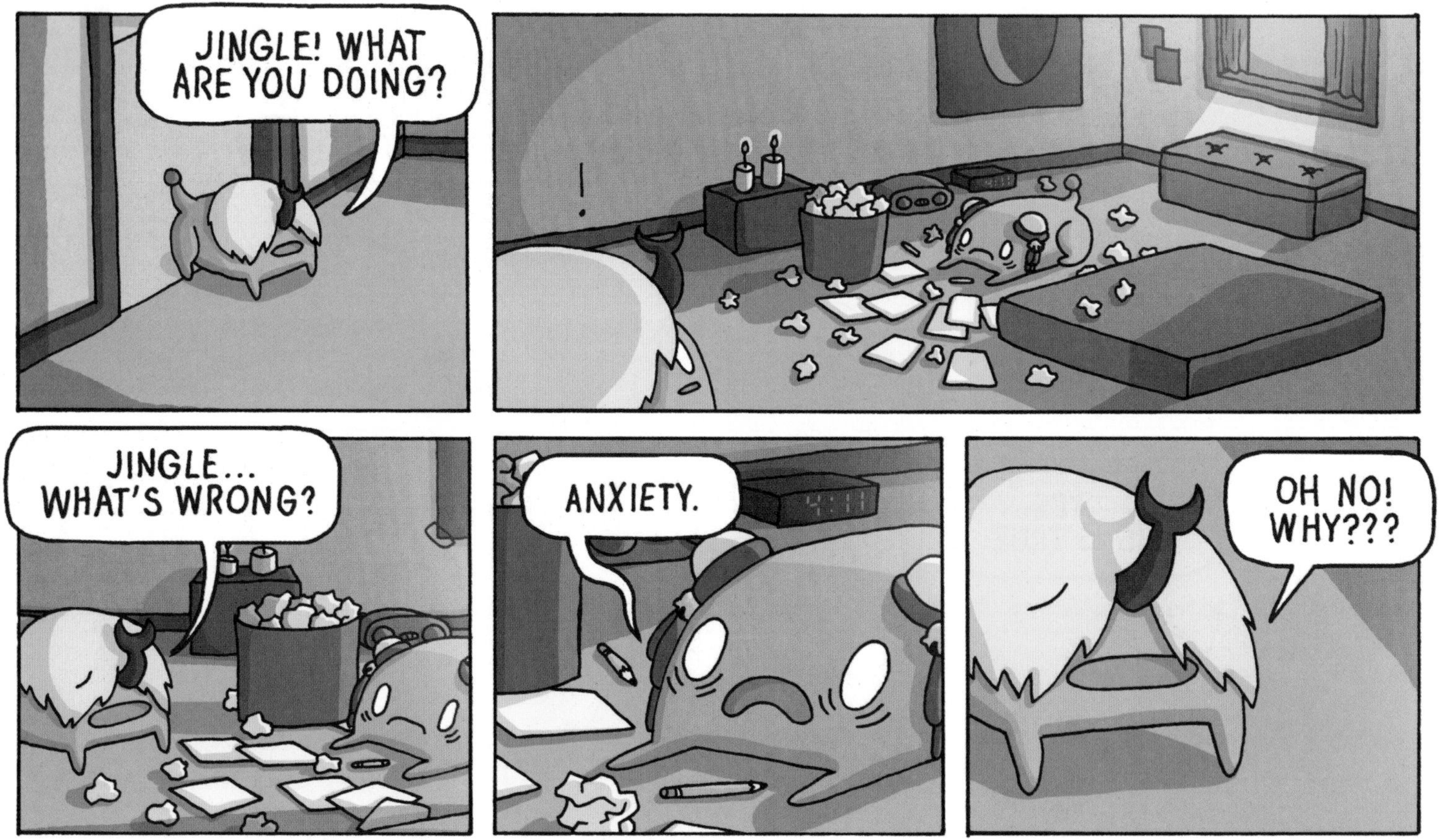
JINGLE! WHAT ARE YOU DOING?
!
JINGLE... WHAT'S WRONG?
ANXIETY.
OH NO! WHY???

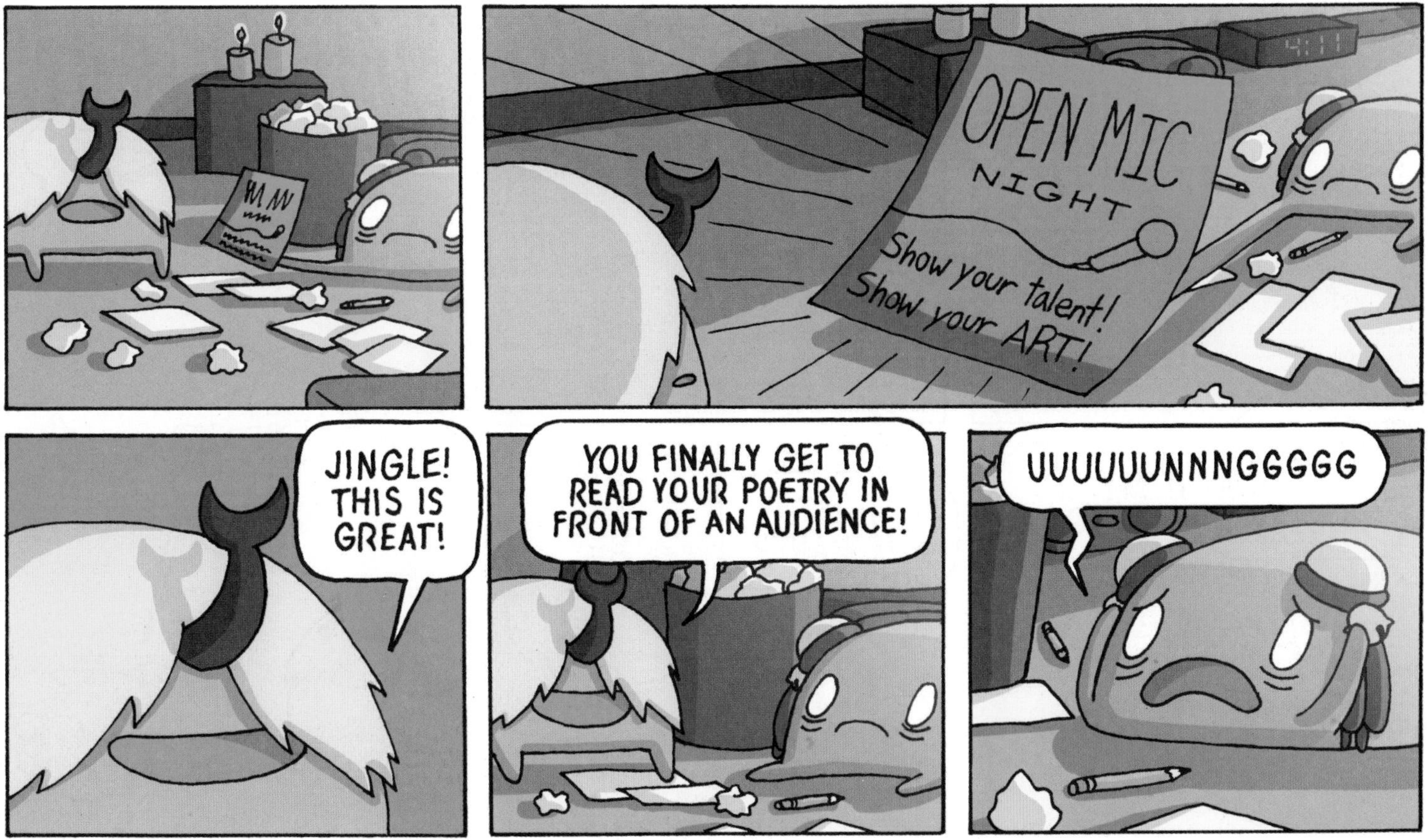
OPEN MIC NIGHT
Show your talent! Show your ART!
JINGLE! THIS IS GREAT!
YOU FINALLY GET TO READ YOUR POETRY IN FRONT OF AN AUDIENCE!
UUUUUUNNNGGGGG

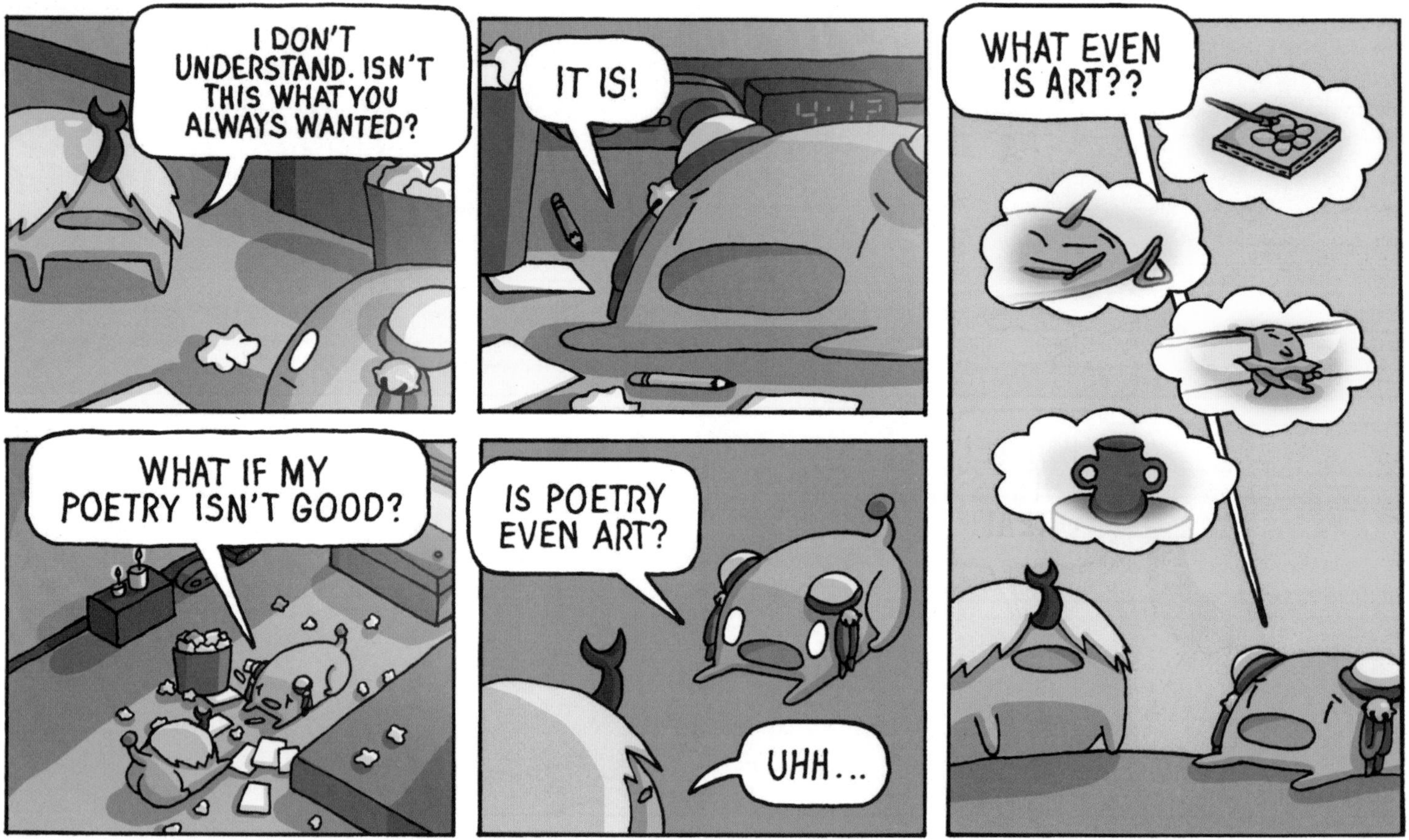
I DON'T UNDERSTAND. ISN'T THIS WHAT YOU ALWAYS WANTED?
IT IS!
WHAT EVEN IS ART??
WHAT IF MY POETRY ISN'T GOOD?
IS POETRY EVEN ART?
UHH...

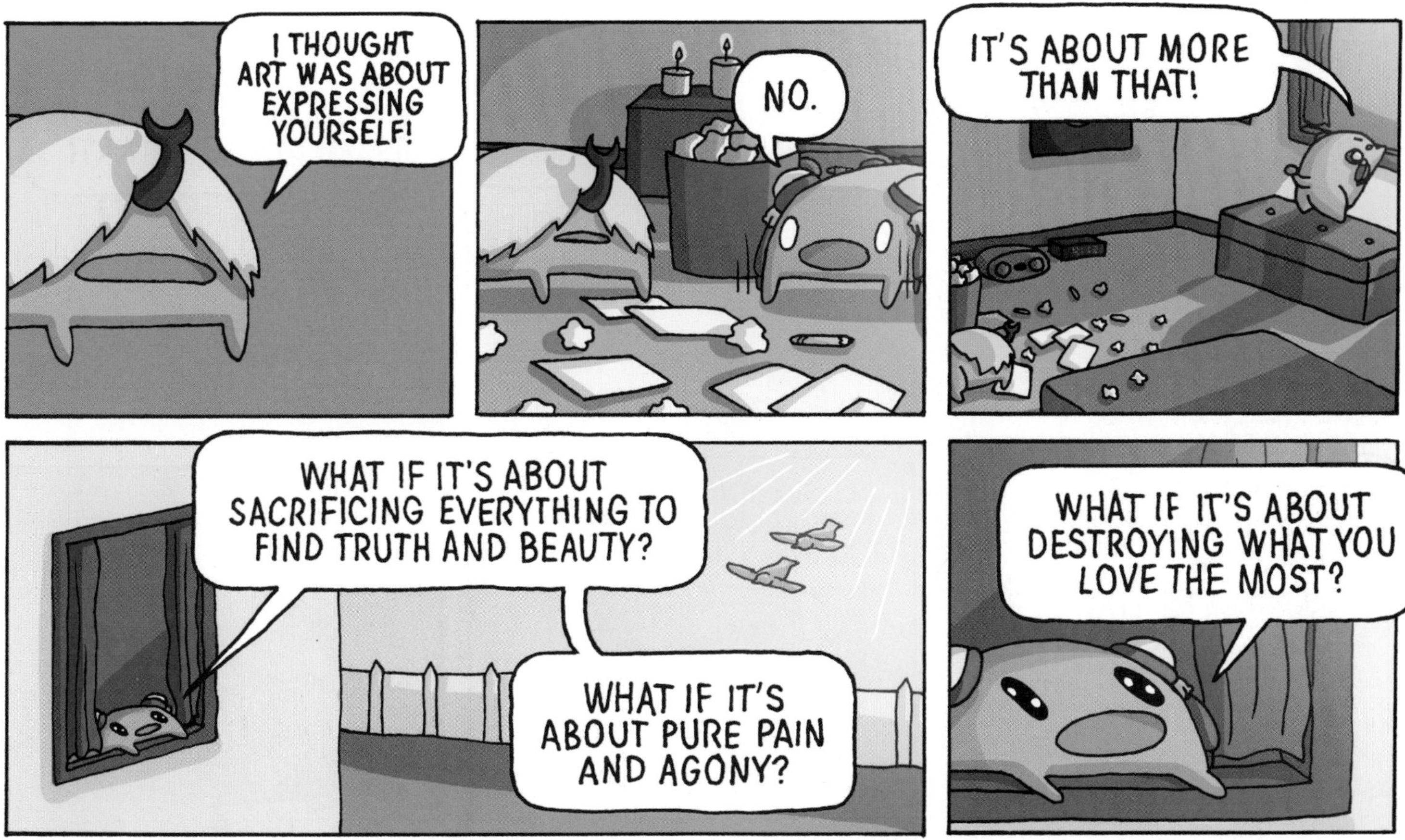
I THOUGHT ART WAS ABOUT EXPRESSING YOURSELF!
NO.
IT'S ABOUT MORE THAN THAT!
WHAT IF IT'S ABOUT SACRIFICING EVERYTHING TO FIND TRUTH AND BEAUTY?
WHAT IF IT'S ABOUT PURE PAIN AND AGONY?
WHAT IF IT'S ABOUT DESTROYING WHAT YOU LOVE THE MOST?

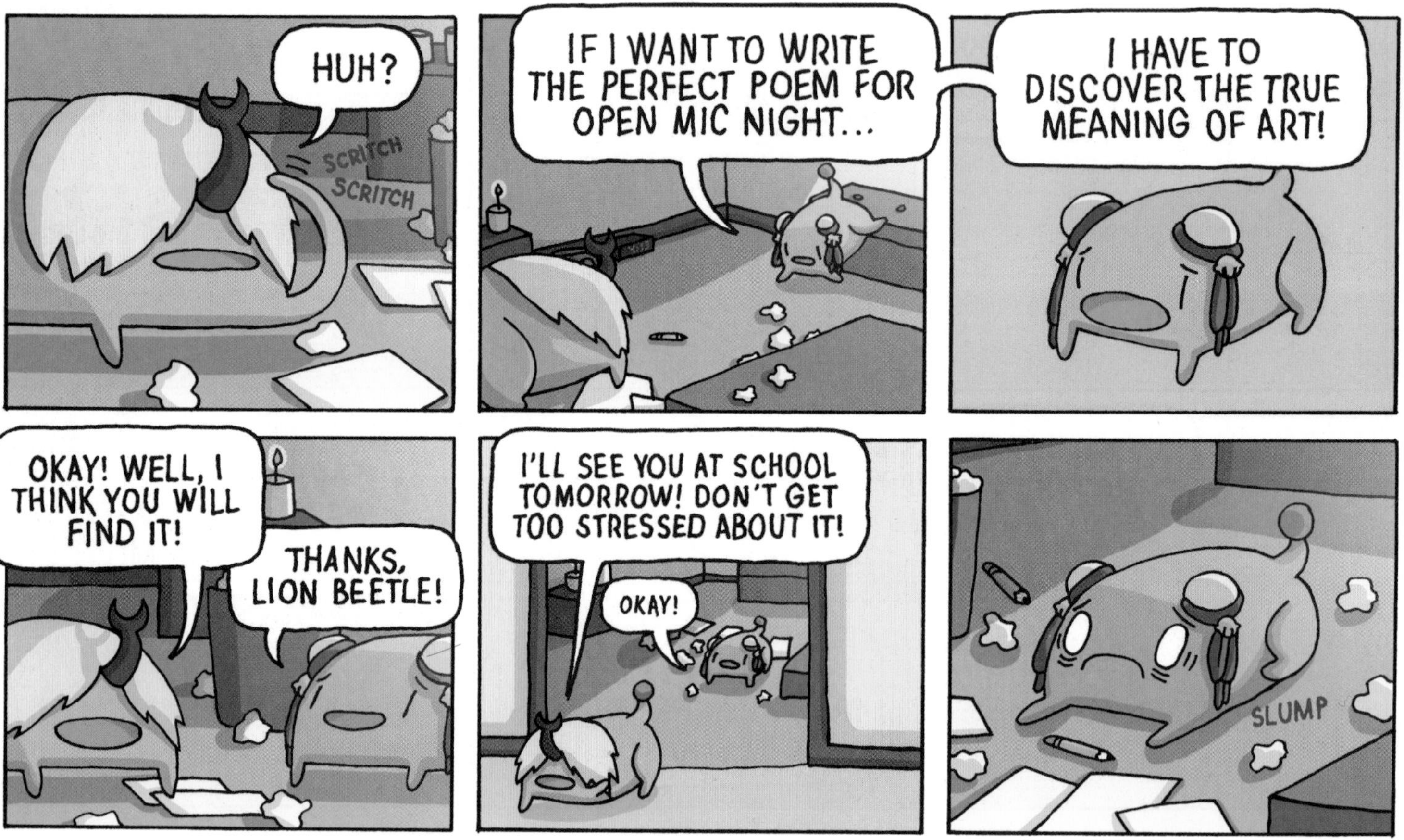
HUH?
SCRITCH
SCRITCH
IF I WANT TO WRITE THE PERFECT POEM FOR OPEN MIC NIGHT...
I HAVE TO DISCOVER THE TRUE MEANING OF ART!
OKAY! WELL, I THINK YOU WILL FIND IT!
THANKS, LION BEETLE!
I'LL SEE YOU AT SCHOOL TOMORROW! DON'T GET TOO STRESSED ABOUT IT!
OKAY!
SLUMP

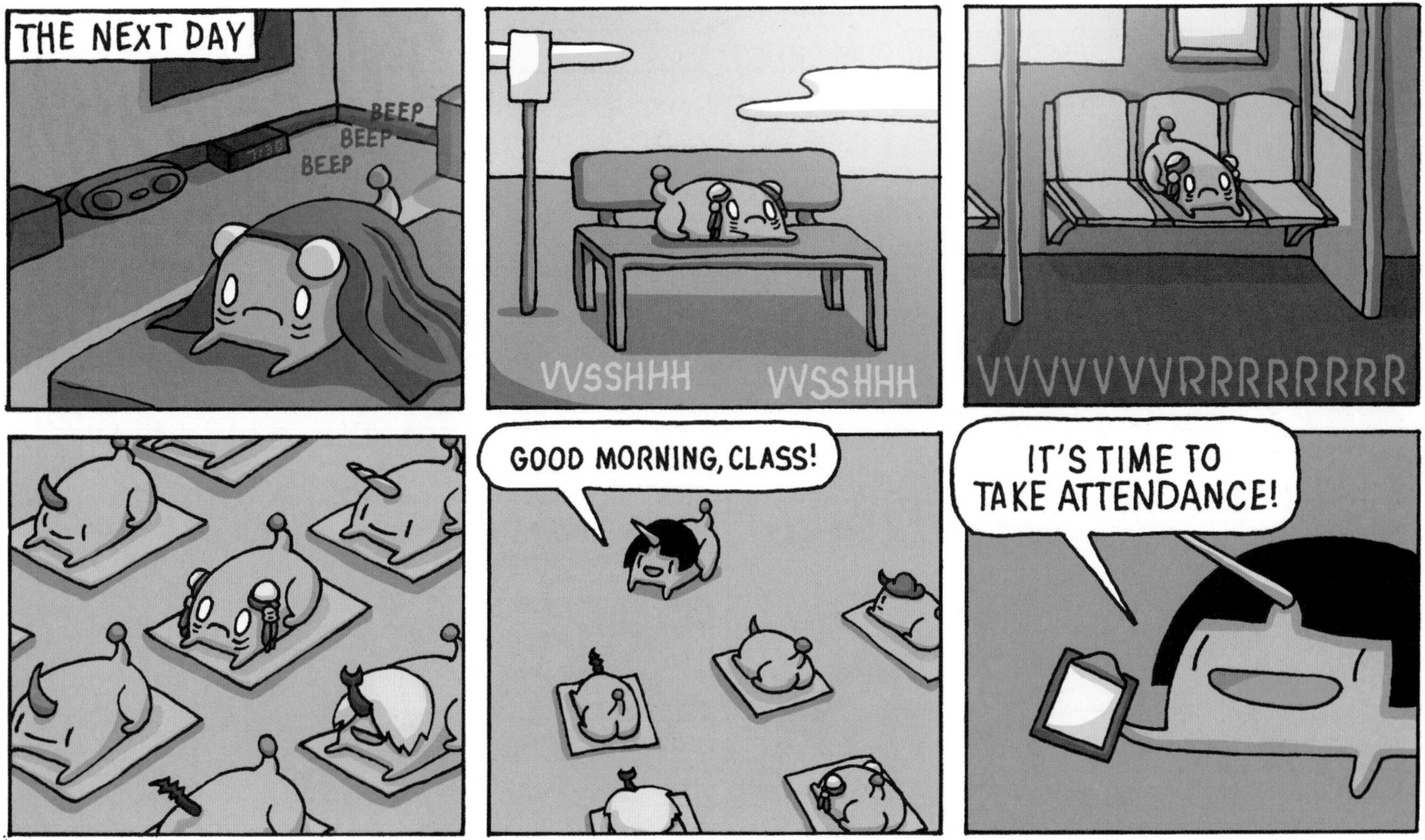
THE NEXT DAY
BEEP
BEEP
BEEP
VVSSHHH
VVSSHHH
VVVVVVVVRRRRRRRR
GOOD MORNING, CLASS!
IT'S TIME TO TAKE ATTENDANCE!

OKAY.

1. Sparkle
2. Journal
3. Knife
4. John
5. Telescope
6. Lion Beetle
7. Jingle
8. Stanley
9. Baby
10. Dingdong
11. Samurai
12. Kate
13. Chong
14. Bilbo
15. Tent
16. Charles

SPARKLE?

HERE!

JOURNAL?

HERE!

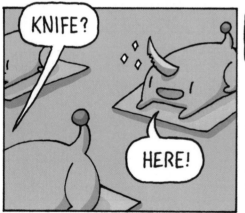

KNIFE?

HERE!

JOHN?
TELESCOPE?
LION BEETLE?

HERE!

HERE!

HERE!

JINGLE?

...

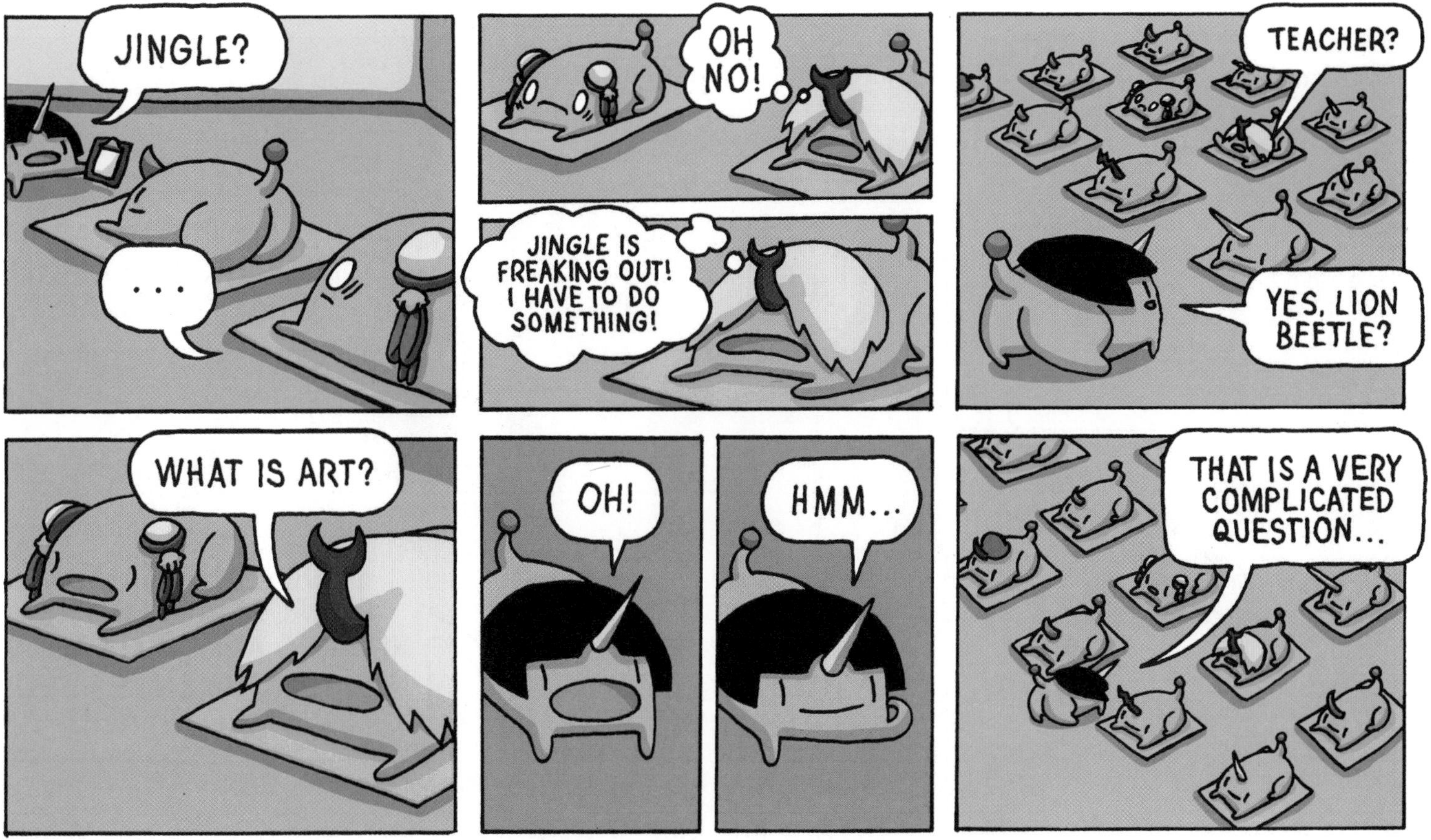
JINGLE?
...
OH NO!
TEACHER?
JINGLE IS FREAKING OUT! I HAVE TO DO SOMETHING!
YES, LION BEETLE?
WHAT IS ART?
OH!
HMM...
THAT IS A VERY COMPLICATED QUESTION...

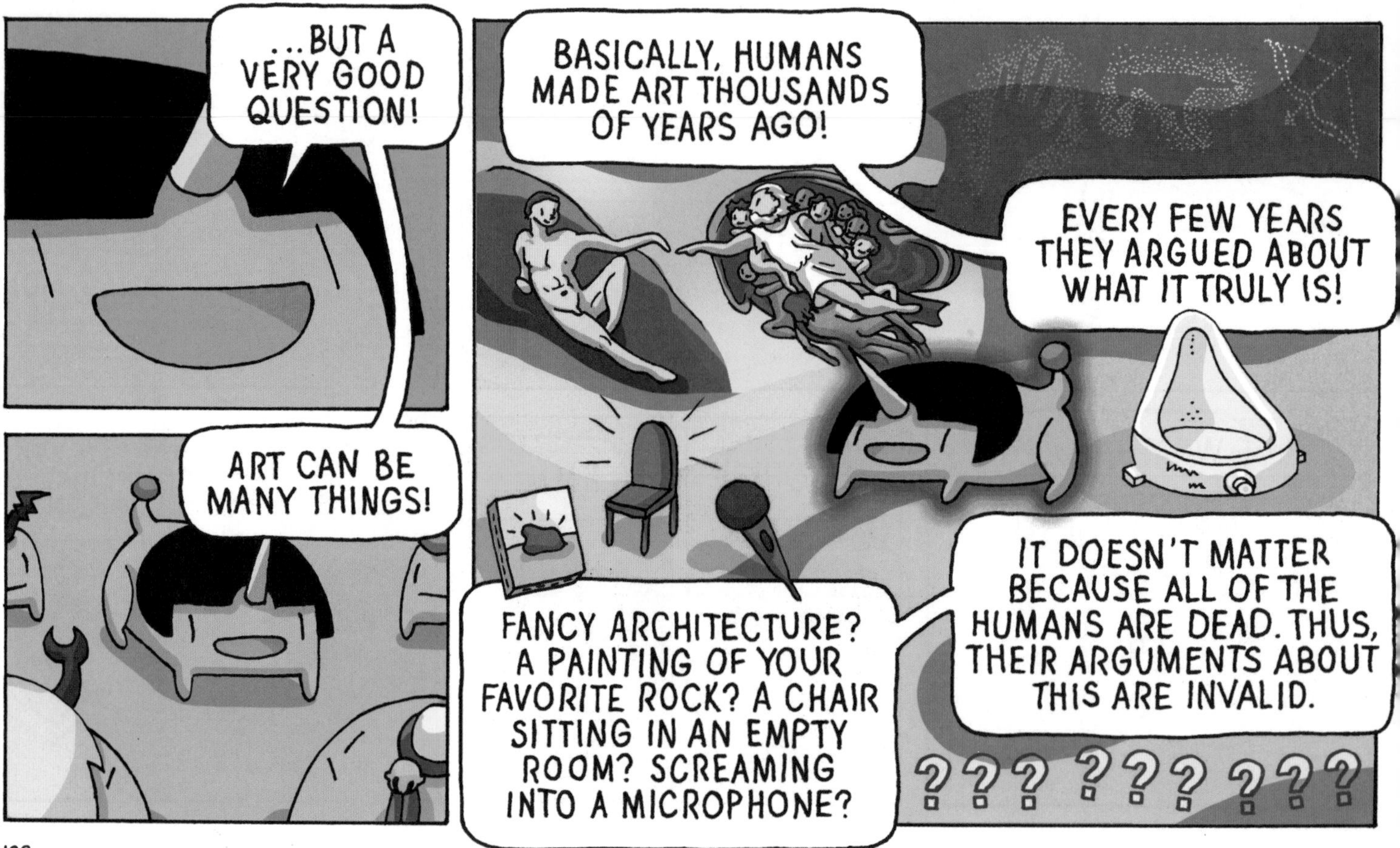
...BUT A VERY GOOD QUESTION!
ART CAN BE MANY THINGS!
BASICALLY, HUMANS MADE ART THOUSANDS OF YEARS AGO!
EVERY FEW YEARS THEY ARGUED ABOUT WHAT IT TRULY IS!
FANCY ARCHITECTURE? A PAINTING OF YOUR FAVORITE ROCK? A CHAIR SITTING IN AN EMPTY ROOM? SCREAMING INTO A MICROPHONE?
IT DOESN'T MATTER BECAUSE ALL OF THE HUMANS ARE DEAD. THUS, THEIR ARGUMENTS ABOUT THIS ARE INVALID.
?????????

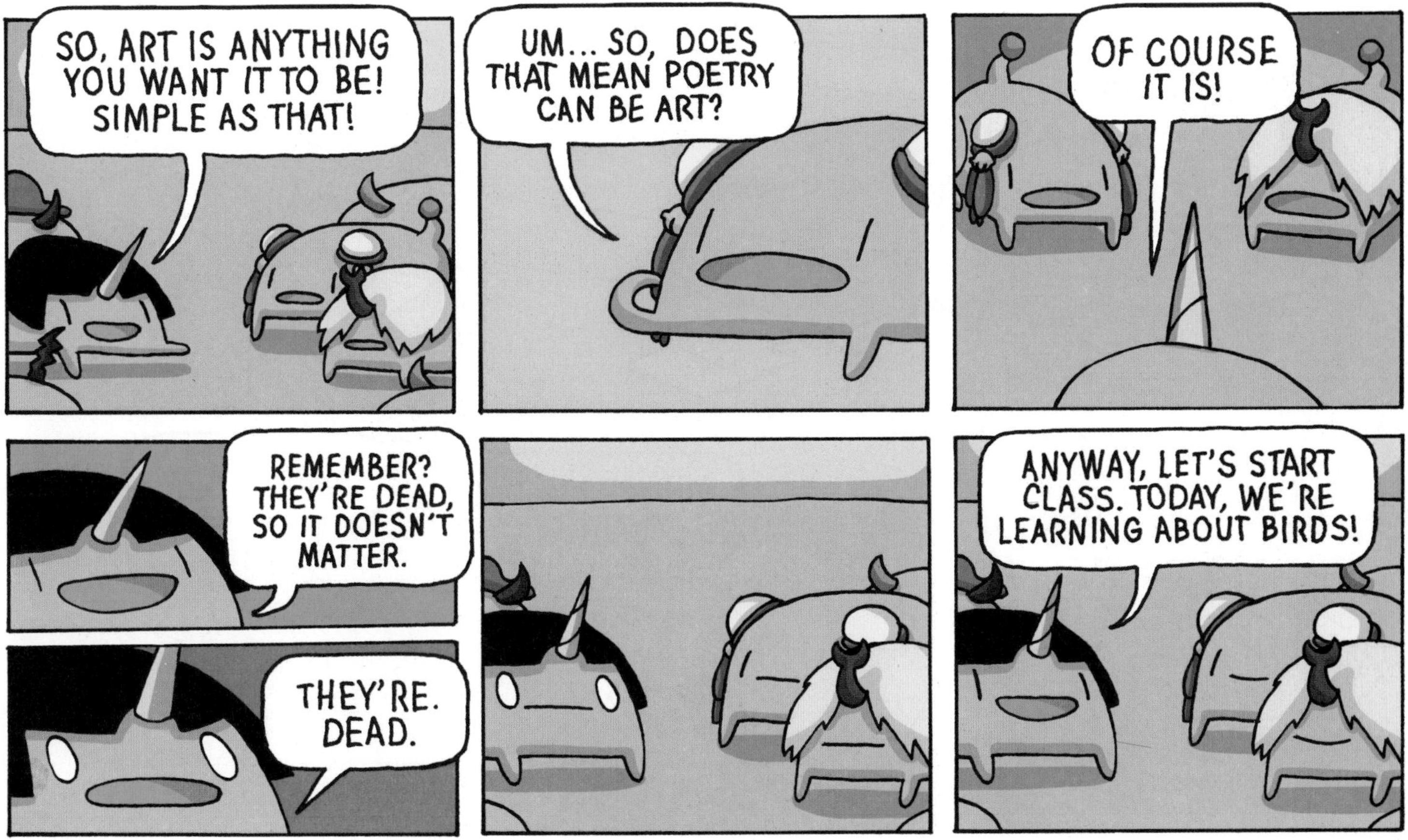
SO, ART IS ANYTHING YOU WANT IT TO BE! SIMPLE AS THAT!
UM... SO, DOES THAT MEAN POETRY CAN BE ART?
OF COURSE IT IS!
REMEMBER? THEY'RE DEAD, SO IT DOESN'T MATTER.
THEY'RE. DEAD.
ANYWAY, LET'S START CLASS. TODAY, WE'RE LEARNING ABOUT BIRDS!

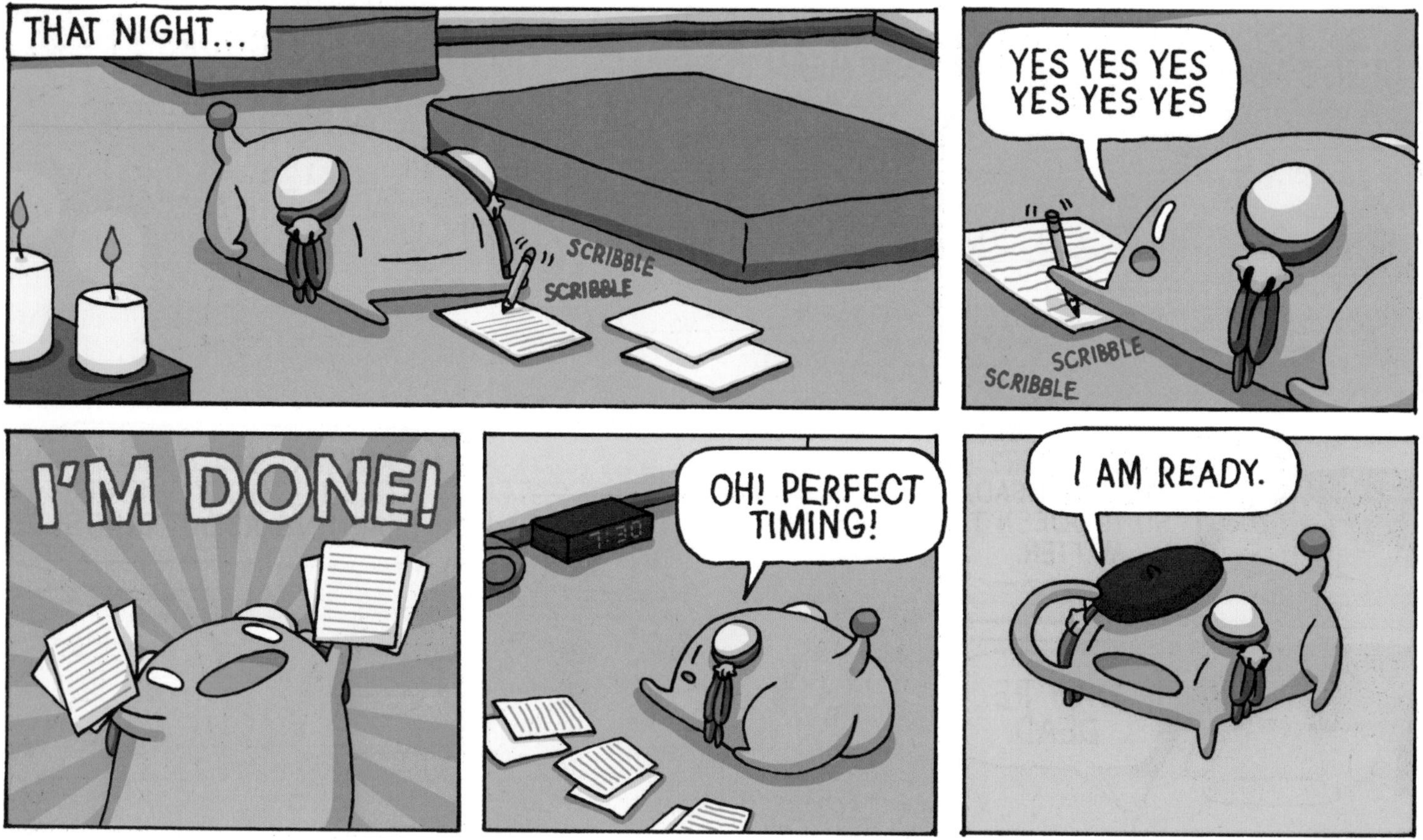
THAT NIGHT...
SCRIBBLE
SCRIBBLE
YES YES YES
YES YES YES
SCRIBBLE
SCRIBBLE
I'M DONE!
OH! PERFECT TIMING!
I AM READY.

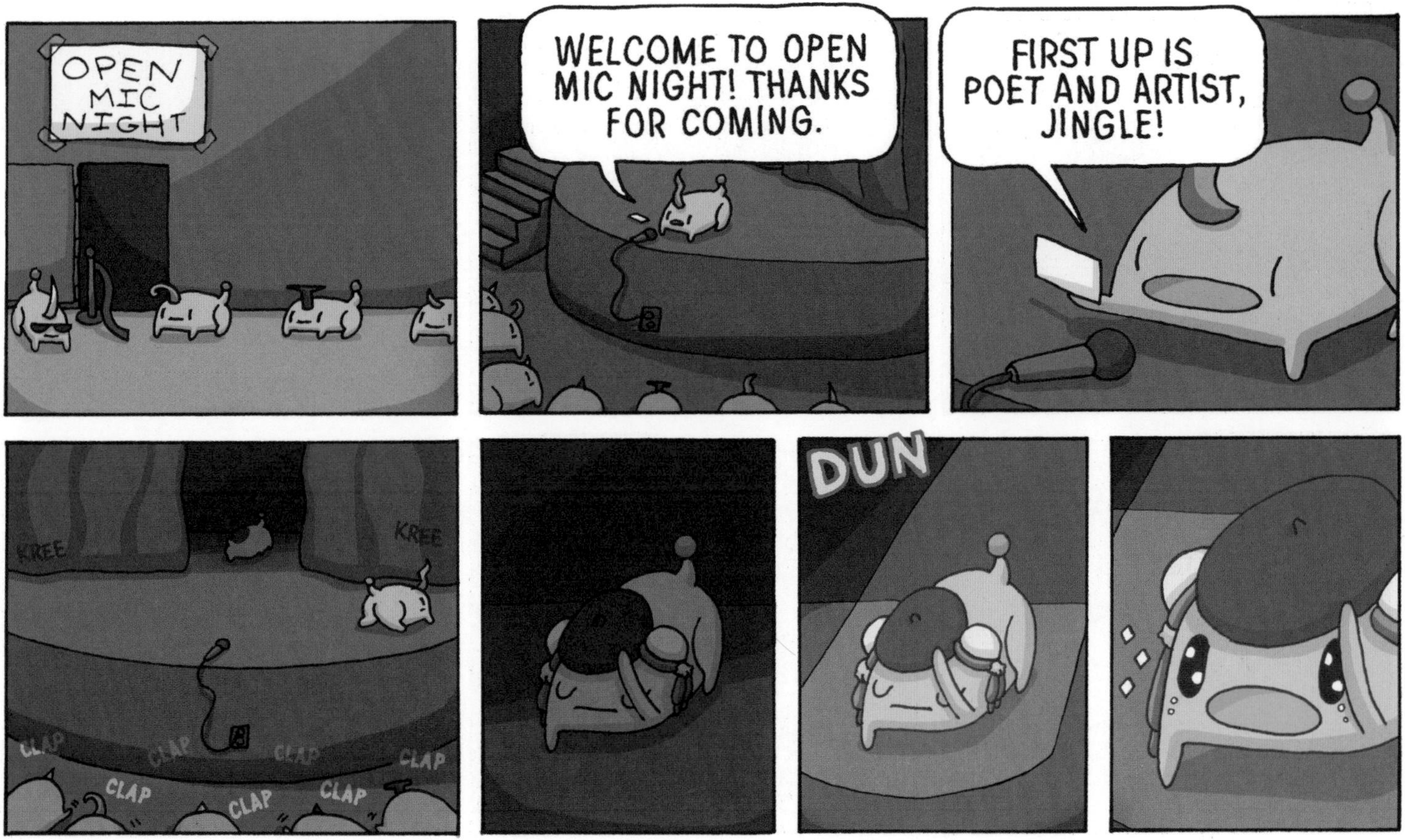
OPEN MIC NIGHT
WELCOME TO OPEN MIC NIGHT! THANKS FOR COMING.
FIRST UP IS POET AND ARTIST, JINGLE!
KREE
KREE
CLAP
CLAP
CLAP
CLAP
CLAP
CLAP
CLAP
DUN

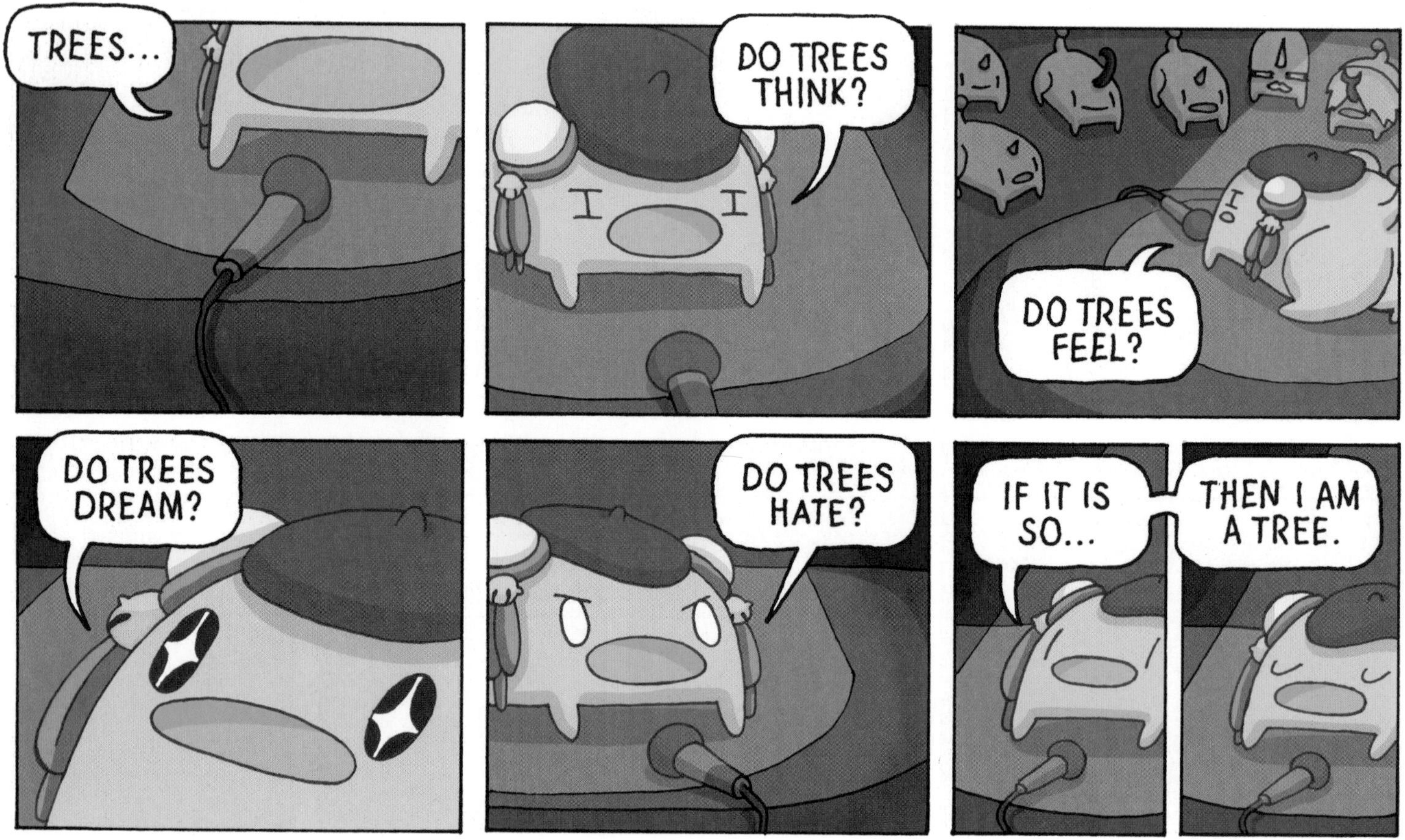
TREES...
DO TREES THINK?
DO TREES FEEL?
DO TREES DREAM?
DO TREES HATE?
IF IT IS SO...
THEN I AM A TREE.

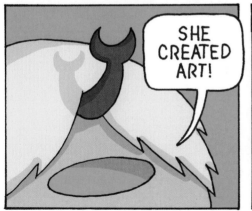

CHAPTER EIGHT

—

WHERE DO YOU LIVE?

HA HA

HA HA

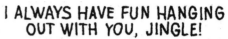
I ALWAYS HAVE FUN HANGING OUT WITH YOU, JINGLE!

I'M HAVING FUN, TOO!

YAY!

PLUS, I LOVE THIS HOUSE!

EVERYTHING HERE IS VERY SOFT AND GOOD!

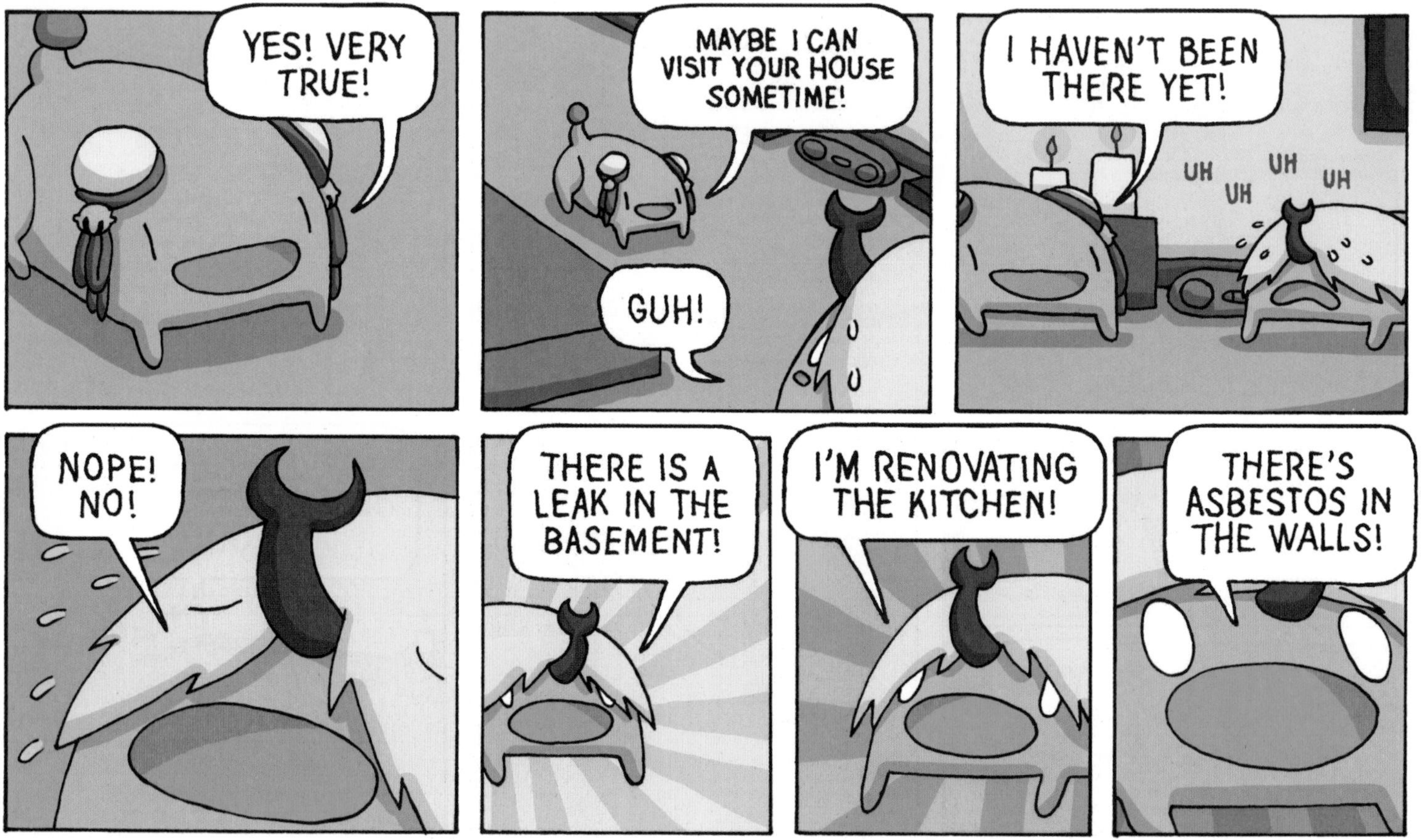
YES! VERY TRUE!
MAYBE I CAN VISIT YOUR HOUSE SOMETIME!
GUH!
I HAVEN'T BEEN THERE YET!
UH
UH
UH
UH
NOPE! NO!
THERE IS A LEAK IN THE BASEMENT!
I'M RENOVATING THE KITCHEN!
THERE'S ASBESTOS IN THE WALLS!

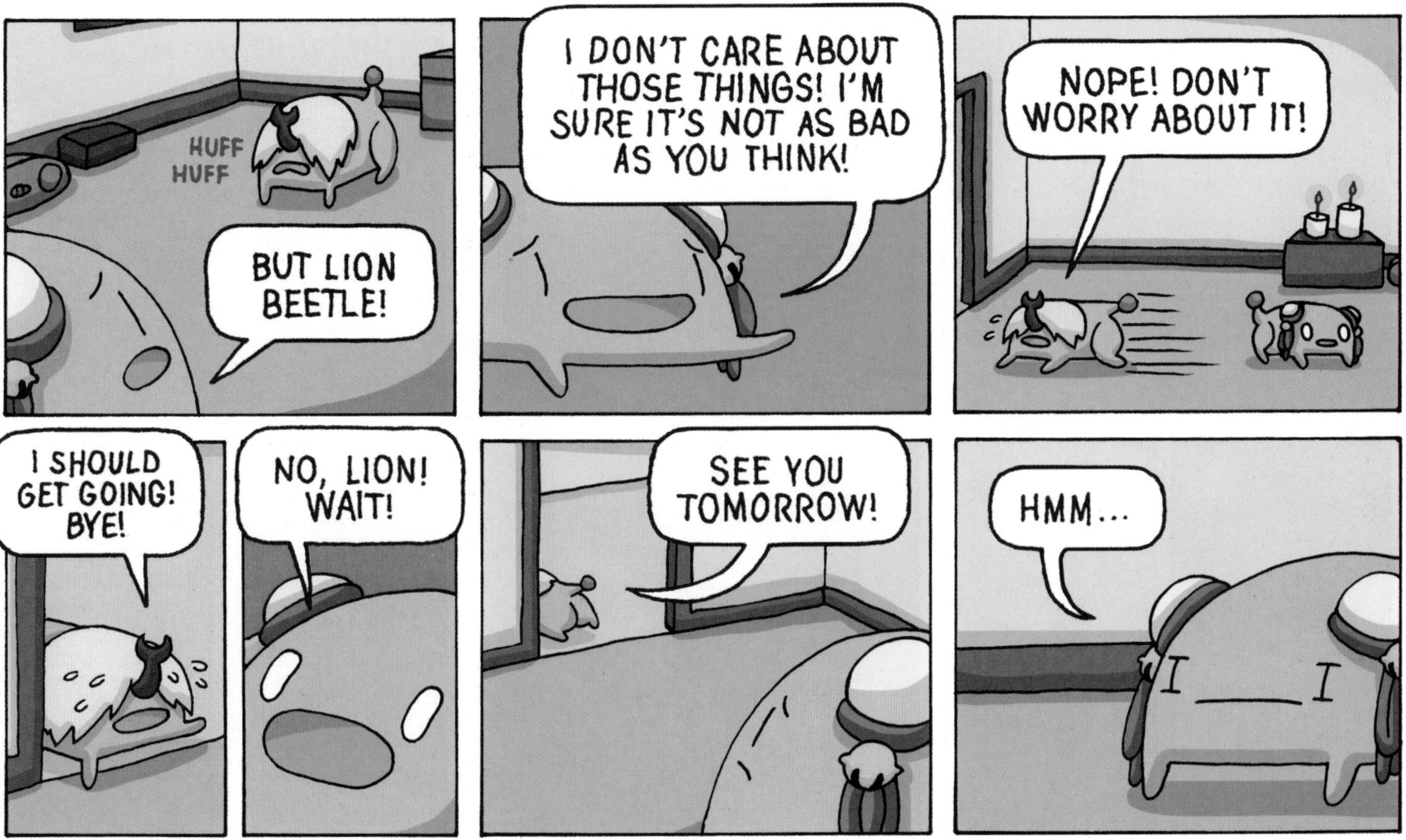
HUFF
HUFF
BUT LION BEETLE!
I DON'T CARE ABOUT THOSE THINGS! I'M SURE IT'S NOT AS BAD AS YOU THINK!
NOPE! DON'T WORRY ABOUT IT!
I SHOULD GET GOING! BYE!
NO, LION! WAIT!
SEE YOU TOMORROW!
HMM...

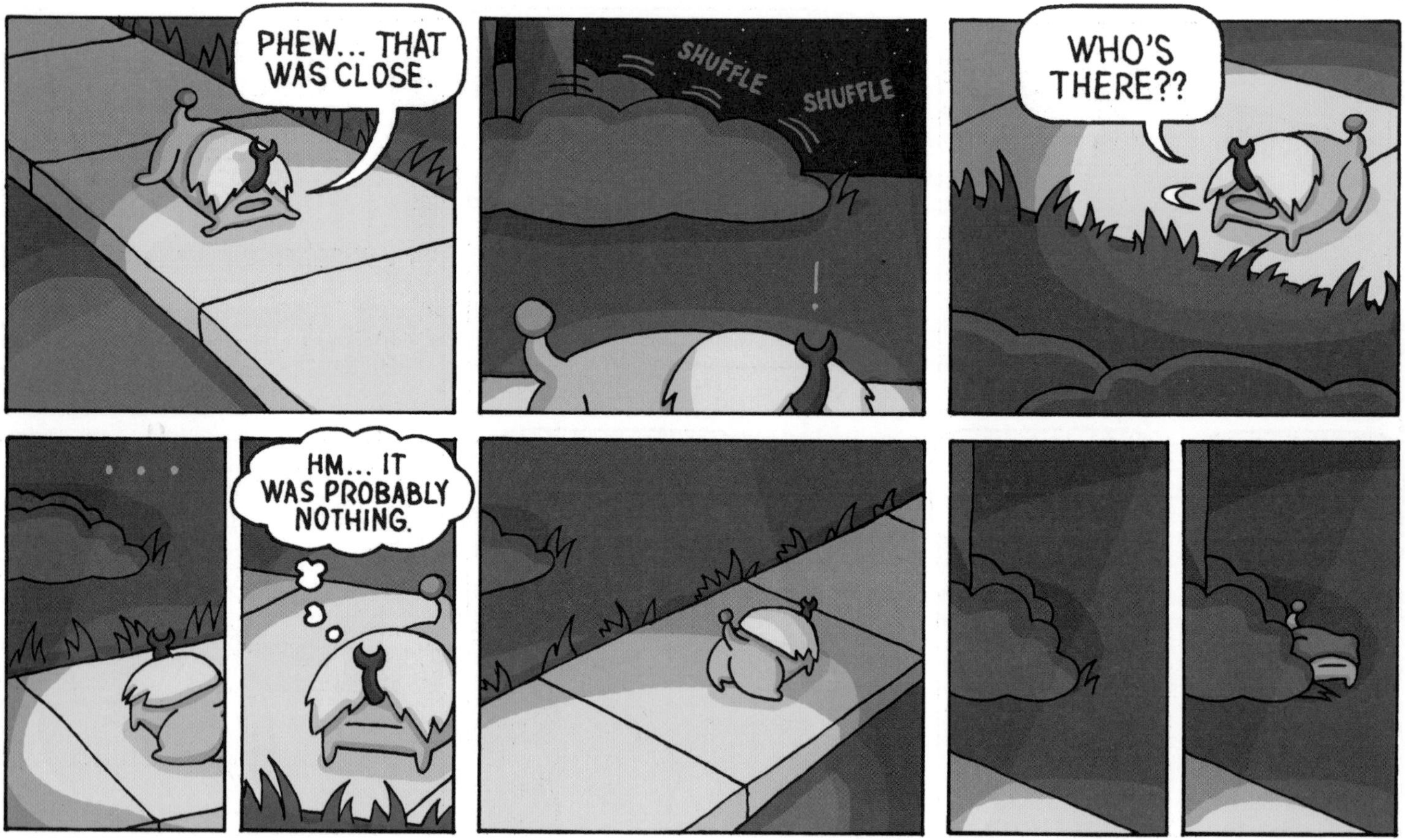
PHEW... THAT WAS CLOSE.
SHUFFLE
SHUFFLE
!
WHO'S THERE??
• • •
HM... IT WAS PROBABLY NOTHING.

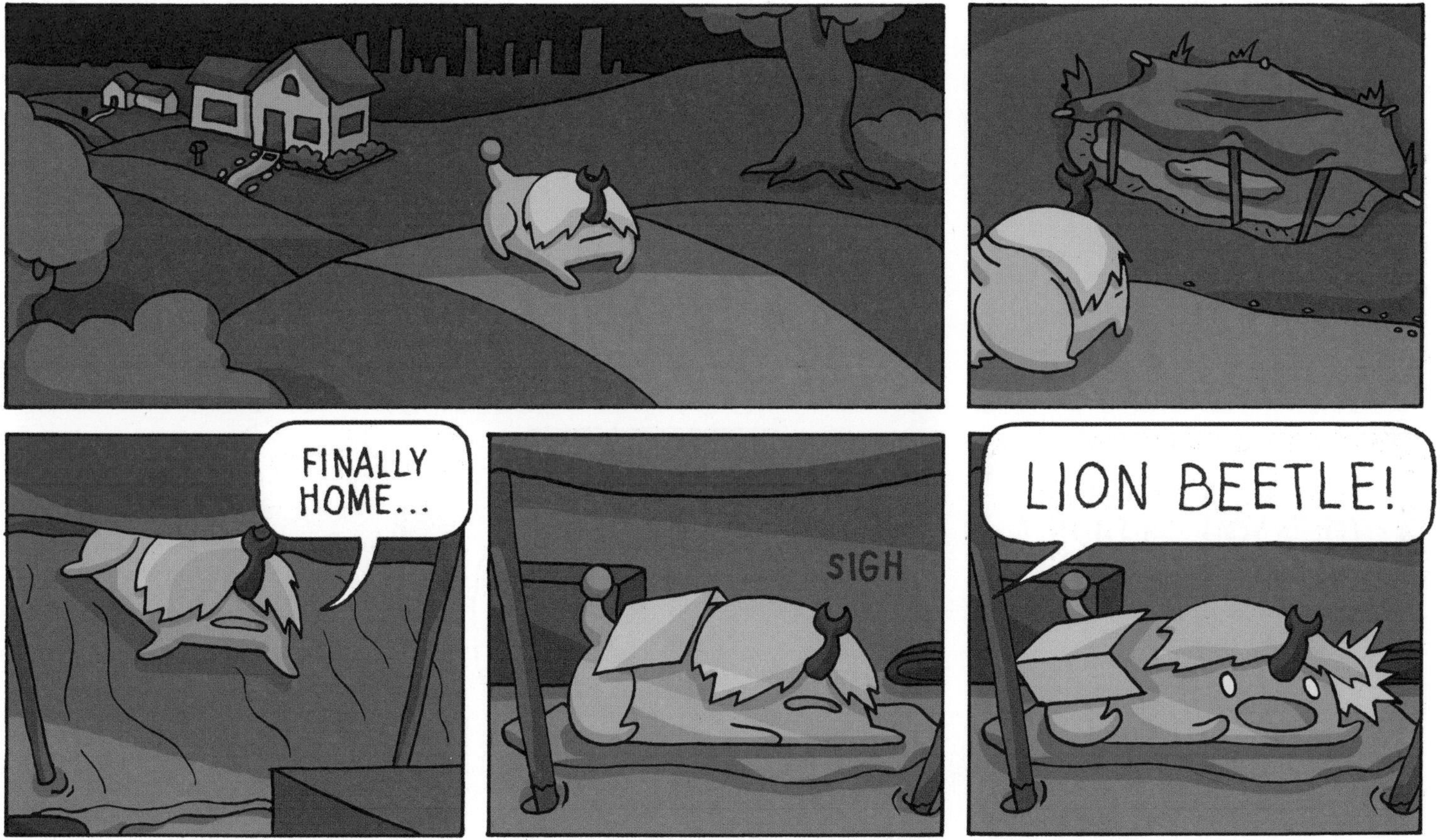
FINALLY HOME...
SIGH
LION BEETLE!

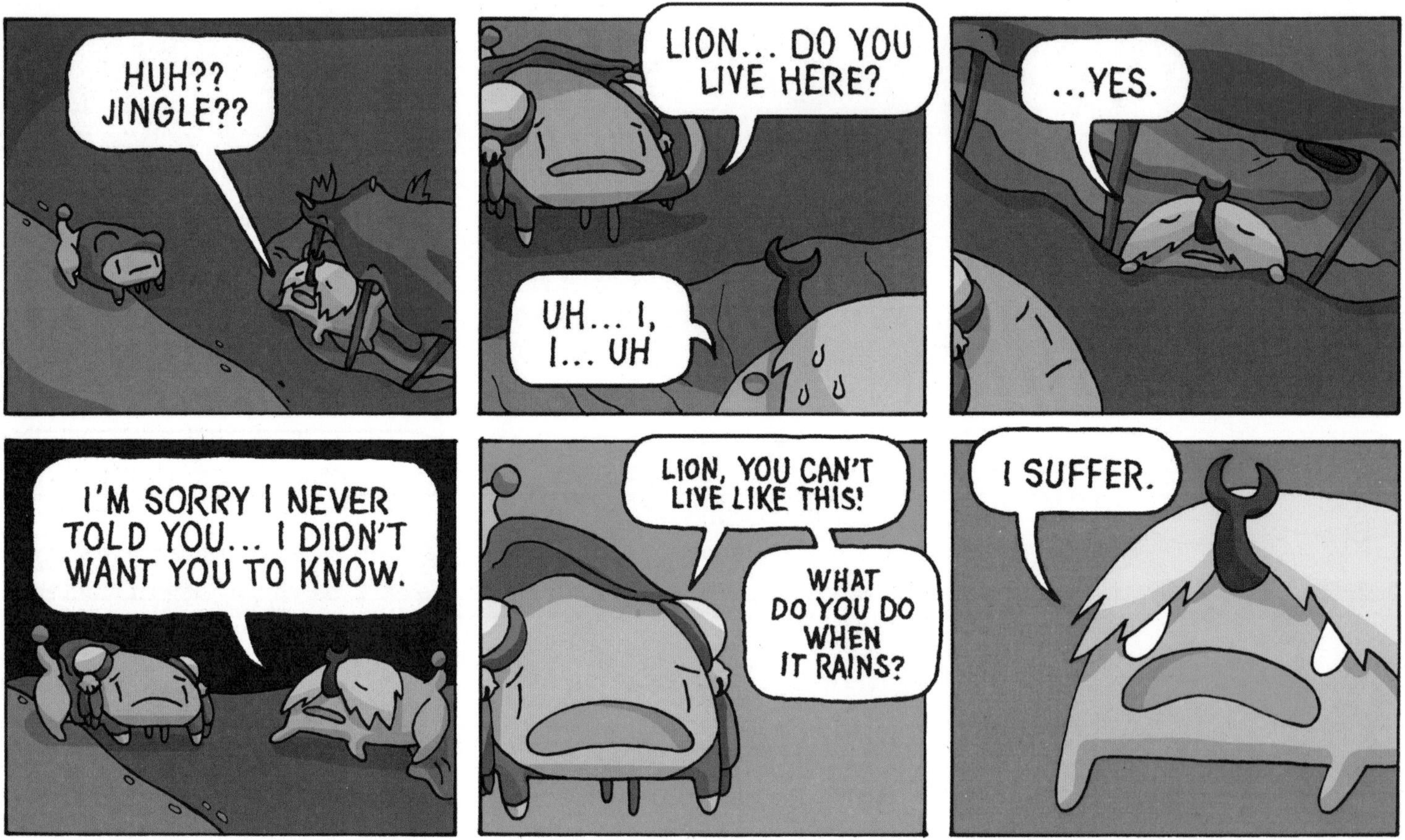
HUH?? JINGLE??
LION... DO YOU LIVE HERE?
UH... I, I... UH
...YES.
I'M SORRY I NEVER TOLD YOU... I DIDN'T WANT YOU TO KNOW.
LION, YOU CAN'T LIVE LIKE THIS!
WHAT DO YOU DO WHEN IT RAINS?
I SUFFER.

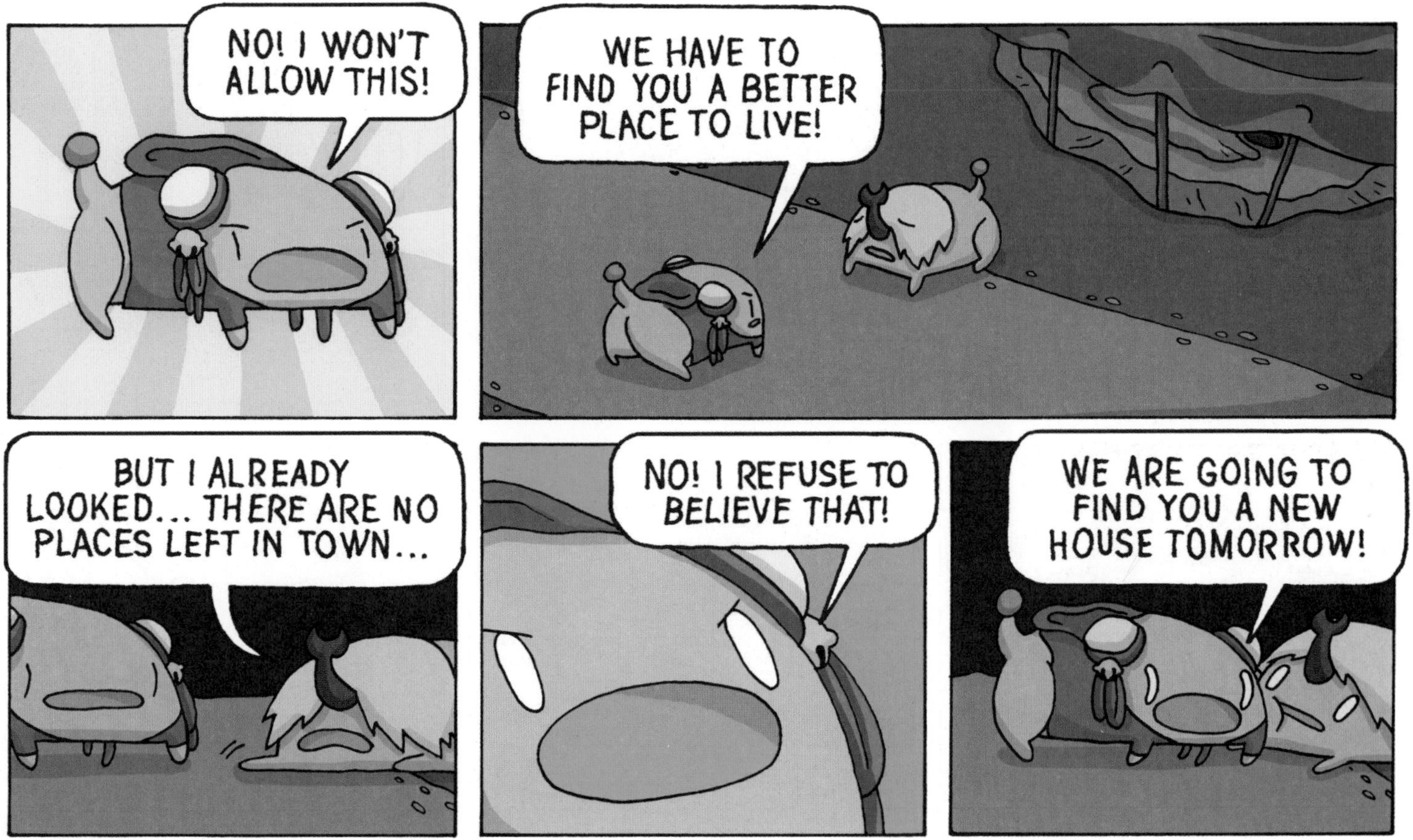
NO! I WON'T ALLOW THIS!
WE HAVE TO FIND YOU A BETTER PLACE TO LIVE!
BUT I ALREADY LOOKED... THERE ARE NO PLACES LEFT IN TOWN...
NO! I REFUSE TO BELIEVE THAT!
WE ARE GOING TO FIND YOU A NEW HOUSE TOMORROW!

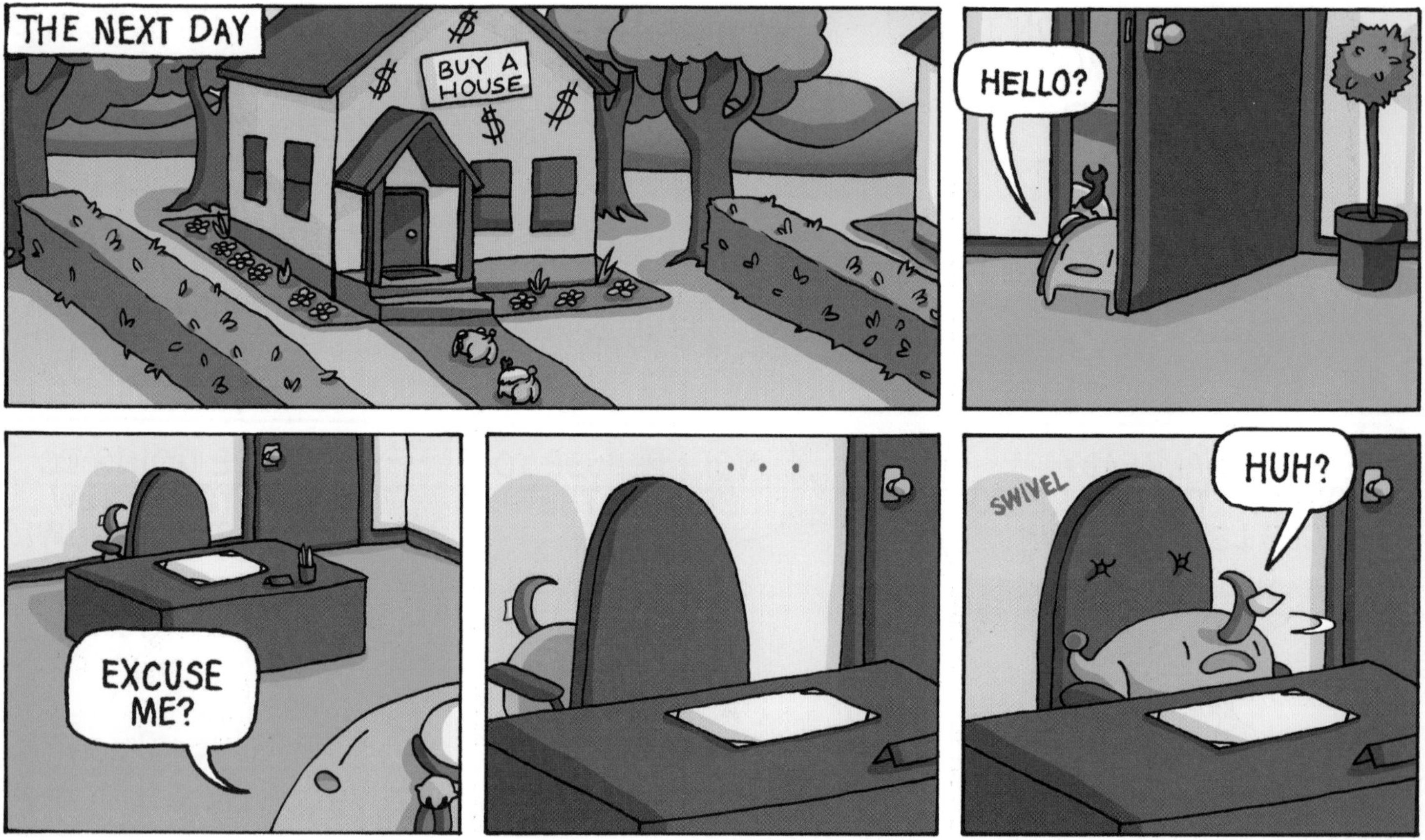
THE NEXT DAY
BUY A HOUSE
HELLO?
EXCUSE ME?
...
SWIVEL
HUH?

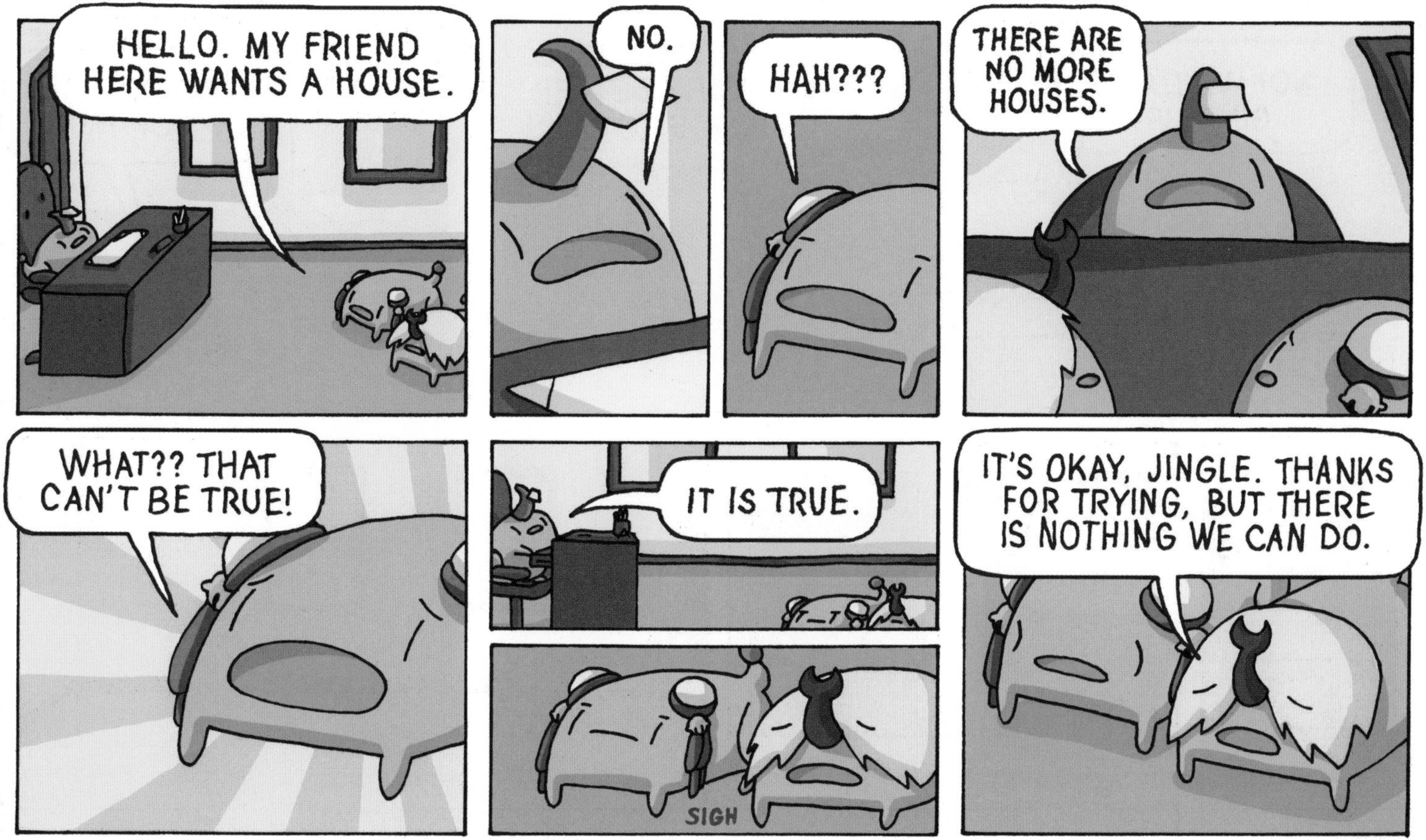
HELLO. MY FRIEND HERE WANTS A HOUSE.
NO.
HAH???
THERE ARE NO MORE HOUSES.
WHAT?? THAT CAN'T BE TRUE!
IT IS TRUE.
SIGH
IT'S OKAY, JINGLE. THANKS FOR TRYING, BUT THERE IS NOTHING WE CAN DO.

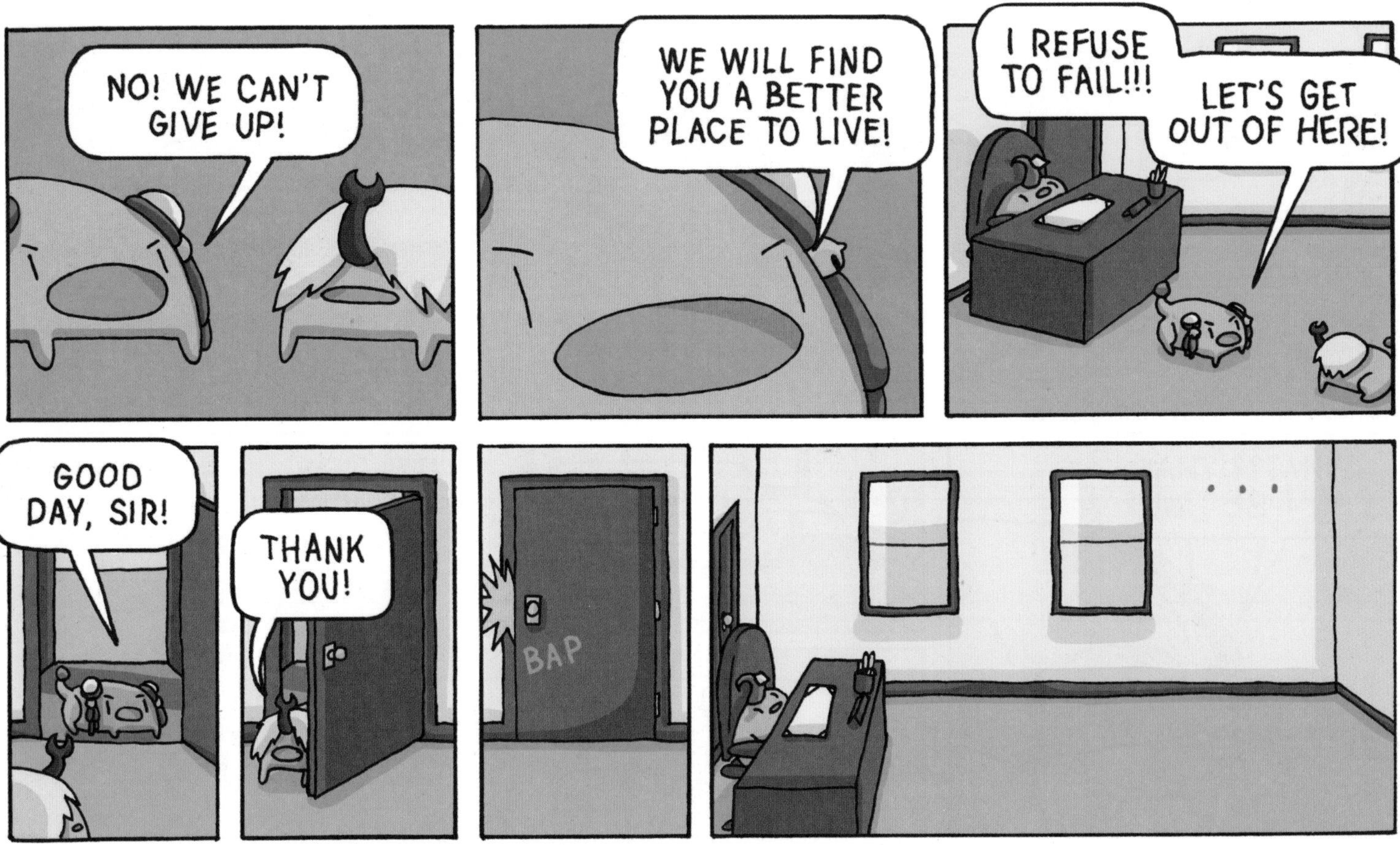
NO! WE CAN'T GIVE UP!
WE WILL FIND YOU A BETTER PLACE TO LIVE!
I REFUSE TO FAIL!!!
LET'S GET OUT OF HERE!
GOOD DAY, SIR!
THANK YOU!
BAP
...

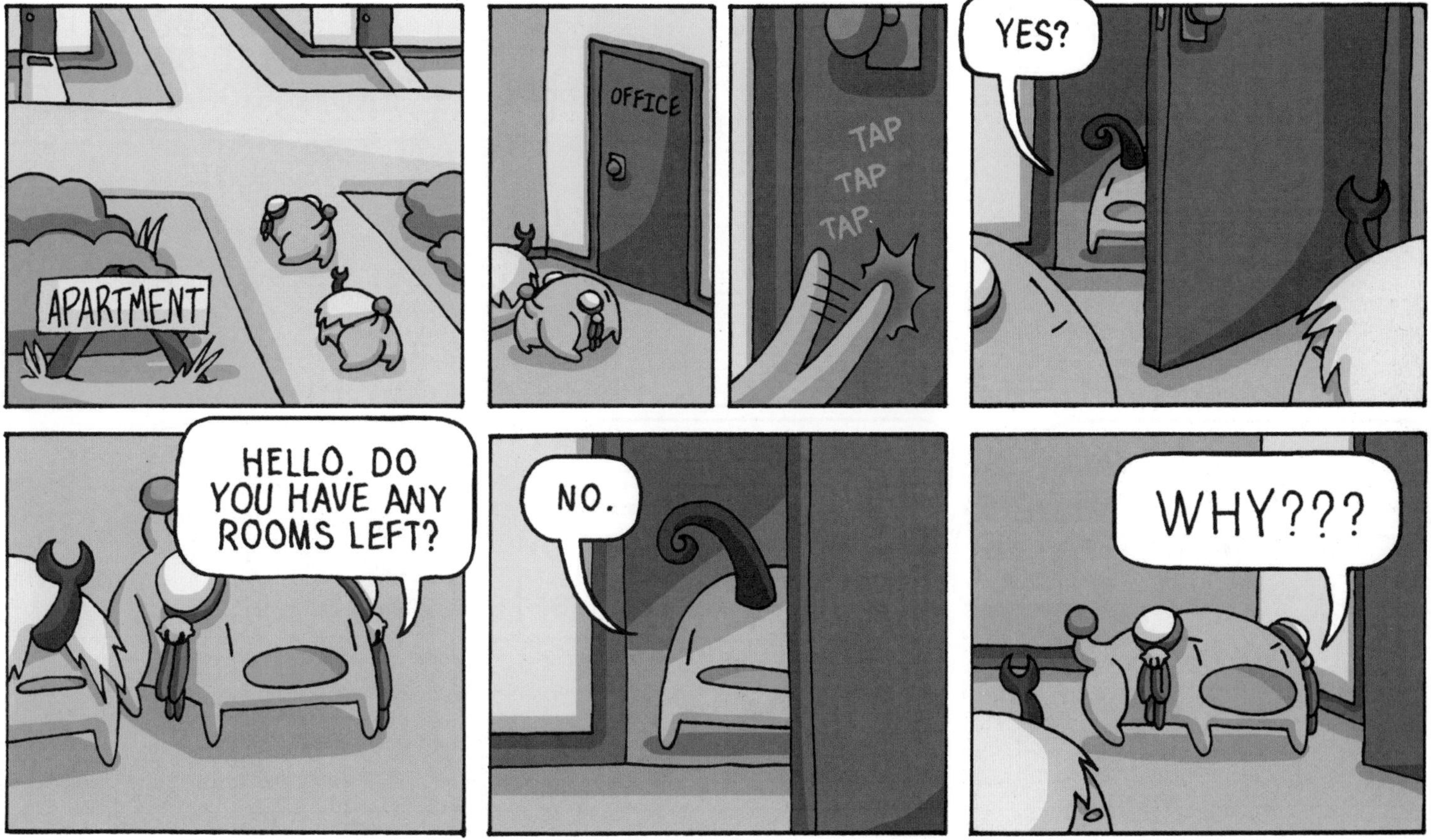
APARTMENT
OFFICE
TAP
TAP
TAP
YES?
HELLO. DO YOU HAVE ANY ROOMS LEFT?
NO.
WHY???

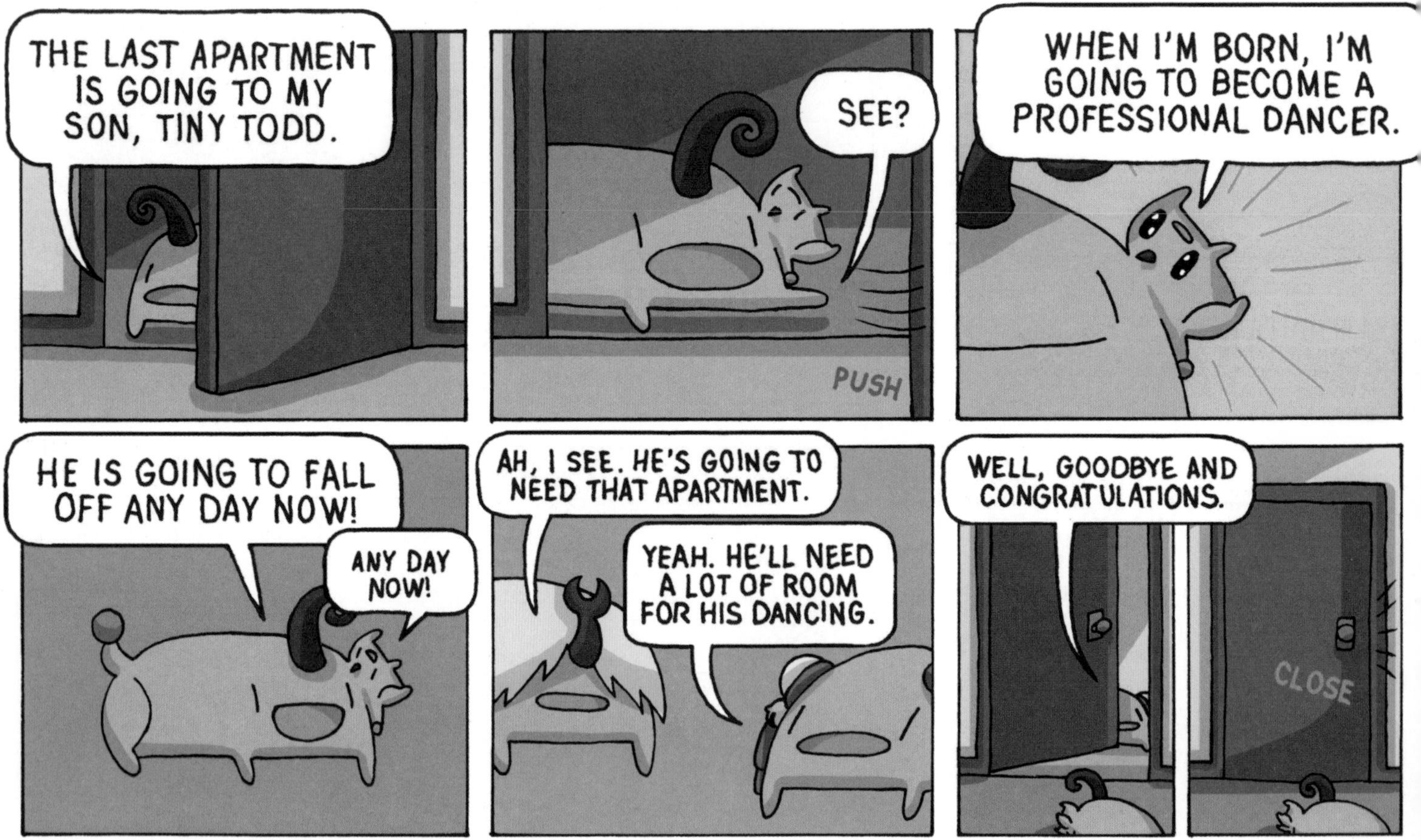
THE LAST APARTMENT IS GOING TO MY SON, TINY TODD.
SEE?
PUSH
WHEN I'M BORN, I'M GOING TO BECOME A PROFESSIONAL DANCER.
HE IS GOING TO FALL OFF ANY DAY NOW!
ANY DAY NOW!
AH, I SEE. HE'S GOING TO NEED THAT APARTMENT.
YEAH. HE'LL NEED A LOT OF ROOM FOR HIS DANCING.
WELL, GOODBYE AND CONGRATULATIONS.
CLOSE

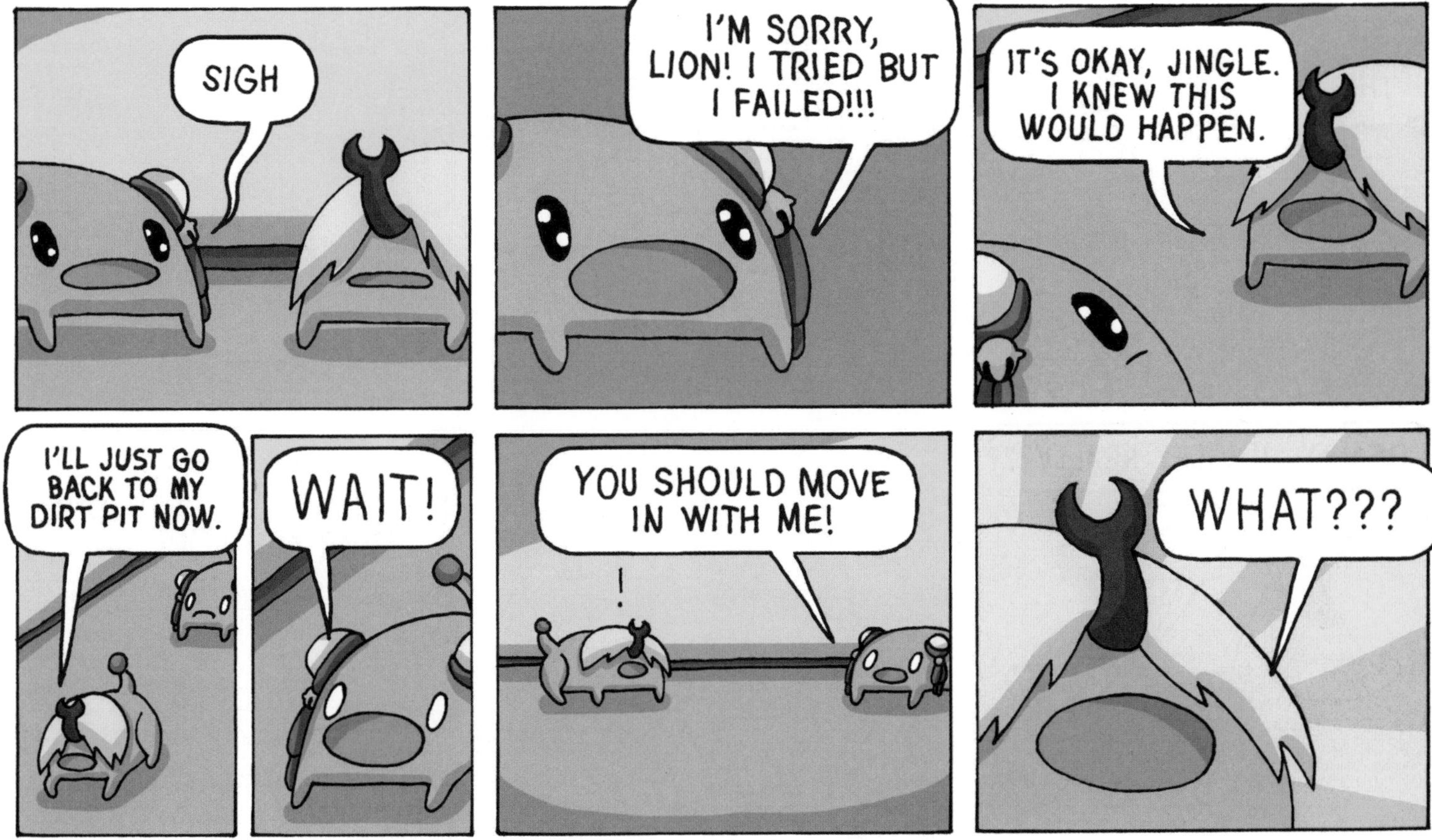
SIGH
I'M SORRY, LION! I TRIED BUT I FAILED!!!
IT'S OKAY, JINGLE. I KNEW THIS WOULD HAPPEN.
I'LL JUST GO BACK TO MY DIRT PIT NOW.
WAIT!
YOU SHOULD MOVE IN WITH ME!
!
WHAT???

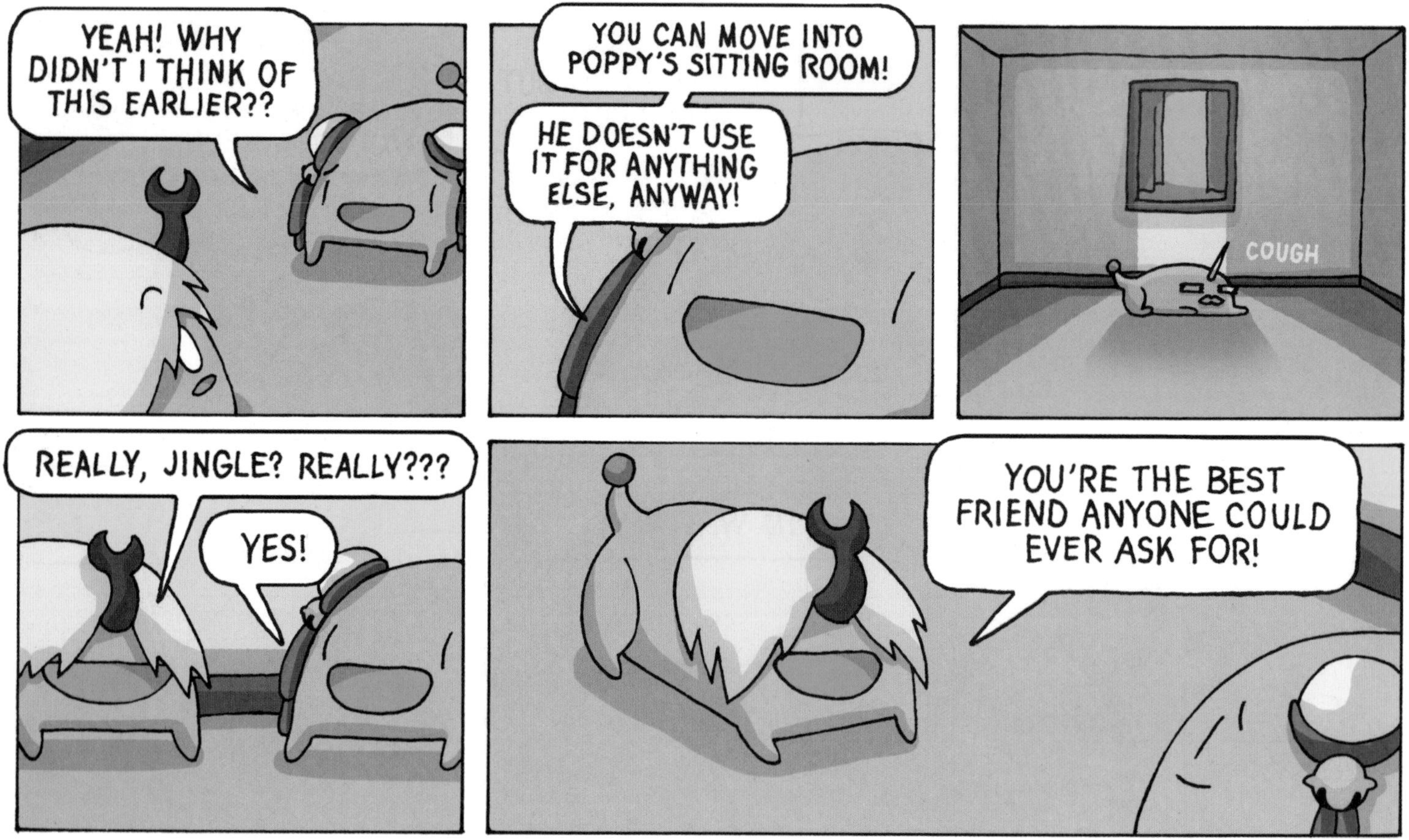
YEAH! WHY DIDN'T I THINK OF THIS EARLIER??
YOU CAN MOVE INTO POPPY'S SITTING ROOM!
HE DOESN'T USE IT FOR ANYTHING ELSE, ANYWAY!
COUGH
REALLY, JINGLE? REALLY???
YES!
YOU'RE THE BEST FRIEND ANYONE COULD EVER ASK FOR!

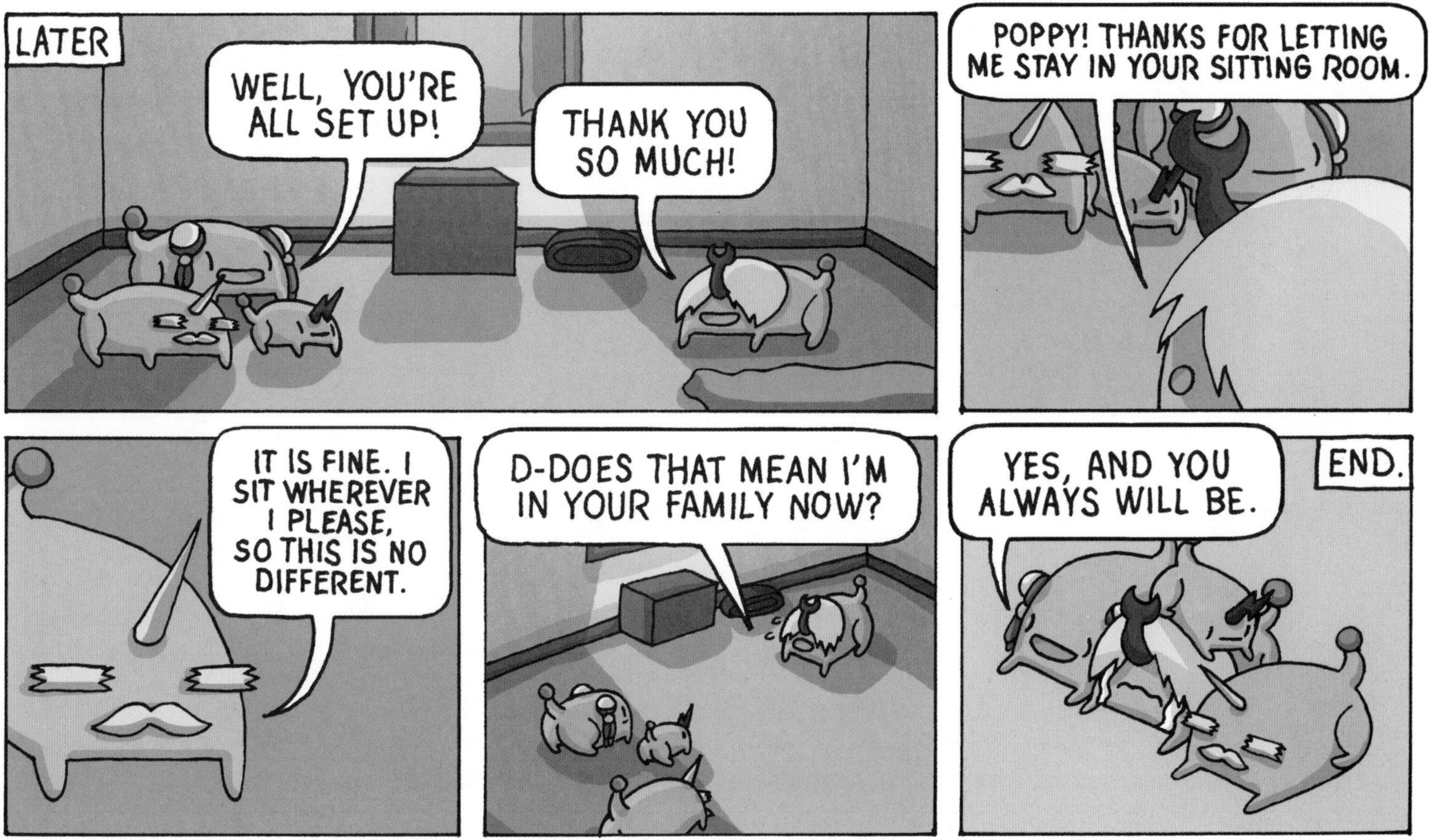
LATER
WELL, YOU'RE ALL SET UP!
THANK YOU SO MUCH!
POPPY! THANKS FOR LETTING ME STAY IN YOUR SITTING ROOM.
IT IS FINE. I SIT WHEREVER I PLEASE, SO THIS IS NO DIFFERENT.
D-DOES THAT MEAN I'M IN YOUR FAMILY NOW?
YES, AND YOU ALWAYS WILL BE.
END.

CHAPTER NINE

—

DO YOU EVER WONDER?

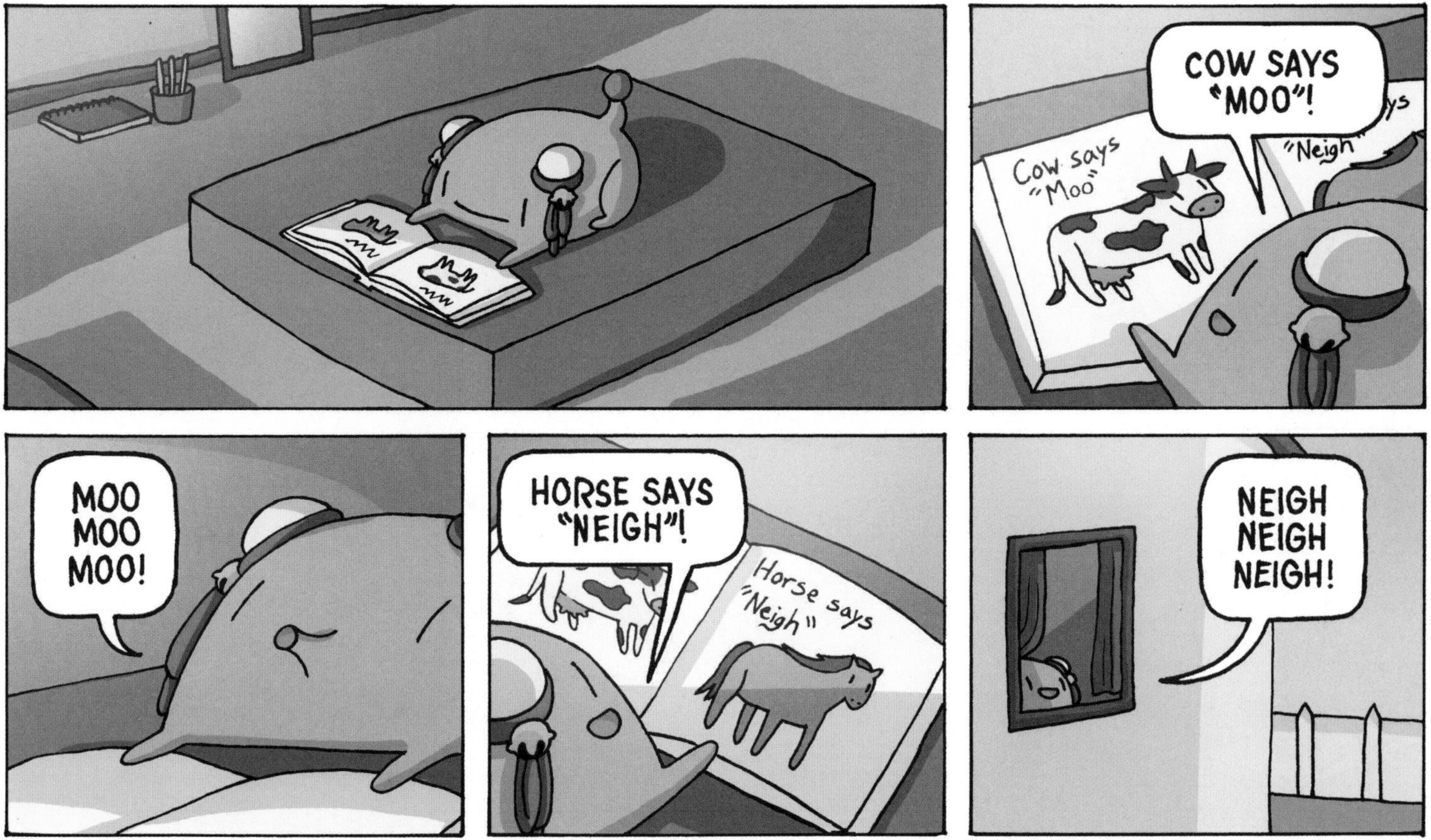
COW SAYS "MOO"!
Cow says "Moo"
"Neigh"
MOO MOO MOO!
HORSE SAYS "NEIGH"!
Horse says "Neigh"
NEIGH NEIGH NEIGH!

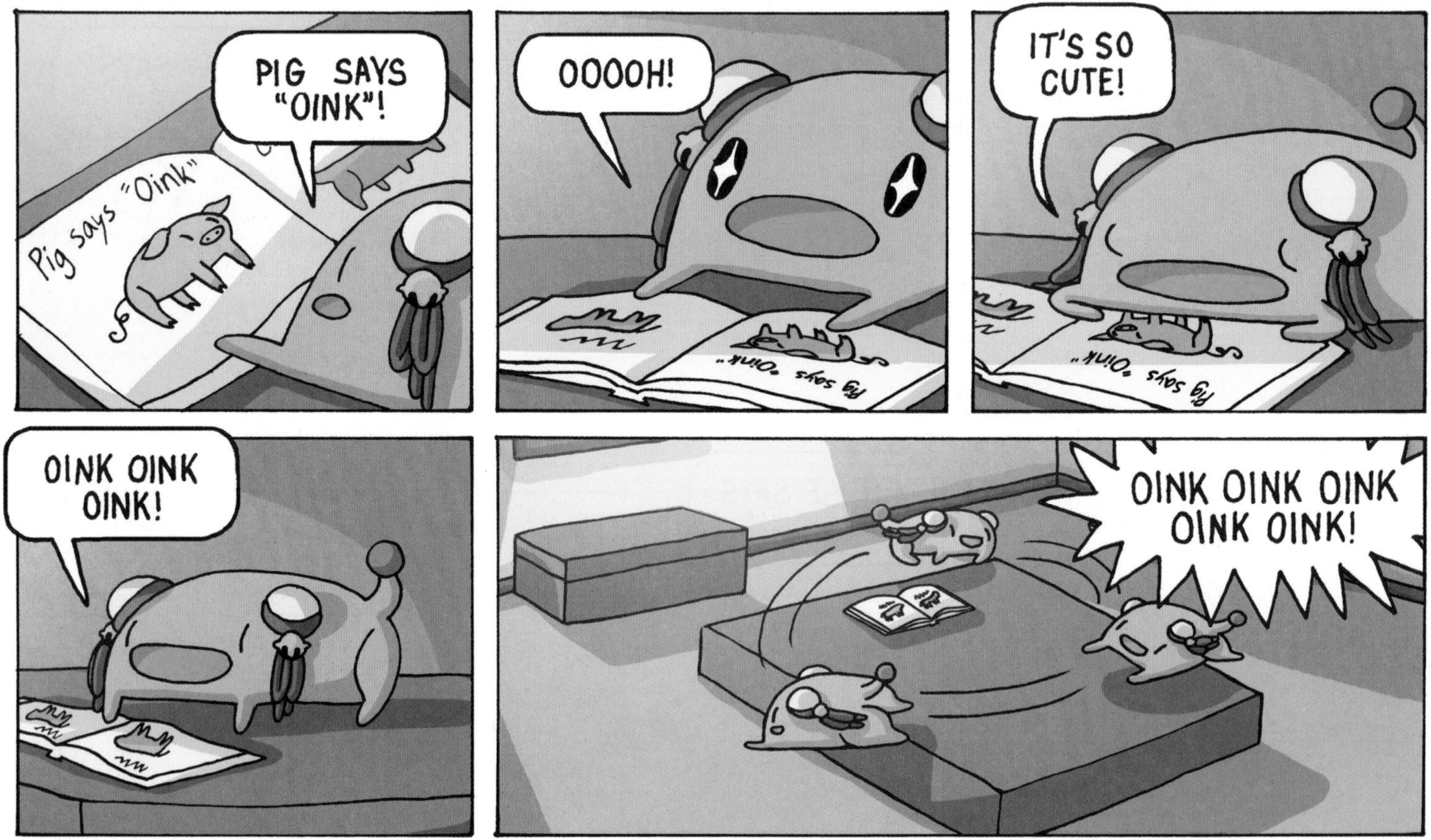
Pig says "Oink"
PIG SAYS "OINK"!
OOOOH!
Pig says "Oink."
IT'S SO CUTE!
OINK OINK OINK!
OINK OINK OINK OINK OINK!

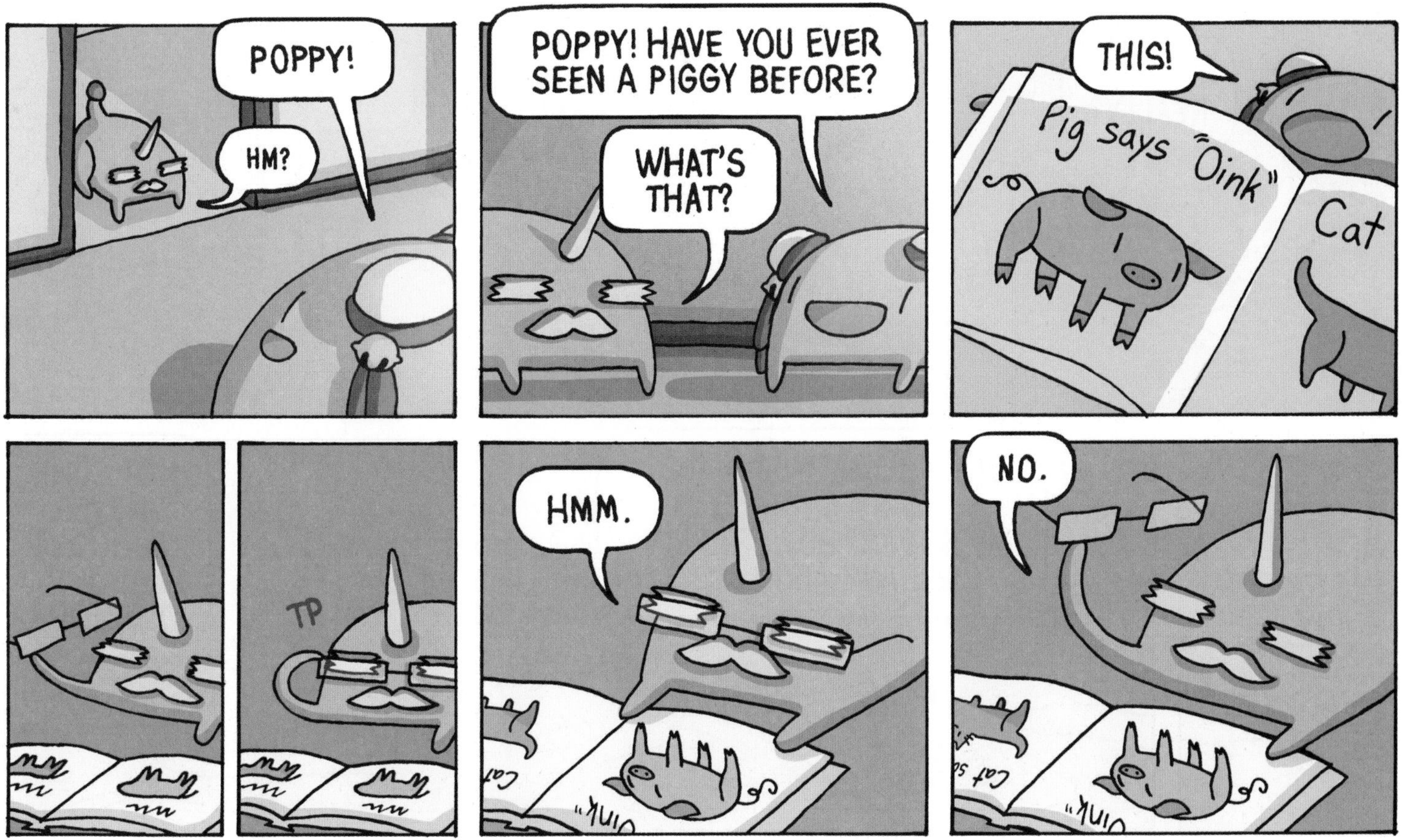
POPPY!
HM?
POPPY! HAVE YOU EVER SEEN A PIGGY BEFORE?
WHAT'S THAT?
THIS!
Pig says "Oink"
Cat
TP
HMM.
NO.

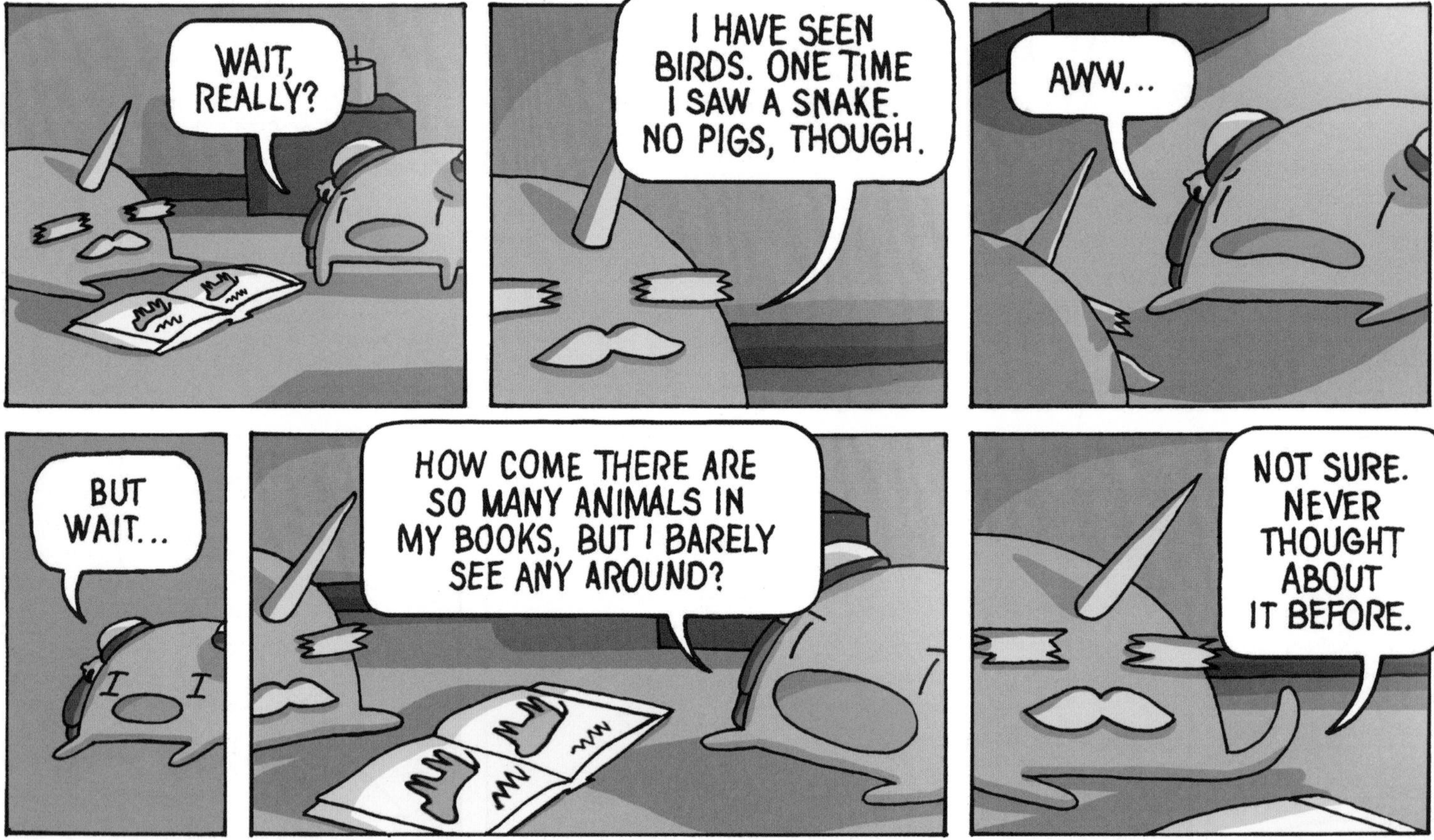
WAIT, REALLY?
I HAVE SEEN BIRDS. ONE TIME I SAW A SNAKE. NO PIGS, THOUGH.
AWW...
BUT WAIT...
HOW COME THERE ARE SO MANY ANIMALS IN MY BOOKS, BUT I BARELY SEE ANY AROUND?
NOT SURE. NEVER THOUGHT ABOUT IT BEFORE.

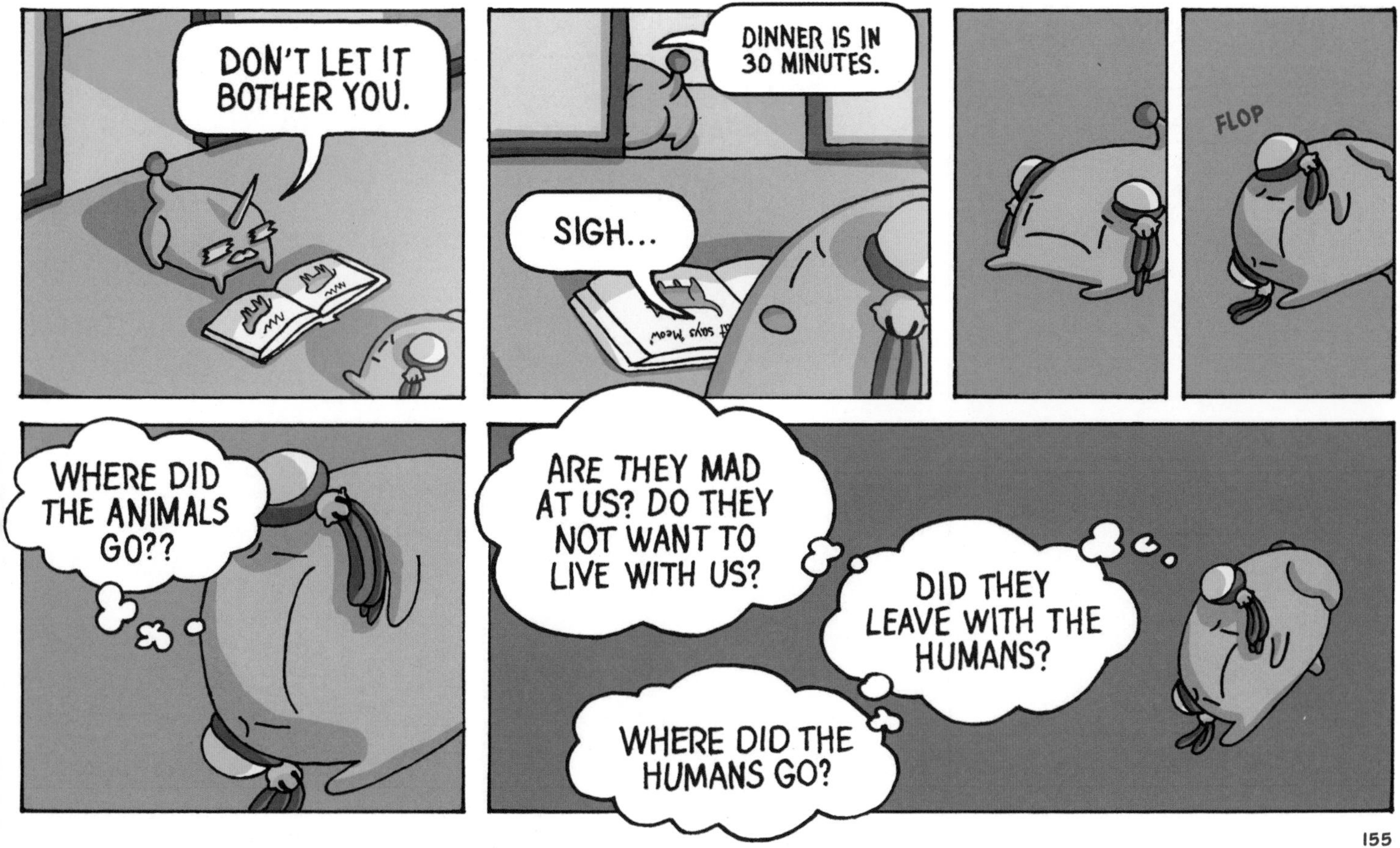
DON'T LET IT BOTHER YOU.
DINNER IS IN 30 MINUTES.
SIGH...
FLOP
WHERE DID THE ANIMALS GO??
ARE THEY MAD AT US? DO THEY NOT WANT TO LIVE WITH US?
DID THEY LEAVE WITH THE HUMANS?
WHERE DID THE HUMANS GO?

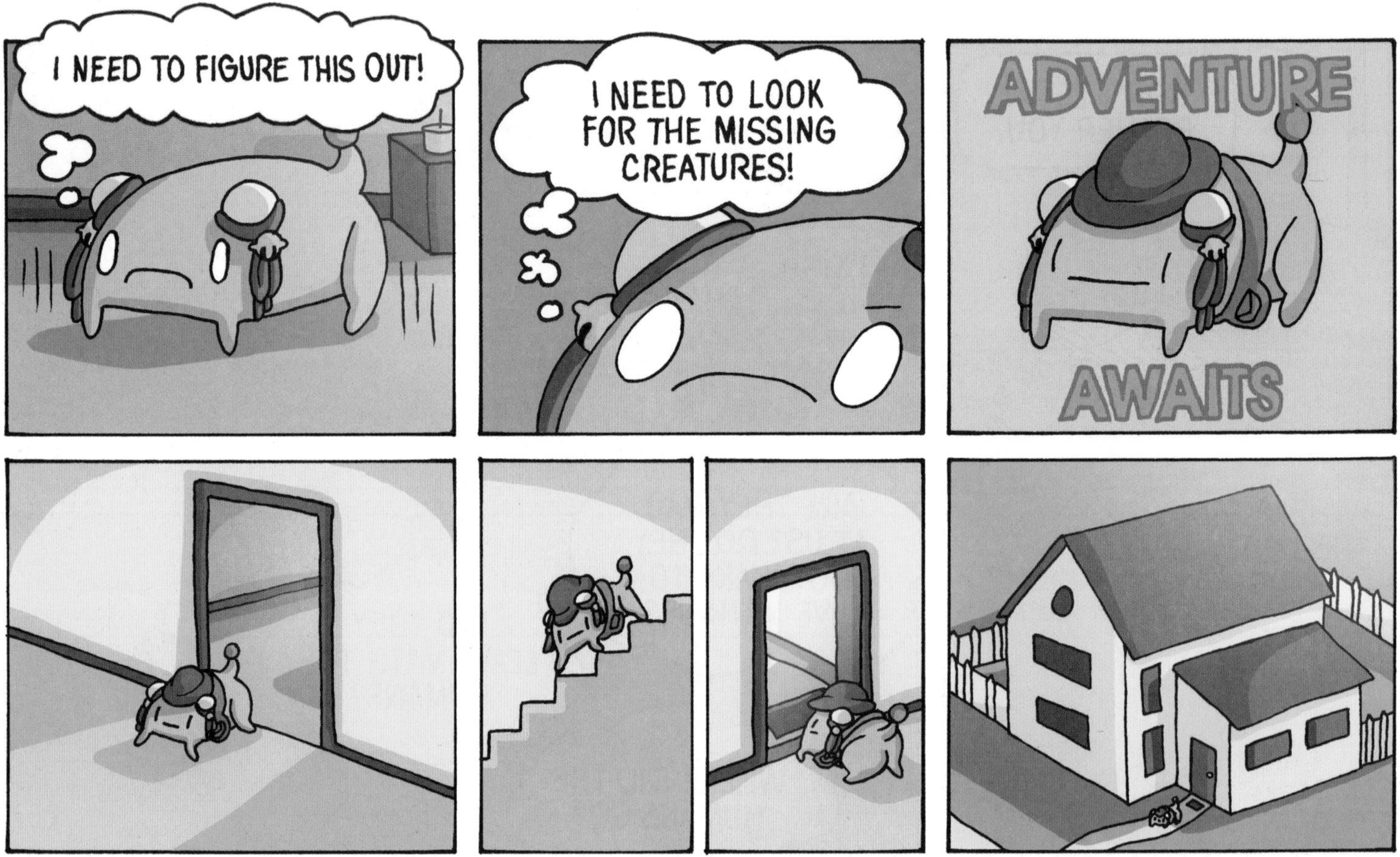
I NEED TO FIGURE THIS OUT!
I NEED TO LOOK FOR THE MISSING CREATURES!
ADVENTURE
AWAITS

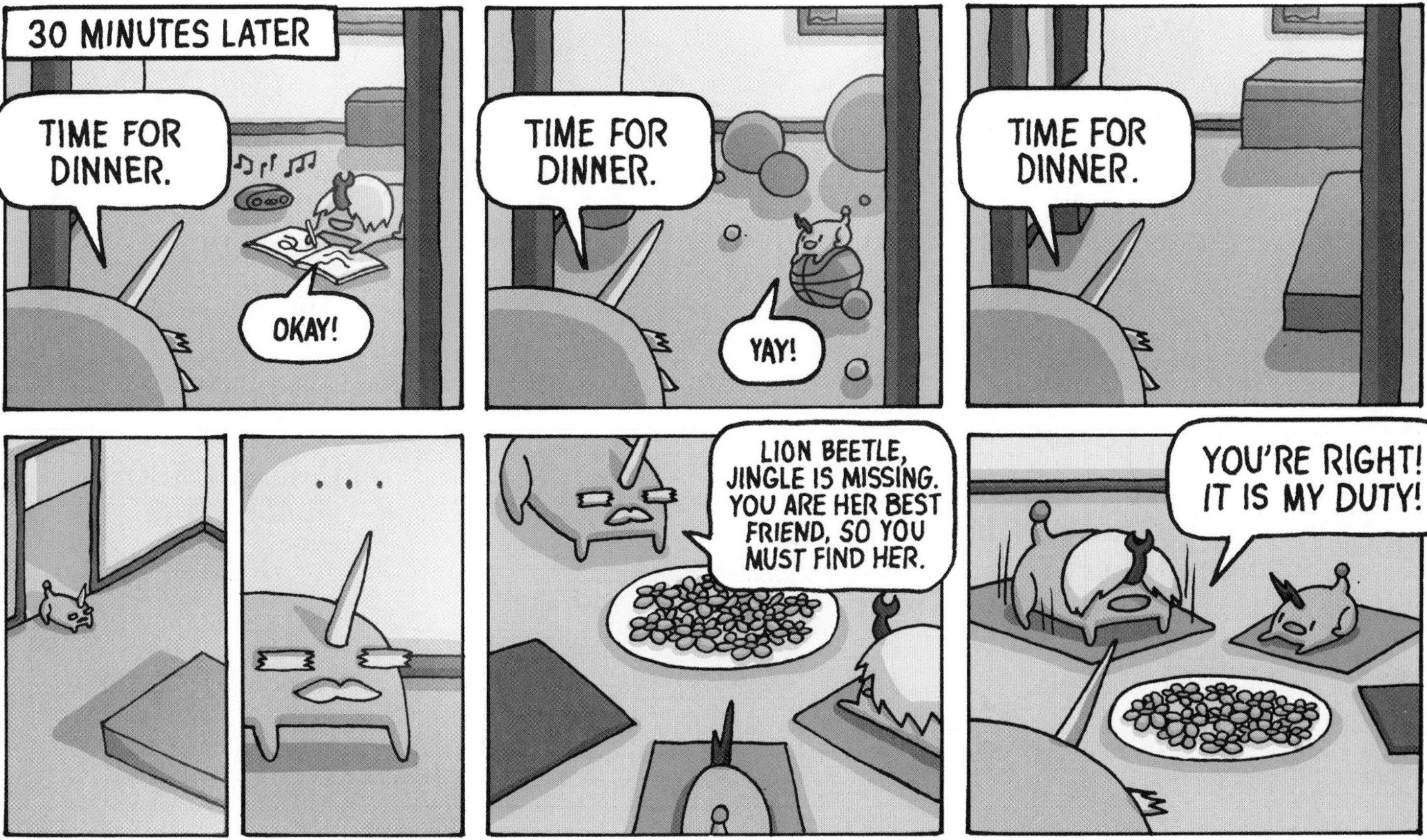
30 MINUTES LATER
TIME FOR DINNER.
OKAY!
TIME FOR DINNER.
YAY!
TIME FOR DINNER.
. . .
LION BEETLE, JINGLE IS MISSING. YOU ARE HER BEST FRIEND, SO YOU MUST FIND HER.
YOU'RE RIGHT! IT IS MY DUTY!

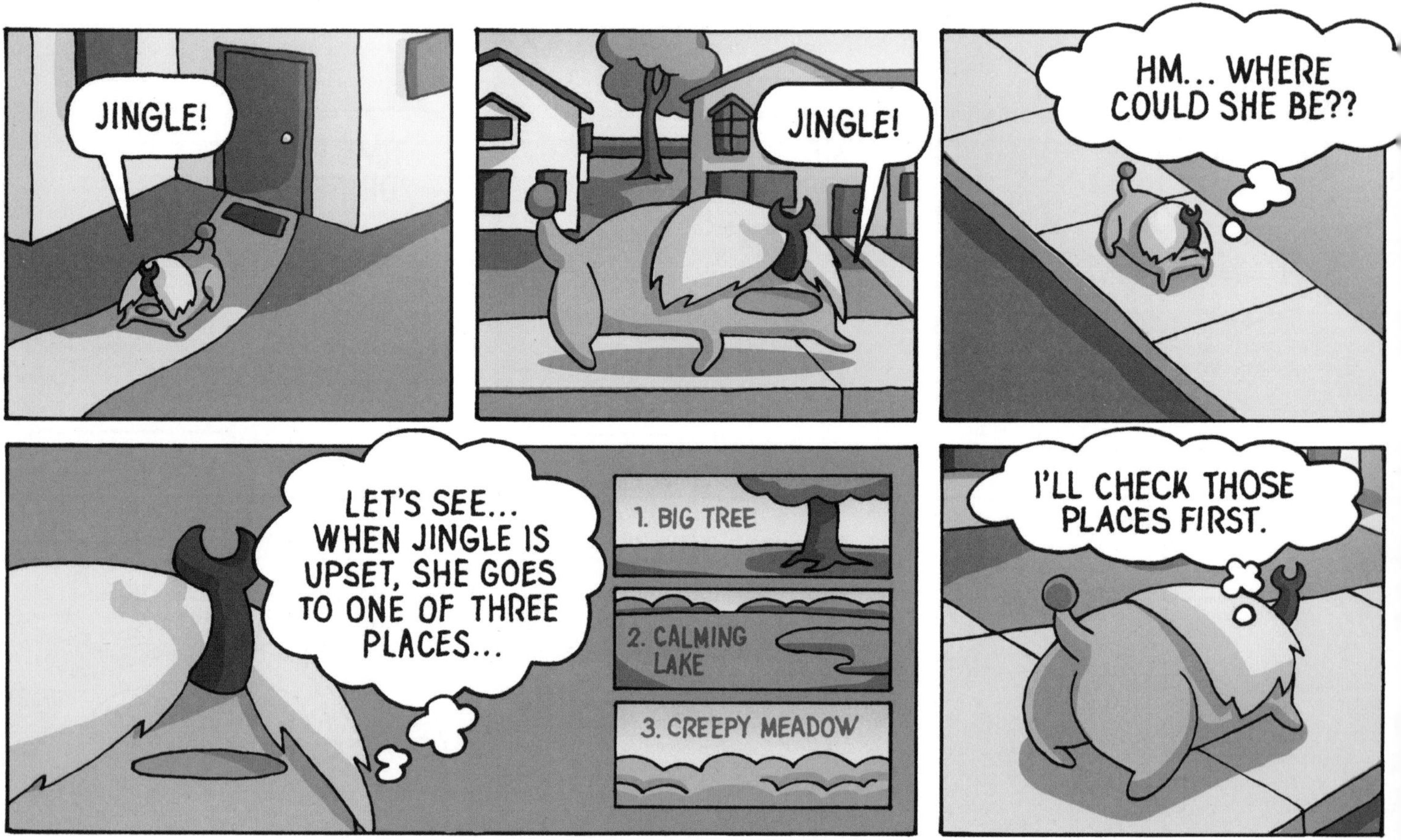
JINGLE!
JINGLE!
HM... WHERE COULD SHE BE??
LET'S SEE... WHEN JINGLE IS UPSET, SHE GOES TO ONE OF THREE PLACES...
1. BIG TREE
2. CALMING LAKE
3. CREEPY MEADOW
I'LL CHECK THOSE PLACES FIRST.

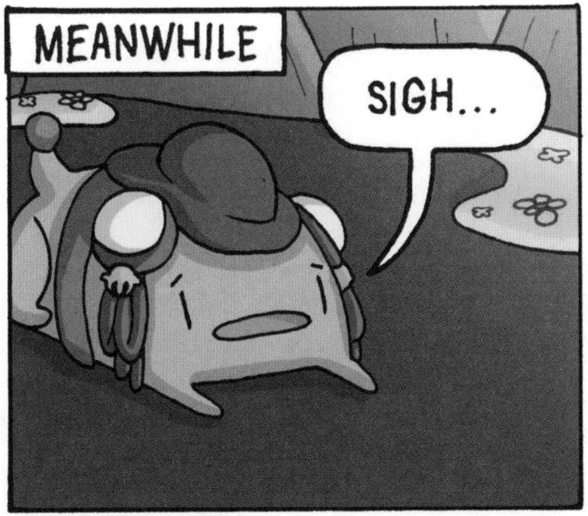
MEANWHILE
SIGH...

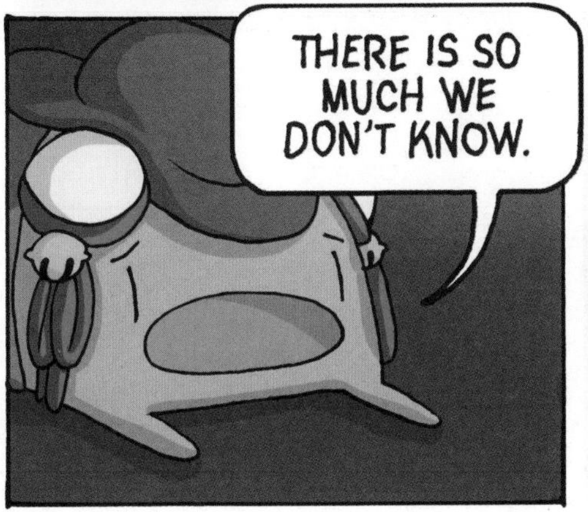
THERE IS SO MUCH WE DON'T KNOW.

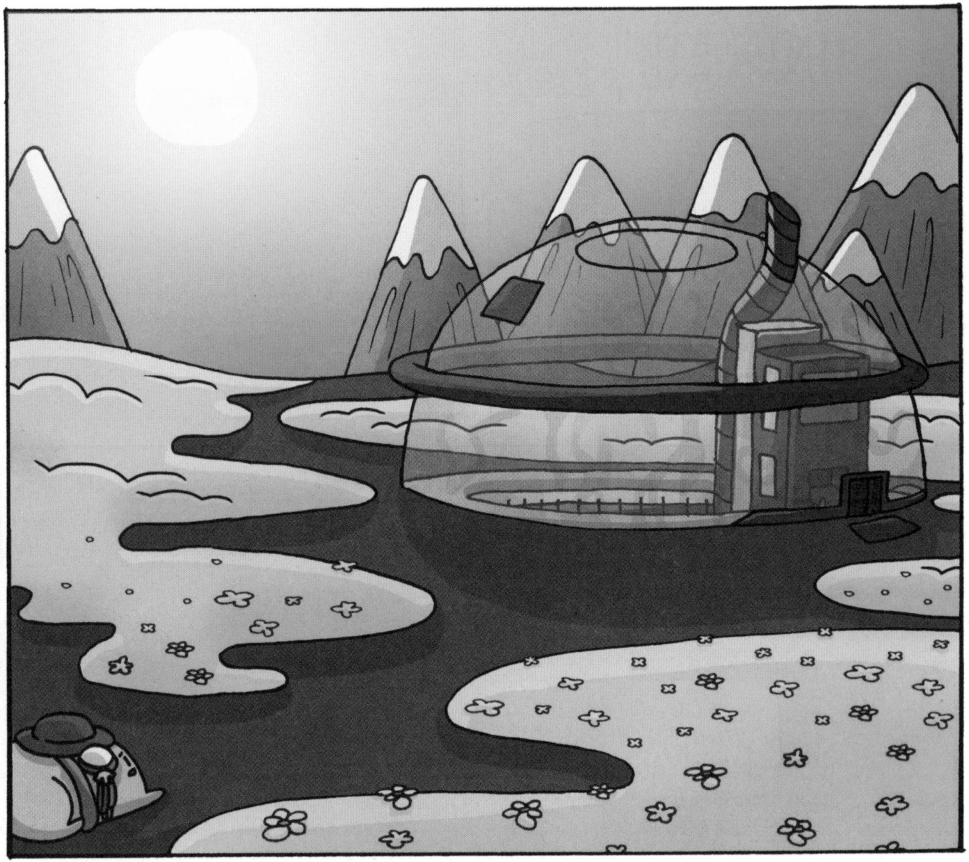

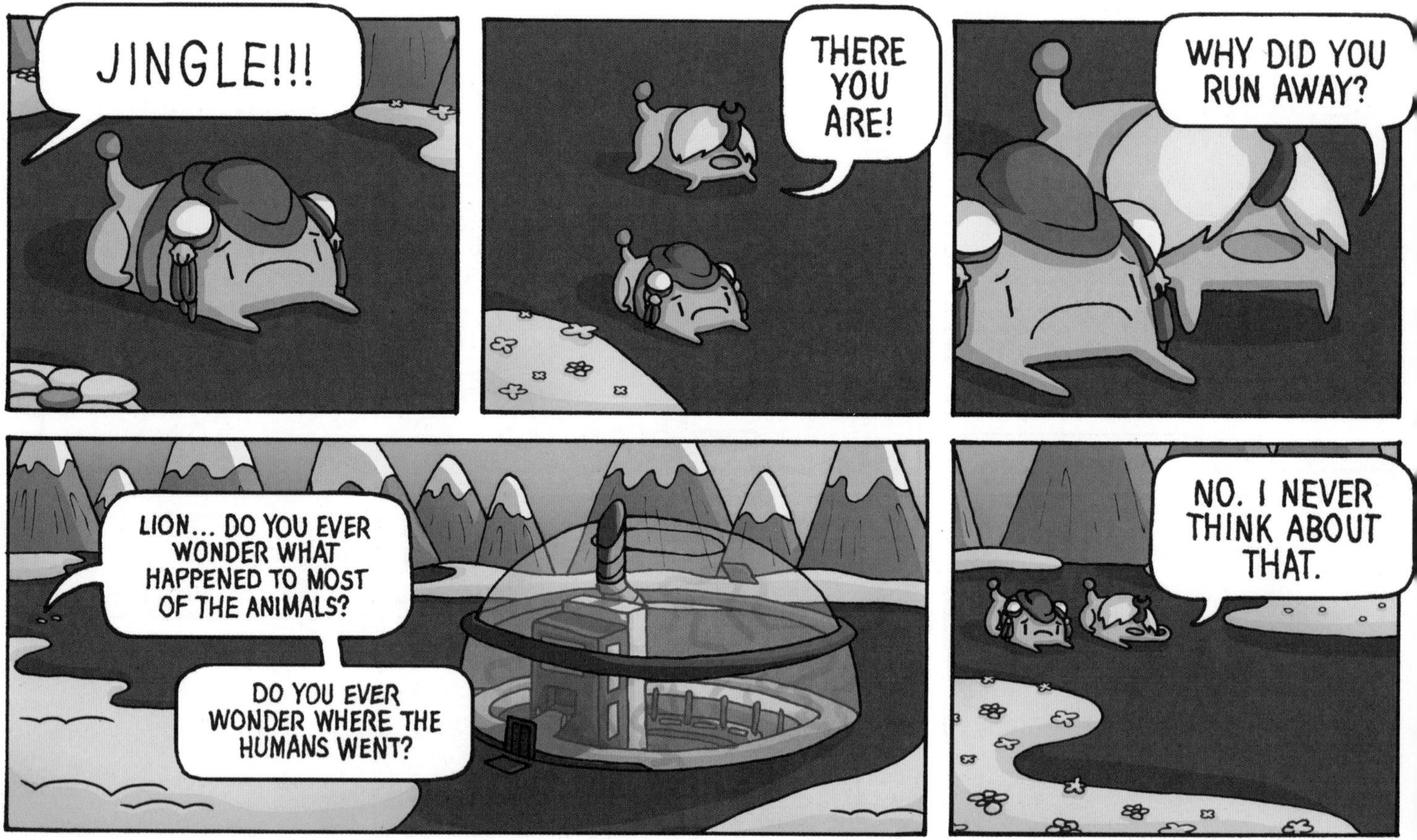
JINGLE!!!
THERE YOU ARE!
WHY DID YOU RUN AWAY?
LION... DO YOU EVER WONDER WHAT HAPPENED TO MOST OF THE ANIMALS?
DO YOU EVER WONDER WHERE THE HUMANS WENT?
NO. I NEVER THINK ABOUT THAT.

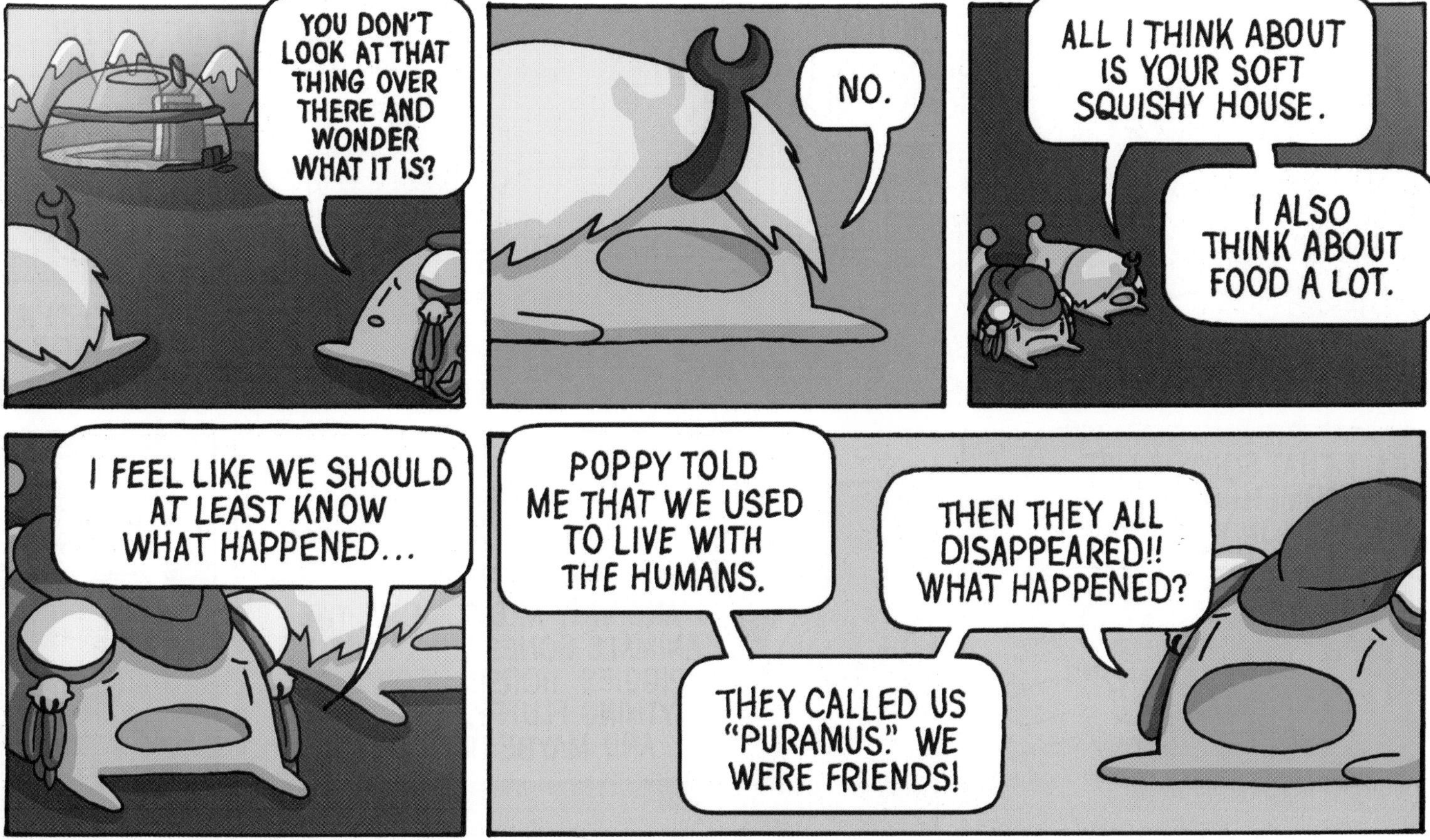
YOU DON'T LOOK AT THAT THING OVER THERE AND WONDER WHAT IT IS?
NO.
ALL I THINK ABOUT IS YOUR SOFT SQUISHY HOUSE.
I ALSO THINK ABOUT FOOD A LOT.
I FEEL LIKE WE SHOULD AT LEAST KNOW WHAT HAPPENED...
POPPY TOLD ME THAT WE USED TO LIVE WITH THE HUMANS.
THEY CALLED US "PURAMUS." WE WERE FRIENDS!
THEN THEY ALL DISAPPEARED!! WHAT HAPPENED?

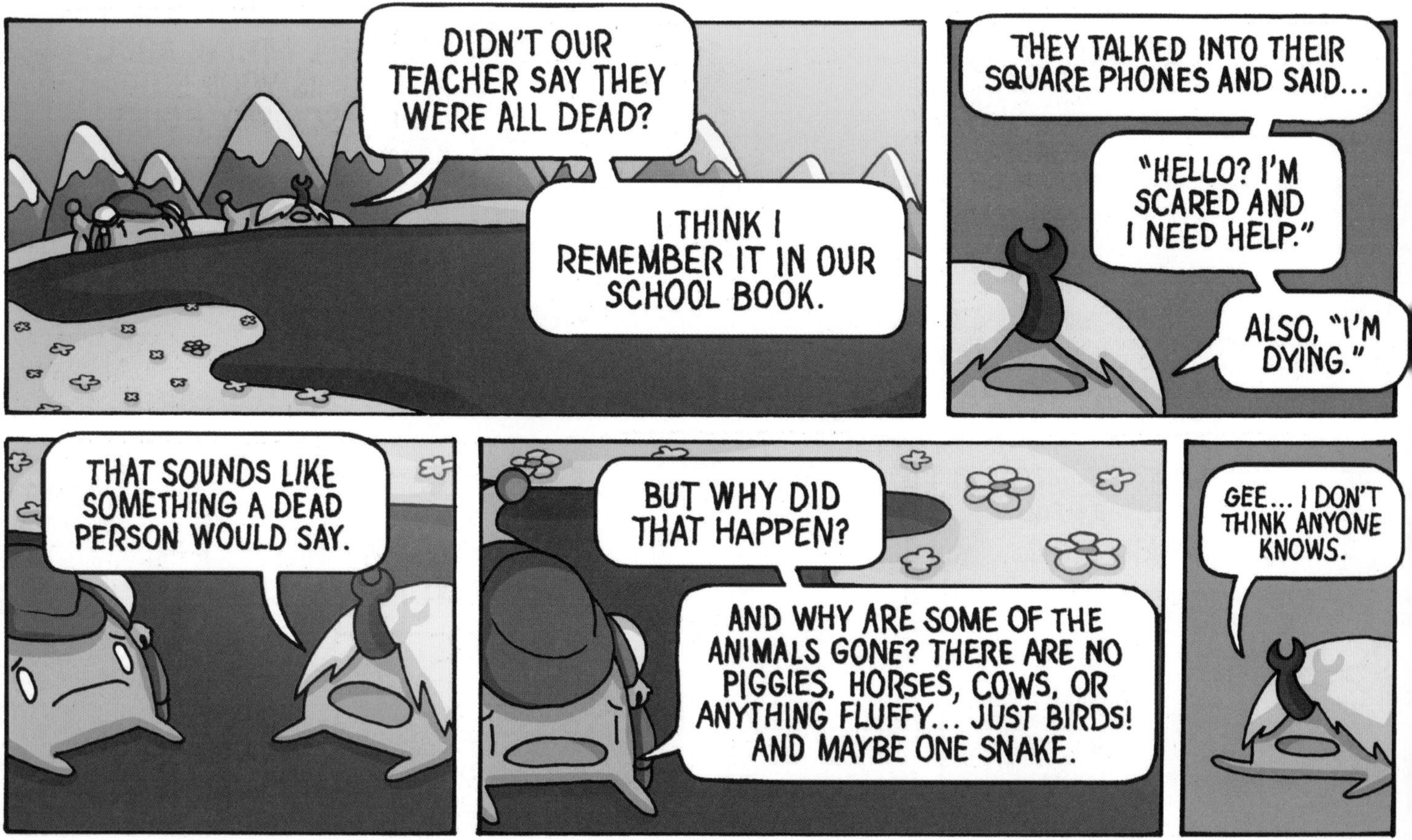
DIDN'T OUR TEACHER SAY THEY WERE ALL DEAD?
I THINK I REMEMBER IT IN OUR SCHOOL BOOK.
THEY TALKED INTO THEIR SQUARE PHONES AND SAID...
"HELLO? I'M SCARED AND I NEED HELP."
ALSO, "I'M DYING."
THAT SOUNDS LIKE SOMETHING A DEAD PERSON WOULD SAY.
BUT WHY DID THAT HAPPEN?
AND WHY ARE SOME OF THE ANIMALS GONE? THERE ARE NO PIGGIES, HORSES, COWS, OR ANYTHING FLUFFY... JUST BIRDS! AND MAYBE ONE SNAKE.
GEE... I DON'T THINK ANYONE KNOWS.

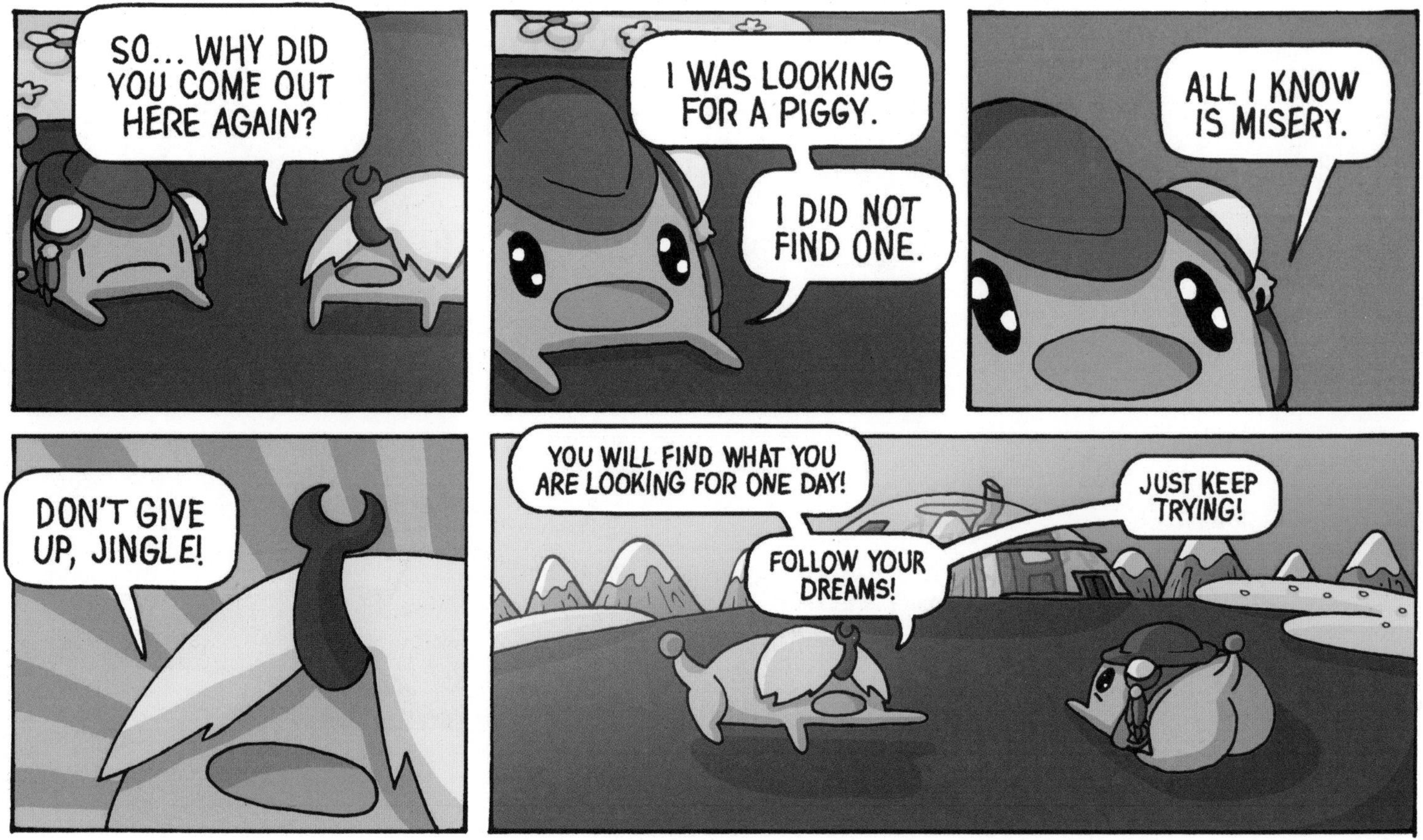
SO... WHY DID YOU COME OUT HERE AGAIN?
I WAS LOOKING FOR A PIGGY.
I DID NOT FIND ONE.
ALL I KNOW IS MISERY.
DON'T GIVE UP, JINGLE!
YOU WILL FIND WHAT YOU ARE LOOKING FOR ONE DAY!
FOLLOW YOUR DREAMS!
JUST KEEP TRYING!

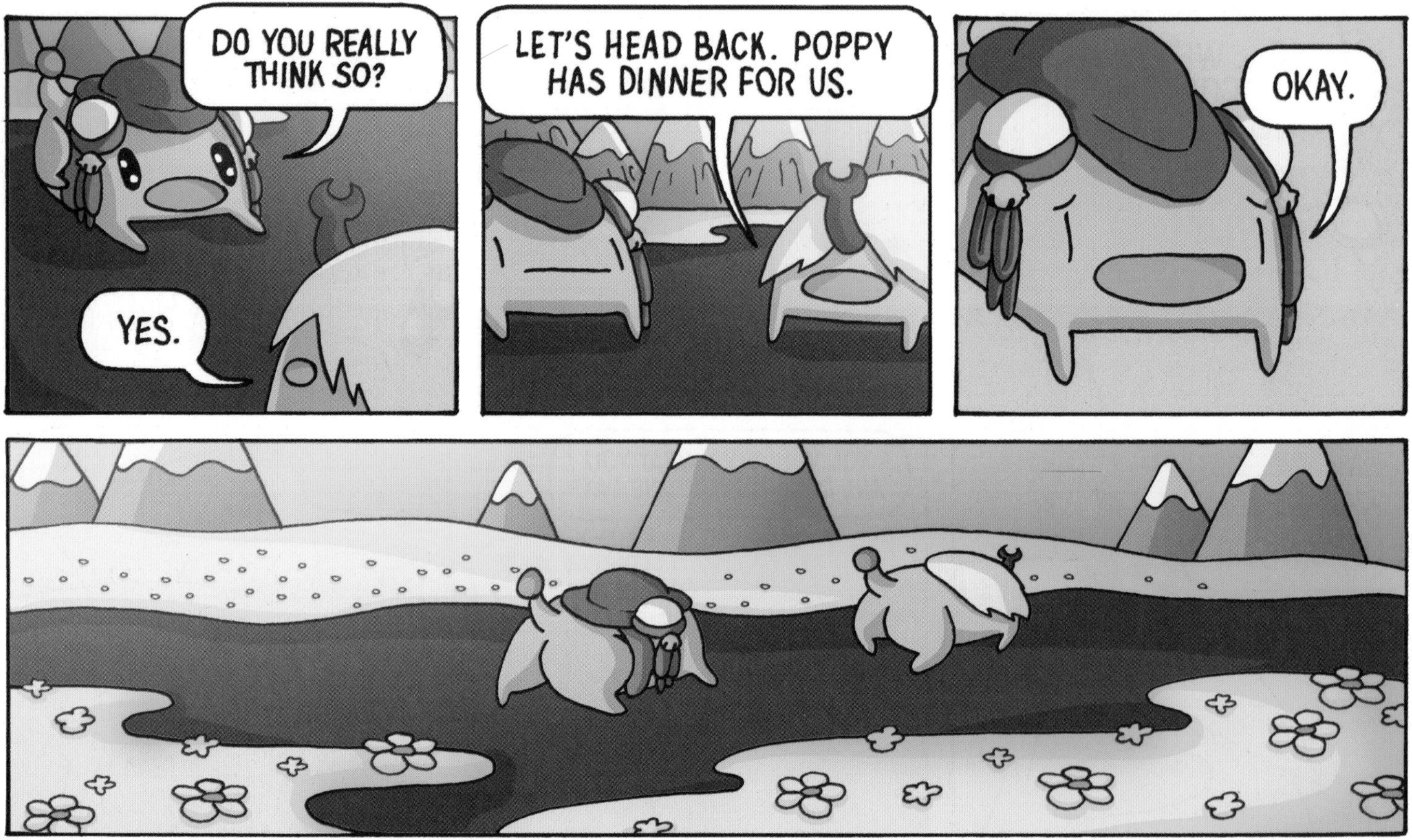
DO YOU REALLY THINK SO?
YES.
LET'S HEAD BACK. POPPY HAS DINNER FOR US.
OKAY.

MUNCH
MUNCH
MUNCH
MUNCH
MUNCH

I HAVE AN ANNOUNCEMENT TO MAKE!

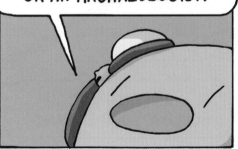

WHEN I GROW UP, I WANT TO BE AN ANTHROPOLOGIST OR AN ARCHAEOLOGIST!

THAT WAY, I CAN LEARN IMPORTANT THINGS ABOUT OUR HISTORY!

I WILL LEARN WHAT HAPPENED! I WILL FIND THE TRUTH!

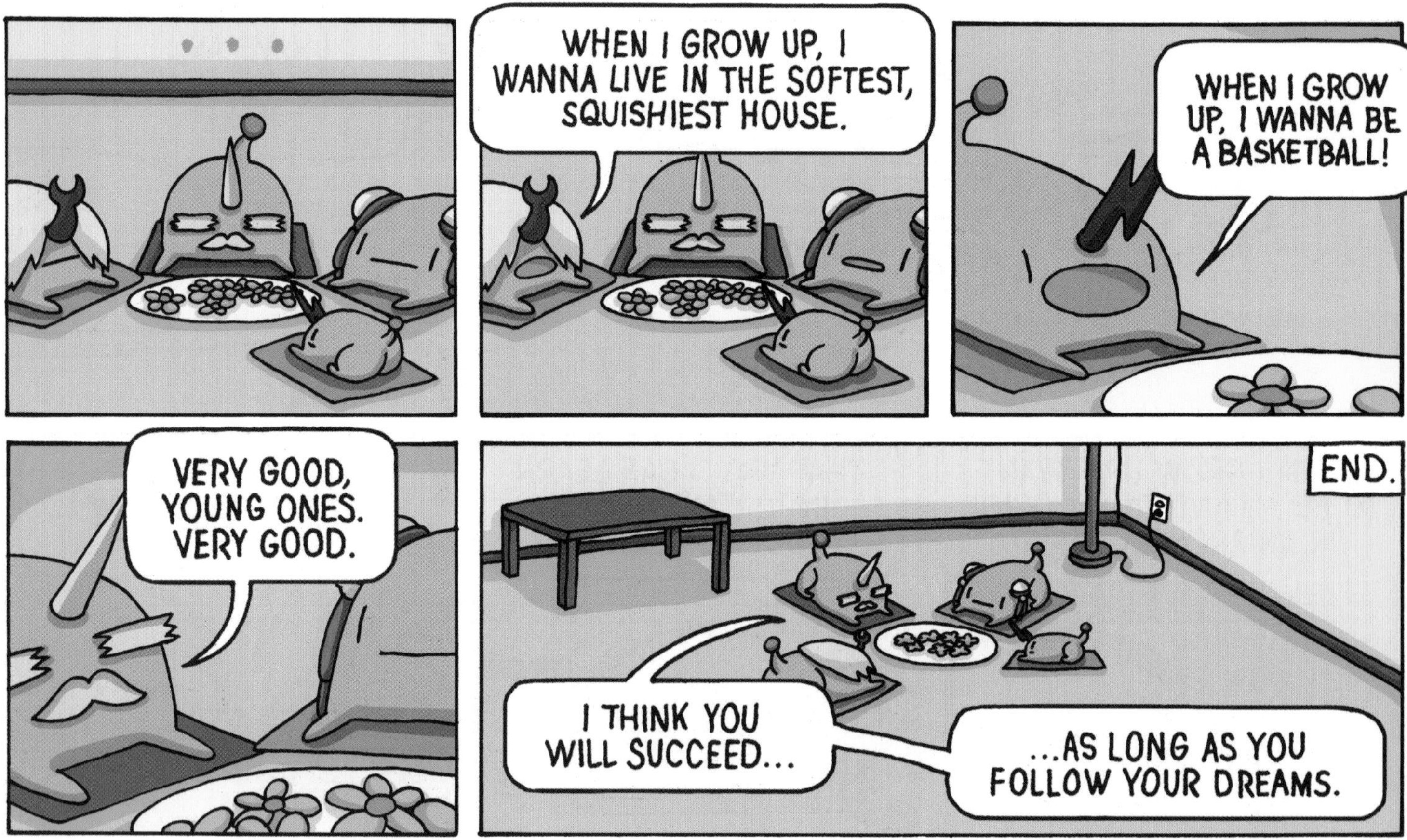

WHEN I GROW UP, I WANNA LIVE IN THE SOFTEST, SQUISHIEST HOUSE.
WHEN I GROW UP, I WANNA BE A BASKETBALL!
VERY GOOD, YOUNG ONES. VERY GOOD.
END.
I THINK YOU WILL SUCCEED...
...AS LONG AS YOU FOLLOW YOUR DREAMS.

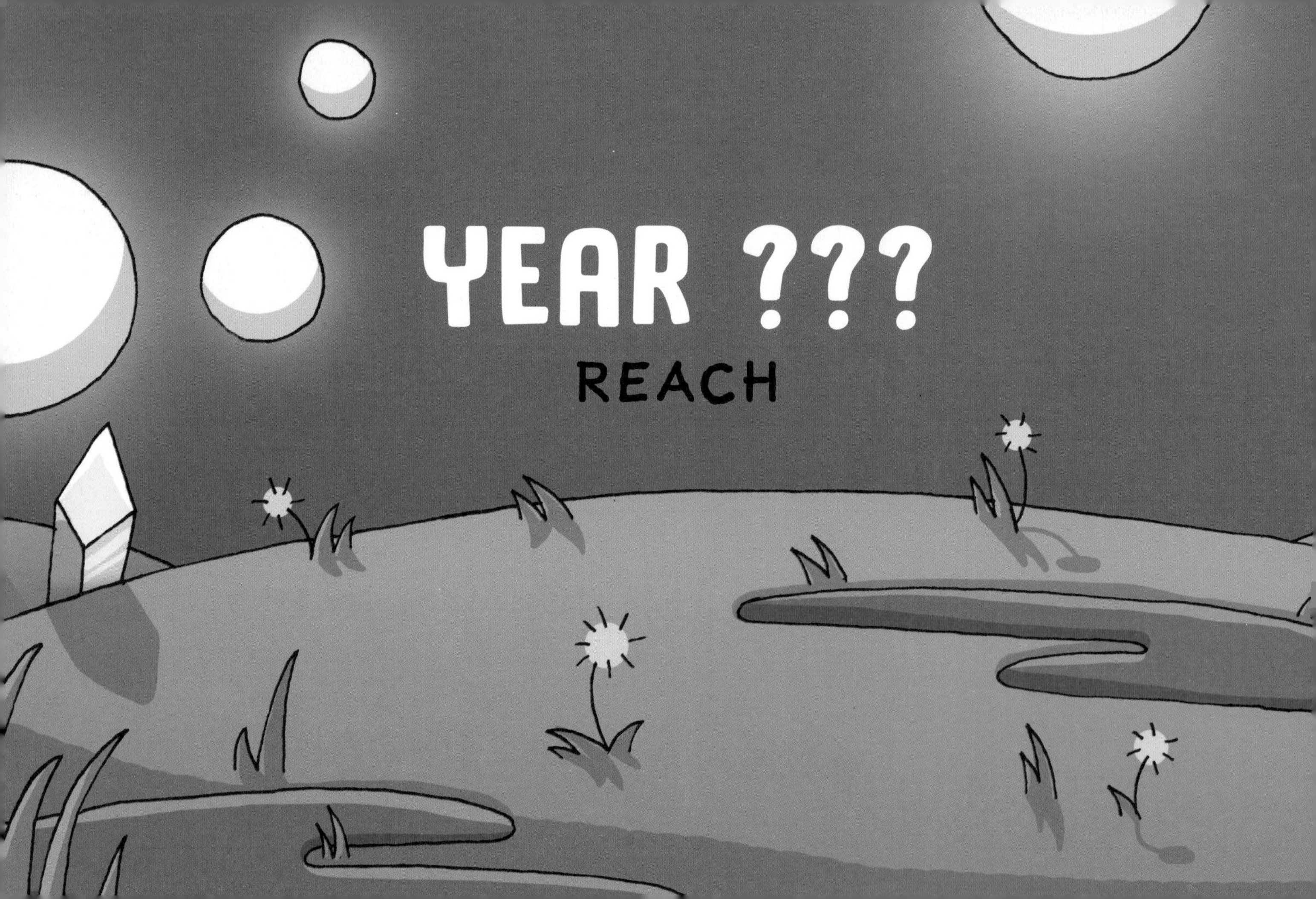
YEAR ???
REACH

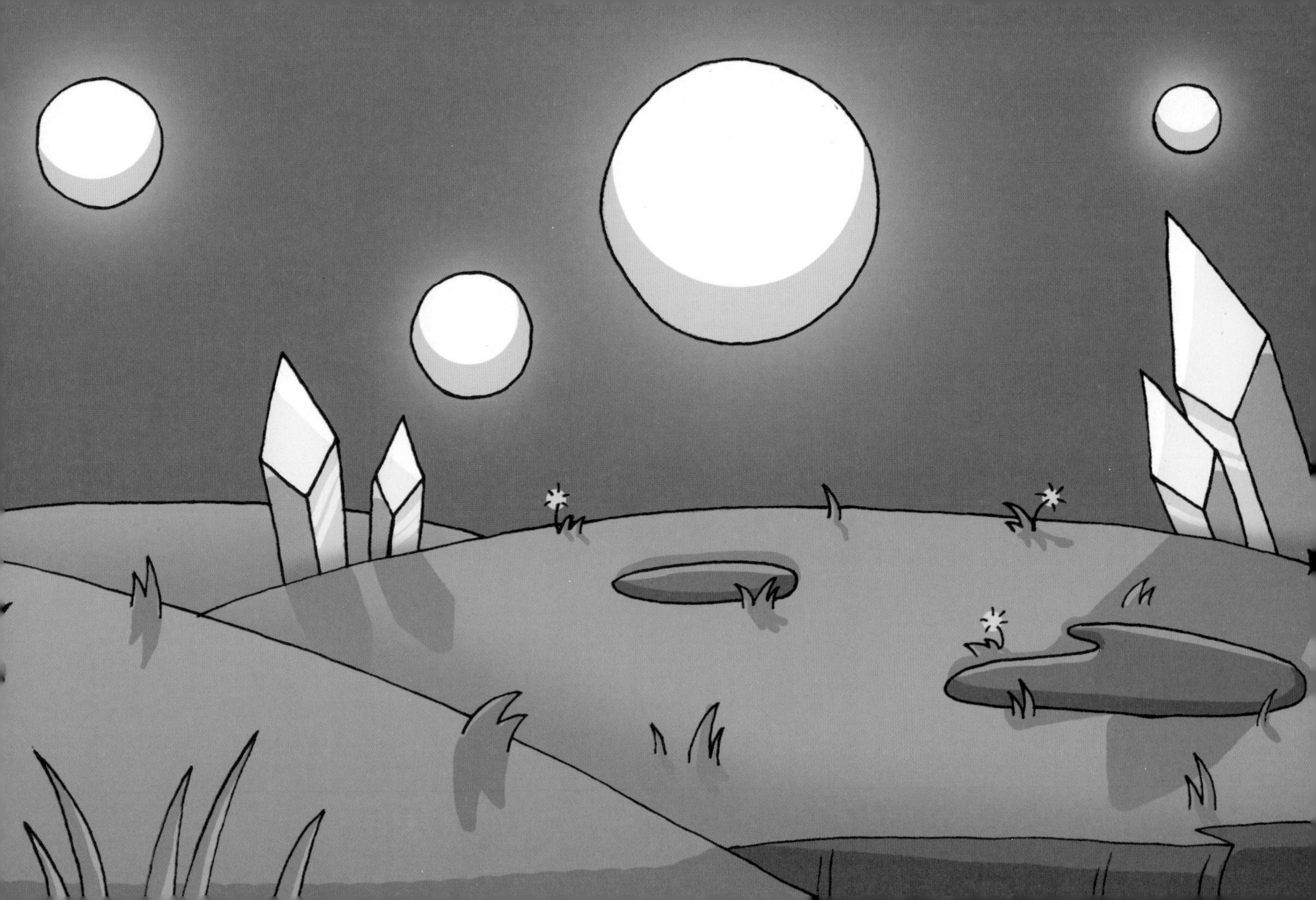

CHAPTER TEN
—

FIND SOME
GOOD THINGS

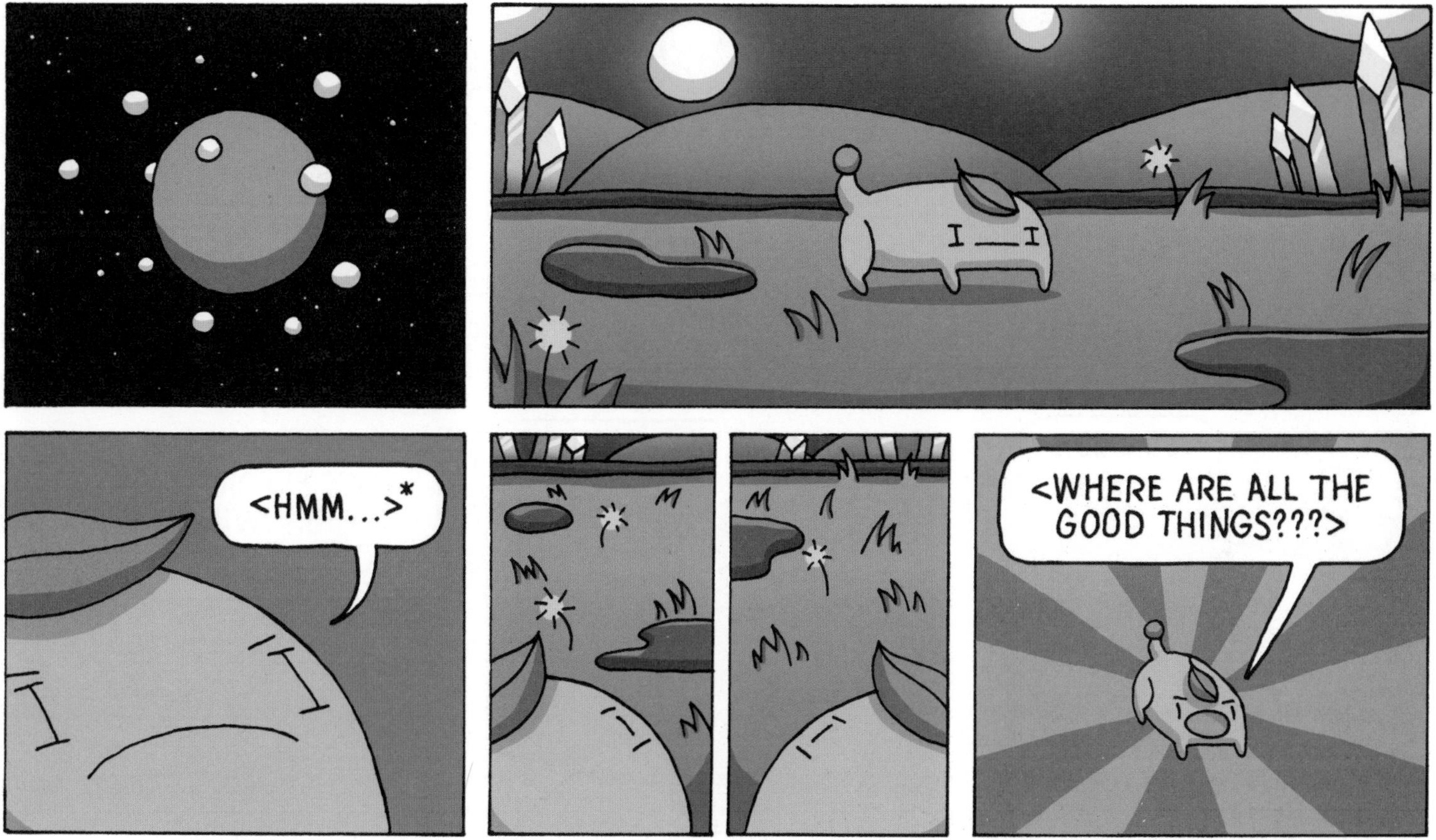
<HMM...>*
<WHERE ARE ALL THE GOOD THINGS???>

*TRANSLATED FROM AN ALIEN LANGUAGE. SOUNDS LIKE "MEH, MEH, MEH, MEH"

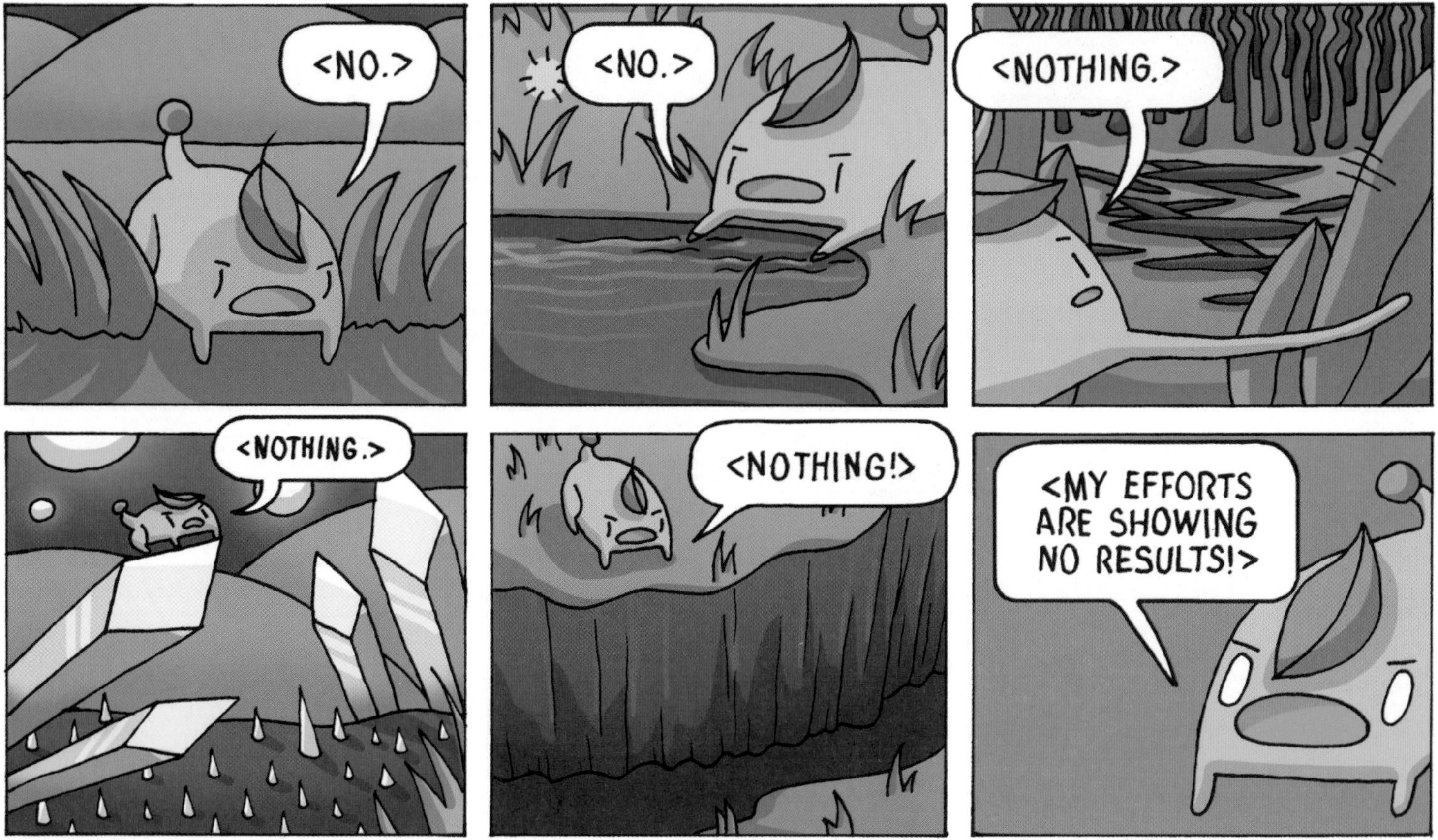
<NO.>
<NO.>
<NOTHING.>
<NOTHING.>
<NOTHING!>
<MY EFFORTS ARE SHOWING NO RESULTS!>

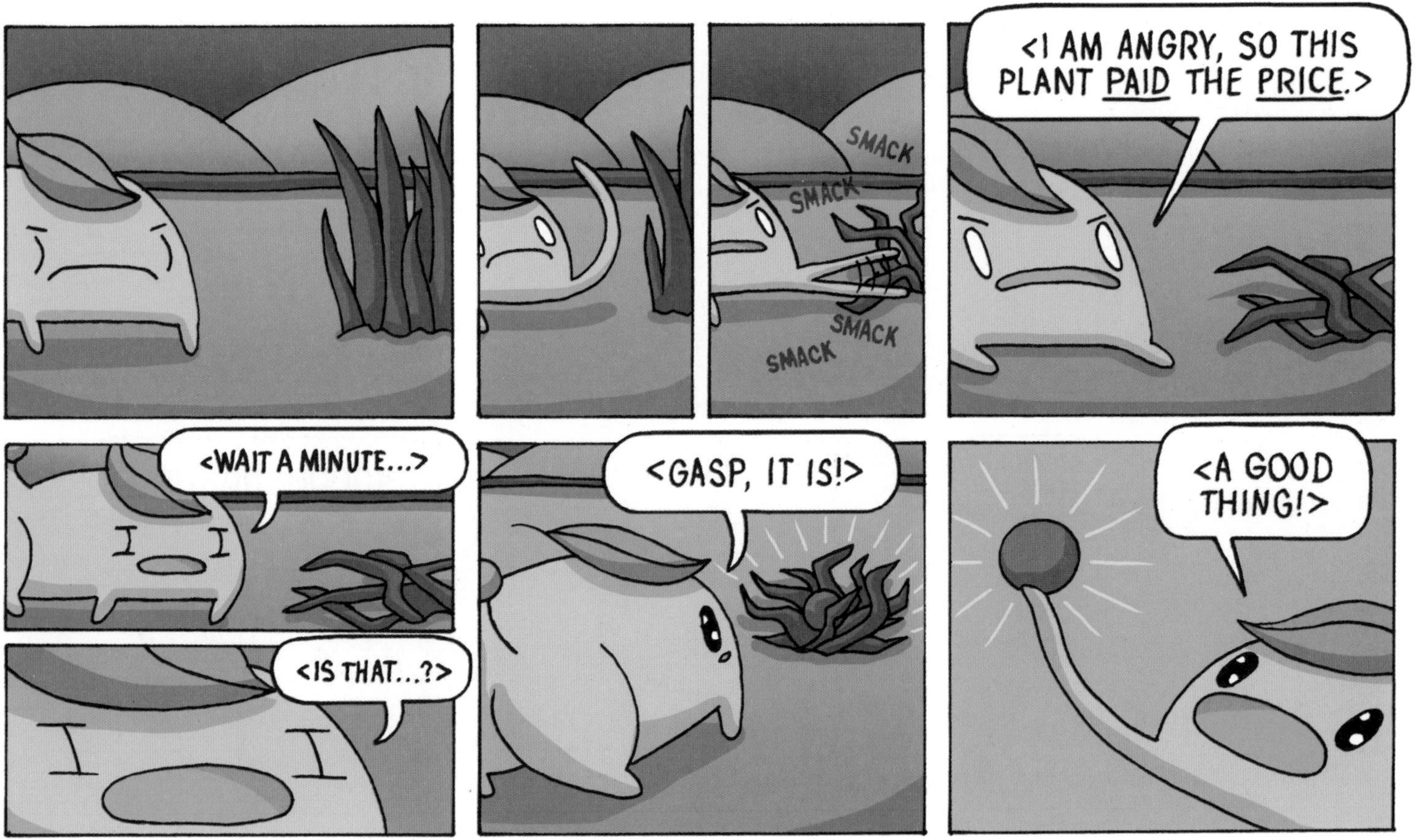
SMACK
SMACK
SMACK
SMACK
<I AM ANGRY, SO THIS PLANT PAID THE PRICE.>
<WAIT A MINUTE...>
<IS THAT...?>
<GASP, IT IS!>
<A GOOD THING!>

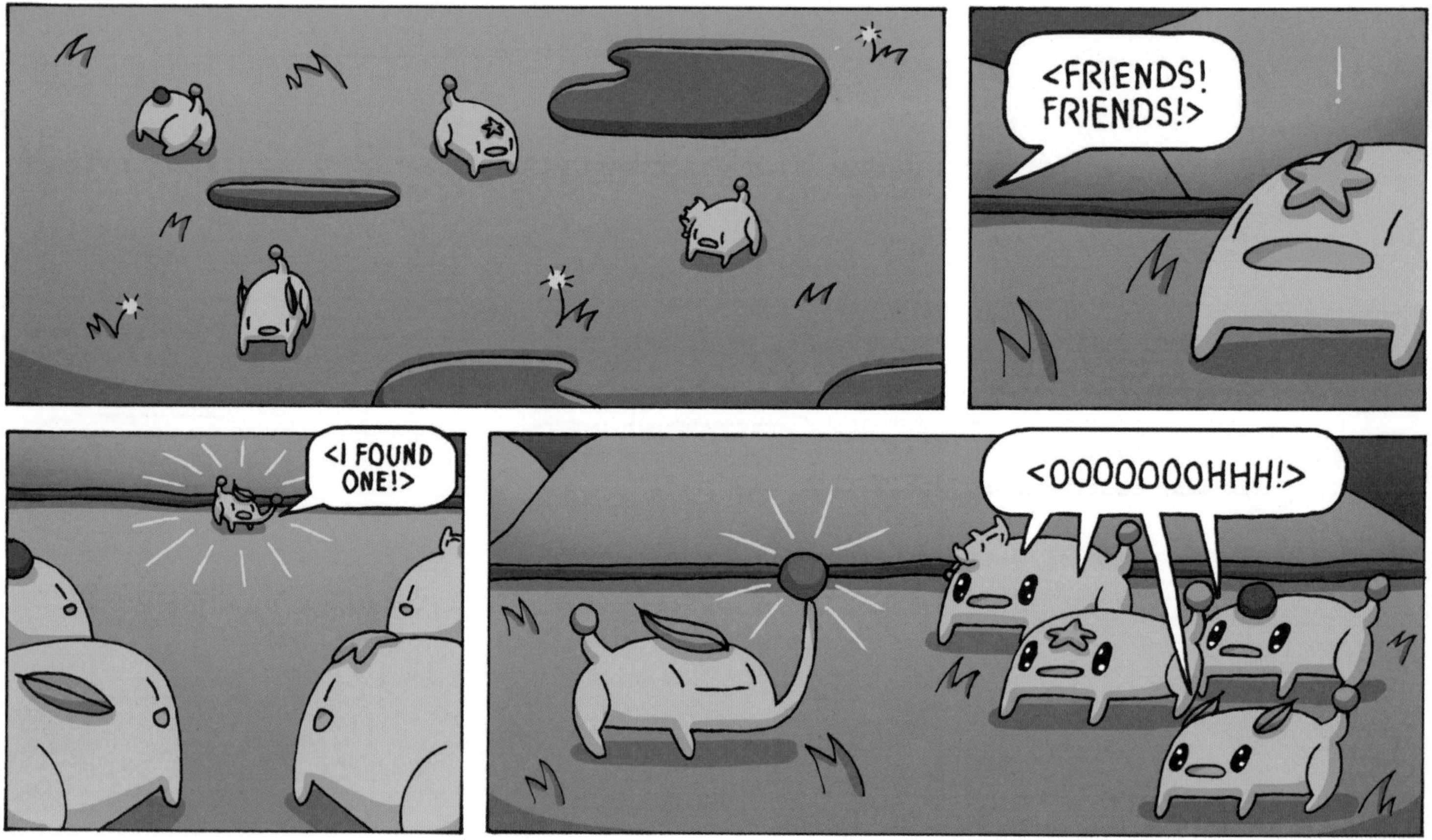
<FRIENDS! FRIENDS!>
<I FOUND ONE!>
<OOOOOOOHHH!>

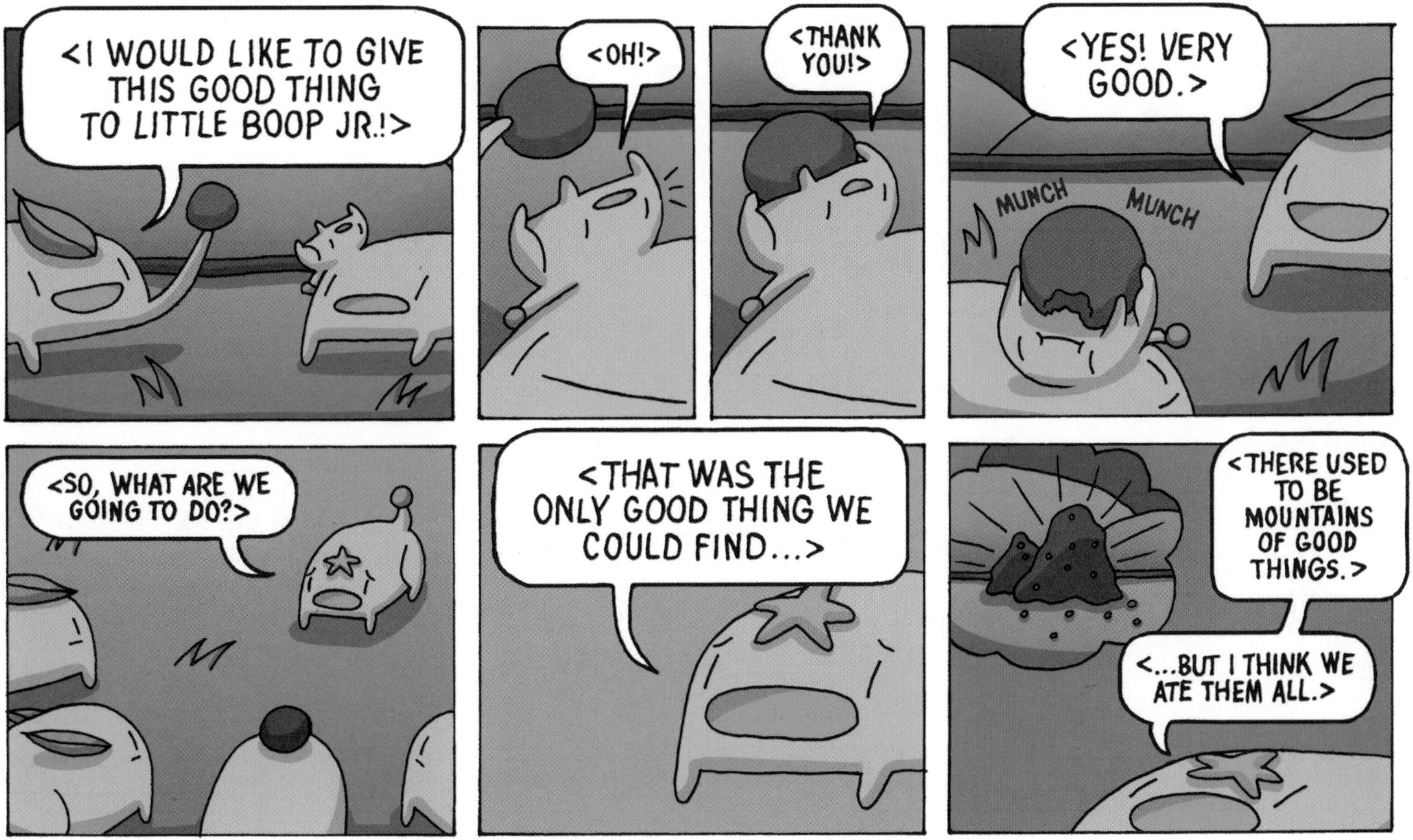
<I WOULD LIKE TO GIVE THIS GOOD THING TO LITTLE BOOP JR.!>
<OH!>
<THANK YOU!>
<YES! VERY GOOD.>
MUNCH
MUNCH
<SO, WHAT ARE WE GOING TO DO?>
<THAT WAS THE ONLY GOOD THING WE COULD FIND...>
<THERE USED TO BE MOUNTAINS OF GOOD THINGS.>
<...BUT I THINK WE ATE THEM ALL.>

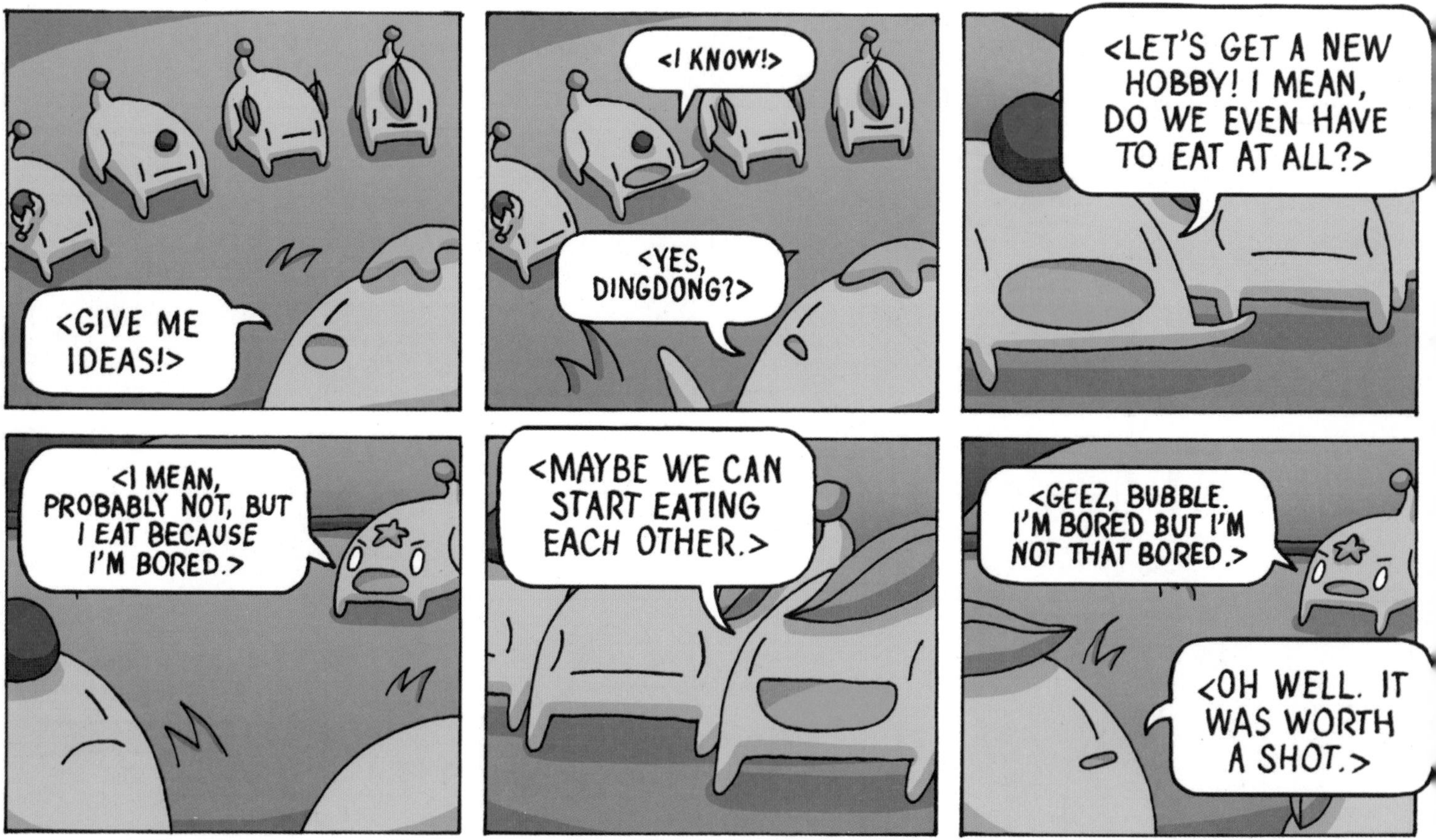
<GIVE ME IDEAS!>
<I KNOW!>
<YES, DINGDONG?>
<LET'S GET A NEW HOBBY! I MEAN, DO WE EVEN HAVE TO EAT AT ALL?>
<I MEAN, PROBABLY NOT, BUT I EAT BECAUSE I'M BORED.>
<MAYBE WE CAN START EATING EACH OTHER.>
<GEEZ, BUBBLE. I'M BORED BUT I'M NOT THAT BORED.>
<OH WELL. IT WAS WORTH A SHOT.>

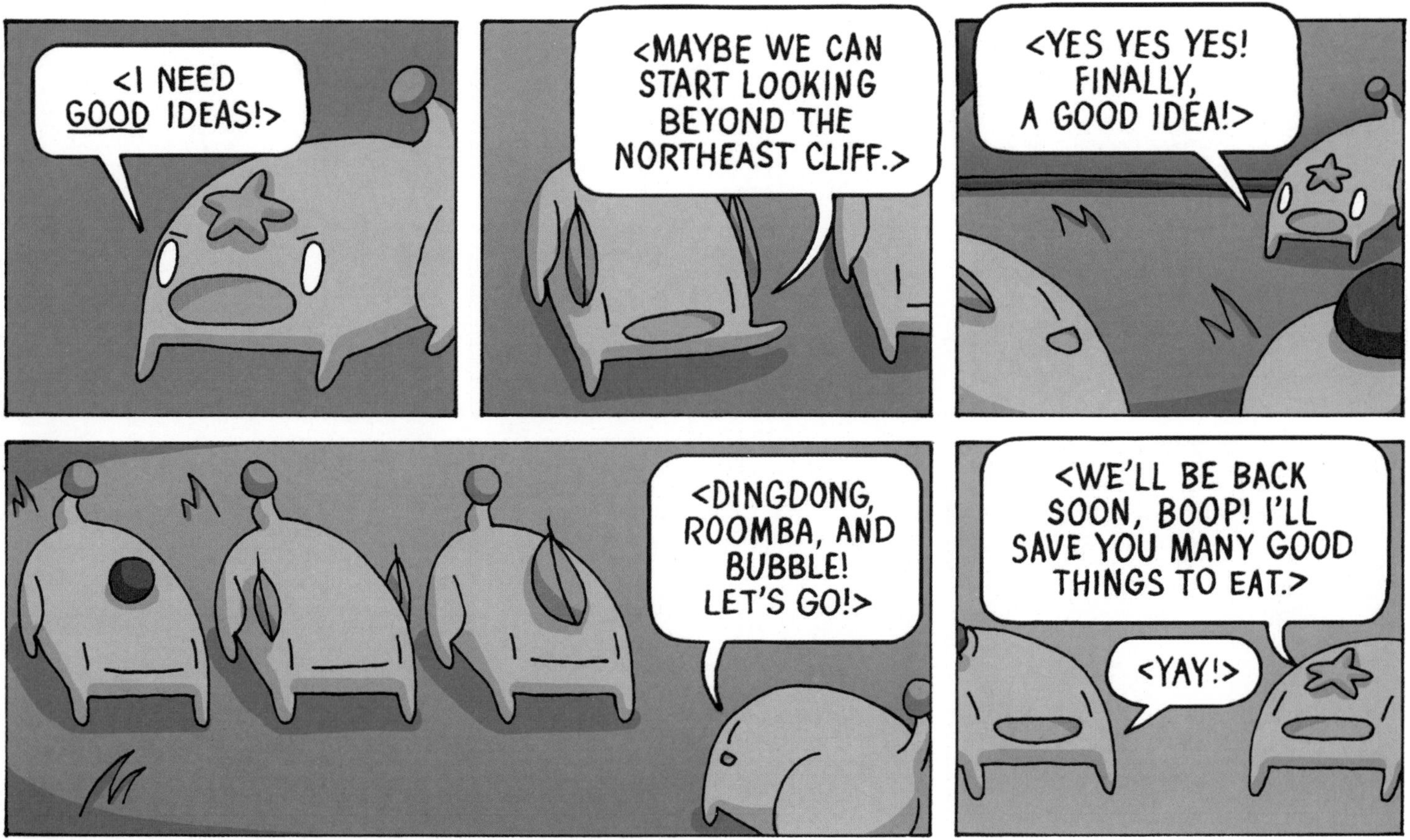
<I NEED GOOD IDEAS!>
<MAYBE WE CAN START LOOKING BEYOND THE NORTHEAST CLIFF.>
<YES YES YES! FINALLY, A GOOD IDEA!>
<DINGDONG, ROOMBA, AND BUBBLE! LET'S GO!>
<WE'LL BE BACK SOON, BOOP! I'LL SAVE YOU MANY GOOD THINGS TO EAT.>
<YAY!>

LEAP
LEAP
BONK
<OOOH!>

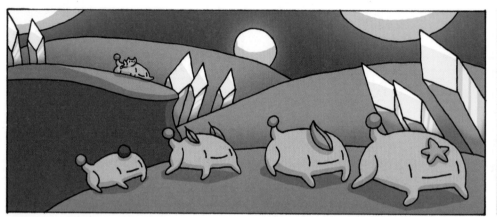

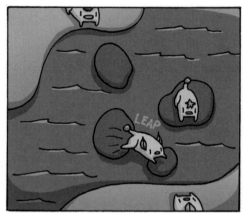

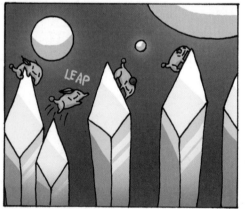

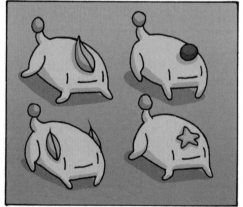

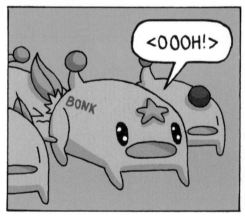

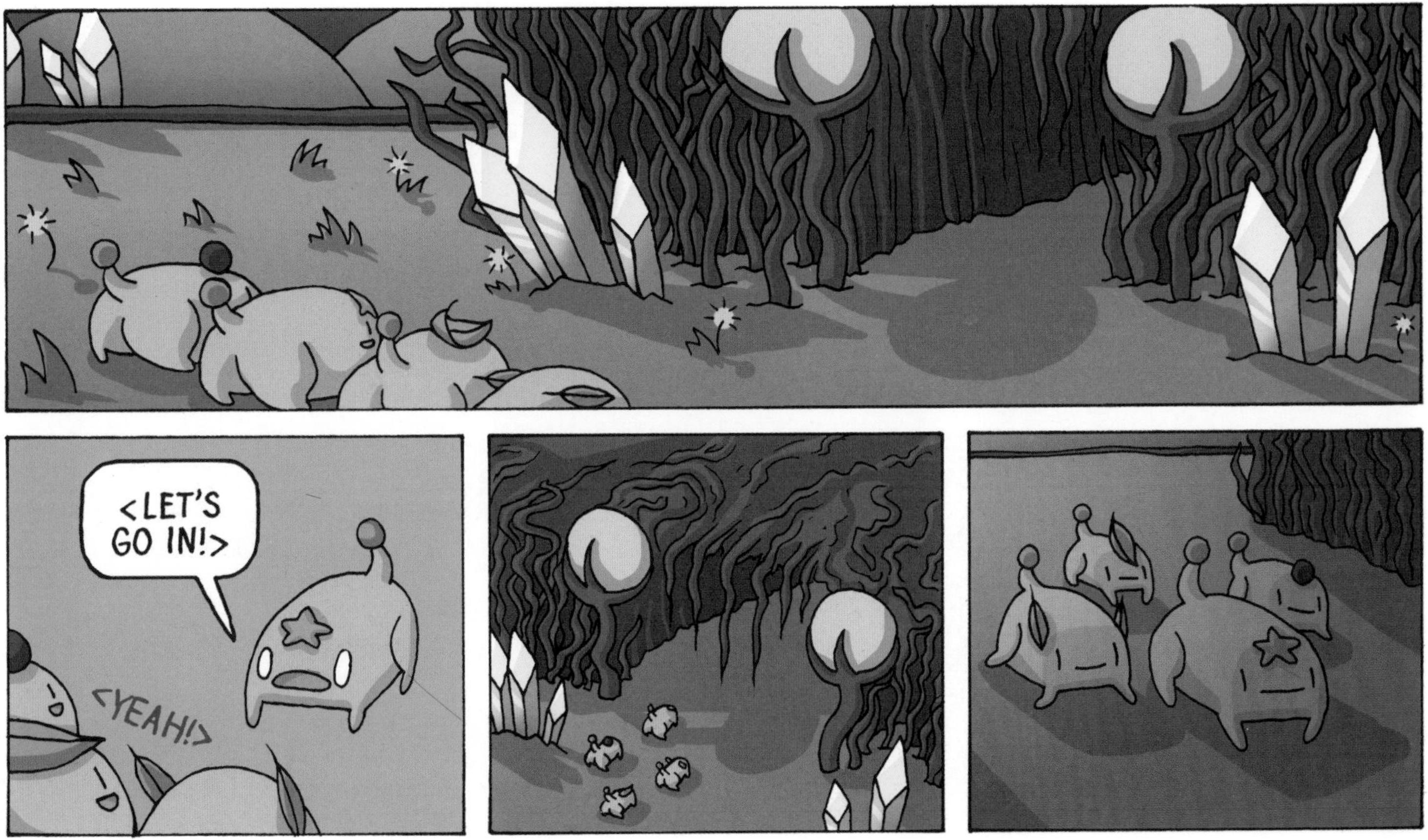
<LET'S GO IN!>
<YEAH!>

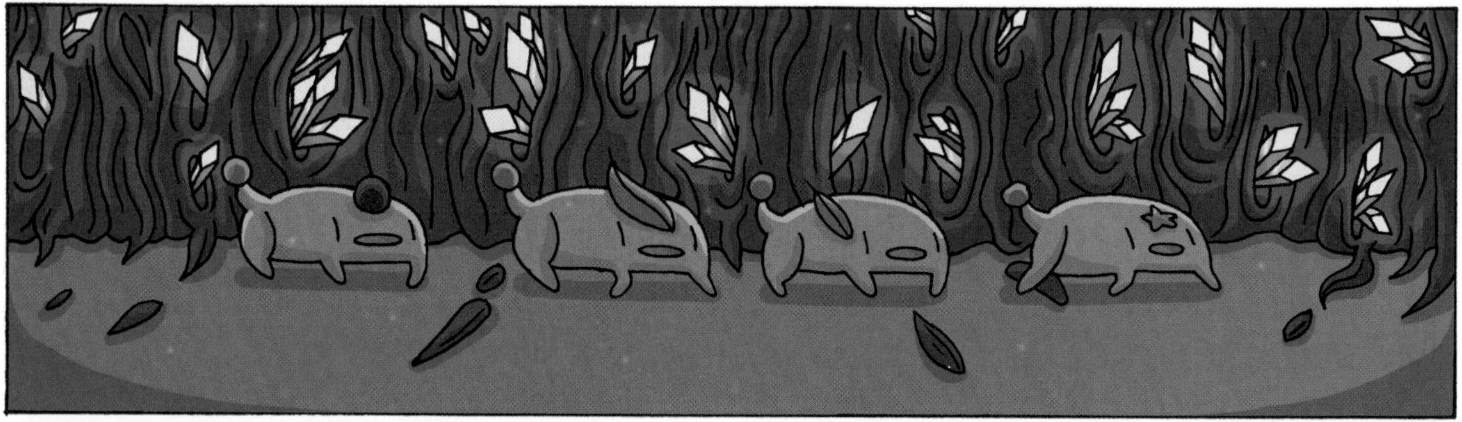

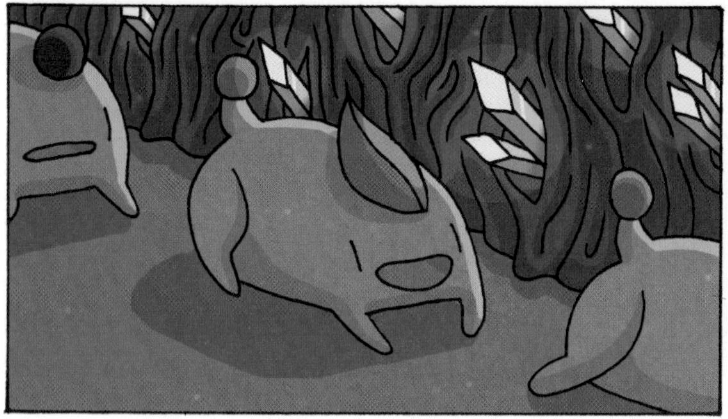

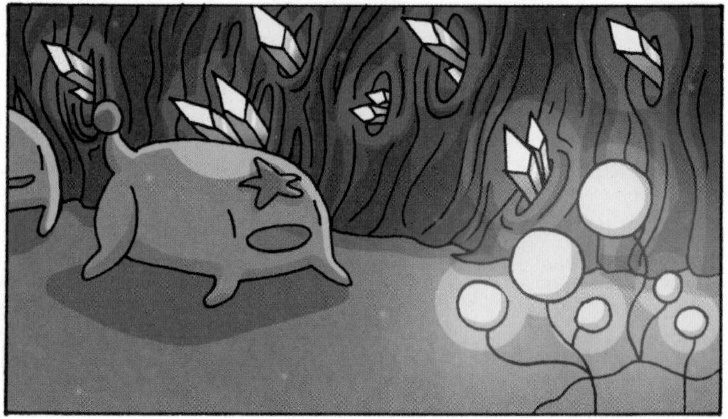

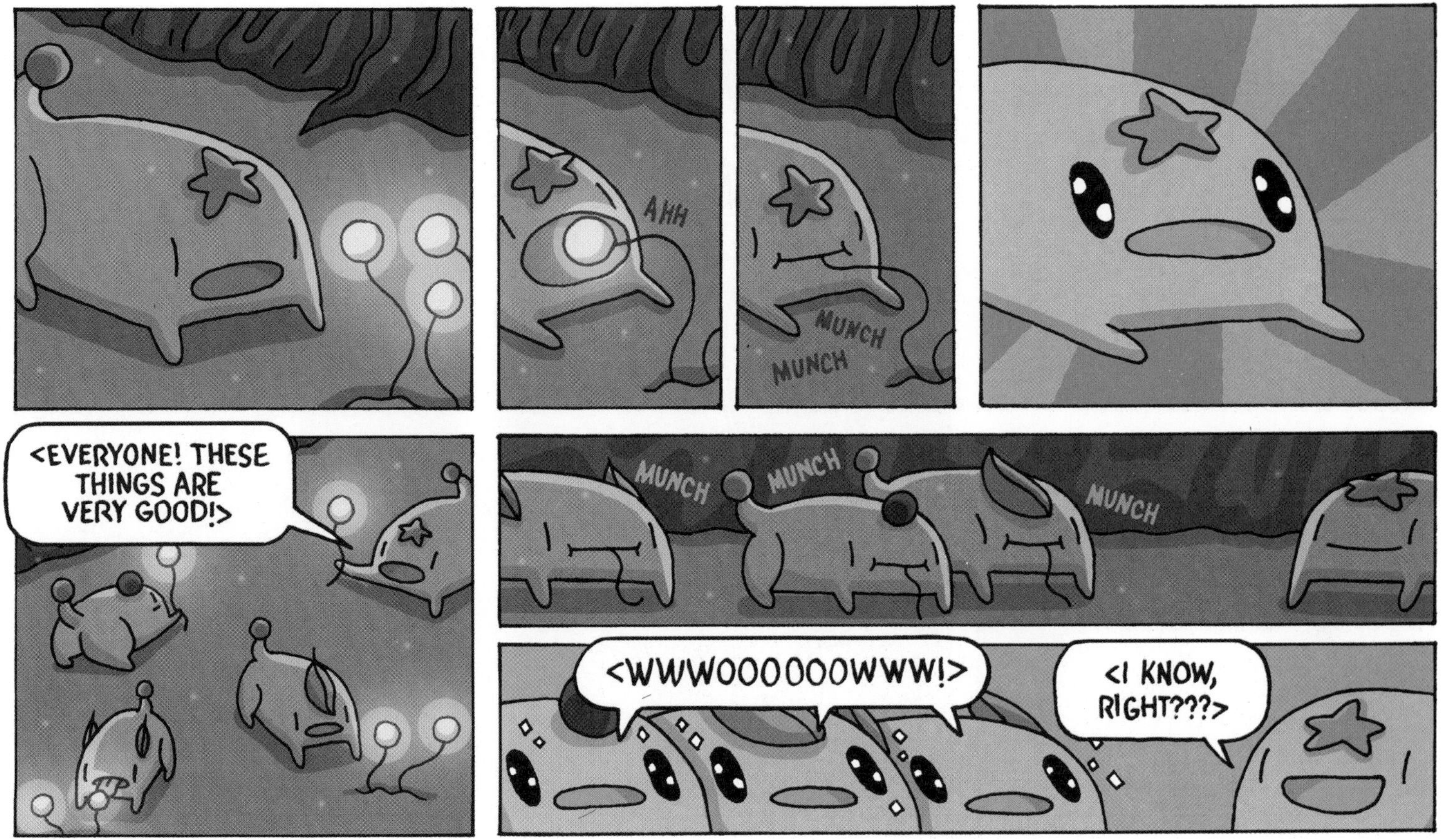
AHH
MUNCH
MUNCH
<EVERYONE! THESE THINGS ARE VERY GOOD!>
MUNCH
MUNCH
MUNCH
<WWWOOOOOOWWW!>
<I KNOW, RIGHT???>

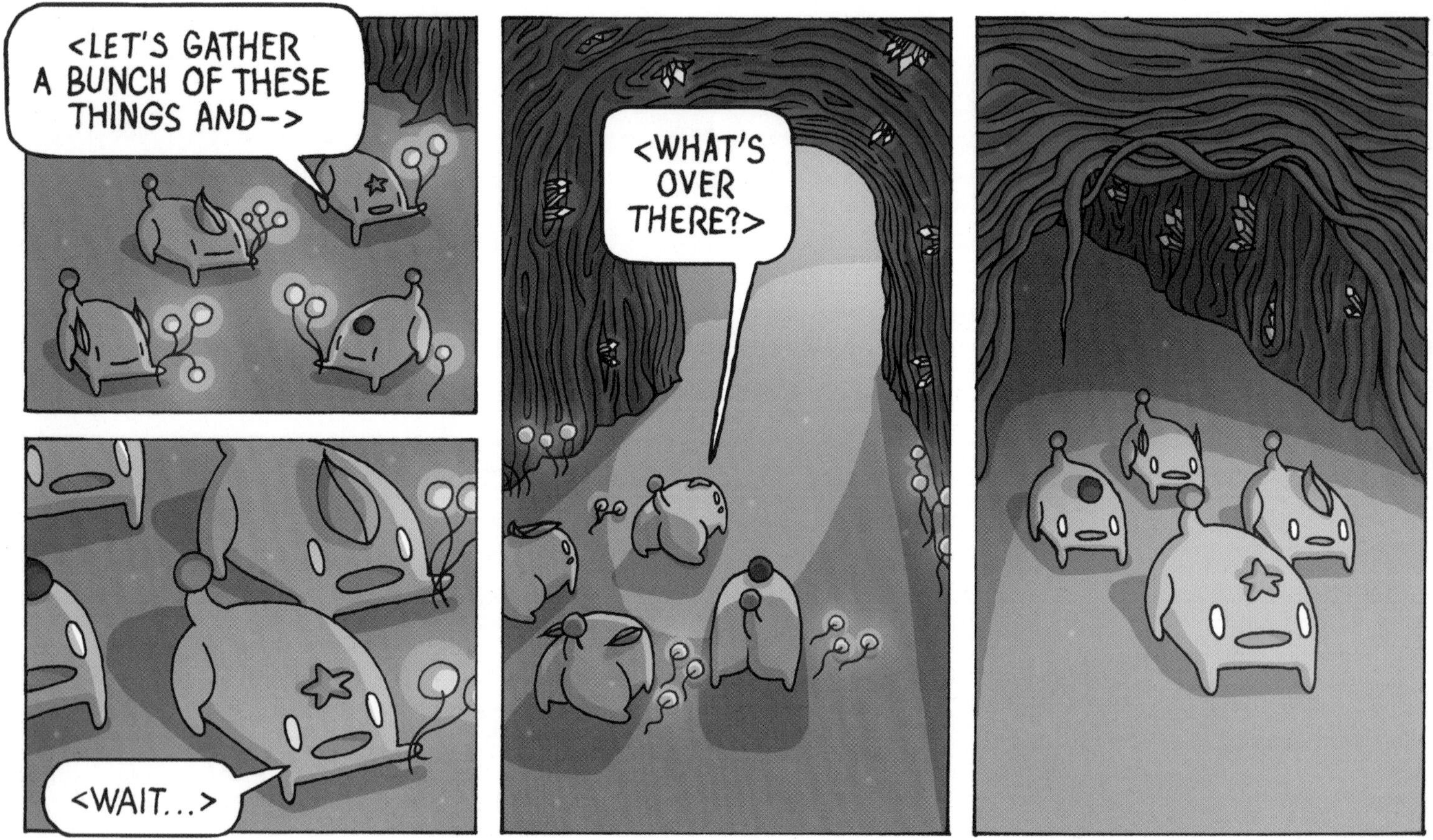
<LET'S GATHER A BUNCH OF THESE THINGS AND->
<WAIT...>
<WHAT'S OVER THERE?>

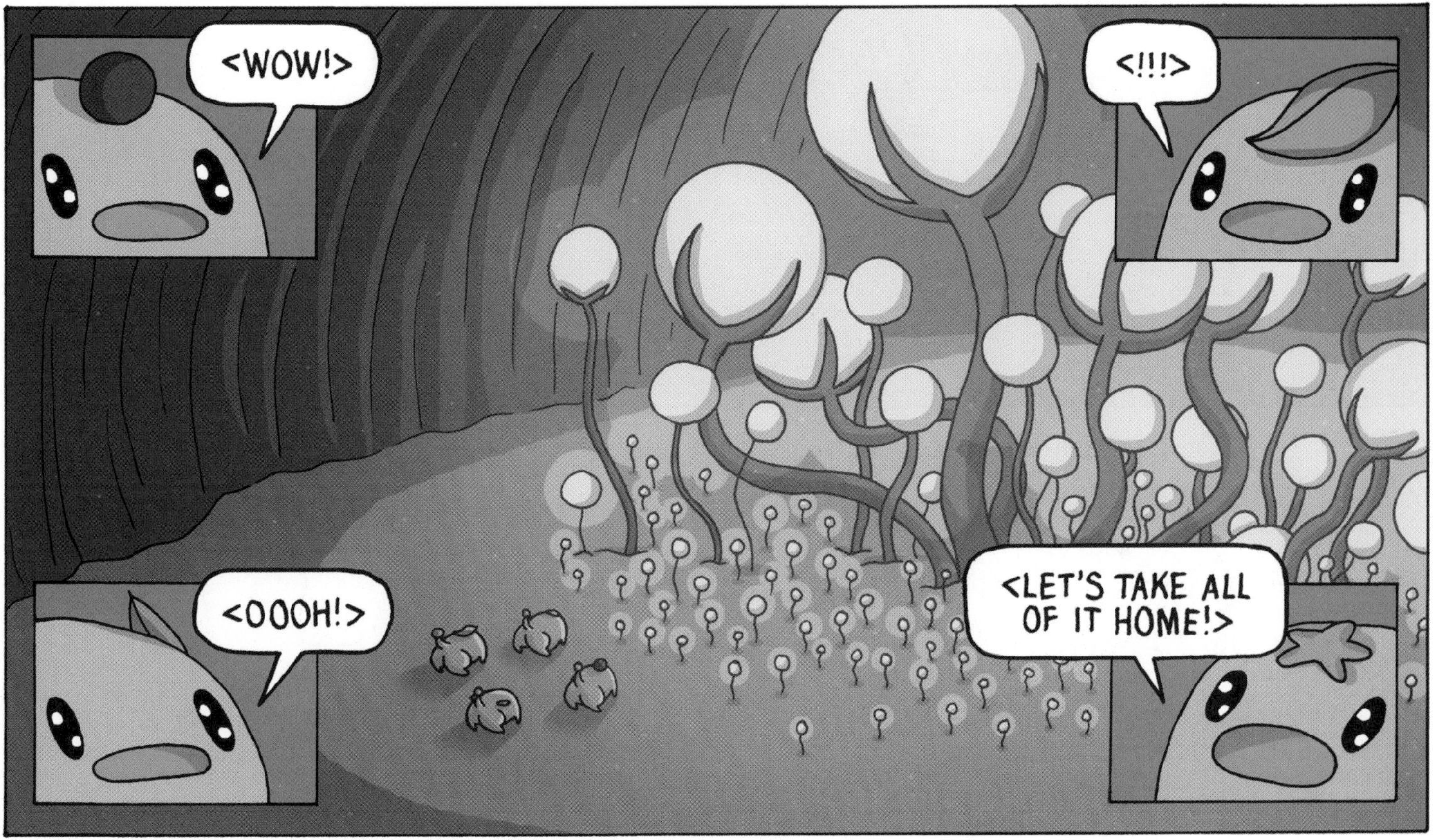
<WOW!>
<!!!>
<OOOH!>
<LET'S TAKE ALL OF IT HOME!>

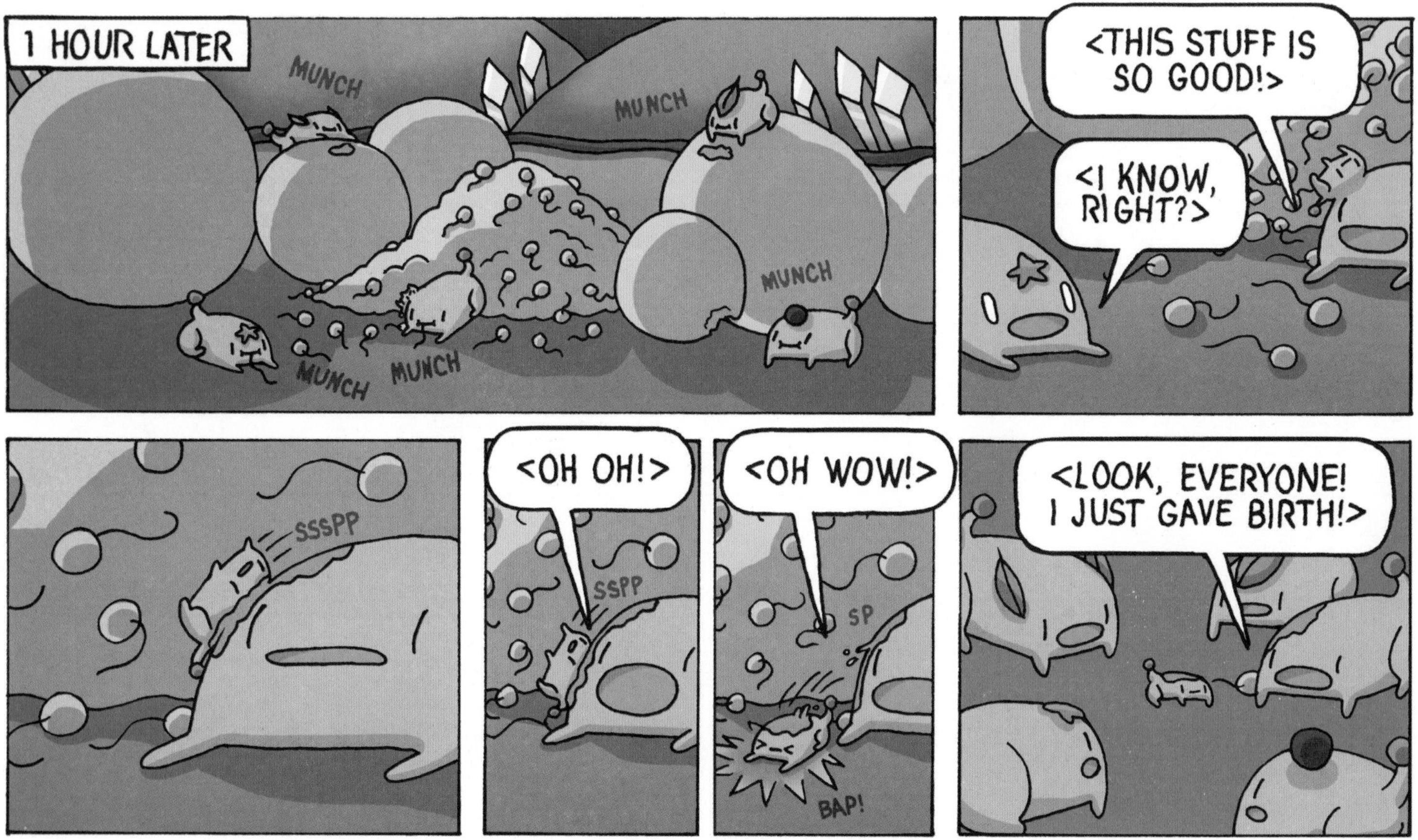
1 HOUR LATER
MUNCH
MUNCH
MUNCH
MUNCH
MUNCH
<THIS STUFF IS SO GOOD!>
<I KNOW, RIGHT?>
SSSPP
<OH OH!>
SSPP
<OH WOW!>
SP
BAP!
<LOOK, EVERYONE! I JUST GAVE BIRTH!>

<WHAT ARE YOU GOING TO DO NOW, LITTLE ONE?>
<I AM GOING TO EXPLORE THE WORLD.>
<ALSO, MY NAME IS GOING TO BE MEEP FROM NOW ON.>
<OKAY!>
DOOT
<GOODBYE!>
<SIGH. THIS IS NICE.>
END.

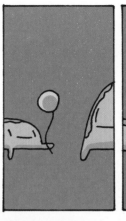

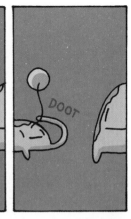

CHAPTER ELEVEN

—

BUBBLE HAS A VISION

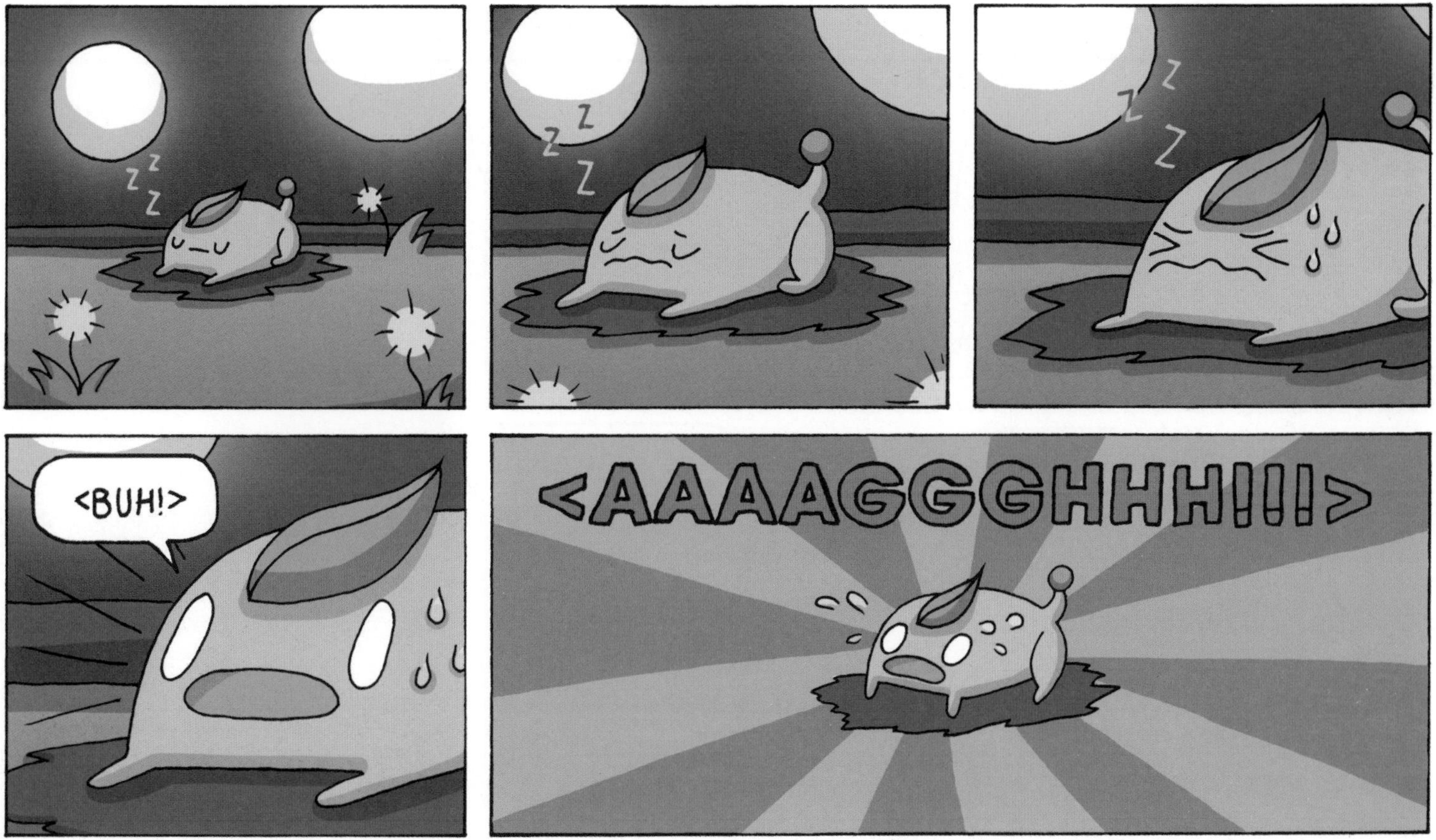

Z Z Z
Z Z Z
Z Z Z
<BUH!>
<AAAAGGGHHH!!!>

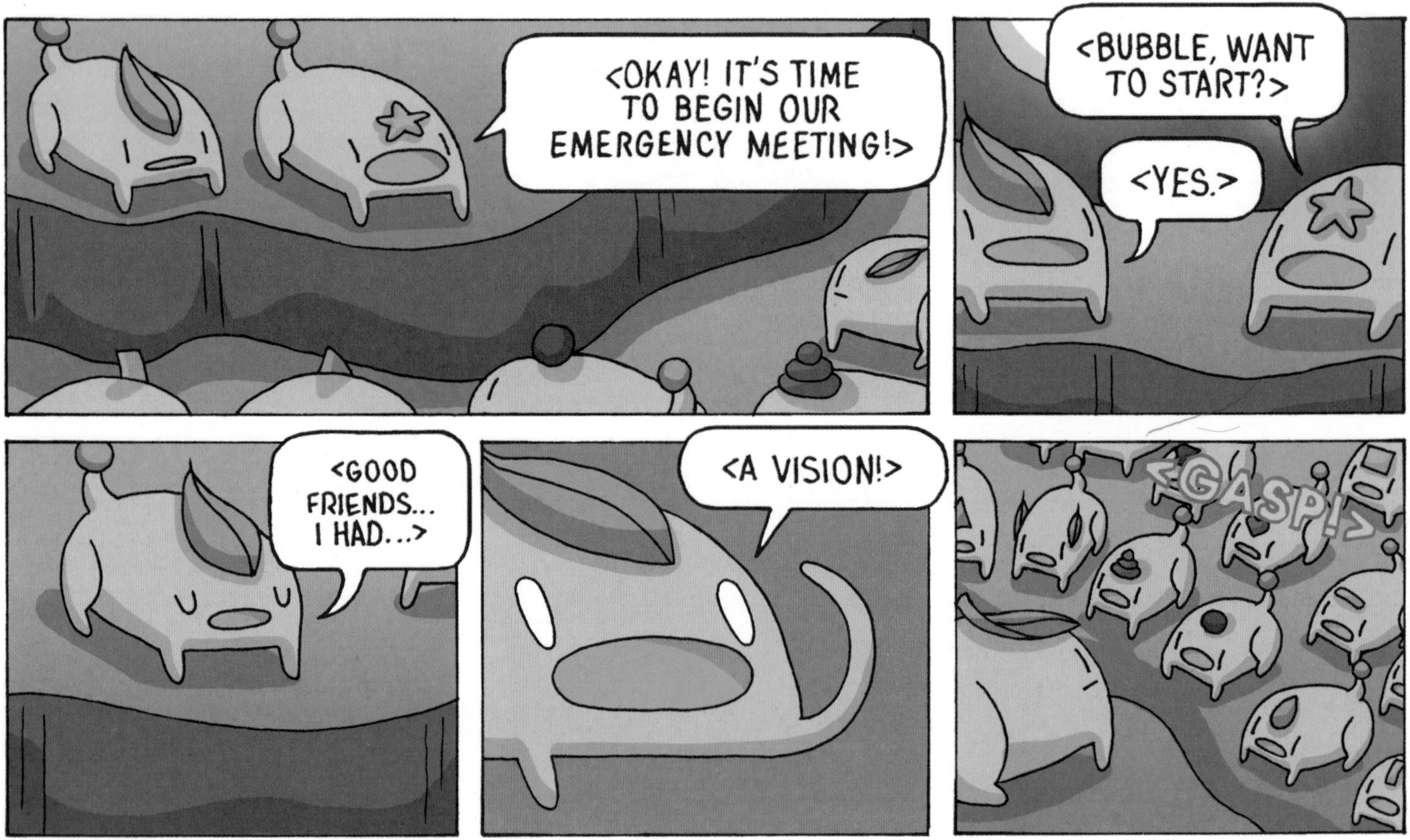
<OKAY! IT'S TIME TO BEGIN OUR EMERGENCY MEETING!>
<BUBBLE, WANT TO START?>
<YES.>
<GOOD FRIENDS... I HAD...>
<A VISION!>
<GASP!>

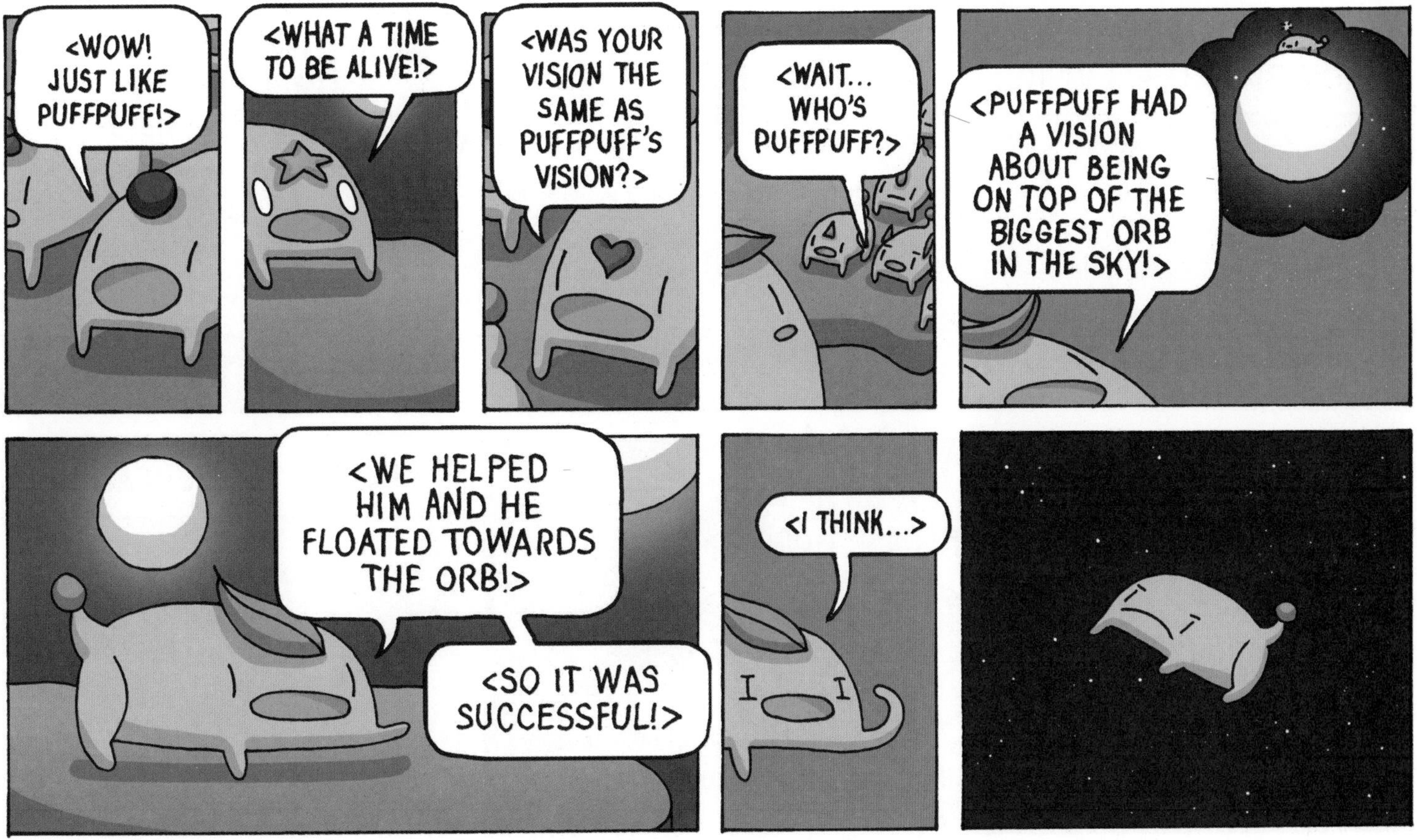
<WOW! JUST LIKE PUFFPUFF!>
<WHAT A TIME TO BE ALIVE!>
<WAS YOUR VISION THE SAME AS PUFFPUFF'S VISION?>
<WAIT... WHO'S PUFFPUFF?>
<PUFFPUFF HAD A VISION ABOUT BEING ON TOP OF THE BIGGEST ORB IN THE SKY!>
<WE HELPED HIM AND HE FLOATED TOWARDS THE ORB!>
<SO IT WAS SUCCESSFUL!>
<I THINK...>

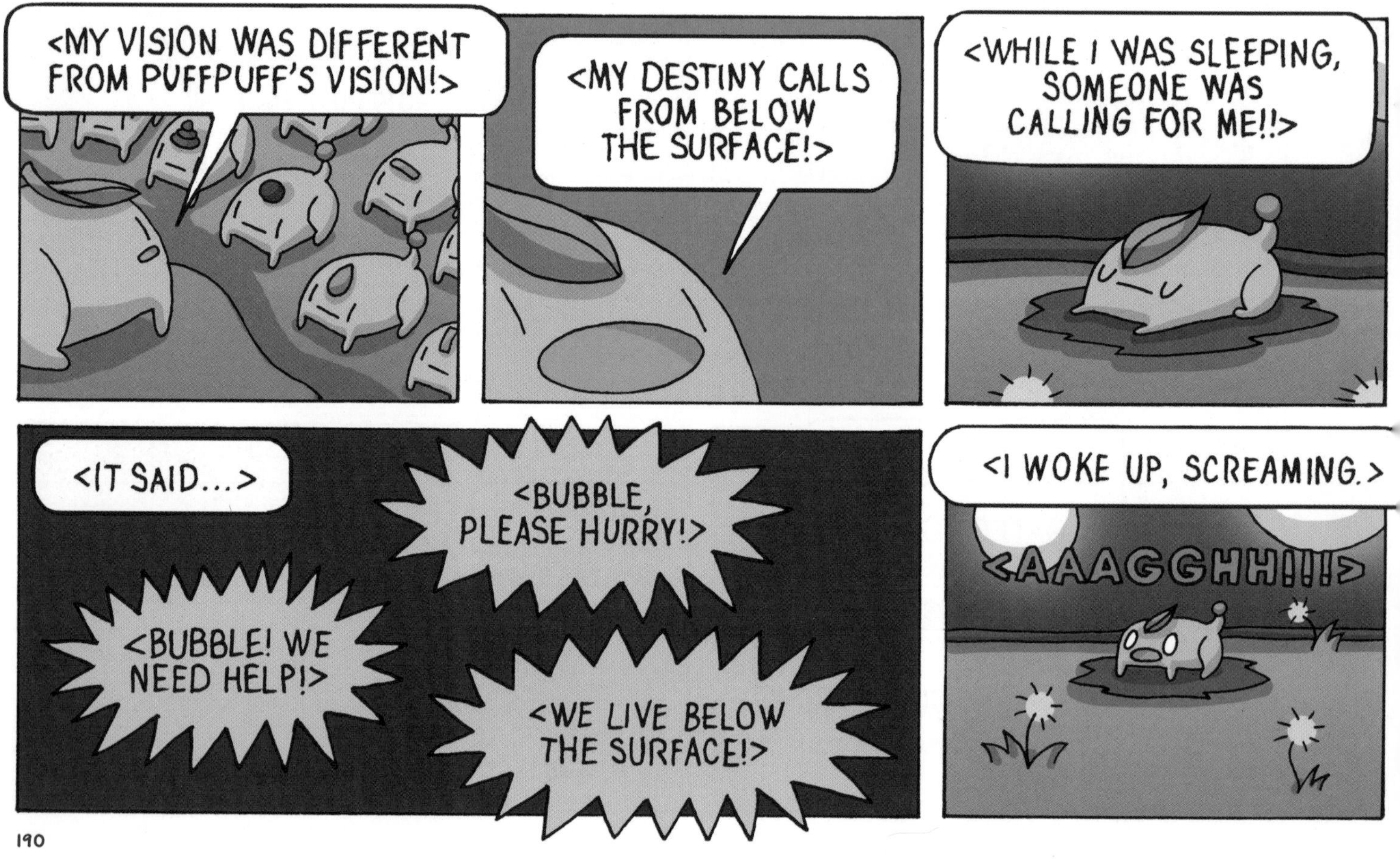

<MY VISION WAS DIFFERENT FROM PUFFPUFF'S VISION!>
<MY DESTINY CALLS FROM BELOW THE SURFACE!>
<WHILE I WAS SLEEPING, SOMEONE WAS CALLING FOR ME!!>
<IT SAID...>
<BUBBLE, PLEASE HURRY!>
<BUBBLE! WE NEED HELP!>
<WE LIVE BELOW THE SURFACE!>
<I WOKE UP, SCREAMING.>
<AAAGGHH!!!!>

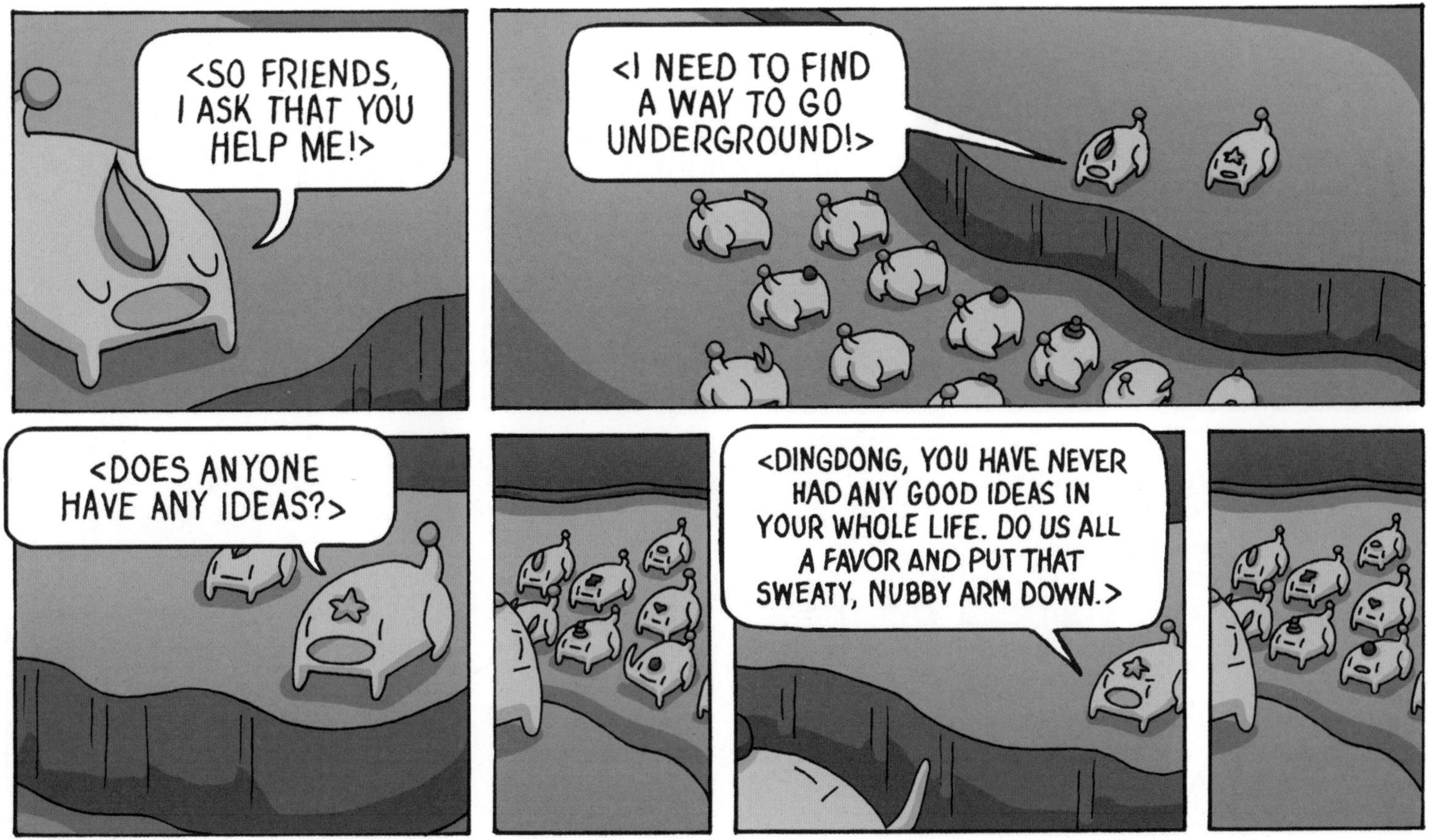
<SO FRIENDS, I ASK THAT YOU HELP ME!>
<I NEED TO FIND A WAY TO GO UNDERGROUND!>
<DOES ANYONE HAVE ANY IDEAS?>
<DINGDONG, YOU HAVE NEVER HAD ANY GOOD IDEAS IN YOUR WHOLE LIFE. DO US ALL A FAVOR AND PUT THAT SWEATY, NUBBY ARM DOWN.>

<YES?>

<I FOUND A DARK, SCARY CAVE THE OTHER DAY. I THINK IT GOES UNDERGROUND.>

<THAT IS A VERY GOOD IDEA!>

<INDEED!>

<LEAD US THERE, PLEASE!>

<OKAY!>

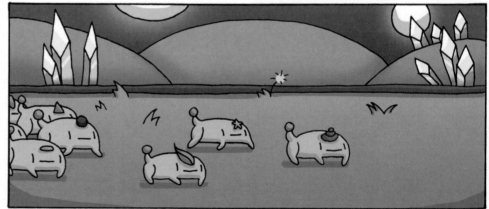

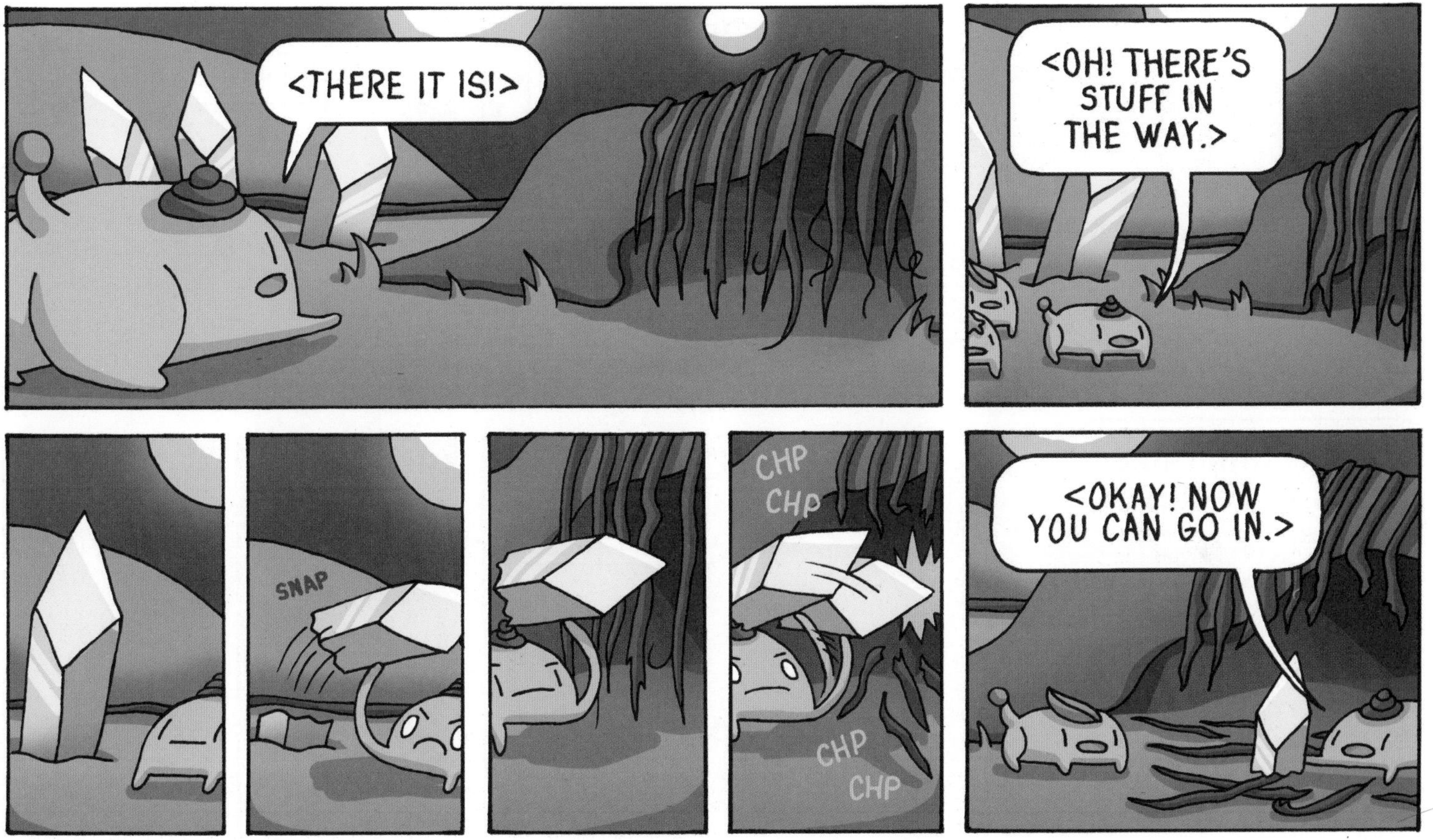

<THERE IT IS!>
<OH! THERE'S STUFF IN THE WAY.>
SNAP
CHP CHP
CHP CHP
<OKAY! NOW YOU CAN GO IN.>

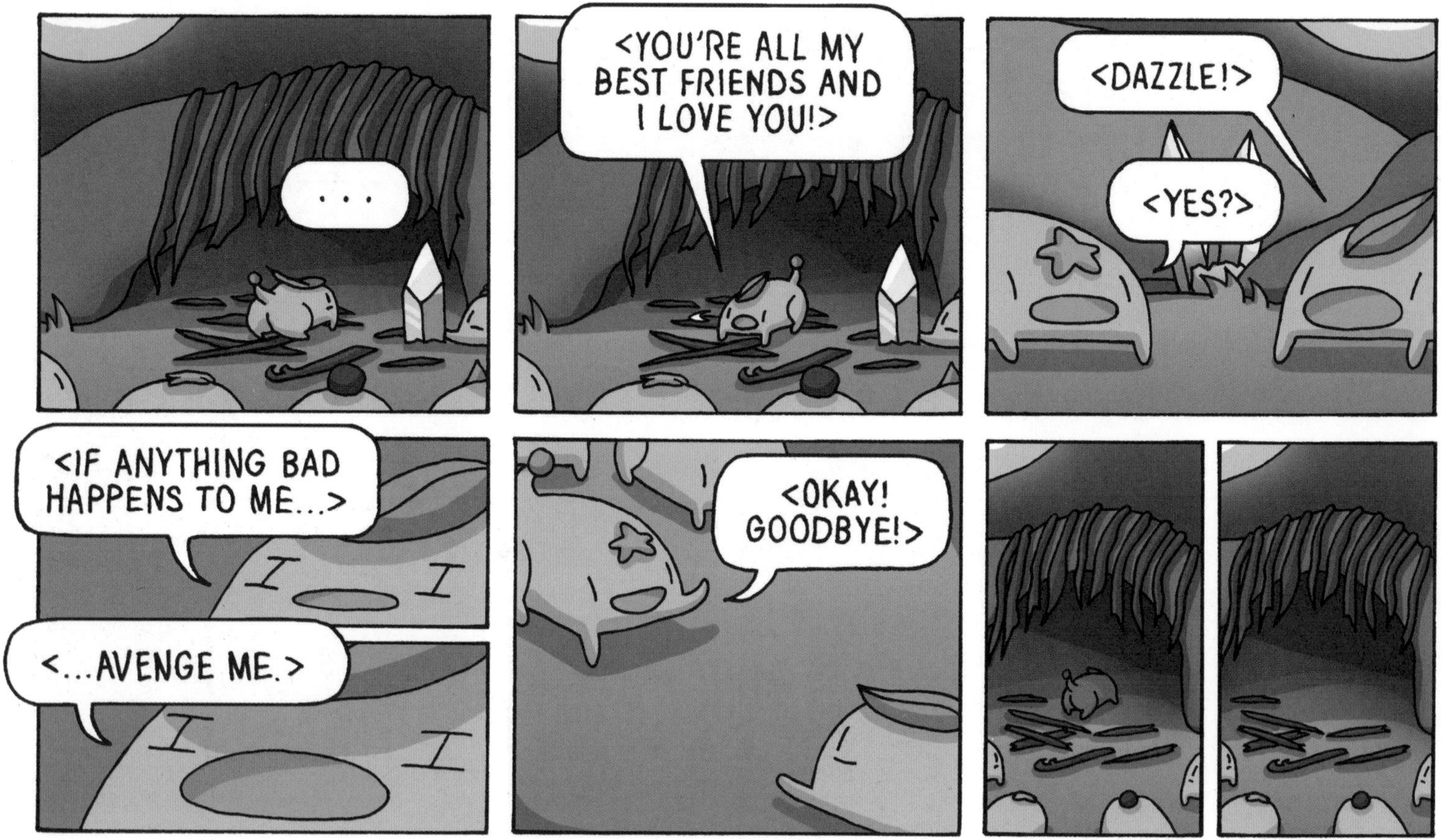
...
<YOU'RE ALL MY BEST FRIENDS AND I LOVE YOU!>
<DAZZLE!>
<YES?>
<IF ANYTHING BAD HAPPENS TO ME...>
<...AVENGE ME.>
<OKAY! GOODBYE!>

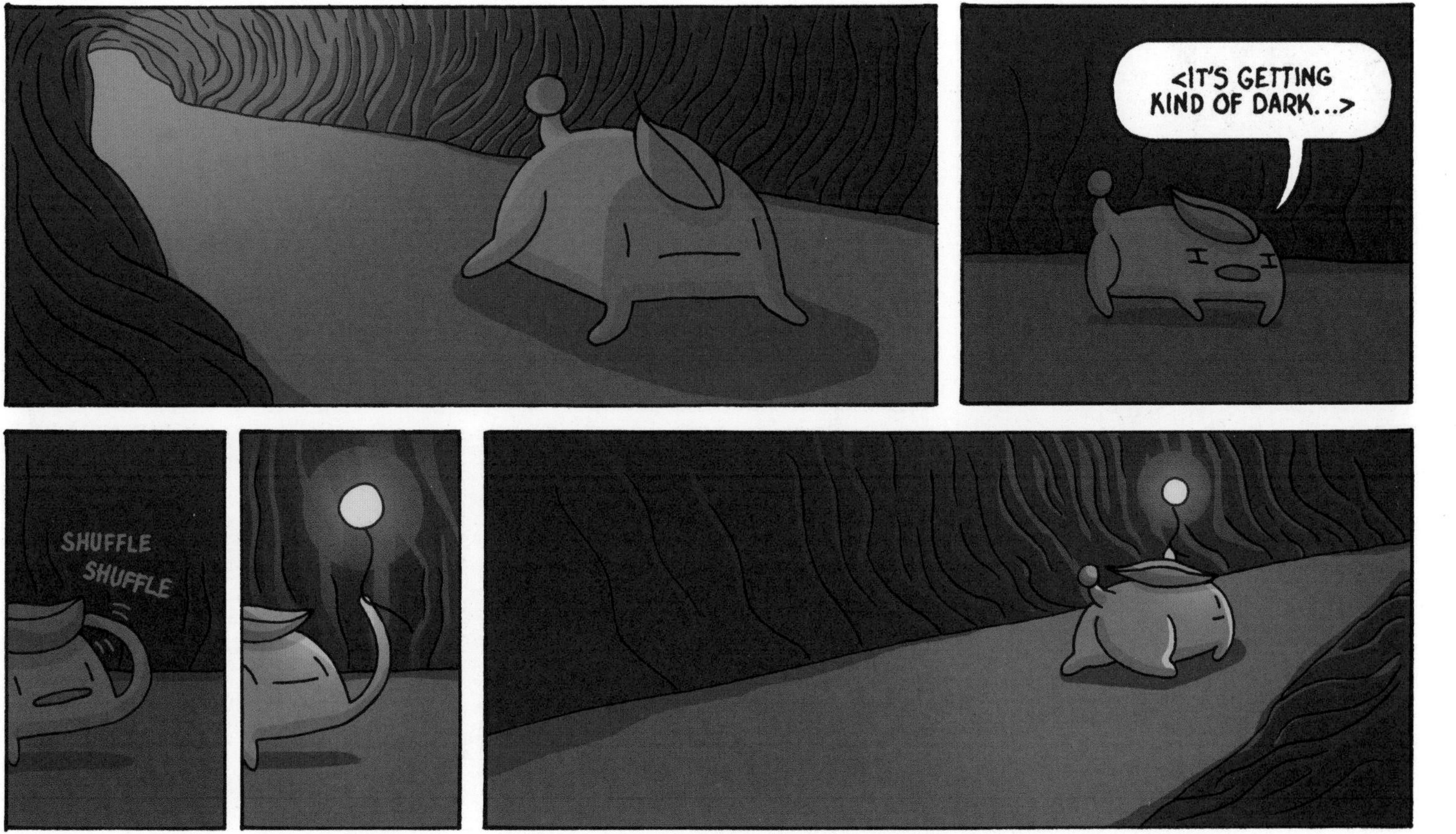
<IT'S GETTING KIND OF DARK...>
SHUFFLE
SHUFFLE

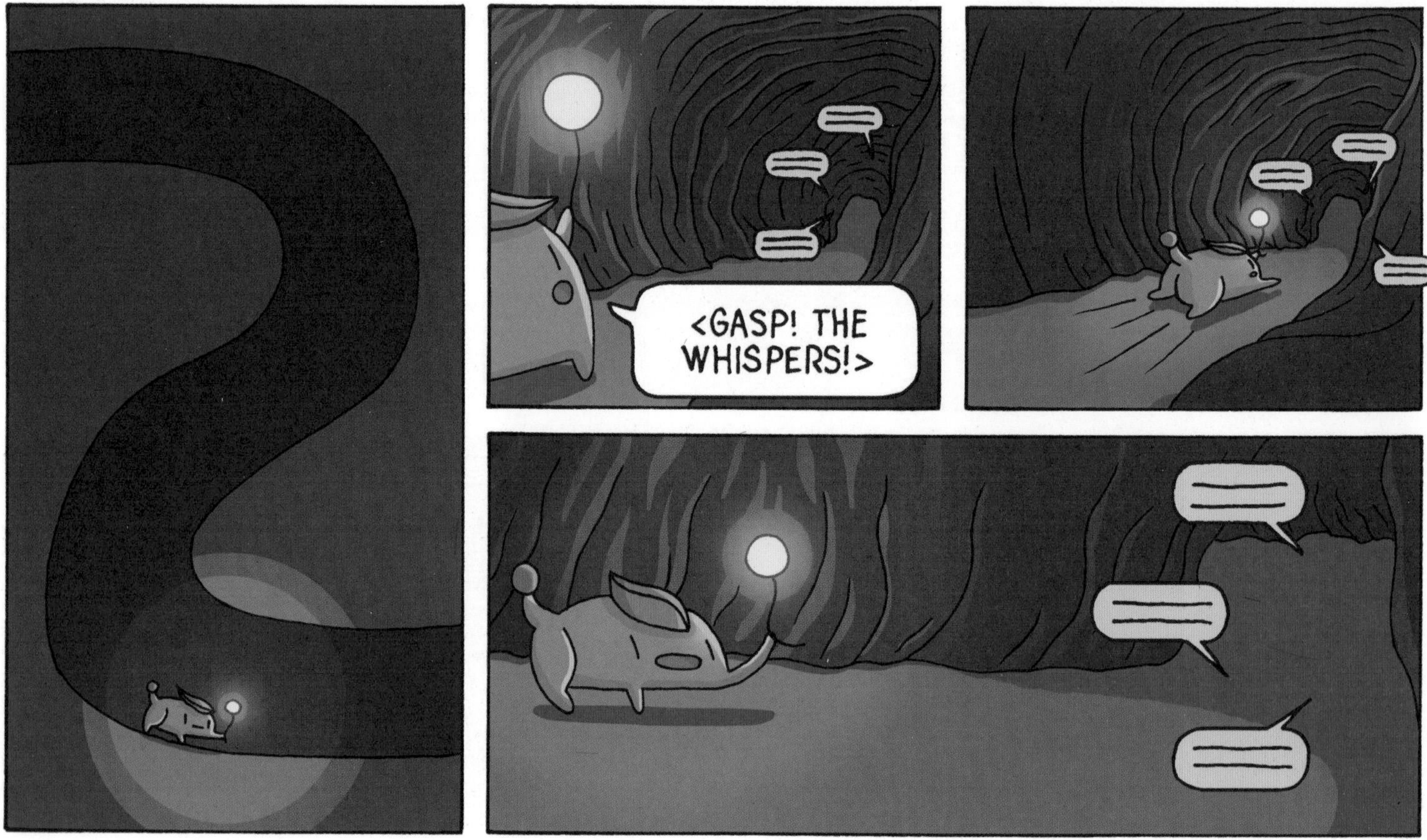
<GASP! THE WHISPERS!>

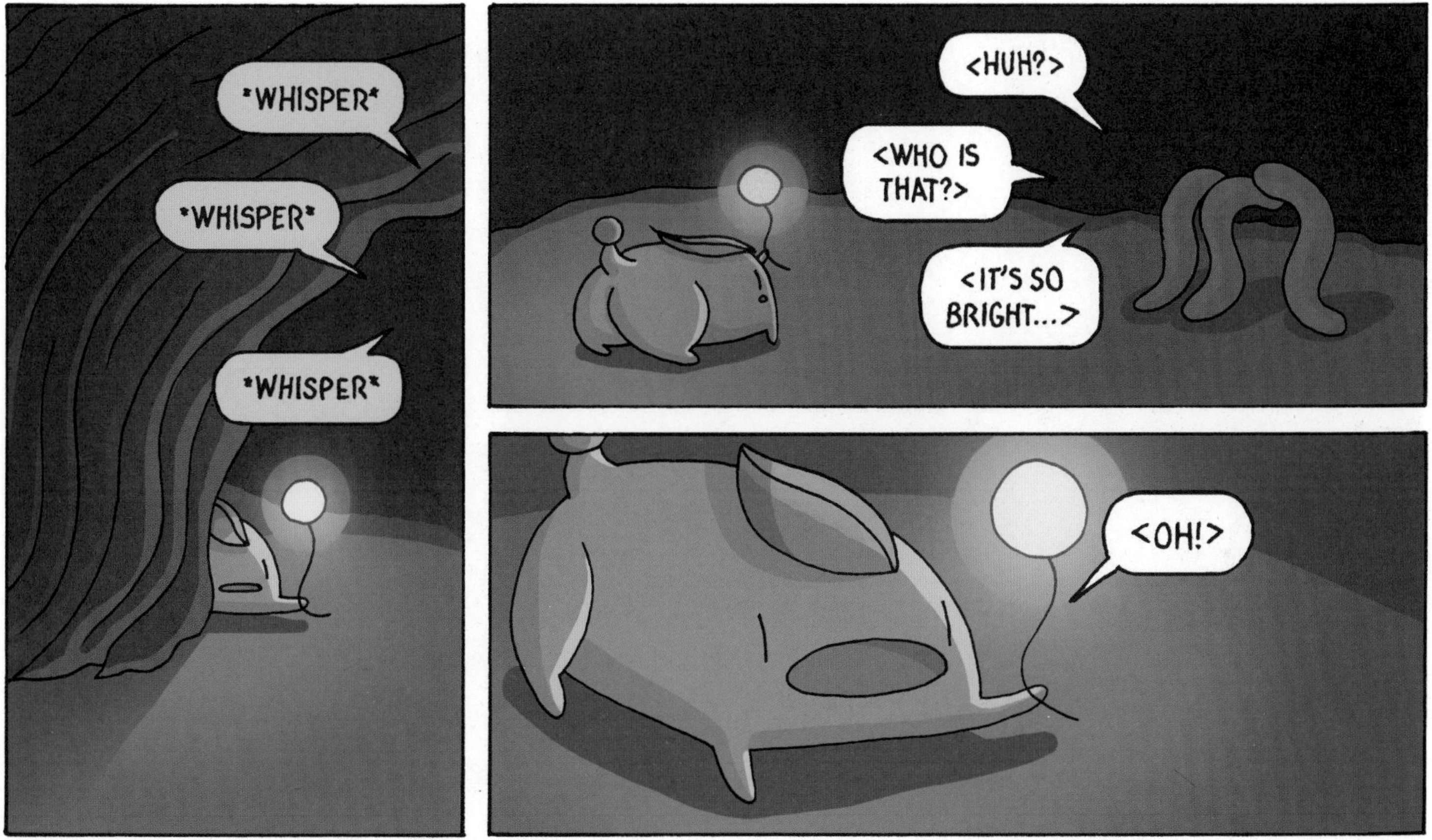
WHISPER
WHISPER
WHISPER
<HUH?>
<WHO IS THAT?>
<IT'S SO BRIGHT...>
<OH!>

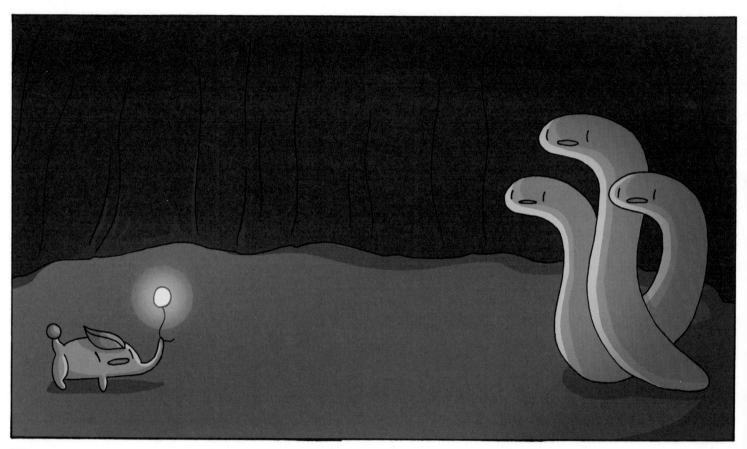

<HELLO! MY NAME IS->
<AAGGHH!!!>
<YOU'RE ONE OF THOSE THINGS!>
<A CREATURE MOST FOUL!>
<MOST FOUL!>
HHSSS
<HUH? WHY WOULD YOU SAY THAT? I'M CUTE, SMALL, AND NICE!>

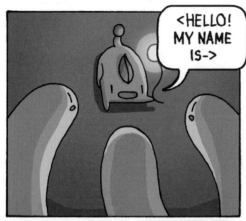

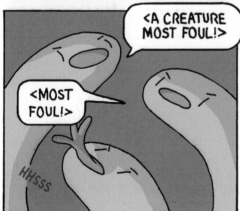

<WAIT, YOU DON'T KNOW WHAT HAPPENED?>
<NO.>
SIGH
<I WILL EXPLAIN.>
<WE USED TO LIVE PEACEFULLY ON THE SURFACE.>
<THEN YOU SHOWED UP.>
<IT WAS FINE AT FIRST.>
<...BUT THEN, SOMETHING ABOUT YOU MADE US SICK!>
<THERE WAS NOTHING WE COULD DO, SO WE MOVED BELOW THE SURFACE.>

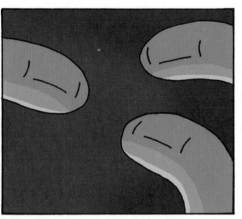

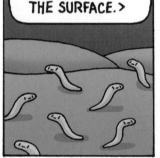

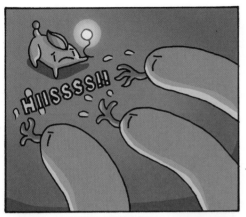

HIISSSSS!!

<I'M SORRY. I'M SURE WE DIDN'T MEAN TO DO THAT.>

<MAYBE YOU'RE ALLERGIC TO US.>

<MAYBE.>

<IS IT HARD LIVING HERE?>

<NO.>

<NOT REALLY.>

<IT'S EASY.>

<WE EVOLVED SO NOW WE CAN SEE IN THE DARK.>

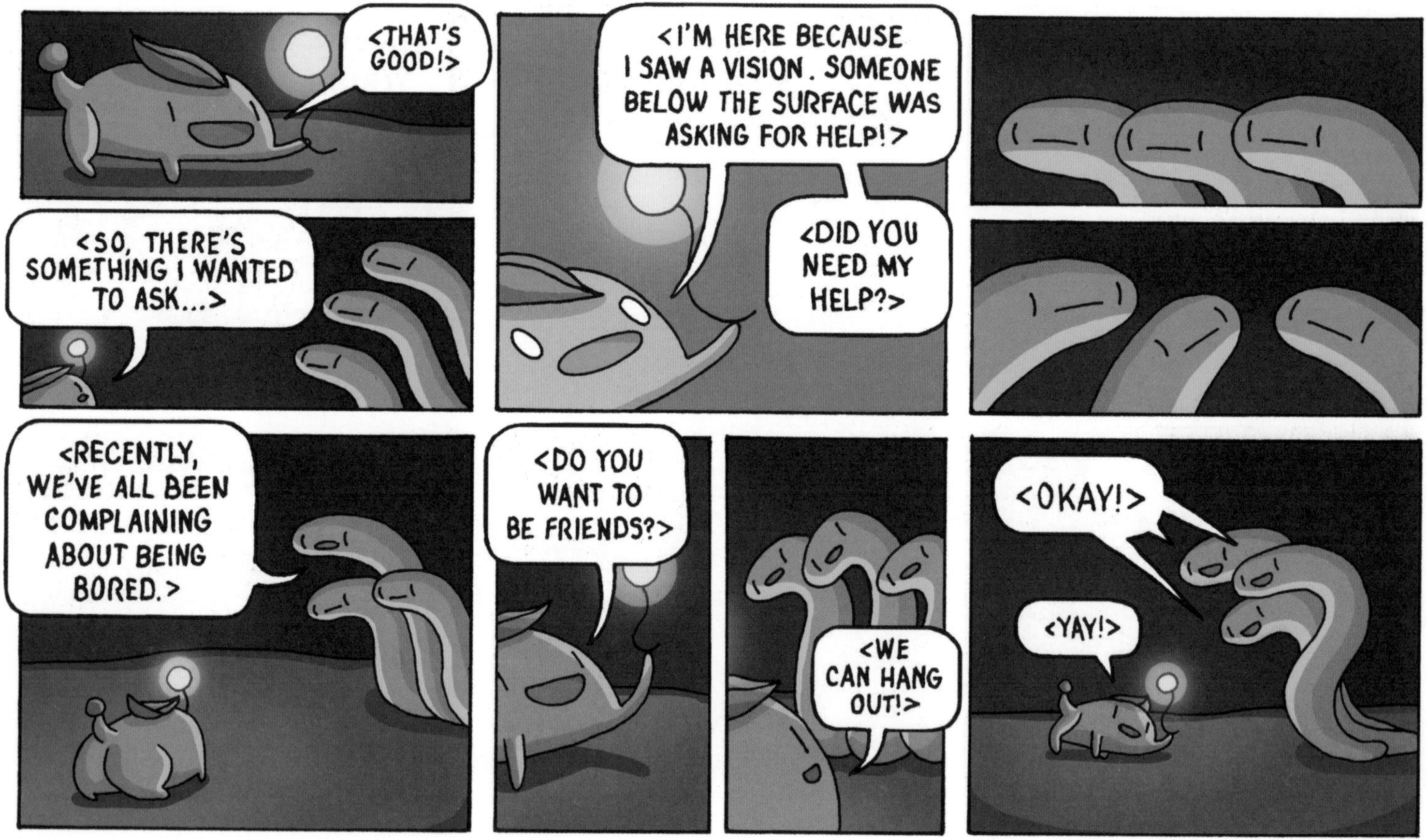
<THAT'S GOOD!>
<SO, THERE'S SOMETHING I WANTED TO ASK...>
<I'M HERE BECAUSE I SAW A VISION. SOMEONE BELOW THE SURFACE WAS ASKING FOR HELP!>
<DID YOU NEED MY HELP?>
<RECENTLY, WE'VE ALL BEEN COMPLAINING ABOUT BEING BORED.>
<DO YOU WANT TO BE FRIENDS?>
<WE CAN HANG OUT!>
<OKAY!>
<YAY!>

<LET'S START OVER. MY NAME IS BUBBLE!>
<MY NAME IS HISS HISS!>
I'M HISSSS-SSSSSSSS!>
I AM HISSSSSS HISS HISS HISSS!>
<IT'S NICE TO MEET YOU!>
<ANYWAY, I NEED TO GO BACK.>
<OKAY!>
<IT'S ALMOST MY BEDTIME.>
<BEFORE YOU GO, I WANT TO SAY SOMETHING.>
<DON'T BRING ANYONE ELSE. YOU CAN VISIT ANYTIME, BUT ALWAYS COME ALONE...>

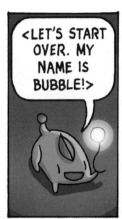

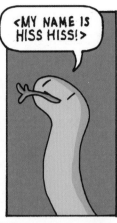

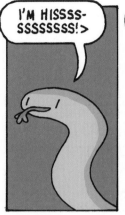

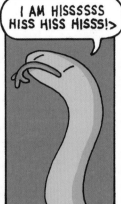

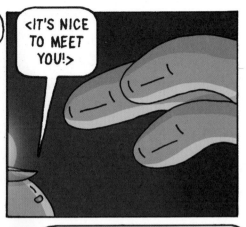

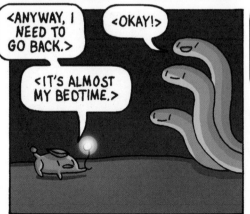

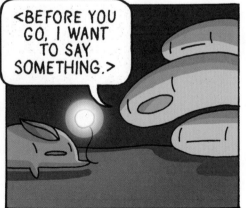

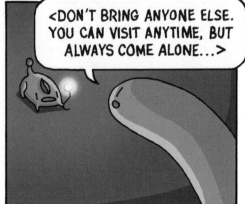

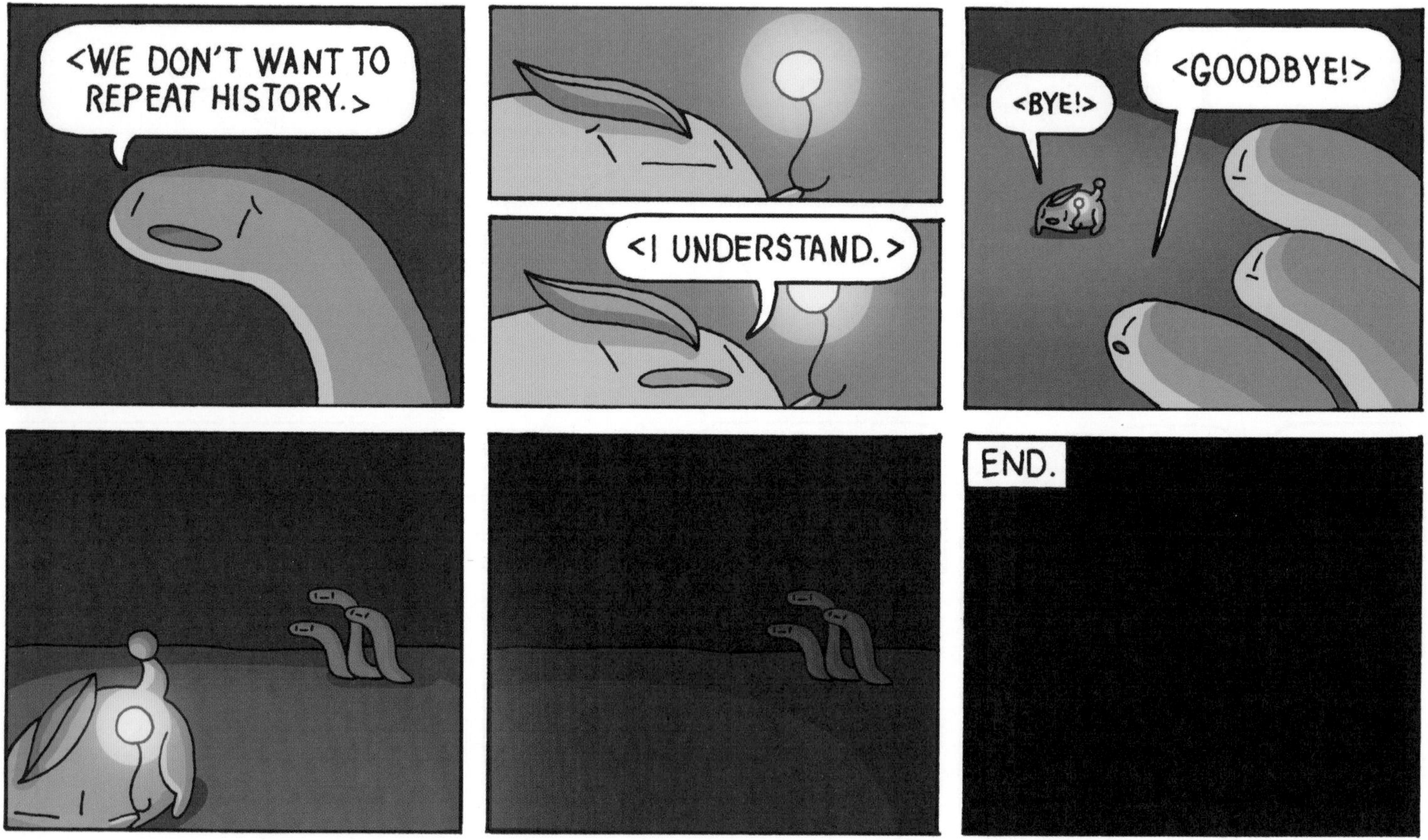
<WE DON'T WANT TO REPEAT HISTORY.>
<I UNDERSTAND.>
<BYE!>
<GOODBYE!>
END.

CHAPTER TWELVE

—

PUFFPUFF'S JOURNEY

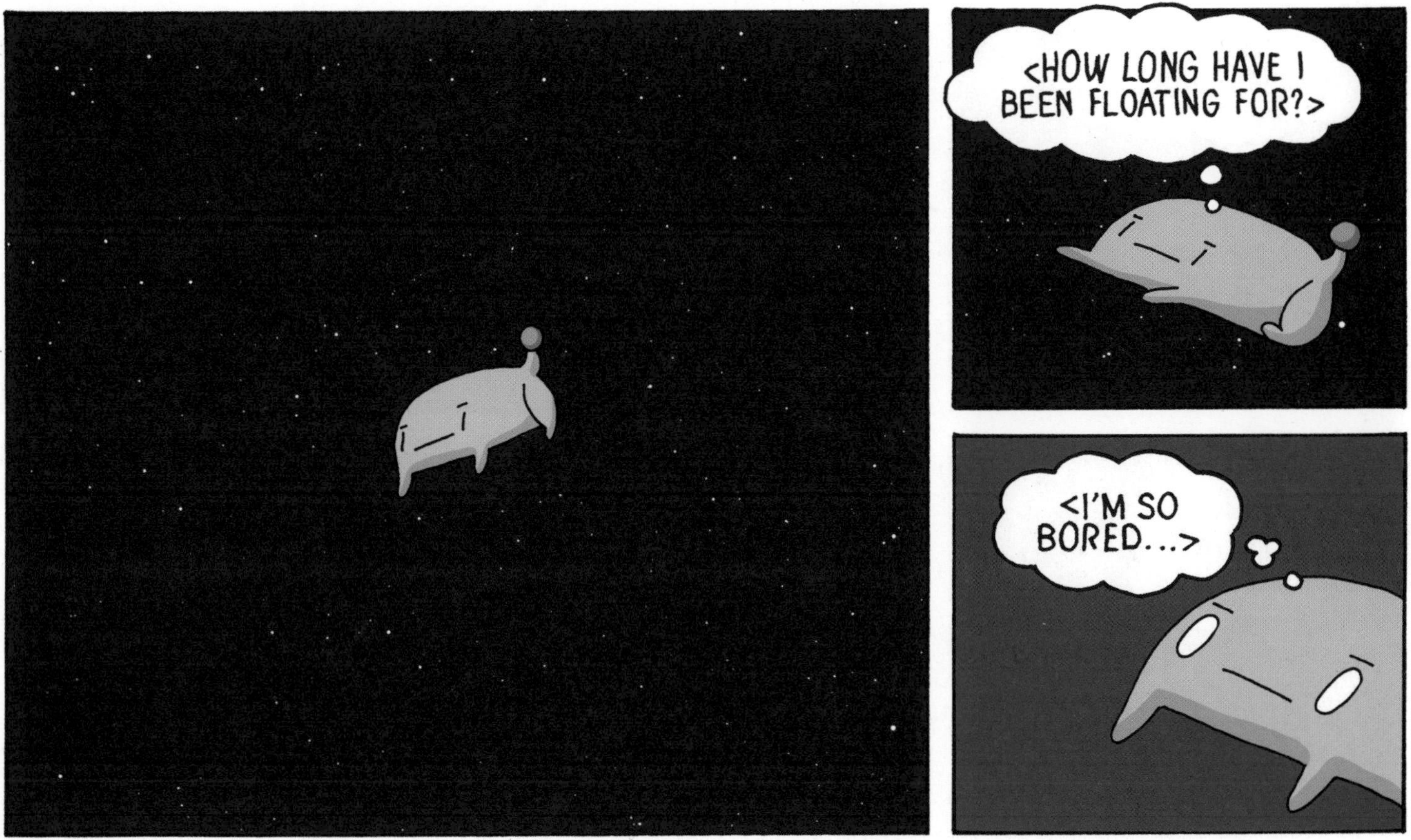
<HOW LONG HAVE I BEEN FLOATING FOR?>
<I'M SO BORED...>

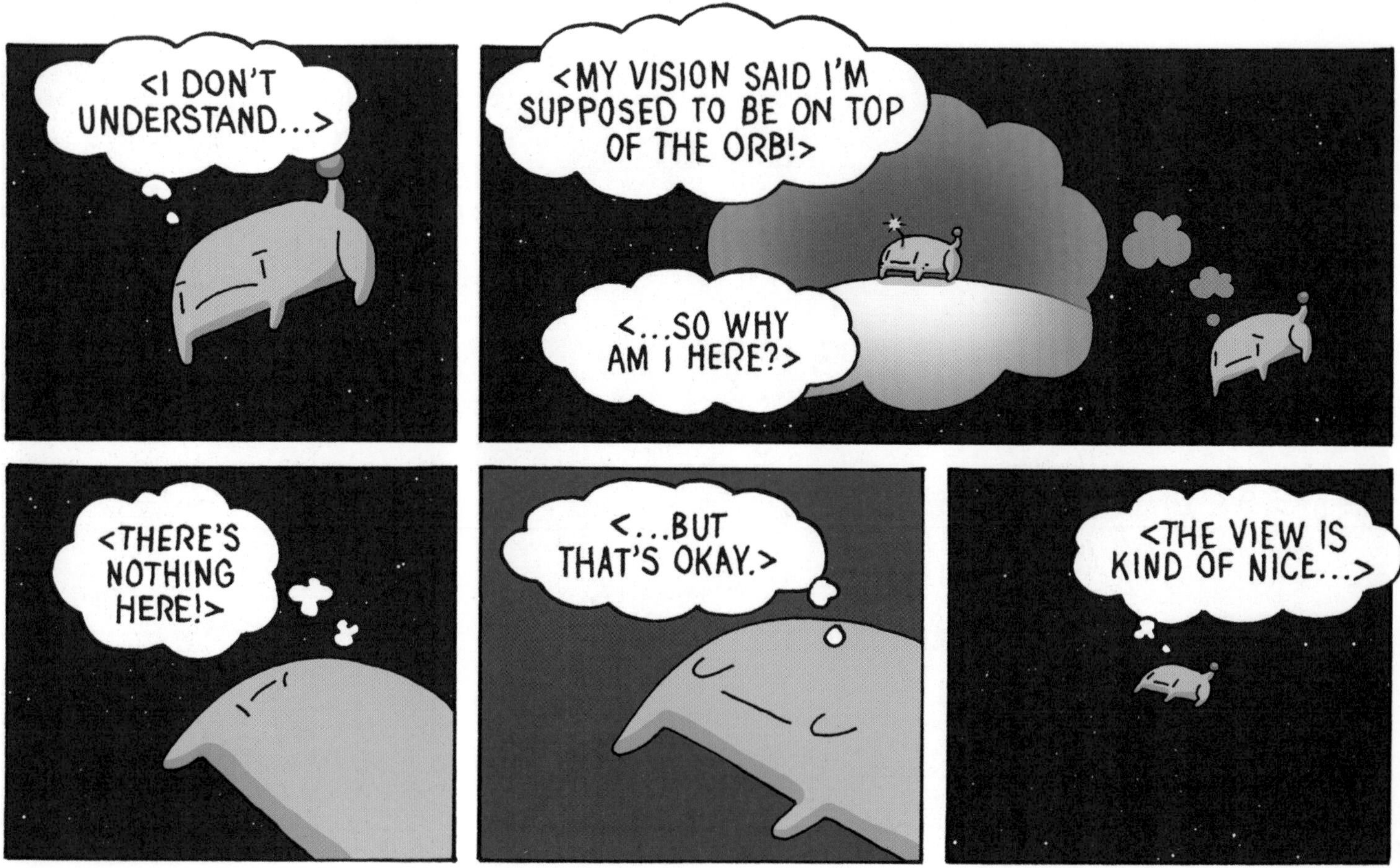
<I DON'T UNDERSTAND...>
<MY VISION SAID I'M SUPPOSED TO BE ON TOP OF THE ORB!>
<...SO WHY AM I HERE?>
<THERE'S NOTHING HERE!>
<...BUT THAT'S OKAY.>
<THE VIEW IS KIND OF NICE...>

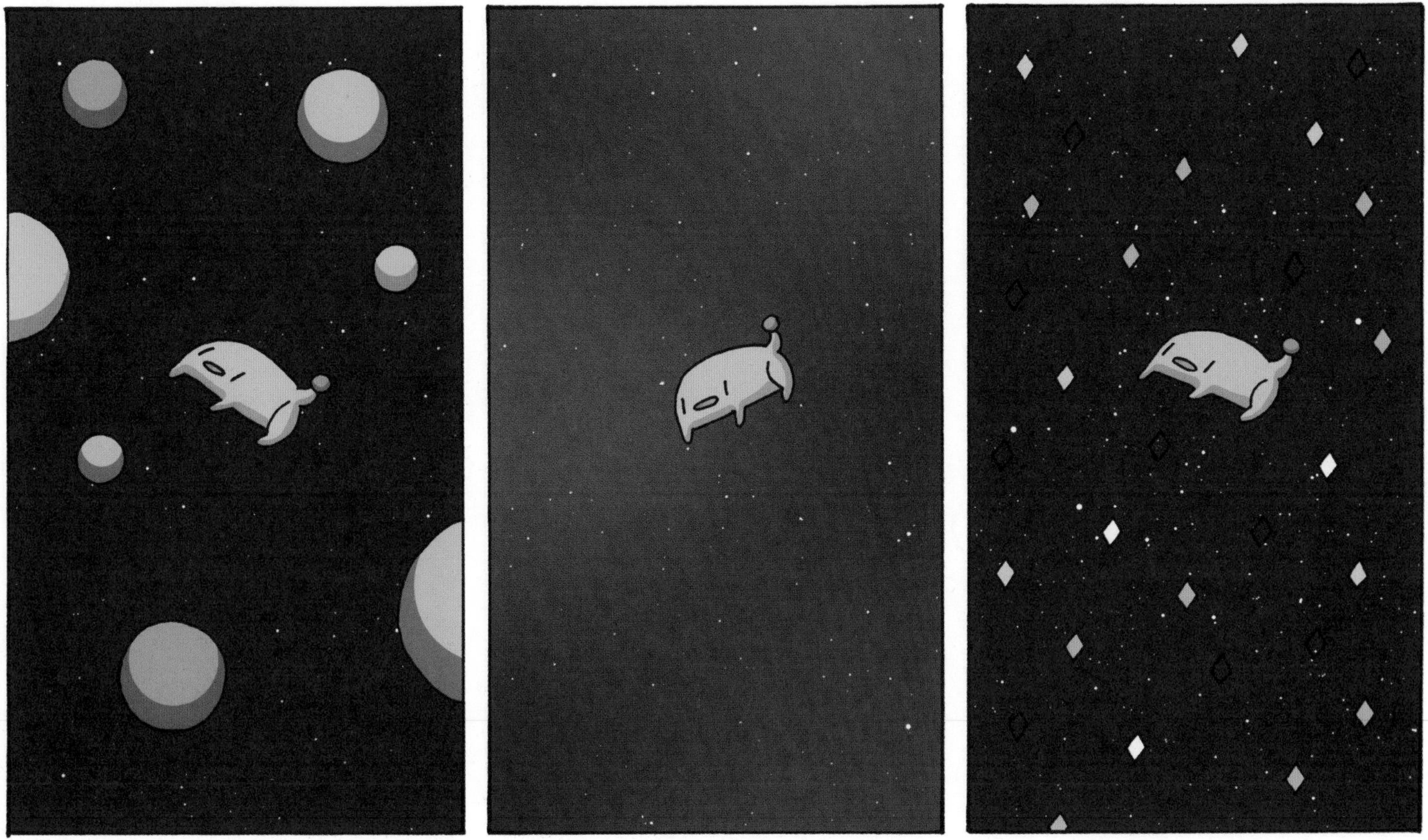

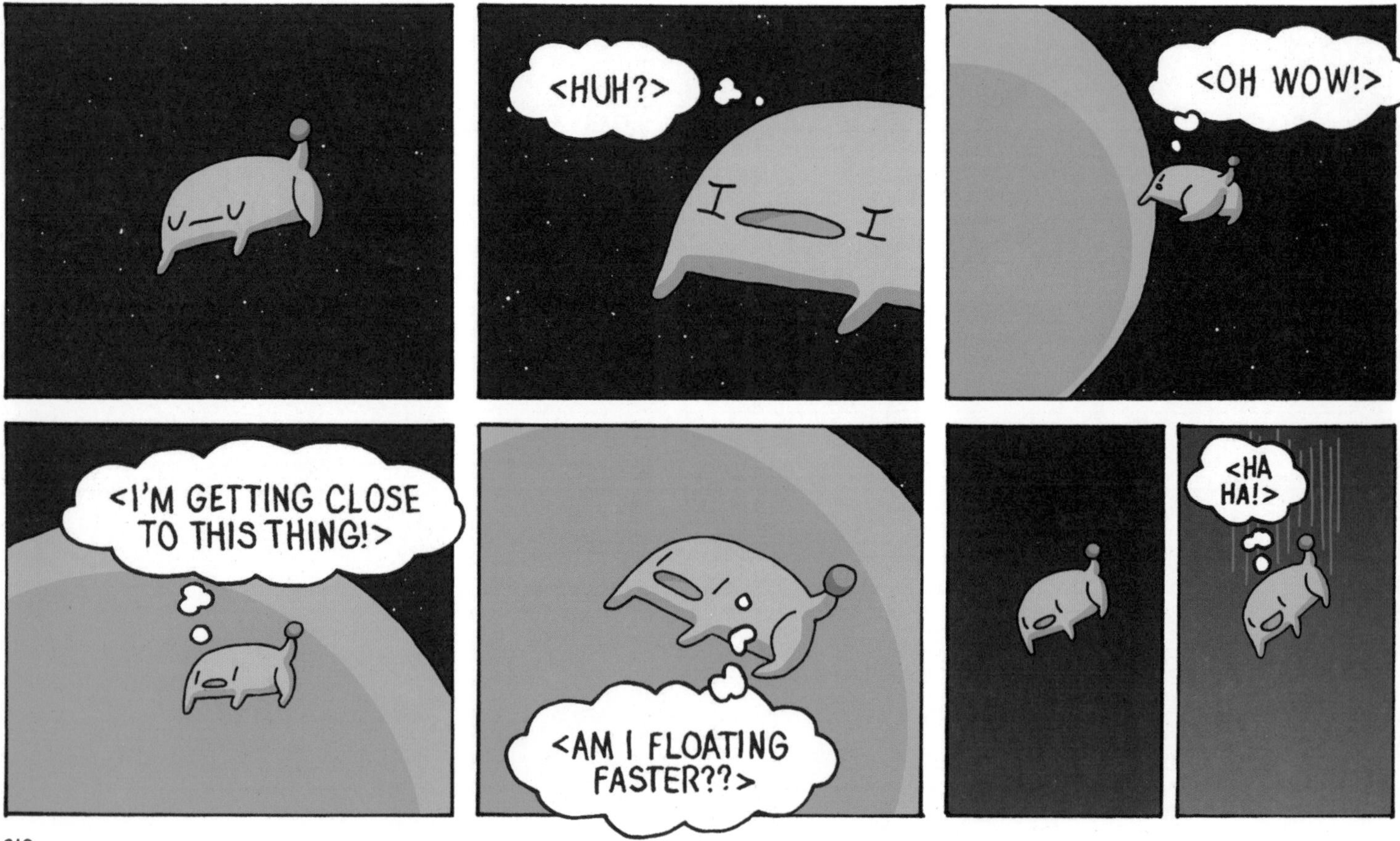

<HUH?>
<OH WOW!>
<I'M GETTING CLOSE TO THIS THING!>
<AM I FLOATING FASTER??>
<HA HA!>

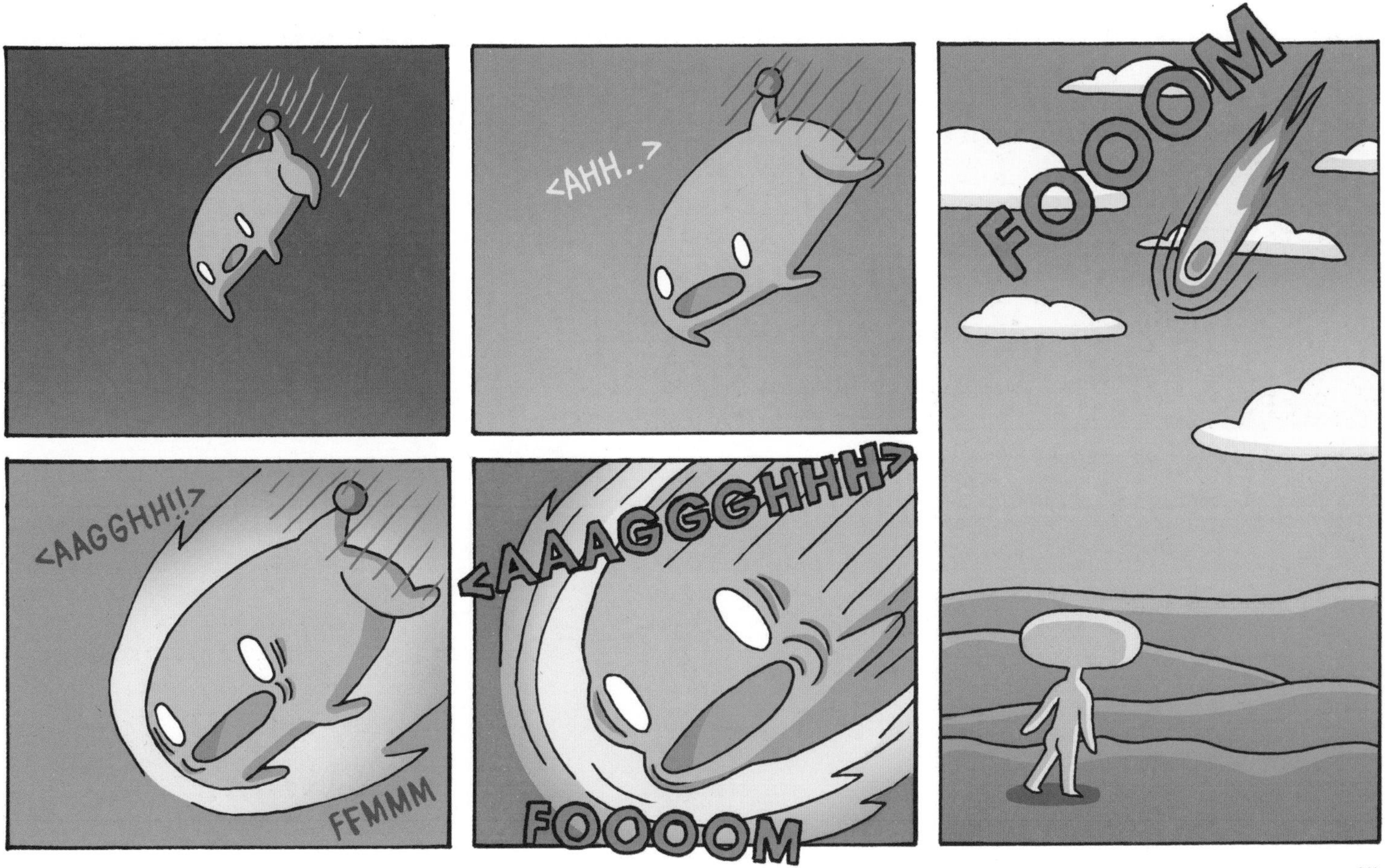
<AHH..>
<AAGGHH!!>
FFMMM
<AAAGGGHHHH>
FOOOOM
FOOOM

POOOMM!!!
TSS
TSS
<UGHH...>
TSS

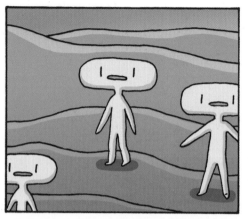

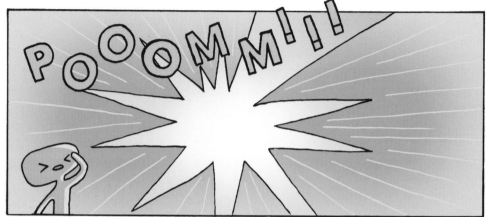

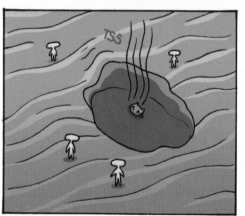

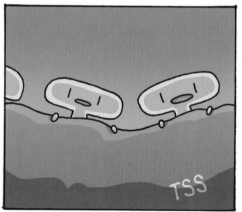

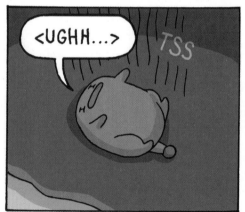

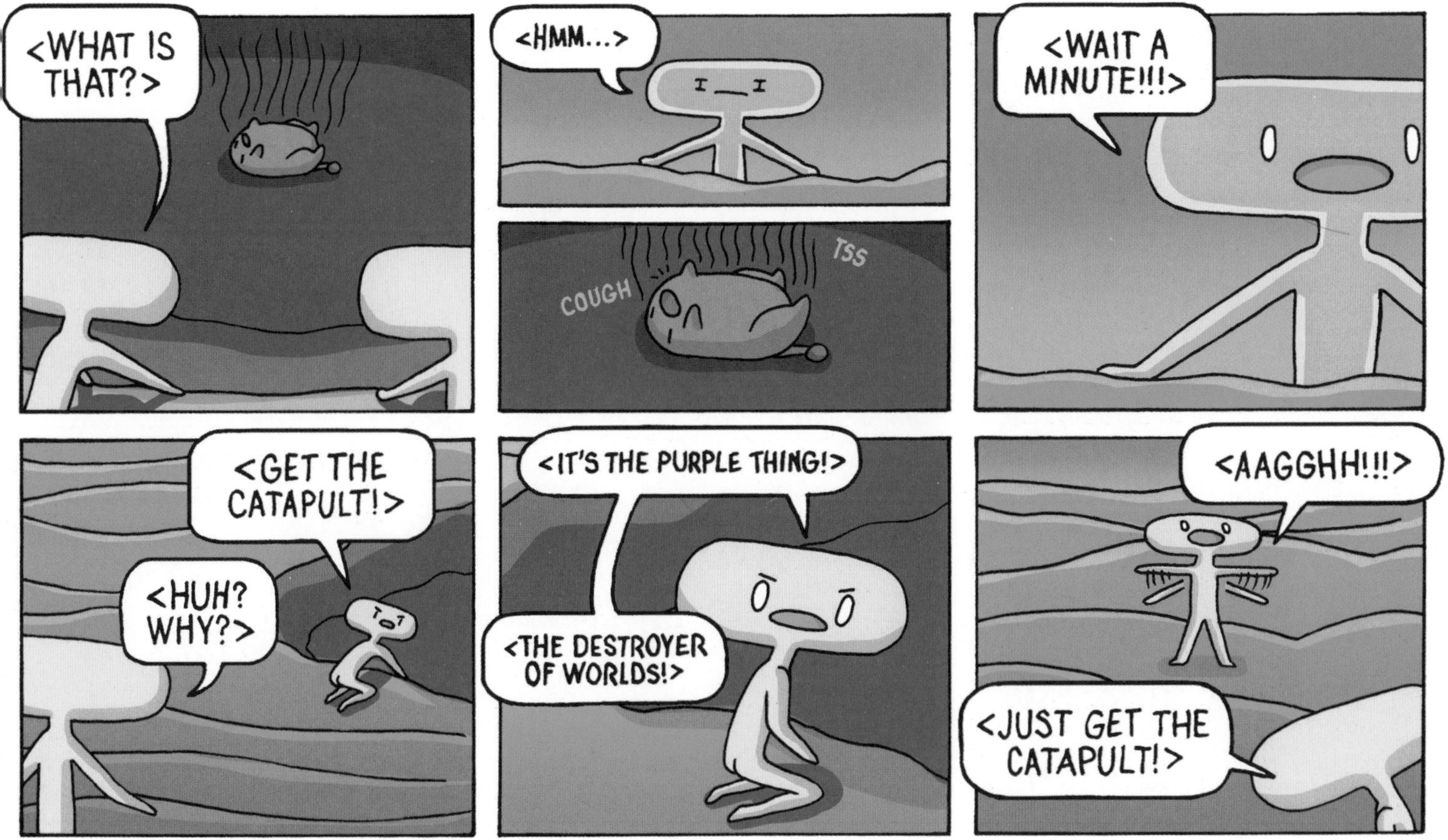

<WHAT IS THAT?>
<HMM...>
COUGH
TSS
<WAIT A MINUTE!!!>
<GET THE CATAPULT!>
<HUH? WHY?>
<IT'S THE PURPLE THING!>
<THE DESTROYER OF WORLDS!>
<AAGGHH!!!>
<JUST GET THE CATAPULT!>

PK.
TP
TUP
<AAGH>
<NEVER AGAIN...>

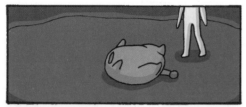

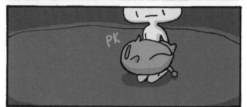

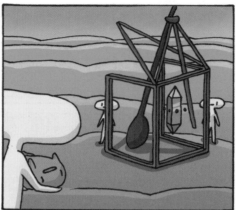

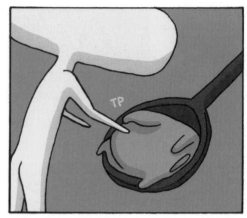

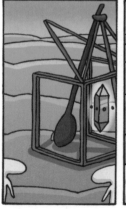

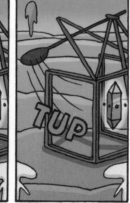

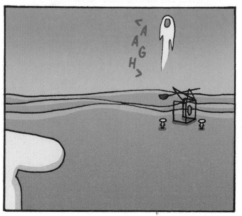

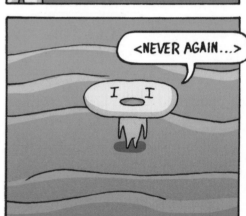

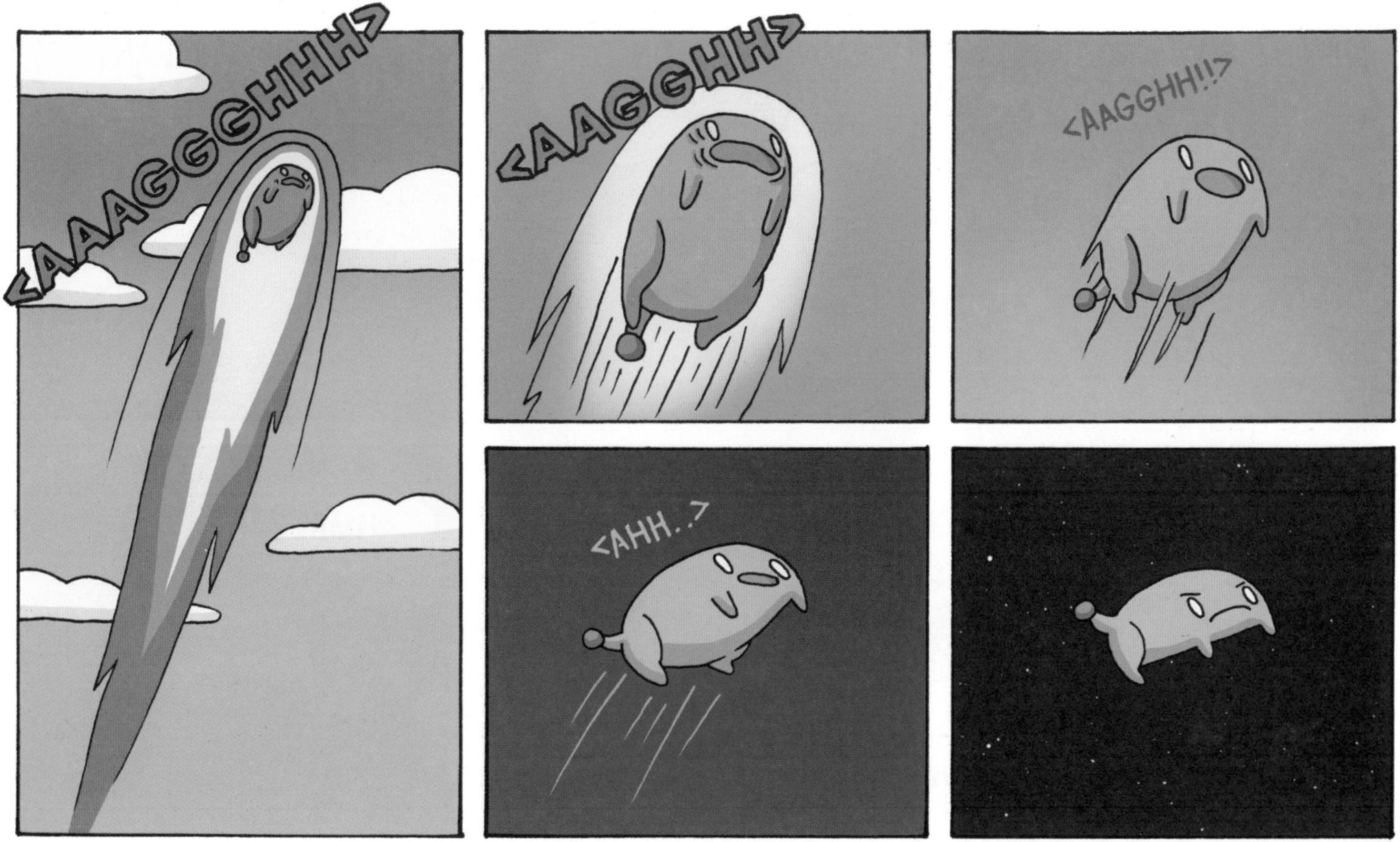
<AAAGGGHHH>
<AAGGHH>
<AAGGHH!!>
<AHH..>

A LITTLE BIT LATER

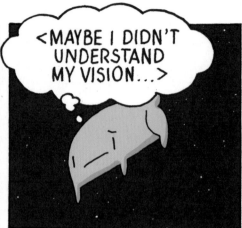

<MAYBE I DIDN'T UNDERSTAND MY VISION...>

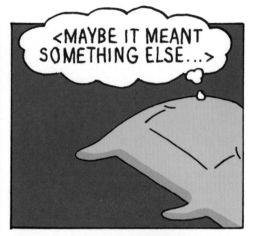

<MAYBE IT MEANT SOMETHING ELSE...>

<THERE ARE SO MANY ORBS IN THE SKY...>

<MAYBE MY DESTINY IS ON ANOTHER ORB...>

<HMM...>

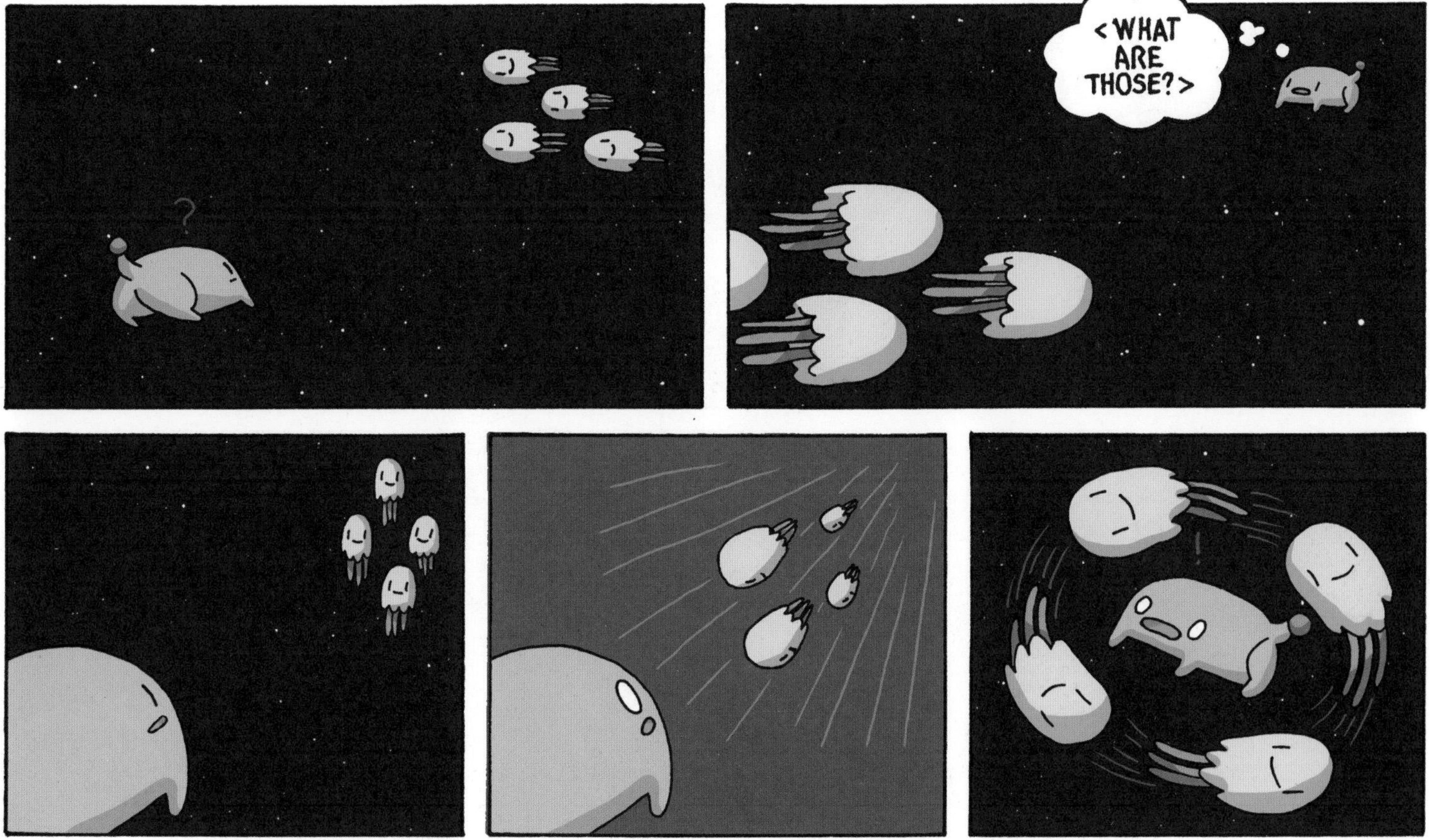
<WHAT ARE THOSE?>

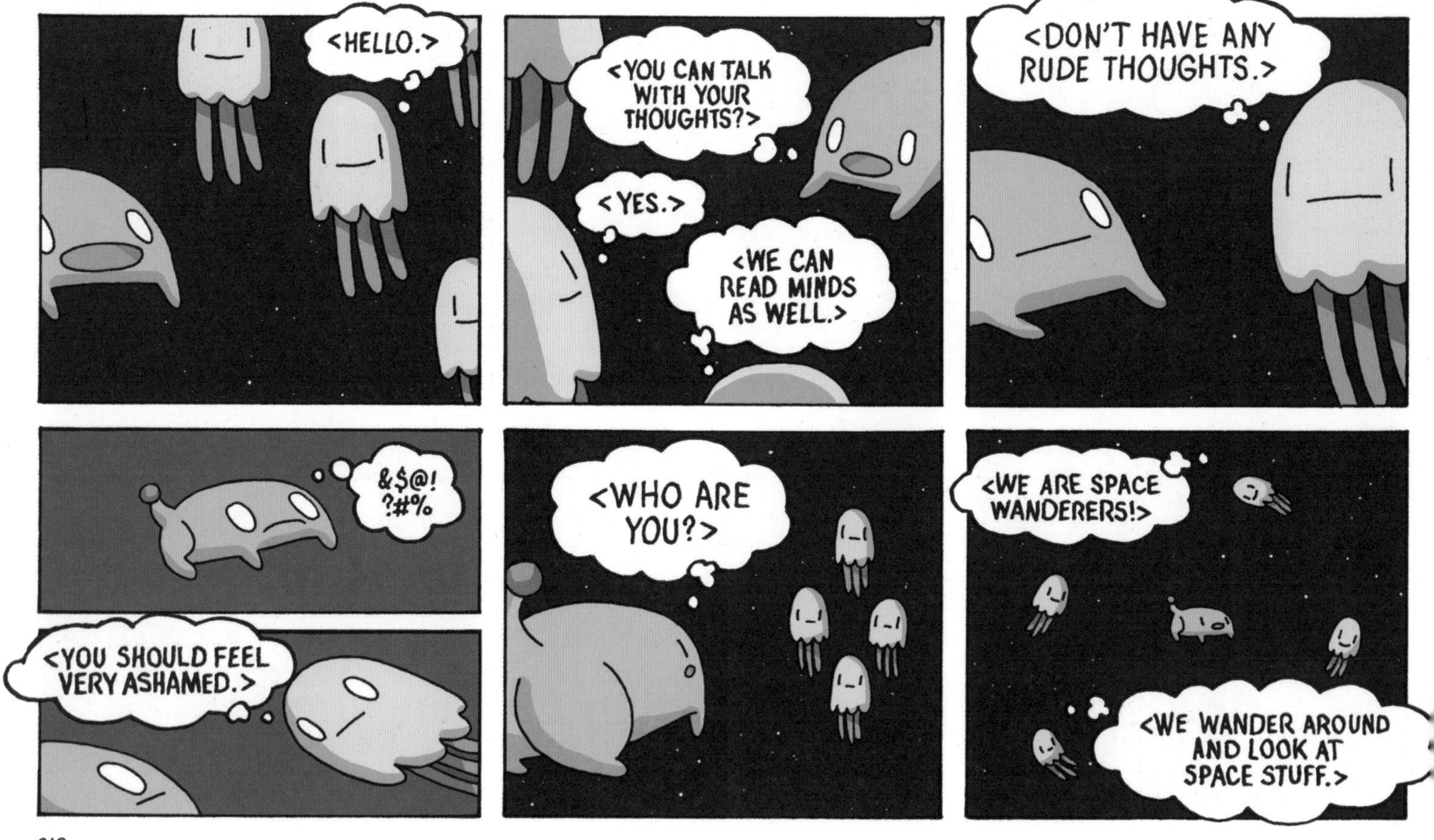
<HELLO.>
<YOU CAN TALK WITH YOUR THOUGHTS?>
<YES.>
<WE CAN READ MINDS AS WELL.>
<DON'T HAVE ANY RUDE THOUGHTS.>
&$@! ?#%
<YOU SHOULD FEEL VERY ASHAMED.>
<WHO ARE YOU?>
<WE ARE SPACE WANDERERS!>
<WE WANDER AROUND AND LOOK AT SPACE STUFF.>

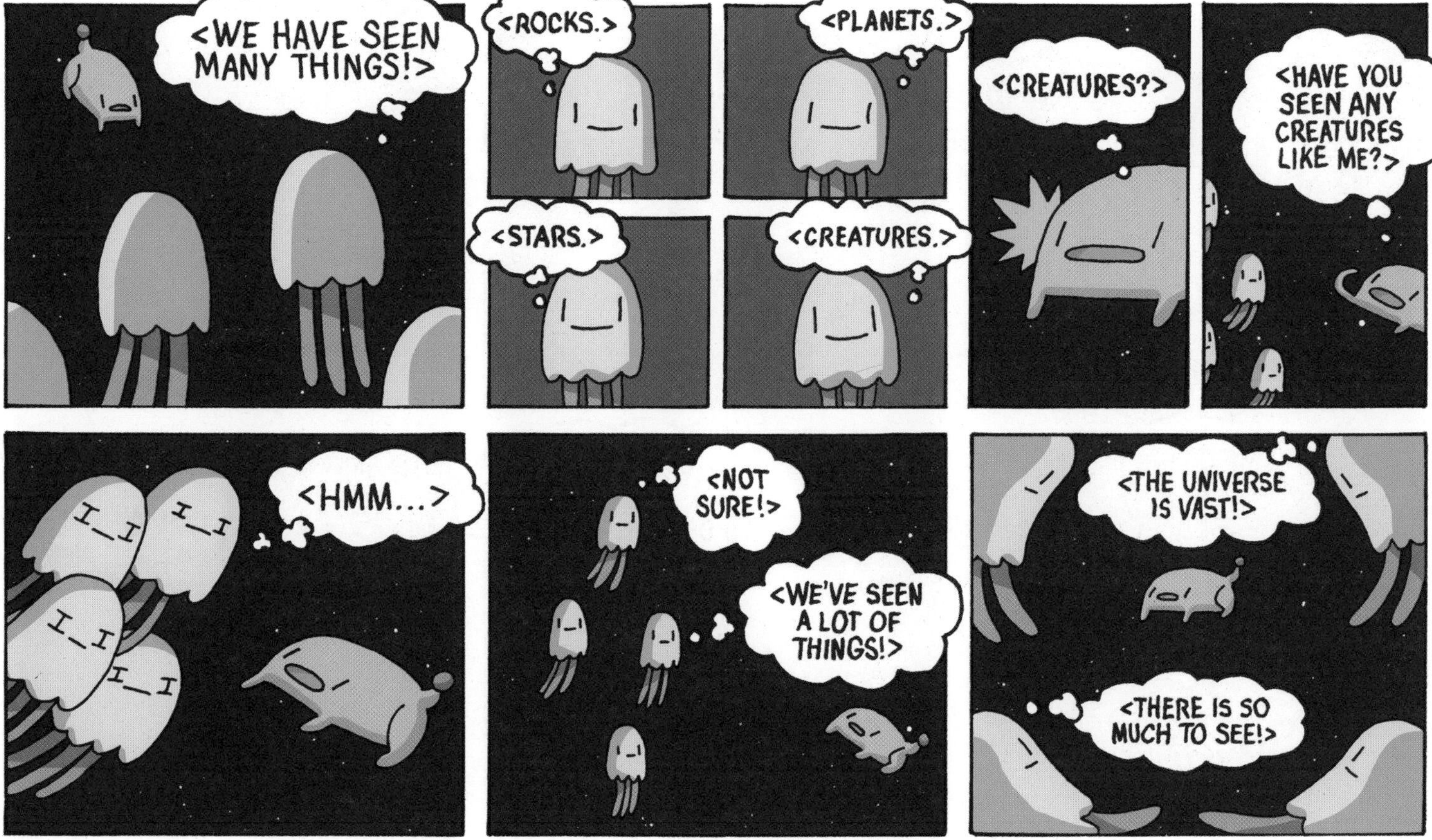
<WE HAVE SEEN MANY THINGS!>
<ROCKS.>
<PLANETS.>
<STARS.>
<CREATURES.>
<CREATURES?>
<HAVE YOU SEEN ANY CREATURES LIKE ME?>
<HMM...>
<NOT SURE!>
<WE'VE SEEN A LOT OF THINGS!>
<THE UNIVERSE IS VAST!>
<THERE IS SO MUCH TO SEE!>

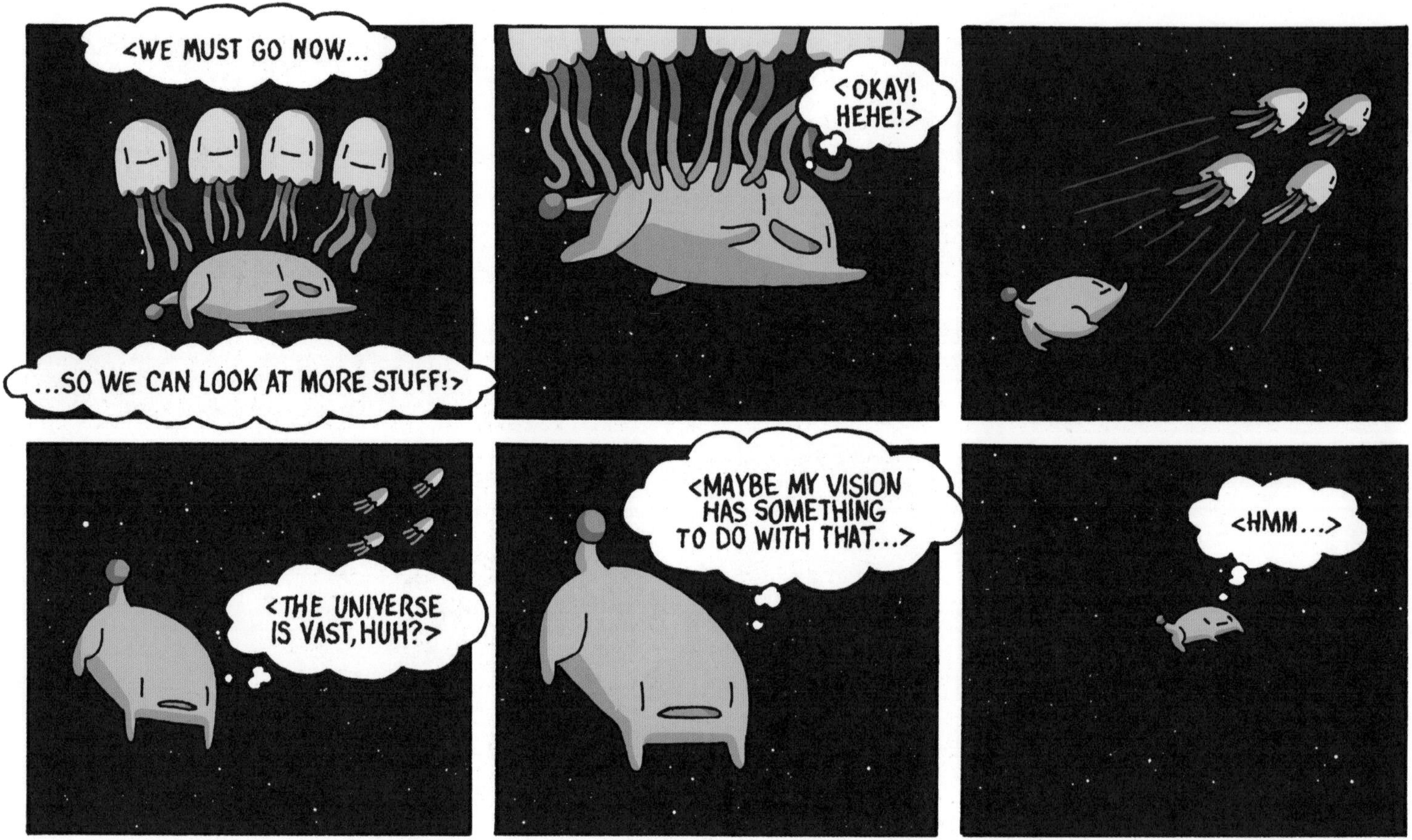
<WE MUST GO NOW...
...SO WE CAN LOOK AT MORE STUFF!>
<OKAY! HEHE!>
<THE UNIVERSE IS VAST, HUH?>
<MAYBE MY VISION HAS SOMETHING TO DO WITH THAT...>
<HMM...>

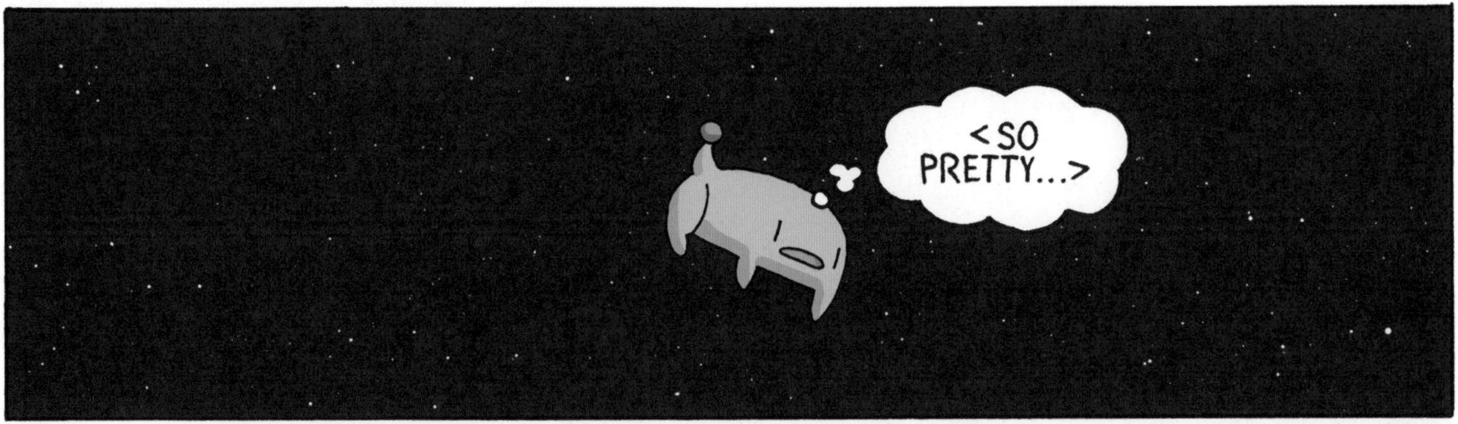
<SO PRETTY...>

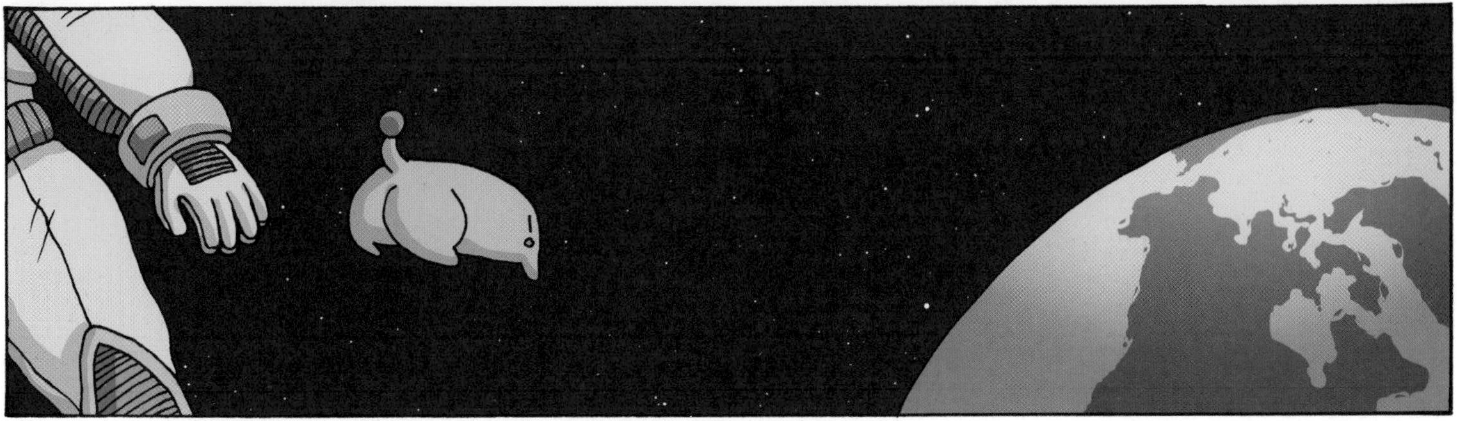

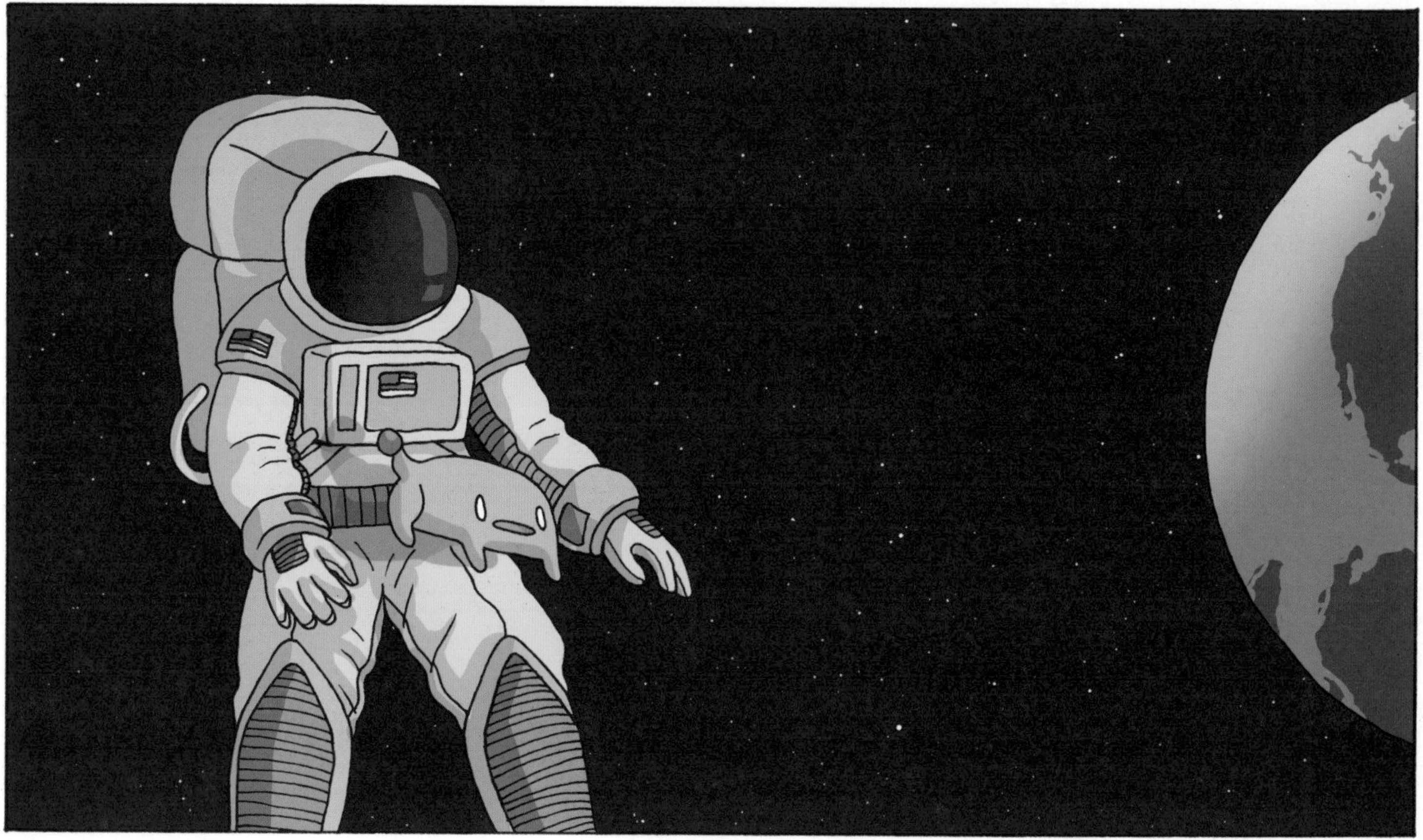

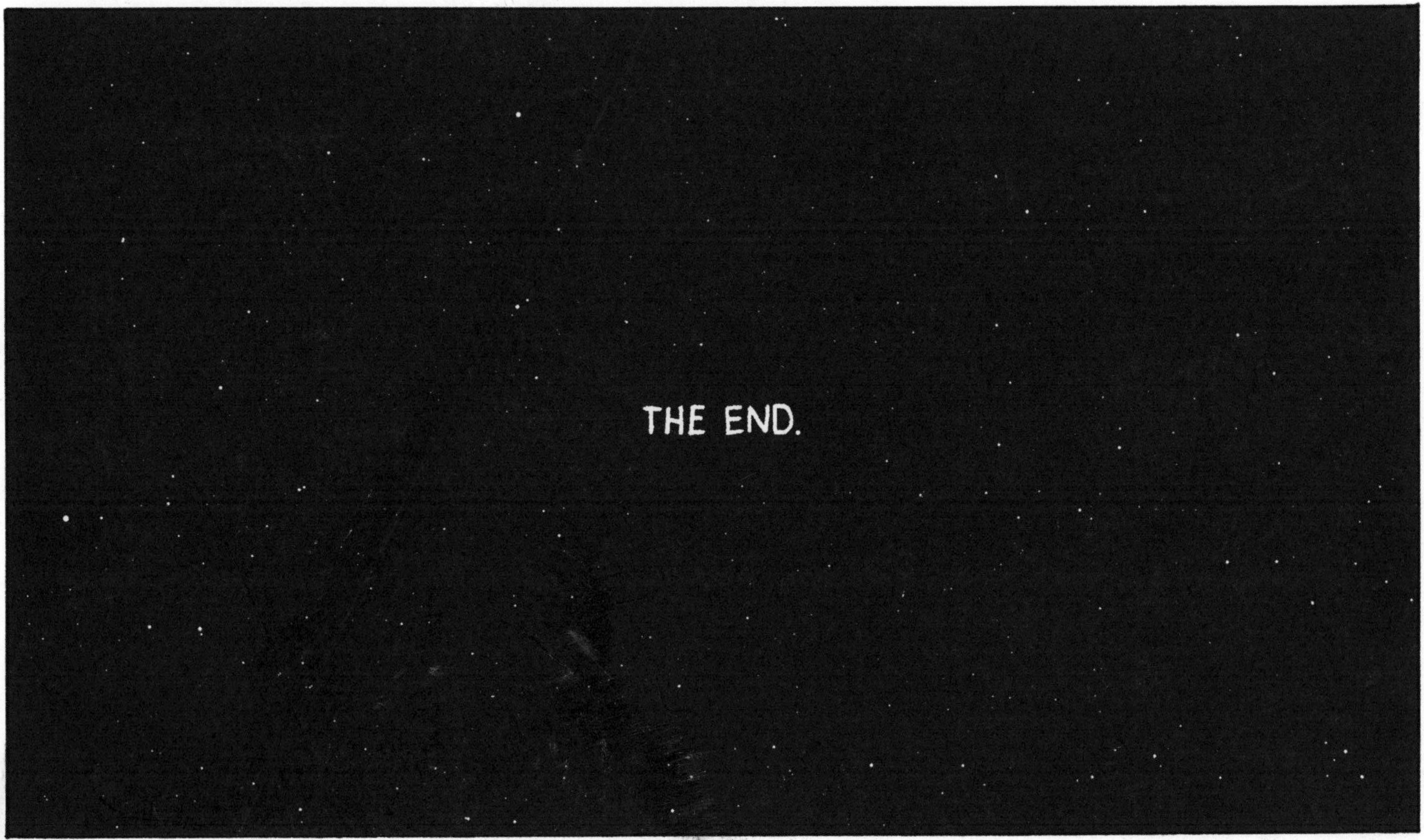
THE END.

ACKNOWLEDGEMENTS

Paul: Thank you for encouraging me to focus on my weird illustrations. You taught me so much during my time at Tyler and I will never forget that.

Sam: Thank you for helping me improve. You're 100% real all the time and it helped me so much. Also, thanks for helping me make my greens more yellow and my blues more vibrant. Everything looks so much better.

Kelly: Thank you for always making me laugh. Your constant positivity helped me throughout this year. Even though I said I didn't need it, I actually really needed it and I appreciate that.

My parents: Thank you for always encouraging me to be the best I can be and helping me through school! I think about that a lot.

Roomba: Thanks for being hilarious and making me laugh every day. Also, thanks for being the best Disney World partner. I can't wait for our next trip!

Knives (the cat): I know you have no idea what a book is, or why I have been ignoring your incessant screaming for pets, but you are the greatest therapy cat. Whenever I am stressed, I just look at you and laugh because of how round you are. I die every time.

Nick: Thanks for listening to me complain and ordering food for me. That meant a lot.

My webcomic readers: I never thought my silly little webcomic would be read by so many. I originally began the project because I thought it would be fun for me to do. Then so many people started reading and sharing it. The response was overwhelming, and I thank each and every one of you.